HEROIC
WITH
GRACE

HEROIC WITH GRACE

Legendary Women of Japan

Edited by
Chieko Irie Mulhern

An East Gate Book
M.E. Sharpe, Inc.
Armonk, New York   London, England

An East Gate Book

All rights reserved. No part of this book may be reproduced in any
form without written permission from the publisher, M. E. Sharpe, Inc.,
80 Business Park Drive, Armonk, New York 10504.

Available in the United Kingdom and Europe from M. E. Sharpe,
Publishers, 3 Henrietta Street, London WC2E 8LU.

Library of Congress Cataloging-in-Publication Data

Heroic with grace : legendary women of Japan /
edited by Chieko Irie Mulhern.
p.   cm.
Includes index.
ISBN 0-87332-527-3— ISBN 0-87332-552-4 (pbk.)
1. Women in public life—Japan—Biography.
2. Women—Japan—Biography. 3. Women—Japan—History.
I. Mulhern, Chieko Irie.
HQ1391.J3H47   1991
305.4′0952—dc20
90-28750
CIP

Printed in the United States of America

MV   10 9 8 7 6 5 4 3 2 1

CONTENTS

PREFACE

Chieko Irie Mulhern

THIS BOOK presents the lives and times of eight prominent women who epitomized the joys and sorrows of being female in Japan. The scope of selection is inevitably limited by the availability and manageability of source materials as well as the specialties and scholarly interest of the coauthors. Each woman subject has been chosen according to four criteria: (1) she is well documented in historical records or literary works; (2) she made some positive and constructive impact on her time and Japan's history; (3) her significant achievements were made primarily in a typically female role; and (4) her causes thrived into the future, unlike the lost causes that Japan's popular male heroes tended to serve.

By no means isolated, unusual cases born of freakish twists of fate or preternatural strength, these are the best-known representatives of many women who exerted their influence on society, people, and nation far beyond the familial sphere. They are not heroes who happened to be female nor who renounced their female identity in defiance to bravely enter the male domain in pursuit of success and power. Rather, their feminine identity was an essential factor in most of their contributions significant enough to alter or shape the course of Japan's history.

Starting with the "oldest profession" in Japan, the shamaness-priestess, the list includes eight of the respected and influential roles in which Japanese women were able to test the limit of feminine potentials and fill the needs of particular times and social conditions as only females could. Each chapter provides the historical background and sociopolitical perspectives necessary for understanding how and why some women found themselves placed in such supreme positions as emperor and acting shogun, fully expected to wield the power attendant to the title.

The book covers the entire chronological span of Japan's history, but each chapter is put into whatever form is most suitable or relevant to the subject and her era. Different form and style allows readers to leave one age and enter a completely new world as they proceed. In this way, this volume serves a tandem purpose: to reconstruct the image of women of each age and to introduce the literary genre that made or preserved the legendary stature of a particular woman. Since each chapter illuminates both the public and private aspects of a woman hero's life, the male hero type of each age is also interwoven or contrasted in the discussion.

Chapter 1 deals with the only nonhistorical character in this book: Empress Jingū, created by the compilers of Japan's first official "histories"—*Kojiki* (Record of ancient matters, 710) and *Nihongi* (Chronicle of Japan, 720). But the Jingū legend, with which the chapter begins, contains many episodes paralleling the events and actions attributed to real-life women rulers and substantiated not only by Japanese sources but also by entries in Chinese and Korean records. By all indications, Empress Jingū is a composite character based on many historical women as well as a mythological shamaness embodying the female leadership in Japan's matriarchal past. In analyzing the legend, Professor Aoki introduces earliest history uncovered by her study of old local gazetteers (*fudoki*), interprets the national mythology with anthropological as well as sociopolitical perspectives focusing on the Sun Goddess Amaterasu, and reassesses women's position in the ancient polity in reference to government appointment rosters and local records.

In chapter 2, Dr. Aoki introduces the life of a strong-willed female sovereign from the pages of *Nihongi*. Jitō literally shaped Japan's history in the seventh century: first as wife dedicating her loyalty to her uncle/husband virtually against her emperor father; next as empress and equal partner in effective joint rule; as empress dowager in her frail son's stead; then as the forty-first *tennō* (emperor) in her own right; and finally as *dajō-tennō* (ruling ex-sovereign) to aid her young grandson on the throne, establishing a precedent to be followed by many powerful male emperors. Appended to this chapter is a brief survey of the ten reigns under eight women tennō.

The third chapter searches the elusive identity of Murasaki Shikibu (flourished ca. 1000), the author of *The Tale of Genji*, through the wealth of prose literature—including her own diary and poetic collection and the memoirs of her contemporaries—that makes the career of court lady come alive. Thanks to these sophisticated women who served at the salons of imperial ladies into their middle and even later years, the Heian period (794–1185) is richly documented with poignant insider views of the aristocratic life at home as well as at court. The second half of chapter 3 follows a composite life course of Heian ladies reconstructed out of their own narrative legacy, replete with visual beauty full of delicate forms and colors, by Dr. Fischer, as expert on oriental art as well as on Heian literature.

Chapter 4 plunges right into the thick of battle that opened the age of warriors and military administration, which would overshadow the elegant court culture for seven centuries to come. Tomoe, the undefeated woman general, took part in the first waves of the all-out war between the two great houses—Taira and Minamoto—in the late twelfth century. Japan's history accords renown to several other female samurai, but Tomoe is the only one whose battlefield prowess and combat skills are delineated with heroic details in two literary genres that are by nature male-oriented: the war tales told by traveling monk-minstrels, and the noh plays performed by male-only troupes.

Professor Tyler enlivens his analytical exposition with his own translation of corresponding passages from various war tales that evoke the warrior ethos and flesh out Tomoe's lord and her brother, imbuing the portrait of this woman shrouded in romantic mist with *mono no aware* (pathos of things). He follows up his narrative presentation with the first full translation of *Tomoe*, the only play about a woman in the *shura* (warrior) category of the noh repertory. In lowering her standing in the moral cosmic order vis-à-vis her failed lord, this play provides fertile ground for a comparative study with the versions in the war tales, with the male hero types favored by the Japanese through the ages, or in terms of recent feminist theories in Western scholarship.

Chapter 5 highlights Tomoe's near contemporary who found the reins of government thrust into her hand time and again and proved herself worthy of the task each time. Hōjō Masako (1157–1225), wife of the first shogun of Japan's first shogunate at Kamakura who earned the appellation dowager shogun in her lifetime, has her modern champion in historical novelist Nagai Michiko (b. 1925). After she won the Naoki Prize for *Enkan* (The ring of flames, 1964), a novel depicting the Taira-Minamoto wars from the Kamakura side, Nagai went on to win even more acclaim with *Emaki* (Picture scroll, 1966), taking up the imperial side to delve into the psychological tactics played against both clans by the seventy-seventh emperor Go-Shirakawa, long retaining power as retired sovereign. In 1969 Nagai achieved great popularity with her newspaper serial novel, *Hōjō Masako*, which became a spectacular hit as a year-long television serial drama on the influential national network NHK.

Dr. Benton incorporates her interview with Nagai into her own analysis of Masako's life, clarifying some of Nagai's new findings that constitute invaluable contributions to the field of Japanese history ungrudgingly acknowledged by academics. One is the *menoto* (nurse-guardian) system, the significance of which has been largely overlooked but which actually motivated many a political upheaval. Another is *uwanari-uchi*, the sanctioned right of the first wife to fight off the later wife, which Masako exercised more than once, giving rise to her reputation as a jealous wife. Nagai, with fresh insights derived from her meticulous research into primary sources, attributes this battle of women to the right and wish of the wife's paternal family to protect their material and other investment in the high-born son-in-law according to the marriage customs of the day.

In terms of universal female psychology, *uwanari-uchi* is echoed with uncanny accuracy in works of other countries, albeit with modern and cultural twists, as in the climax of the 1987 Hollywood hit, *Fatal Attraction*, which also makes ingenious use of the self-immolation motif from *Madama Butterfly*. Dr. Benton's study of Hōjō Masako's relationship with her husband and her shogun sons sheds light on transcultural anatomy of female jealousy and the myth of maternal instinct. The last section, by Chieko Mulhern, measures Masako's caliber against that of two contemporaries who locked horns with her more than once over matters that affected the imperial and shogunal bloodlines, while wielding untold political power at court as Go-Shirakawa's concubine and as his grandson Emperor Go-Toba's menoto.

Chapter 6 enters modern times with Hani Motoko (1873–1957), who rode the crest of Japan's transition from a feudal society ruled by the samurai class to a parliamentary monarchy dedicated to industrialization. Interwoven into Hani's life are an overview of women's history, the state of modern career fields at the time women broke into them, and various ways women carved out a meaningful existence and attained career satisfaction during the Meiji (1868–1912) and Taishō (1912–26) periods. In her autobiography translated herein, Hani provides a portrait of a Meiji woman maturing from her childhood in the underdeveloped Northeast to the formative years at a higher school in Tokyo, moving from an ill-matched early marriage to one of the best-known and most fruitful unions, and flowering from a housemaid into Japan's first newspaperwoman, publisher of the longest-living serious women's magazine, and founder of a thriving educational institution.

Chapter 7 covers a new profession—acting—that became available to Japanese women only in modern times and thanks to the imported media, namely, the New Theater, which staged Western drama in translation, and the cinema. Takemine Hideko (b. 1924) grew up with the cinema industry, from a child star in silent films to a popular idol bursting upon the bleak postwar scene in Japan's first color movie, to one of the most respected and beloved actresses of all time. Since the 1970s, she has been out of the public eye except through her highly acclaimed essays, but the memories of her superb acting and the natural charisma of her screen personality remain. In a recent large-scale popularity poll (taking male votes only), Takamine Hideko came in second among 150 Japanese actresses named, paralleling Audrey Hepburn in a separate list of 150 foreign stars (*Joyū besuto 150* [Bungeishunjū bunko, 1990]).

Professor O'Brien retells the anormal life of this star, vivid and enlightening for her personal observations of prominent artists and self-insights gleaned from her notable memoirs. His expertise on the conventions of Japanese autobiographical literature informs his running comments that add dimension and perspective helpful to Western readers. Along with some complicated family situations not uncommon in Japan of her time, and the fate of illustrious role models in her profession, Takamine delineates the slices of life in wartime as well as postwar Japan with genuine anguish and grief for the young soldiers, many of whom carried her photograph into battle, no Betty Grable but literally a pin-up *girl*.

Social concerns and women's issues are some of the most conspicuous hallmarks of Ariyoshi Sawako (1931–84) covered by the concluding chapter. Since Ariyoshi is among the handful of Japanese novelists whose works are best represented by translations in various Western languages, Professor Tahara, who is responsible for the bulk of Ariyoshi's works available in English, concentrates on providing guideposts through her career course packed with significant literary and social achievements. It is too early to sum up Ariyoshi as a writer, and the sheer volume of her opus and the vast range of her themes defy a ready treatment in one chapter. To encourage and aid further study, Dr. Tahara gives objective synopses of major stories and reveals glimpses of this enigmatic public figure as a woman and a personal friend.

Anyone familiar with Japanese history must have noted an enormous gap in chronology by now, and many would be tempted to decry the seeming oversight of this editor in skipping over 650 years between the death of Hōjō Masako in 1225 and the birth of Hani Motoko in 1873. In between lie the rest of the Kamakura period (1185–1333), which is essentially a continuation of Masako's age, and the entire Muromachi period (1338–1573), a variation on the warrior administration only more urbanized and refined, ending in the free-for-all armed strife. Next came the interminable Tokugawa period (1603–1868), when both men and women were discouraged from taking action on their own, under strict codes of behavior.

The glaring omission of these centuries in this study of women heroes is intentional and for a simple reason—the absence of women accorded a legendary stature in the positive sense. True, each age produced some women whose names are etched in history and even recognized by the Japanese public today. Yet closer examination betrays too many negative factors that disqualify them as women heroes by the standard applicable to the eight women presented in this book. Hino Tomiko (1440–96), for instance, who was gifted with extraordinary financial acumen and amassed vast wealth in her own right, cannot possibly be considered a hero by today's criteria. She is said to have run the shogunate after her husband, the eighth shogun Yoshimasa, became bored with his duties, but only to abuse power and spread moral chaos over the country. As a shogun's consort, she is no more than an unsuccessful copy of Masako.

One Japanese woman who was known to the West even during her lifetime and has been featured in plays and fiction ever since is Hosokawa Tama Gracia (1562–1600). As the principal wife of a *daimyo* (overlord), Gracia may be conducive to a role study; and as a noble Christian lauded as a virtual martyr by her fellow believers, she can represent the staunch and courageous Japanese Christians, many of them women and children, who died for the faith during the long proscription period. Nevertheless, Gracia's religious convictions and her death to safeguard her husband's honor did not shape history or leave lasting marks in society at large. A tragic heroine rather than a woman hero, Gracia has inspired many Western writers. Thorough coverage of her life is available in Chieko Mulhern's "Hosokawa Gracia: A Model of Mariko," in *Learning from Shogun* (Santa Barbara: University of California Press, 1980), which elucidates the historical facts behind James Clavell's characterization in his best-seller *Shogun*; and two articles also by Mulhern, "Cinderella and the Jesuits: An Otogizoshi Cycle as Christian Literature," *Monumenta Nipponica* (Winter 1979), and "Analysis of Cinderella Motifs Italian and Japanese," *Asian Folklore Studies* (Spring 1985), both of which trace the key motifs of some medieval tales to real-life experiences of Gracia, who was glorified by the Jesuits stationed in Japan.

In Gracia's generation, but far removed from her class, lived a woman who is credited with originating a type of performing art that would eventually culminate in the Kabuki theater, combining music, dance, and drama. Beyond the name she went by and her possible former occupation as priestess at Izumo Shrine, nothing much is recorded about this woman performer, Okuni of Izumo (1527?–1613). Ariyoshi Sawako, in her novel *Izumo no Okuni* (1967), gives an account of her achievement in popularizing new acts called Okuni Kabuki before the shogunate banned women (and later young men as well) from theatrical troupes.

By far the most prominent female name in Tokugawa history may be Kasuga no tsubone (1579–1643), the menoto of the third shogun Iemitsu. Born of a fairly high-ranking samurai family, Kasuga is said to have been instrumental in getting her charge declared the heir over his younger brother, favored by their parents, and in converting Iemitsu from a homosexual to at least a bisexual willing and able to sire future shoguns (two in fact). Kasuga commands an impressive body of legend, partly rooted in historical incidents but consisting mostly of behind-the-scenes maneuvers and tight control of a vast female domain that was the shogunal harem, facts about which are totally blacked out. In 1629 Kasuga was sent to the court as a shogun's emissary to dissuade the emperor from abdicating in protest against the shogunate policies, but she was unsuccessful, and a child princess who was Iemitsu's niece became tennō (Meishō), putting an end to his hope of seeing her marry and bear a future emperor of the Tokugawa blood. Kasuga's life, famous or notorious as the case may be, is included in *Her Place in the Sun: Women Who Shaped Japan*, by Higuchi Chiyoko, English version by Sharon Rhoads (Tokyo: East Publications, 1973). She may have shaped Japan through shaping a powerful shogun who ruled as much as reigned, but she falls short of qualifying as a positive role model.

What our book intends to offer is not a historical theory but a survey of the changing images of Japanese women heroes more as national legends than historical facts, for it is through legends that these women achieved their immortality and exerted their greatest influence on the Japanese imagination down through the ages. Nevertheless, the concrete examples of eight women touch on a number of issues, including the state of women in broader perspective; factors formative to women's status in various ages; social climate conducive to positive female actions; the concept of Japanese womanhood in relation to that of manhood; the popular need for such strong female figures to be glorified; and situations peculiar to Japan such as those that defined, for example, fiction writing as a feminine pursuit and acting as a male-only profession until modern times.

Even in the modern West, being female takes a measure of heroic perseverance and gracious tolerance. These eight Japanese women were indeed exceptionally heroic in their achievements but without sacrificing grace or their full life as women. It is hoped that *Heroic with Grace: Legendary Women of Japan* can meet the increasing need for comprehensive reading materials focused on women, by presenting the ultimate female role models and reviewing the paradox of Japan's male-dominant past that yielded them.

CONTRIBUTORS

MICHIKO Y. AOKI. Having concentrated on scholarly research and publication for many years, Dr. Aoki recently returned to college teaching as assistant professor of Asian studies at Clark University. Her works related to the subject of this volume are *Izumo Fudoki* (1971); *Ancient Myths and Early History of Japan* (1974); *As the Japanese See It: Past and Present,* co-editor (1981); an on-going series of translations and articles on novelist Shibaki Yoshiko in *Proceedings of the International Symposium on Asian Studies—9* (1987: "Three Generations of Tokyoites in Four Stories"), 10 (1988: *"Dance Entitled Snow:* Excerpts and Synopsis"), and 11 (1989: "The Role of Geisha in Japanese Society"); and entries on Nogami Yaeko, Hayashi Fumiko, Hirabayashi Taiko, and Shibaki Yoshiko in *Japanese Women Writers: A Bio-critical Source Book* (forthcoming).

MARGARET FUKAZAWA BENTON. A resident of Tokyo since 1970 and fully bilingual, Dr. Benton has published scholarly articles in Japanese journals as well as translations into English, such as the two essays by novelist Nozaka Akiyuki in *Honyaku no sekai* (April and November 1981). Her works available in the United States include "Kawabata Yasunari's Style: The Use of Yamato Kotoba," Master's thesis, Columbia University, 1970; "Kitahara Hakushū: The Man and His Poetry," Ph.D. dissertation, Columbia University, 1980; and *"Suzume* and *Suiboku:* Kitahara Hakushū's Turn to Monochrome," *Journal of the Association of Teachers of Japanese* (Summer 1989).

FELICE FISCHER. Associate curator and acting head of the Far Eastern Art Department at the Philadelphia Museum of Art, Dr. Fischer has written many articles in art books and museum journals and organized a number of exhibits on Asian themes, such as "Arts of Tea" (1988) and "The Theme and Variation—Japanese Design Motifs" (1989). Her expertise on the Heian period in particular is encapsulated in "Ono no Komachi: A Poetess of the Ninth-Century Japan," Ph.D. dissertation, Columbia University, 1971; "If You Were a Heian Lady," *Ikebana International* (February 1985); and entries on Ono no Komachi, Murasaki Shikibu, and Sei Shōnagon in *Japanese Women Writers: A Bio-critical Source Book.*

CHIEKO IRIE MULHERN. Professor of Japanese and comparative literature at the University of Illinois at Urbana-Champaign, Dr. Mulhern served as editor-in-chief of this volume. Her recent works relevant to women's studies range from studies of popular culture in *Japanese TV Drama for, by, and about Women,* Michigan State University WID Forum-III, 1985, and "Japanese Harlequin Romances as Transcultural Woman's Fiction," *Journal of Asian Studies* (February 1989); to literary analyses in "Japanese Cinderella as a Pubertal Girl's Fantasy," *Southern Folklore Quarterly* (March 1984), "Joycean Narrative Consciousness in *The Tale of Genji* and Enchi Fumiko," *Hikaku bungaku kenkyū* (Fall 1988); to comprehensive expositions such as a survey of Japanese women writers in *Longman Anthology of World Literature by Women* (1988) and coverage of women novelists in "Introduction: The Japanese Business Novel," in Arai Shinya, *Shōshaman: A Tale of Corporate Japan,* trans. Chieko Mulhern (1991). Dr. Mulhern is editor-in-chief of Greenwood Press's forthcoming *Japanese Women Writers: A Bio-critical Source Book,* which will comprise article-length entries on more than fifty women authors, past and present.

JAMES O'BRIEN. Professor of Japanese literature at the University of Wisconsin-Madison, in 1990 Dr. O'Brien completed two three-year terms as president of the Association of Teachers of Japanese. Among his numerous publications are recent translations of modern poetry by Takamura Kōtarō and Murano Shirō, to be followed shortly by critiques of the two poets as well as of Kitahara Hakushū and Miyoshi Tatsuji. His expertise on the Japanese tradition of autobiographical writing culminated in two books: *Dazai Osamu* (1975), in the Twayne World Authors Series, and *Crackling Mountain and Other Stories by Dazai Osamu* (1989). His study of fiction is continued in monograph-size works on Murou Saisei and Akutagawa Ryūnosuke.

MILDRED TAHARA. Associate professor of Japanese literature at the University of Hawaii, Dr. Tahara has published several articles on historical figures featured in Heian literature, in addition to *Tales of Yamato: A Tenth-Century Poem-tale* (1980). Her translations of Ariyoshi Sawako's fiction include three full-length novels, *The River Ki* (1980), *The Twilight Years* (1984), and *Her Highness Princess Kazu* (forthcoming), as well as a collection of short stories in preparation. Dr. Tahara was trained in the art of tea ceremony at the Urasenke School.

ROYALL TYLER. Educated in France and the United States, Dr. Tyler has conducted research in Japan and taught in Canada and the United States before moving to Norway. Since 1984, he has been senior lecturer at the University of Oslo, serving several times as chairman of the East Asian Institute. His scholarly activities encompass North America, Japan, and Europe, and his publications are numerous in various languages. To cite those with direct bearing on the subject of this book: *Pining Wind: A Cycle of Nō Plays* and *Granny Mountain: A Second Cycle of Nō Plays* (Cornell University East Asian Papers no. 17 and no. 18, 1978); *Japanese Tales* (1987); "Women in Japanese Zen Buddhism," "Priestess (*miko*) in Japanese Religion," "Women in Premodern Japan," and "Japanese Women Writers," in *Kvinnenes Kulturhistorie* (A cultural history of women) (1988); "Upper-class Heian Society and Japanese Folk Religion," *Proceedings of the 1987 Venice Symposium Rethinking Japan;* and *The Miracles of the Kasuga Deity* (forthcoming). Dr. Tyler studied kyōgen with the master actor Shigeyama Sennojō and in February 1989 performed the play *Suhajikami* at the Kanze Kaikan noh theater in Kyoto, where he was visiting professor at the International Research Center for Japanese Studies for 1988–89.

HEROIC
WITH
GRACE

1

EMPRESS JINGŪ
The Shamaness Ruler

MICHIKO Y. AOKI

IT TAKES two genealogical tables to trace the lineage of Empress Jingū, daughter of Prince Okinaga Sukune and Katsuraki Takanuka. Her paternal line is impressive enough, for she is a sixth-generation descendant of the ninth emperor, Kaika. Her maternal line, however, can boast more mystical origins delineated in a fairy tale–like story.

The Legend in Japanese History

Long ago in the Korean Kingdom of Silla, a low-born woman was taking a nap by a pond. Suddenly a rainbow-colored shaft of sunlight penetrated the warm place between her loins. A low-born man witnessed this strange phenomenon and kept secret watch over the woman. In due time she gave birth to a red jewel. The man asked for and was given the jewel, which he hung around his waist. One day Ame no Hiboko charged him with using his ox as a pack animal and intending to eat it afterward. To buy his way out of the predicament, the low-born man offered the jewel to the prince.

At Prince Hiboko's bedside, the red jewel turned into a beautiful maiden. He made her his formal wife. She waited on him attentively until he grew disdainful and flung abusive words at her. ''I was born of the sunlight, so I shall go to my parent's country,'' she said. She crossed the sea in a small boat and settled in Naniwa (present Osaka) in the Land of the Rising Sun. Prince Hiboko tried to follow his wife, but the god of the Naniwa Narrows would not let him pass. He landed in Tajima Province and married a local woman.

Hiboko's great-great-grandson Tajimamori became a legend in his

own right: at the command of the eleventh emperor Suinin, Tajimamori sailed to the south seas in search of the "ever shining citrus,"
believed to be an elixir of immortality; ten years later he accomplished
his mission and returned, only to find his sovereign already dead; the
loyal emissary died of grief in front of the imperial tomb.
Tajimamori's brother married his own niece and sired Katsuraki
Takanuka, the mother of Empress Jingū.

Jingū married the fourteenth emperor in the second year of his
reign. Chūai was a nephew of Emperor Seimu (13th) and a son of the
legendary Prince Yamato Takeru. Chūai had already taken two consorts and sired sons. One boy posed no threat to Jingū, because his
mother was merely a daughter of a local magistrate. The other consort,
Princess Ōnakatsu (Great Intermediary; possibly a powerful shamaness), however, was of noble birth so that her two sons, the princes
Kagosaka and Oshikuma, were eligible to ascend the throne.

One month after their marriage, Jingū and Chūai moved to Tsunuga,
a port town on the coast of the Sea of Japan in the region called Koshi
(Land Beyond). There Chūai built a temporary palace overlooking a
beach fringed with thick pine groves and named it Kehi no miya (the
present site of Kehi Shrine in Fukui Prefecture). While in Tsunuga, he
succeeded in bringing the chief(s) of Awaji Island to his side and
established *miyake* (royal granary land or territory directly controlled
by the imperial house). Then he headed south on a hunting tour (a
euphemism for "tour of inspection," which could also mean "tour of
pacification") and reached Kii Province. He was staying at Tokorotsu
Palace when his deputies in the western provinces sent a report that the
Kumaso (Recalcitrants) in Tsukushi (present Kyushu) were rebelling
and refused to pay tribute to the central Yamato state that year. Chūai
immediately set out on a chastising campaign against the Kumaso. He
sailed with his fleet toward the port town of Anato (present
Shimonoseki at the southwestern tip of the Main Island), after dispatching a message to Jingū in Tsunuga.

Jingū embarked for Anato to join her husband at the harbor of
Toyora. At the strait called Nuta (probably the present Wakasa Bay,
known for its fishing industry), Jingū performed divination aboard her
ship. A great many snappers assembled around her ship, and Jingū
sprinkled rice wine over them. The fish became drunk and floated on
the water, thus giving the local fishermen a great catch, which they
called "the gift from Our Wise Sovereign." Within two months of her

arrival, Jingū and her husband moved into their new residence, Toyora Palace of Anato.

In the spring of the eighth year of Chūai's reign, he decided to cross the strait to Tsukushi Island and start an all-out offensive against the Kumaso. A man came to his court volunteering to be his pilot. The seaman displayed a *sakaki* (evergreen pulled out with roots) on the stern of his boat; on its branches he hung a few strings of jewels, a bronze mirror, and an iron sword. Guided by this pilot, Chūai sailed to Tsukushi. At one point of their sea journey, Chūai's ship became immobile. The emperor pleaded with local deities to release his ship and appointed one of his followers to serve them as a priest. Thereupon his ship was freed to proceed on its way.

Jingū's boat experienced a similar difficulty. When it entered the Bay of Kuki, the tide became too low to carry the boat forward. Chūai's pilot came over and made ponds stocked with fish and birds. When Jingū saw them sporting, her anxiety was eased. Then the high tide came, and her ship made it into the harbor of Na (present Hakata), the seaport on the northern tip of Tsukushi.

In autumn Chūai summoned his generals for a war council. That night Jingū was visited by a dream, or she fell into a trance. A deity appeared to her and said, "Why should the emperor worry about the Kumaso not surrendering to him? The Kumaso have little to offer. It is not worth your while to raise an army against them. There is a better land called Silla, which lies on Mukatsu (the other side of the ocean). There you can find treasures in plenty, for Silla is a rich country full of marvelous things dazzling to the eye—gold, silver, and bright-colored jewels. . . . If you worship me with proper offerings, I shall see to it that Silla will yield. Your soldiers will not even have to draw their swords. Victory is yours. In return, I merely claim as offerings your husband's ship and the rice field which he has acquired from a chieftain of Anato."

Chūai could not believe what he heard from his wife. He at first dismissed her story as a fanciful dream. But on second thought, he climbed to the top of a nearby hill to have a look. Even from that vantage point, he could see nothing in the great seas. He therefore concluded that if his wife really heard the voice of a god suggesting that she persuade him to give up his ship and the rice field, it must be a treacherous god.

Jingū again fell into a trance, and the indignant voice of the slighted god was heard coming through Jingū's lips: "I see this land of Silla lying outstretched like a reflection of heaven on the water. How can you say that I promise what does not exist, accusing me of deception?" Finally, the angry god announced, "Since you disbelieved my words, you shall not have this land by any means. However, your wife—I shall call her empress from now on—has just become pregnant. The child she bears will one day secure that land."

Chūai was still unable to believe the voice. He refused to change his policy of pacifying the Kumaso by military means. As far as he was concerned, his mission was a legacy from his father, Prince Yamato Takeru (the Brave of Yamato), who had come to Tsukushi before Chūai was born and quelled the recalcitrant Kumaso for the Yamato state by killing Kumaso Takeru, the powerful chieftain of his day. Now Chūai had to do the same in honor of his father—such was his sense of mission and reasoning. He mustered a large army of soldiers and attacked the Kumaso. The battle was fierce, and Chūai lost many of his men. But the outcome did not prove to be decisive, and he returned empty-handed.

Early in the following year, Chūai suddenly fell ill and soon died. Since he was only fifty-one years old, the people whispered, "Perhaps he met such an early death because he had not acted according to the god's will." There were also rumors that he was fatally struck by a Kumaso arrow. Jingū sent her great uncle Takeuchi back to Anato with Chūai's remains for a secret burial, and she personally took command of the Yamato forces. Now empress of the Yamato state by the god's will, Jingū had to amend the sins of her husband and comply with the god's wish. Also, it was necessary for her to cleanse her person of the defilement caused by his death. She ordered her councillors to perform purification rituals in repentance of transgressions against the deities.

On the most auspicious day of the third moon, Jingū entered the newly constructed purification hall. She asked Takeuchi to play the *koto* (translated variously as zither, lute, or harp), and Nakatomi, the minister of rituals, to interpret the god's oracle. In a hypnotic state induced by the sound of the string instrument, Jingū asked for the name of the god in whose honor she wished to make offerings and erect shrines. For seven days and seven nights she continued her prayer while abstaining from all the pleasures of this world. When the eighth day dawned, a voice was heard identifying the deity as the goddess who resided in the Isuzu Shrine of Watari in the Land of Divine Wind, Ise. "My name is

Princess Mukatsu (the Other Side of the Ocean)," announced the voice.

Jingū was still in a trance, Takeuchi continued to strum the koto strings, and Nakatomi waited, ready to catch whatever words that might come out of Jingū's lips. The empress asked in her own voice, "Are there any more deities besides this goddess?" Then a different voice spoke through her. "Yes. I am the deity of Oda no Agata, also known as Waka Hirume." "Are there any more gods to whom we should make offerings?" The answer to Jingū's question came from her mouth, but this time the voice was masculine: "I am the spirit of Kotoshironushi, who rules in heaven and in the void." "Are there more?" "I am not certain if there are any more," the male voice said and fell silent. Nakatomi, who was interpreting the oracles, pondered awhile and said cautiously, "These must be all the answers for now, but there may be more later on." "We shall wait," said Jingū in her own voice. Soon they heard another ethereal voice: "There are three gods who have settled at the bottom of the water in Himuka (the Land of the Sun) by the name of Upper, Middle, and Lower Tsutsunowo (Cylinders). They are in charge of every level of the abyss." "Are there any more?" "Whether or not there are more gods to be worshipped is not known at this moment." Then there were no more words.

The gods having been identified thus, envoys were promptly dispatched to make proper offerings to them. Jingū appointed a general to be the commander-in-chief of an expeditionary force. The troops attacked the Kumaso, and before long Jingū received news of the Kumasos' surrender.

In the early summer, Jingū arrived at the town of Matsura in Hinomichi no kuchi (the Path to the Land of the Sun; the area including the present Nagasaki Prefecture and part of Saga Prefecture). It was a thriving fishing village. There Jingū performed divination after partaking of a meal on the bank of a small river in the village of Tamashima (Jewel Island). The empress bent a needle to fashion a fishing hook and made a line with the threads from her garment. She used cooked rice as bait. Hoisting herself nimbly onto the top of a rock in the middle of the river, she held up the fishing line toward heaven and prayed aloud: "I wish to attack Silla and take possession of her treasures. May an *ayu* fish be caught on this line as an omen if my plan is to succeed, and if I am to bring my troops safely home!" Jingū cast the fishing line into the water. Before long an *ayu* fish was leaping at the end of it. Jingū was now convinced that she must undertake a campaign against Silla according to the god's command given to her in the first of the divine revelations.

Upon returning to her headquarters at Kashihi Beach (present Hakata), Jingū performed another divination. This time she waded into the sea and loosened her hair, letting it fall into the water. When she lifted her head up, the long hair parted of its own accord in the middle. Jingū bound it up into bunches over her ears in the way men wore their hair. It was now clear that the god wanted her to be dauntless and take on a manly appearance. She donned a masculine attire and summoned her councillors. To the assembly she said: "Mobilizing troops to make war is a grave decision that affects our state and our future. If I entrust the task of this expedition entirely to you, my lords, you alone will have to be held accountable for the outcome of our venture. If it ends in success, fine. Should it fail, however, you will be obliged to take the blame and suffer the consequences. I cannot let that happen. Therefore, I wish to assume full responsibility. Although I am a woman and weaker than men, I will adopt a masculine appearance and character. I expect to receive support from the divine spirits as well as from you. We will declare war. Crossing the strait where towering waves await us, we shall move our fleet to take the Silla treasures. If our expedition proves successful, it will be to your credit, my lords. If it does not, I will take all the blame. Now, please deliberate among yourselves."

The councillors unanimously voted in favor of her proposal.

On the ninth moon, Empress Jingū ordered various provinces to muster ships and train soldiers in the use of weapons. It was never an easy task to recruit enough men for a campaign. This time Jingū forestalled possible trouble with proper procedures: in invocation of divine help, she sent offerings to the Great God of Miwa in Yamato Province. Thereupon, soldiers began arriving in droves. By divination, the best day for the departure was selected, and Jingū addressed the three full divisions that assembled on the beach. The soldiers were elated when they saw their female leader appear dressed like a man and carrying a battle-ax in her hand.

"As you all know, we are going to war," the empress began. "I have a few things to say about tactics. Order among the ranks is of critical importance if we are to win the battle. If the drums are beaten to inappropriate time and the flags flutter in confusion, order cannot be preserved. Don't underestimate the enemies even if they are smaller in number; but don't be afraid of them either, even if they outnumber us. You must not engage in atrocities: avoid unnecessary killing and spare those who surrender. Follow my instruction faithfully, and I will reward you when the battle is over. But, of course, I must punish you if you show cowardice and flee before your foes."

After her speech, a god spoke through Jingū: "My gentle spirit will attach itself to the empress's person and keep her safe; my violent spirit will play the vanguard and lead her troops." The soldiers responded with a battle cry.

Jingū felt the child in her womb leap. She closed her eyes and prayed for a sign. Before long a voice told her to pick up a narrow stone lying on the beach and to insert it into her loins. She prayed aloud: "Oh, myriad gods of heaven and earth, let my child be born in this land on the day we safely return from this campaign!" She felt stronger and better. The fetus stopped kicking inside her womb. Then she set sail for Tsushima (islands between Japan and the Korean peninsula), stepping stones leading to their ultimate destination.

On a fine morning in early winter, Jingū's fleet left Tsushima for Silla. The wind god made favorable winds and the sea god directed the billows to carry the ships onward. Large sea creatures such as dolphins and swordfish swam around the ships, as if escorting the fleet to the shores of Silla. The direction of the winds remained right, and the tidal waves caused by their wake reached far inland. As the townsfolk of Silla watched, the Yamato troops landed and marched straight to the palace of the Silla king.

The swift movement of the Japanese troops took the king by surprise. Upon learning that the invaders were led by a woman with great magical powers, he decided to surrender immediately. He could see no point in resisting the forces under the command of a leader in divine grace; besides, his men believed that such an army would be invincible. The wise king of Silla promised Empress Jingū that he would become the keeper of her horses, which meant that Silla would furnish Japan with the superior continental horses that she wanted. He also promised to send one hundred craftspeople, male and female, every year as tribute to Japan.

Some of the Japanese troops clamored to kill the Silla king, but Jingū stopped them by saying, "No. We will not kill him. Remember I told you to spare those who surrender. Now that we have won our objective without fighting, it is not right to kill the king. If we harm him, misfortune will befall us.'' Even the blood-thirsty among the soldiers fell silent.

Jingū sent her men to the town offices of various localities and confiscated cabinets filled with treasures along with local maps and family registries. Those papers would become useful for the Japanese in collecting annual dues from Silla. When all was done, Jingū ceremoniously planted her spear in front of the Silla king's palace as the symbol of her victory.

One warm winter day the Japanese fleet left the Silla port. The sea was calm, the winds favorable, and Jingū arrived in Tsukushi without trouble. She gave birth to a male baby. The royal son was named Prince Homuda (Arm Piece), because he had on his arm a birthmark in the shape of an archery arm-guard. He would be known in history as Emperor Ōjin (Fifteenth). People called the place of his birth Umi (Birthing).

Early in the following year Jingū returned to her palace in Anato, where her husband had been temporarily interred. She collected his remains from the tomb to take back to the Yamato capital.

In the capital region there was much concern about the two sons of Princess Ōnakatsu, a high-ranking consort of the late Emperor Chūai. The princes were now full-grown men. Rumors ran rampant that they were plotting to remove the infant half-brother by Jingū from the list of succession candidates. The two mobilized troops under the pretext of constructing their father's burial mound. Then they lay in wait along Jingū's return route. The brothers held a ritual hunt for divination, saying, "As an omen of success, please let us catch some good game." They were sitting, each in his own shed, when a wild boar sprang out of the bush. The animal climbed over the shed of Prince Kagosaka and killed him. Now that an unlucky sign was manifested in his brother's death, the surviving prince Oshikuma decided not to wait for the empress there and moved to Suminoye.

When Jingū heard about this development, she consulted Takeuchi. They agreed that the baby should travel by a separate sea route to foil the enemy's plan. Takeuchi took the little prince to Kii Peninsula while Jingū proceeded to the port of Naniwa. When the empress's fleet was nearing the Akashi strait, her ship started to go in circles. She resorted to divination again. This time she was warned by the Sun Goddess Amaterasu not to allow the violent one of her spirits to get close to

Jingū's person but to arrange for it to dwell peaceably in the land of Hirota. Jingū inquired where the land of Hirota was and learned that it was in the vicinity of Muko harbor. To serve as priestess at the dwelling place of Amaterasu's violent spirit, Jingū selected Lady Hayama, daughter of Yamashiro Neko (chieftain of Yamashiro Province).

Soon another deity made her will known through an oracle. This goddess, Waka Hirume, who had spoken to Jingū once before, asked the empress now to enshrine her at Nagawo in Settsu Province (present Osaka). Accordingly, Jingū designated Unakami Isachi as priest of that shrine. Then God Kotoshironushi, who had also appeared to Jingū prior to her Silla expedition, reappeared. This ruler of the heavens and the void wanted to be worshipped at Nagata in Settsu. Jingū appointed Naga, sister of Lady Hayama, as priestess of that shrine. Lastly, the three deities—Upper, Middle, and Lower Cylinders—reappeared and revealed their wish to be enshrined at Suminoye of Settsu Province. Jingū complied with all of these divine requests and respectfully made offerings to them. Only after all the requirements were fulfilled did Jingū set sail again.

Meanwhile, Prince Oshikuma had withdrawn as far as Yamashiro and encamped at the Uji River. Jingū went south first to see her young son and great uncle Takeuchi in Kii. Upon her arrival, she consulted Takeuchi and summoned the councillors for a conference. The council reached a decision on how to deal with Prince Oshikuma. On the fifth day of the third moon, Jingū ordered Takeuchi to attack the prince's forces. Together with another general, Takeuchi took the best of their soldiers to Yamashiro and encamped across the Uji River. The prince came out of his camp to challenge Takeuchi, and one of his followers sang a war song aloud to uplift the men's morale:

> *Beyond the river is the pine field,*
> *Where the pine trees are thinly scattered.*
> *Let us proceed with strong catalpa bows and booming arrows*
> *To start the battle, each selecting his equal as his foe,*
> *A peer against a peer. Come all, let us go to battle.*

In Jingū's camp, Takeuchi deliberated on his plan of action. He told his men to bind up their hair in such a fashion as to conceal spare bowstrings in it. He also told them to wear wooden swords. Takeuchi's forces then advanced toward Oshikuma's line. "I am not planning to take away the country from you, my lord," Takeuchi called. "I am only trying to obey your command while rearing this infant prince. Why should I fight with you when there is no need for it? Let both our armies cut the bowstrings, cast down the swords, and make peace with each other. Then I urge you, my prince, to ascend the throne yourself." Takeuchi turned round and ordered his men to cut their bowstrings. Instantly all the soldiers took out their knives and cut their bowstrings. "Throw your swords into the water," said Takeuchi, and his men took off their wooden swords and threw them into the river. Prince Oshikuma observed these acts and believed Takeuchi's words. He ordered his troops to cut their bowstrings and throw their swords away.

When he saw the enemy completely disarmed, Takeuchi had his men produce the spare bowstrings concealed in their hair. He gave them real swords, which had been transported separately. Now Jingū's troops were fully armed again. At Takeuchi's command they crossed the river and charged into Oshikuma's lines. "Alas, I have been deceived. We have no spare weapons!" The prince ground his teeth in vexation but could do nothing but retreat.

Takeuchi pursued Oshikuma and his army and overtook them at the Afusaka Pass in Ōmi Province. Most of Oshikuma's troops perished. The prince and his remaining followers plunged into the water at the ferry port of Seta and drowned themselves. Hearing this news, Jingū sent her men in search of Oshikuma's body, but they could not find it. Takeuchi expressed his anxiety in a poem:

> *The birds plunged into the water*
> *At the ferry of Seta*
> *By the Lake of Afumi (Ōmi).*
> *With my own eyes I cannot see them.*
> *Can they be still alive?*

Jingū ordered the search continued. Several days later her men found the bodies of their enemies near the bank of the Uji River.

In the tenth moon, Jingū's councillors honored her with the title of Empress Dowager. Early in the following year, the remains of Emperor Chūai were formally buried in the tomb in Kawachi Province. In the first moon of the following year, that is, the third year of Jingū's regency, she installed her son as the heir apparent. She established her capital at Ihare (an area covering parts of the present cities of Kashiwara and Sakurai).

In the third moon of the fifth year of her regency, Jingū received three envoys bearing tribute from the king of Silla. They had a secret mission to retrieve a Silla man who was being held hostage in Japan. The envoys met this man, Mi-cheul Hochi-polhan, and coached him to plead with Jingū. Mi-cheul said to the empress dowager, "The envoys tell me that the king has impounded my wife and children to make them his slaves. Please give me a leave so I can go home to save my family." Jingū granted his request and appointed Katsuraki Sotsuhiko, a general with a distinguished military reputation established both in Japan and on the Korean peninsula, to escort Mi-cheul home. The Korean envoys, Mi-cheul with his own entourage, and Katsuraki Sotsuhiko traveled together as far as the harbor of Tsushima, midway between the Korean peninsula and the Japanese islands. Then the Silla envoys secretly provided a separate boat for Mi-cheul and sent him back to Silla alone. The enraged Katsuraki, instead of going home as planned, proceeded to Silla and attacked the castle of Chhora. Only then did he return to Jingū's court with captives and booty to present to the empress dowager.

In the spring of the thirteenth year of her regency, Jingū sent Prince Homuda to make offerings to the Great God of Kehi, whom she had enshrined at Tsunuga in Koshi. When Homuda returned to the capital nine days later, his mother gave a fabulous banquet in his honor. She sang a song:

This marvelous liquor is not my liquor,
But the liquor that is presented to this august prince,
He who dwells in the eternal land as firmly as a rock;
The liquor that was brewed and blessed by the honorable deities
Of Sukuna with words of divine blessing.
Drink it deeply and rejoice.

In the forty-sixth year of her regency, the empress dowager sent Shima no Sukune to Thak-syn in Mimana on the Korean peninsula. Shima no Sukune returned to report the situation he had observed on his tour, to her great satisfaction: "When I met the prince of Thak-syn, I learned that the King of Paekche meant to send envoys to Japan but did not know the way. So I sent one of my men to the king of Paekche to convey our best wishes. It seems that the king was very pleased by my gesture. He himself took my man around to show his treasure house and told him that he wished to pay tribute to Japan. This Paekche king, Syo-ko, entrusted to me these rolls of silk cloth, a Tartar bow and arrows, and forty bars of precious iron to be presented to you.''

In the forty-seventh year, Jingū received envoys from the Paekche court bearing tribute from their king. Along with them came a Silla envoy also with tribute. Jingū and Prince Homuda were extremely pleased. They said, "It was our former sovereign Chūai's wish to receive envoys from these countries. How delighted he would have been to see them for himself, but alas, he cannot do so now.'' When they examined the articles of tribute, however, the empress dowager and the heir apparent were surprised: tributary goods from Silla looked superb, while those from Paekche suffered so much in comparison that they seemed to be of no value. They asked the Paekche envoys, "Why is it that your gifts appear so poor in quality?'' They answered, "Now that you asked, we must tell you the truth. We did not come here directly from our country. We lost our way on route and strayed into one of the Silla ports. Officials there arrested us, put us in prison, and tried to kill us. So we looked toward heaven and invoked a curse on them. The Silla authorities became scared and spared our lives, but they took our tribute meant for you. They gave us goods of inferior quality as replacements and told us to take them to you as tribute from our king. They warned us that if we told you the truth, we could not expect to return home without a serious mishap.''

Deeply offended, Jingū and Homuda reprimanded the Silla envoy, but they knew it was useless to blame him. After some deliberation, they prayed to heavenly deities asking for instruction through divination. The gods ordained the matter to be entrusted to Takeuchi's discretion. He thereupon devised some excellent plans. Within two years his plans proved fruitful: Silla was chastised by an expeditionary force, and the Japanese troops pacified seven tribal units on the southern part of the Korean peninsula. They also pacified the people on the island lying off the southwestern coast of the peninsula (present Chejo Island), which Jingū gave to Paekche. Thereafter Paekche sent annual tributes to the Japanese court.

Upon receiving the Paekche envoy in the fifty-first year of her regency, Jingū said to her son and Takeuchi: "We owe it to Heaven and not to man that we have a friend like Paekche. It is by Heaven's grace that we have their tribute regularly. Every time I see the Paekche envoys at our court, I cannot help but rejoice in the sight. We should hold Paekche in great favor. Continue likewise even after I am gone from this life.''

In the fifty-second year, Jingū was further surprised by a special gift from the king of Paekche—a sword made of excellent steel, expressly meant for Jingū to pass onto her descendants down through generations. Because it had six small decorative blades attached to the main blade like tree branches, it was named the Seven-branched Sword.

In the sixty-second year, Silla failed to pay tribute. The Japanese court decided to send a punitive expedition. Katsuraki Sotsuhiko was appointed commander-in-chief. [In the *Records of Paekche*, this man's name appears as Sachihiko instead of Sotsuhiko.] When he reached Silla, the king and his courtiers devised a countermeasure: they sent two beautiful women from court to Sotsuhiko's camp. The Japanese general fell in love with them and forgot all about his mission. Instead of pressing the Silla king to make amends to Japan, Sotsuhiko turned around and attacked Kara, a tribal state in Mimana, surprising the royal family of Kara who had always assumed that Japan as their master posed them no threat. Now under attack by a Japanese general, they fled to take refuge in Paekche, where the king received them cordially. A sister of the Kara prince came to Jingū's court with an appeal for help. Outraged by the news, Jingū immediately dispatched an army to regain the lost territory. When Sotsuhiko heard that Jingū was angry with him, that her general had recaptured Kara, and that the royal family had been reinstated there, Sotsuhiko returned home stealthily and sent word to his sister, who was serving at Jingū's court.

In her effort to obtain a pardon from the empress dowager, the sister spoke of her brother to Jingū: ''Last night I had a dream in which my brother Sotsuhiko appeared.'' A mere mention of the name enraged Jingū into exclaiming, ''How dare he appear even in your dream!'' Sotsuhiko's sister was so frightened that she could say nothing more. When the sister explained the situation to her brother, he realized that he could not be forgiven for his transgressions. It is said that he hid himself in a cave and committed suicide.

In the sixty-ninth year of her regency, Empress Jingū died at the age of one hundred.

Jingū in Early Japanese History

Empress Jingū was one of the best-known female names in Japanese history, spotlighted in the first half of the twentieth century in particular. An alleged biography of Empress Jingū is found in the earliest "history" books compiled under imperial auspices in the eighth century, *Kojiki* (Record of ancient matters, A.D. 712) and *Nihongi* (or *Nihon shoki*, Chronicles of Japan, A.D. 720). It is this biography that is related in the preceding section.

The Japanese had had no written record, or no writing system of their own for that matter, until the sixth century, when they officially adopted the Chinese scripts brought over from China and the Korean peninsula through diplomatic channels and by immigrants. Prior to the importation of the continental culture, the ancient Japanese had relied on the memory capacity of the reciters, whose hereditary job was to preserve and orally disseminate the stories of their forebears and records of public events. One extant example of their earliest efforts to transcribe the oral accounts into writing is *Teiki* (Imperial chronicle), a genealogy of the imperial family. Members of the aristocracy were also motivated to delineate the achievements of their own ancestors and show their connection with the imperial family. Such "house histories" were later collected to survive as *Kuji* (Ancient tales). The oldest, handwritten texts of these two books date back to the mid-sixth century. The collective desire of the literate ruling class to establish national identity by chronicling or fashioning a worthy past culminated in the production of *Kojiki* and *Nihongi*. These books had been considered history down through the ages and touted as sacred truth by the twentieth-century militarist regime until their historicity was disclaimed in the aftermath of Japan's defeat in the Pacific War of 1941–45.

Most *ki-gi* (also known in Japan as *ki-ki*, an abbreviation of *Kojiki* and *Nihon shoki*) tales tend to reflect historical facts but coat harsher realities with the mist of romantic myth. The eighth-century authors of the Jingū legend obviously combined, scrambled, and otherwise tampered with facts and personal identities known to them at the time, for such is the usual way in which myths and legends are made out of specific events in history. *Kuji*, which served as one of the primary sources for *Kojiki*, is filled with traces of such attempts. Well-doctored tales must have proliferated in the late seventh and early eighth centuries, as each prominent family made earnest efforts to compile its own "house history." An event that took place in a time long past would lose its realness in the course of being told and retold. The harshness of an event would be diminished as each reciter colored the story so as to emphasize the positive side of someone's exploits. A man who rose from an insignificant background would attempt to connect himself with the bloodline of some family known to have a glorious past. He would tell his friends what he desired to be remembered for and order his house reciters to memorize and transmit it as fact. Some of these stories assumed the form of ballad while others were refined into poetry. An imaginative author or poet might appear at some point in this creative process and elaborate on some story to make it more plausible or impressive.

Like many of the personal "biographies" presented in *Kojiki* and *Nihongi*, the legend of Empress Jingū is a blend of history and fiction. The account of Japanese contact with the Korean peninsula, for example, is a compressed rendering of events that occurred over the latter half of the fourth to the seventh centuries, as corroborated by Korean sources. Similarly, Empress Jingū herself is by no means a pure invention. An undeniably strong current runs through all the extant historical evidence pointing to the existence of a polity in which women exercised great influence and power for a long span of time. Jingū is most likely a composite figure who reflects the personalities and deeds of several real-life female rulers in Japan. As such, the legend of Empress Jingū has a historical validity of its own.

Female Worship

Perhaps the single most important source contributing to the formation of the Jingū legend was the description in Chinese documents of a female leader referred to as the Queen of Wa (Japan). *The History of the Kingdom of Wei* (*Wei chih*, ca. 297) reports that there was a country called Yamatai, or Yamato, across the sea beyond the Korean peninsula:

> The country formerly had a man as ruler. For some seventy or eighty years after that, there were disturbances and warfare. Thereupon the people agreed upon a woman for their ruler. Her name was Pimiko. She occupied herself with magic and sorcery, bewitching the people. Though mature in age, she remained unmarried. She had a younger brother who assisted her in ruling the country. (Tsunoda, *Sources of Japanese Tradition*, pp. 5–6)

Compiled by Ch'en Shou (A.D. 233–97), this document records the location of the power center, the manner and customs of the people of Wa, and their relations with the Chinese court. Pimiko, the ruler of some part of Japan from around A.D. 180 to 240, had long been regarded as a Chinese perception of Empress Jingū by premodern Japanese scholars. This theory was questioned by an eighteenth-century scholar of the National Learning (Kokugaku) school, Kamo Mabuchi (1697–1769). The identity of Pimiko's federation has remained a fascinating puzzle tantalizing scholars and amateur historians ever since. Had the Chinese sustained their interest in Japan beyond the third century, the Japanese would have been deprived of this eternal mystery to ponder and enjoy, but provided instead with excellent sources from which to piece together an accurate picture of this island nation so powerful in its early days. As it was, because of the widespread and prolonged turmoil caused by social and political upheavals affecting all Eurasia, the Kingdom of Wei was soon rocked with internal strife that left their scholar-officials with no time or inclination to observe and write of the happenings in the remote islands far from their own shores. Consequently, the half-century following Pimiko's reign is shrouded to this day in the romantic mist of imagination.

It was not until the early fourth century that the formation of the Yamato state of federation took place. Most Japanese historians agree that a leader called Prince Mima headed a new federation that had its base at the foot of Mount Miwa in the Nara basin. Archaeological finds from the area suggest a political change after some armed conflicts around A.D. 300. Recent scholarship concedes that Prince Mima was probably the same man as the tenth emperor, Sujin (r. ca. 300), though his reign being the tenth in the imperial genealogy is still in dispute.

Sujin's presence in the Yamato region coincides with the beginning of a new cultural era now known by the archaeological term "the Old Tumuli" (kofun) period. Sujin extended his power from Yamato to Kii, Owari, and finally to Izumo. As in the case of Pimiko's federation, the regions that fell under Sujin's sovereignty seem to have had female chieftains previously. Evidence shows that the Yamato region itself had once been under the strong influence of a shamaness whose functions were very much like those of Pimiko in the previous century. But apparently most male chieftains of early fourth-century Japan were warriors. They had just learned how to make steel blades and tried hard to obtain iron ore from the Korean peninsula. Only a few men on the Japanese islands possessed iron implements and steel weapons, which naturally made their owners very powerful. Thus were the warrior chieftains able to rule over the dwellers in peaceful villages and evolve into aristocracy in ancient Japan.

Most likely, however, this kind of polity had existed long before the third century, when the world's first written record about Japan appeared in the Chinese kingdom of Wei. The cultural changes that occurred in the days of Prince Mima, or Emperor Sujin, were not necessarily results of a radical shake-up of the political structure in the Yamato region. The political changes at the inception of the Tumuli period, when new technology began to bring new work methods and new products to the area, seem to have affected a tiny segment of the society, which constituted their ruling class. As the chieftains spread their influence and added new districts under their control, they discovered that arms alone could not contain the population from whom taxes and tithes must be levied to sustain the aristocracy. Women were found to make excellent local leaders, quite willing to collect taxes in return for protection against armed invaders. In time, therefore, a system evolved in which the strongest man served as a deputy to the priestess (or female chieftain) of each area. The rank-and-file soldiers recruited from among the farmers and fishermen were commanded by the deputy strongman. The duties of the female chieftain centered on the spiritual concerns of the people, while the male deputy handled the political and economic matters, as in the case of Pimiko and her younger brother.

Vestiges of the ancient matriarchal society have been noted in northern Kyushu, especially along the coast. One such example is Ominayama (Female Hills), supposedly once visited by a man called Prince Ōtarashi, later known as Emperor Keikō (Jingū's grandfather-in-law; 12th; r. ca. 330). The *Gazetteer of Hizen Province* (compiled ca. 735) notes:

> Female Tsuchikumo [recalcitrant wizards] were living on top of these hills. They would not submit to his royal order to disband and continued to resist him. So the prince sent an army to destroy them. These hills are still called Ominayama [Female Hills] after the women Tsuchikumo who had dwelt there.

Undoubtedly there lived in northern Kyushu some seafaring people who had the custom of electing female chieftains in ancient times. They frequently fought off newcomers who wished to settle there. In time, armed invaders succeeded in overcoming native resistance, but they could not entirely eradicate the practice and beliefs of the older society. Cultural conflicts between the newcomers and the indigenous people often centered around religious observances. An episode in the *Gazetteer of Hizen Province* vividly illustrates a problem that the technologically superior newcomers encountered. In the District of Ki in Hizen (present Saga-Nagasaki area), there was a small town called Himekoso (Maiden's Grove).

> In ancient times a wild deity dwelled on the west bank of the Yamaji river. Many travelers had been killed by this deity. . . . Only half of those who passed this place survived. Divination was held to find the cause of this curse. The deity ordained, "Find a man named Kazeko in Munakata District in Tsukushi. He must serve at my shrine. Only then will my violent spirit be appeased."

Kazeko was sent for and installed as priest at the shrine. At Munakata, a major shrine for the sea deities stood. The language of this myth definitely suggests that these deities preferred to be worshipped by their own seafaring people.

> Kazeko dedicated a *hata* [banner] and prayed, "If this deity really wishes me to serve him, may this banner fly off in the wind and drop at his feet." The priest hoisted the banner high in the air and let the wind carry it. The banner flew away and landed at the grove of Himekoso. It then flew back to the Yamaji River.

By studying the course of the banner's flight, Kazeko located the god's residence. That night he was visited by a dream—a typical means for the ancient gods to communicate with humans. In his dream Kazeko saw a weaving tool and a spinning wheel, which seemed to indicate that he was dealing with the manifestation of female deities. Soon apparitions of the goddesses started dancing in front of him; then they assaulted him and overpowered him—at this point Kazeko woke up. Apparently the female deities were pleased with his interpretation of the banner's flight and his subsequent services. It was assumed that they would no longer kill those who traveled along the western bank of the Yamaji River. The Hizen people named this town Himekoso and worshipped at the shrine.

Etymology of place names constitutes a conspicuous element in the

Jingū legend, along with explanation of Japanese manners and customs, origins of shrines, and evolution of ritual practices. Closer examination of some anecdotes in the legend provides interesting insights. Take, for instance, the story that before crossing Tsushima Strait, Jingū soothed the pain caused by the fetus kicking in her womb with a slender stone applied to her loins. This practice is known to have been prevalent in northern Kyushu in the eighth century. By the same token, the episode of Jingū seeking an omen by catching an *ayu* fish before her Korean expedition reflects the custom of women's participation in fishing during the spawning season. The *Gazetteer of Hizen Province* reinforces this theory by emphasizing that fishing is a ritual act reserved for women only during the spawning season, for "it is said that try as they might, men would never be able to catch fish here." Such historical sources prove that women were respected citizens with a considerable social role to play in those days, when men were mostly sailors and explorers traveling along the coasts, leaving to women such responsibilities as securing food, raising children, and keeping harmony in the community.

As recently as in 1965, a significant discovery was made in northern Kyushu not far from Hakata (where Jingū performed divination through fishing) in the town called Hirabaru in Fukuoka Prefecture. The massive burial mound uncovered there was obviously built for a female of extremely high status. Common objects such as bronze mirrors and swords were found outside the coffin, but their absence around the corpse within the coffin strongly indicates that this was a woman who had had a special role to play yet not belonged to the Tumuli cultural sphere. The Tumuli period (from the late third to early seventh century) is believed to have been characterized by a male-dominant culture on the whole, but this excavation shows there had been exceptions. This particular female corpse was surrounded by jewels of great value, nearly one thousand pieces in all. It is obvious that the female so buried was reverently regarded by her people and lavishly honored both in life and after her death.

Another Tumuli mound (ca. 300) located to the east of Osaka Bay yielded even more revealing evidence of female worship. There were three coffins found under this mound lying side by side. The middle one, the largest of the three, contained the remains of a richly dressed adult female who appeared to have been a shamanistic ruler of her people. The coffin on the east side encased an adult male skull among many funerary objects, such as iron swords, battle axes, an armor, a helmet, leather shields, and spears. In contrast, the contents of the female's coffin included bronze mirrors, necklaces, bracelets, and the remnant of an object made of crystal. The most significant is this last item, which is believed to have been the handle of a decorated staff used in religious ceremonies. This object strongly suggests that the woman was a shamaness who had ruled as queen. The third coffin, which was smaller than the other two and placed far apart from them, contained iron swords, arrowheads, armor, and a helmet, along with the remains of an adult male.

The most intriguing speculation about this find concerns the possible relationship between two of the corpses. The man in the larger coffin seems to have had close ties with the woman buried next to him. Were they brother and sister as Pimiko and her secular administrator had been? Or a married couple like Jingū and Emperor Chūai? But why was his head severed? There is no question about his head having been separated from the body before he was buried, for his torso was nowhere to be found. The skull was surrounded by neatly arranged beads and covered by a mirror. Was he perhaps beheaded when the woman died? If so, why did he have to be killed? There are no definitive answers as yet, but future revelations and further study along this line can provide some insight into larger questions, such as why Japanese history boasts a surprising number of strong and politically effective women both in the mythological age and in the early historical period.

It seems probable that the man whose skull was unearthed beside the shamaness queen was her deputy in charge of political affairs. Burying a man of high social standing in a temporary grave at the time of his death was a custom in ancient Japan. Suppose he had died first. Later, when the woman leader passed away, his head may have been removed from a temporary burial site to be laid to rest beside her. Such a scenario is not an idle hypothesis of an armchair archaeologist, for *Kojiki* tells of an ostensibly historical case that closely parallels the burial of this fourth-century woman and her male companion found in the same Tumuli mound.

The background of this torsoless man seems comparable to that of Emperor Chūai, the husband of Empress Jingū. Chūai was a leader of the Yamato state chosen by consensus of the ruling class. When he stubbornly insisted on attacking the Kumaso against the majority will, he had to be eliminated, as made clear by *Kojiki*'s account of the events leading up to Chūai's demise. Whereas the later *Nihongi* is mute about the minister Takeuchi's role in interceding with the ancestral god in behalf of Chūai, *Kojiki* goes into detail: when Chūai refused to accept the divine message to stop fighting the Kumaso and invade the Korean kingdom of Silla instead, Takeuchi said to him, "Be respectful of the god, my lord. Please hear him speak through the *koto* strings once more"; the emperor reluctantly tried to listen to the god's words, but too late, for he perished soon afterward. *Kojiki* interprets his premature death as a divine punishment—an ancient euphemism for the tribal punishment meted out to a ruler who would not accede to the decision of the majority. In this case, the body of the fallen emperor was buried in a temporary grave, while his wife Jingū was carrying out the majority will. After she completed her campaign against Silla with great success, Chūai's remains were transported to Yamato and respectfully interred in a special tomb. All in all, the excavated tumulus and the Jingū legend in official history books serve as mutually reinforcing evidence of the ancient polity operating on the coalition of a shamaness and a warrior administrator.

Amaterasu the Sun Goddess

The highest being in Japan's ancestral pantheon is the Sun Goddess. Japanese mythology owes its cohesive form and literary flair to the hereditary reciters and the eighth-century compilers of *Kojiki* and *Nihongi*. The Sun Goddess, however, did not start out being the Originator or the Supreme Deity, but was more like a divine priestess in the service of prior deities.

According to the Japanese creation myth, their deities, called *kami*, are not radically different from human beings, except for the first seven heavenly kami who emerged spontaneously and later hid their bodies, while the universe was still shapeless as oil on the water, floating like a jellyfish. Then came five sets of male and female (referred to as brother-sister) kami, including Izanagi and Izanami, who would carry out procreation. Unlike the first female in Genesis, Izanami was not created of the male kami Izanagi's rib bone but appeared spontaneously in her own right out of natural elements, as did Izanagi.

The deities in the Plain of High Heaven gave this couple the Heavenly Spear and charged them to go below. Standing on the Heavenly Bridge (rainbow, boat?) that connected Heaven and Earth, Izanagi and Izanami thrust the spear down into the ocean and stirred. When they pulled it up, the drips of salt water from the spear tip formed an island, Onogorojima (self-coagulated island). The two kami descended upon it and planted a pillar to build their residence. Izanagi said to Izanami, "I find my body to be made nearly perfect but for one superfluous part. I want to beget a country (land) by fitting it with the deficient part of your body." (*Nihongi* renders this passage as "uniting the male source in my body with the female source in your body.") The two kami went round the Heavenly Pillar from opposite directions. As they met on the other side, Izanami exclaimed, "What a beautiful man you are!" "What a beautiful woman you are!" Izanagi responded but on second thought remarked, "It may not have been proper for you to speak first." Indeed, their first mating produced a malformed, leech-like child. They cast him away on a reed boat and ascended to Heaven to seek the gods' counsel. The council of heavenly kami performed a divination rite and concluded that the female had done wrong in speaking first, and that they should go back and try again. The divine couple returned to the island and went round the pillar once more. This time Izanagi spoke first, "What a beautiful woman you are!" and his mate responded in kind. From this union Awaji Island was born, then the present Shikoku, followed by Oki and Tsukushi (the present Kyushu), and lastly the main island of Japan (Honshu). Izanagi and Izanami gave birth to eight major islands that would constitute Japan, the Land of Eight Great Islands.

This is the creation myth in *Kojiki*, which is actually a transcript of an oral version narrated by a reciter called Hieda no Are. Most members of the government reciters' office are believed to have been women, but Are's known title *toneri* (imperial attendant) indicates a normally male position. So this particular reciter's gender remains a matter of scholarly controversy. At any rate, Hieda no Are memorized *Teiki* and *Kuji*, and her recitation was transcribed and edited by a male scribe into *Kojiki*. Eight years later, *Nihongi* was compiled under a heavy influence of Chinese traditions using the borrowed language of Chinese. These two official "histories" covering a roughly similar span of time are a study in contrast. For one thing, *Kojiki* is more detailed in description, more episode-oriented, and more rounded in characterization. For another, *Nihongi* is more male chauvinistic, as in the case of the creation myth. In *Nihongi*'s version, the male kami becomes indignant as soon as he hears his mate speak first and says, "I am a male and by birthright I should have spoken first. How dare you, a female, do the contrary and speak the first words!" The two kami do not turn to Heaven for counsel but immediately go round the pillar again in the "correct" manner.

After creating the land of Japan, in any event, Izanagi and Izanami produced numerous kami whose functions related mostly to natural phenomena, geographical conditions, agricultural technology, and household devices. Finally Izanami "divinely ceased to be" due to the burn she suffered in giving birth to the Fire God. Crying profusely, her husband buried her at the foot of Mt. Hiba. Then he went right on making offspring all by himself. When he cried, his tears became the goddess of Mt. Kagu. When he killed his son Kagutsuchi with a sword, the blood from Kagutsuchi's head turned into deities of swordsmithing and of iron ore–producing mountains. One day Izanagi descended to the Realm of the Yellow Spring (Yomi) and called out at the gate of the Palace of the Netherworld, "My beloved wife, we have yet to accomplish our assigned tasks. Pray come back to life." "Alas, it is too late," Izanami lamented. "If only you had come sooner, before I ate the food cooked by the fire of the Netherworld! But, wait, my beloved husband, you have come this far to see me. I will negotiate with the gods of this realm, but do not try to look on me in the meantime." Eventually losing his patience, Izanagi took a comb off his hair, broke off one of its teeth, and lighted it. Peering into the forbidden chamber in the Palace of Death, he found his wife's body in a state of decomposition, infested with worms. Horrified, he ran for his life, as did Orpheus in the Thracian myth, which the Japanese version closely parallels.

Back on the earth's surface, Izanagi performed ritual purification of his body in a river. When he washed his left eye (considered more important than the right according to Chinese beliefs), the Sun Goddess Amaterasu was born. Next he washed his right eye and the god Tsukiyomi (Moon Reading) emerged. Lastly, as he washed his nose, the god Susanoo (Impetuous Male) sprang to life. Overjoyed at their birth, Izanagi said, "I have produced countless children, but none are as precious as these three." He took off a string of jewels from his neck and handed over to Amaterasu, saying, "I bestow on you the Plain of High Heaven. Go and rule there." He told the Moon God to govern the Realm of the Night, and Susanoo the seas.

Significantly, the ancient Japanese believed that the kami who ruled the night was a male, and the kami who represented the sun was a female. This moon god is given no prominent role to play in the mythology. It is the Sun Goddess and her younger brother Susanoo who are the principal characters. A constant troublemaker, Susanoo would not go to the Realm of the Seas but cried on and on until all the mountains withered and rivers dried up. When the alarmed father demanded explanation, Susanoo said, "I want to go to the Netherworld, where my mother is." Izanagi was outraged. In the first place, Susanoo was not born of Izanagi's late wife, yet he was calling her his mother! Susanoo was promptly expelled from his father's land.

Instead of going directly to the Netherworld, he headed for the Plain of High Heaven to see his sister Amaterasu. The violent one of Susanoo's spirits caused mountains and rivers to tremble and the earth itself to quake. Greatly alarmed by all the commotion, Amaterasu said to herself, "My brother cannot have a good intention in coming here in this manner. He must have it in his mind to take over my domain." The Sun Goddess untied her hair and put it up into two bunches over the ears in a manly fashion, and entwined strings of jewels around her hair and wrists. She armed herself with a large quiver and sturdy archery shoulder-pieces, a bow in one hand and her sword in the other. (This attire of the Sun Goddess is echoed later in the description of Empress Jingū at her departure on the expedition against Silla.)

Amaterasu stamped her feet and asked in a mighty voice, "Why are you here?" "My heart is pure," her brother declared. "I have come to tell you in person why I wish to visit the Netherworld. I mean no harm." "How can you prove the sincerity of your heart?" "Let us make an oath to gods," Susanoo suggested, "and produce children separately. If the children I produce are females, it may be taken that I have an impure heart. But male children will prove my heart is pure." The Sun Goddess broke Susanoo's sword into three pieces, rinsed them in water, and chewed on them. When she blew them out, three goddesses appeared from the mist of her breath. Susanoo took the strings of jewels off the Sun Goddess's person, washed them one after another in the well of Heaven, and crunched on them. He produced five male children in all. Amaterasu said, "Those five male children were born of my possessions, so they are mine. The female children born of your possession are yours." Thus the sister and brother divided the children between them.

Does this episode indicate that the sex roles had been reversed in ancient Japan? Were the early Japanese females Amazons who battled and subdued males, as implied by Amaterasu's high-handed manner, which seems to betray a victor's arrogance? One plausible interpretation of this scene is that Japanese society underwent a slow but painful process in shedding its long-held tribal and matriarchal customs. Before the advent of the familial and patriarchal principles from the continent, a married couple had lived apart; their material properties belonged respectively to his or her kinship group, but their children to the wife's tribe. As Chinese culture rapidly permeated Japanese society, male chauvinism and the practice of private ownership challenged the custom of communal living centered around matrons. Countless disputes occurred between married couples backed by their respective kins. For a long time *loco parentis* remained a nagging issue as it involved inheritance rights.

The Sun Goddess claimed the male offspring created by Susanoo on the ground that they issued from her belongings. "Belongings" can be interpreted as "seeds" that had long been identified with procreative forces in the early agrarian society. But how could Amaterasu, a female kami, assert parental rights over the children born out of Susanoo's mouth? Such biological logic was insignificant for the ancient people. More important for them was reverence toward the female authority, especially in the matters of spiritual nature. As an arbiter judging guilt or innocence of a suspect by divination, the priestess/deity had the right to demand the items submitted as evidence for herself.

Another thing that must be taken into account is the notion of harvesting rights. Amaterasu reaped the crops grown from the seeds that she provided. The Taihō Code, drafted in A.D. 701 and promulgated in the following year, stipulates to the effect that in case of a dispute, the one who sowed the field in question should be granted expressive rights to harvest regardless of a subsequent change in landownership.

In any event, Susanoo surrendered these male offspring after "proving" his innocence and winning permission to stay in Amaterasu's domain. Emboldened by his acquittal, however, he began to commit religious and agricultural offenses. He broke down the divisions of Amaterasu's rice fields, destroyed dikes and ditches, and even desecrated the holy of holies by excreting in the food-offering hall where his sister was to set up an alter. One day while she was weaving cloth for heavenly deities, he tore open the roof of the sacred room and dropped a flayed horse on her looms. A frightened young girl weaver was pierced in the loins by a shuttle and divinely ceased to be (died). The angry Sun Goddess hid herself in a cavern, plunging the world into interminable night and total chaos.

Thereupon myriad gods assembled on the riverbed in High Heaven to devise a plan to lure her out. They set up a makeshift stage in front of the cavern and called on a comic shamaness, Ame no Uzume, to perform a dance. She wore a formal headdress made of spindle-tree and held bush bamboo in her hands. Climbing atop a coop laid upside-down, she danced, stamping her feet and waving bamboo branches. Soon the entire assembly was drawn into a seance. Ancestral gods descended onto Ame no Uzume, who shed her upper garment and loosened her skirt to expose her female parts (believed to be the seat of magical powers). The congregated deities laughed and sang to their hearts' content. Growing increasingly curious about the merrymaking outside, Amaterasu inched open a huge boulder blocking the cavern entrance and peered out. A god who had been waiting for just such a moment held up a mirror in front of her. As she leaned forward to take a better look at what she thought was a strange noble goddess, a strong male kami pulled her out of the cavern, ending the first eclipse and restoring light to the grateful world.

The stage is reminiscent of the ritual performed to mark the winter solstice, but more remarkable is the indication that the kami who participated in this liturgical drama were all of equal status. Unlike the Mediterranean and Chinese pantheons, which make a definite distinction between the ruler and the ruled, Japanese theogony attributes supreme power to no single deity. The Japanese pantheon seems to have maintained a comparatively egalitarian order rather than a hierarchical one. Even when Japanese civilization advanced in time, the basic structure of their government remained unchanged, still echoing the mythological society. As late as in the fifth century, the nobles at the Yamato court still believed in deliberation by a council, or group decision making, without setting any one person at the top with absolute power to dictate to the council. When the group failed to reach consensus, the leading nobles resorted to various forms of divination. A person endowed with charisma performed sacerdotal duties and communicated with spiritual beings for guidance. In yet earlier times, women had been considered to possess more charismatic quality than men, so that shamanesses served as actual leaders in various localities. As male chauvinism brought in by immigrants from the continent inevitably took root in Japanese society, female leadership gradually lost its effectiveness. But the residues of female worship persisted so strongly even in the eighth century that the female Amaterasu was assigned the highest place in the official imperial theogony.

Through a similar process, Amaterasu came to be defined also as a goddess rather than a high priestess. In other words, when the Japanese ruling class adopted the sophisticated continental institutional structures in forming a centralized government, the native religion was formalized into a structured theogony with female kami of various localities incorporated as relatives of the Sun Goddess. The propagation of the newly organized theogony was expedited through local people who came to work for the central government for a certain period of time. Above all, sisters and daughters of local chieftains played a crucial role in the two-way dissemination of religious ideas and customs. Called *uneme*, these women served at the central court in the capacity of low-ranking ladies-in-waiting and returned home after their tour of duty. They contributed greatly to propagating politically inspired dictums and theology throughout Japan.

Creation of Empress Jingū

Many of the continental immigrants who settled in Japan in the mid-fourth century were skilled in metallurgy and in rice farming, and well acquainted with engineering techniques needed for the construction of irrigation ditches and drainages. It was the descendants of these settlers who so ardently insisted in the eighth century that they were related to Empress Jingū, the mother of Emperor Ōjin.

One key component of the Jingū legend that has been accepted as indisputable historical fact is Japanese aggression against the states on the Korean peninsula in the late fourth century. Also authentic, though anachronistically set in the third century in the narrative, is the political climate reflecting the actual international situation of the late sixth and early seventh centuries, during which the Japanese princes whose families would later claim descent from Jingū were conducting serious campaigns against the Korean peoples. Despite the paucity of reliable Japanese sources, which makes it difficult to pinpoint exactly what happened on the Japanese islands during this period, it is not impossible to reconstruct a simulative model of the Japanese society of the day. The Japanese princes were comparable to their Korean counterparts in characteristics and shared much in social values, political ambitions, and high regard for ancestral gods. These armed men were often politically and militarily involved with one another across national borders, sometimes amicably and other times antagonistically, but mostly with inevitable cross-cultural intercourse.

In A.D. 367 and 369, Paekche, with Japanese aid, attacked the neighboring Silla. In 372 the king of Paekche paid his allegiance to the Japanese emperor by sending a sword with six decorative blades attached to the main blade, which is extant in Iso no Kami Shrine in Nara Prefecture. This is the very gift that Empress Jingū's biography claims was presented to her in the fifty-second year of her regency. It is 75 centimeters long and bears inscriptions in gold inlay on both sides of the blade, one of which reads: "On the seventh day of the sixth month in the fourth year of Taiwa we made this seven-branched sword of excellent steel. This sword has the power to subjugate all enemies. We dedicate it to Your Grace." The date corresponds to August 1, 369, in the Western calendar.

Although not all of the Japanese commanders who led military campaigns against and/or with the states on the Korean peninsula have been identified to date, at least one of them seems to have been Emperor Ōjin, according to *Nihongi* entries and the inscription on a stone monument extant in Korea that mentions an aggressive Japanese prince. These two sources reinforce each other in recounting earlier historical events as well. Emperor Ōjin, who emerged as a strongman in the Yodo-Yamato delta, well deserved the title of the first king of the Yamato state. In fact, scholars have long agreed that the fifteenth emperor Ōjin was likely to have been the first in the imperial genealogy with a historical and personal identity, in contrast to the composite or mythological personality of his alleged predecessors.

Power struggle among Japanese nobles continued in Korea as well as in Yamato, while the princes were taking advantage of their access to the riches of the Korean peninsula. What made Ōjin the strongest of them all was his control of the sea lane, thanks largely to the support of the Katsuraki tribe, which had amassed power and wealth through maritime commerce across the Sea of Japan to the Yellow Sea.

Some historians suggest that Ōjin was the founder of a new dynasty.

Others claim that he was the head of the invaders who came from northern Eurasia and conquered the Japanese islands on horseback. Attractive and intriguing, if disturbing to contemporary Japanese, as such theories are, they do not solve the mystery of Empress Jingū.

The compilers of Ōjin's family history expressly accord him an abnormal birth myth befitting a hero: he was born in Kyushu after having remained in Empress Jingū's womb mystically plugged up by a slender stone for the duration of her Korean expedition. As a young boy, Ōjin was escorted by the minister Takeuchi to the Koshi region. This episode is apparently intended to show that Ōjin had been already associated with Koshi before he entered Yamato as a victor. The implication may be that Koshi had come under his command as well before he reached the Yamato region. Thus, when he paid respects to Kehi Shrine in Koshi, his mother had rice wine made and dedicated it to him upon his return. Dedication of new wine as a gesture of good will was a widely practiced custom at the time. "The liquor that is presented to this august prince. . . . The liquor that was brewed and blessed by the honorable Sukuna deities," sang the empress. Since "Sukuna" (minor) meant lesser local chieftains at the time, the dedication of such wine symbolized the submission of Yamato chieftains to Ōjin.

This emperor was not merely a great warrior. He invited skilled craftsmen and artists from the continent to propagate crafts such as weaving, pottery, saddlery, and painting. Ōjin and his descendants also welcomed experienced farmers from the continent to settle in the outlying areas, thereby expanding reliable sources of revenues for the government. Ōjin's descendants inherited his hegemony over lesser princes within the Japanese islands and maintained a foothold on the Korean peninsula as well. The borders of this Japanese territory, traditionally called Mimana, shifted from time to time according to the balance of power among Mimana's Korean neighbors and the Japanese princes. By the end of the fifth century, Mimana had become a troublesome liability to Japan, as it frequently provided some overambitious Japanese prince with a hotbed for rebellion. Then, too, neighboring Korean states started asserting their claims over this Japanese land on the continent under administration by remote control. Its territory reduced by stages, Mimana was finally lost to Silla in 562.

It was to fill this period of Japan's history that the image of an aggressive Japanese woman, fictional yet realistic, came into the literary vision of the reciters more than a century later. Did these reciters fabricate entirely imaginary tales of the past? Or were the scholars who had compiled Japan's "national histories" under the auspices of the reigning emperors in the seventh and eighth centuries actually liars, as the "Father of History" Herodotus was once accused of being? The answer is "not totally." When the scholar-officials embarked on their task by order of Emperor Temmu (40th; r. 673–86), they had at their disposal a vast amount of information on the distant past stored in the memories of the professional reciters in the employ of prominent families as well as those in the government office. In addition, they all knew of some historical women whose lives were documented. There had been a female *tennō* (emperor, reigning sovereign) called Suiko (33d; r. 593–628), during whose reign the leading nobles joined forces to strengthen the central government and carried out several military actions against Silla. At least one of them was successful in making the king of Silla surrender without a fight—it is this campaign of A.D. 600 that served as a model of Jingū's exploits. Even closer to the compilers' own time had been Jitō Tennō (41st; r. 690–97), who not only helped her husband in winning a succession dispute by force and ascending the throne to become Emperor Temmu, but also ruled the country in her own right after his death. Evidence indicates that Jitō performed the duties of a leading shamaness for her royal husband, as described in the next chapter of this book.

The eighth-century scholars were well aware that half a millennium earlier, there had been considerable contact between the Japanese and the Koreans. When they had access to the accounts of Queen Pimiko in the *History of the Kingdom of Wei*, they endeavored to locate Pimiko's tomb and trace her bloodline by studying *Teiki* and the stories collected for the planned *Kojiki*. They searched for the historical identity of Pimiko on one unshakable assumption: someone as prominent as Pimiko must have been born into a great family, which went on to produce illustrious figures in Yamato politics down through generations. Their efforts were well rewarded. In the family history of a tribe known as the Okinaga, they found a girl child borne by a Katsuraki woman.

The Katsuraki were the seafaring tribe that had played a prime role in promoting the historical Emperor Ōjin into a position of supreme political power in the late fourth century. The Okinaga tribe, moreover, was the trade group that had brought advanced iron metallurgy first to Lake Biwa and then to the iron-rich Kameyama Basin. As their name, which meant "Sustained Air," indicates, they made iron implements by means of forges and bellows that they had brought with them from the Korean peninsula. The coalition between the Okinaga "people of the bellows" and the Katsuraki "sea traders" eventually yielded generations of leaders who held hegemony in Japan. When the compilers found a historical entry noting the birth of a girl with an Okinaga father and a Katsuraki mother, they proceeded to predate and Japanize her into a double-image of Pimiko the historical shamaness queen and the mystical mother of Ōjin.

While the aggressive side of Empress Jingū distinctly encapsulates actual Japanese dealings with the Korean states, the dates of her reign and the names of the kingdoms Silla and Paekche defeat her legend's credibility. Around A.D. 200, which *Nihongi* identifies as Jingū's first year of regency, neither Silla nor Paekche existed as yet on the Korean peninsula—both came into being under these names only in the fourth century. The scholar-officials of the eighth century, however, were dealing not only with history but also with theology. Their most important mission was to establish the theogony of Japan with the Sun Goddess presiding at the top. It was a time when the Japanese felt a pressing need for national unity. The court historians molded whatever materials they had available to conform to consensus. Painful memories relating to the Japanese strife with the Korean people and the subsequent loss of Mimana were transformed into tales of glory attributable to a composite or fictional figure of Jingū to bolster national confidence and demonstrate newly achieved cultural maturity of eighth-century Japan.

Historical Assessment

The ki-gi compilers had strong motivations to be convinced of Jingū's existence in the remote past. First, they were laboring under a deep-seated inferiority complex as they learned more and more about China's history and acutely felt their own lack of knowledge about the past. The "discovery" of a heroic female leader who was victorious in dealing with foreign states would be one effective means of uplifting national morale. Second, they had to explain the sudden emergence of a strongman named Ōjin, whose lineage was obscure or even dubious. Providing him with an illustrious mother such as Jingū could solve this problem. Third, and most significantly, it was necessary for them to justify all the deities housed in the principal shrines as indispensable members of the national pantheon and to legitimize the sovereign's exclusive rights to preside over the rituals honoring those deities as the highest ranking priest(ess) in the land. Empress Jingū was a perfect personification or synthesis of the political, military, social, and sacerdotal roles of the sovereign.

The appearance of Empress Jingū in Japanese history would not have occurred had there not been strong vestiges of matriarchal society. The concept of male supremacy, introduced first by the bearers of the iron implements and reinforced by successive waves of immigrating farmers from the continent, seems to have taken root in the Japanese soil as the majority of the population gradually became rice-producing farmers. Yet the tradition of female worship lasted long enough to accord the Sun Goddess the highest position in the theogony. By creating such a jingoistic character as Jingū set in earlier times, Japanese historians satisfied a collective need. Their sense of national shame in losing the Japanese territory of Mimana to Silla was assuaged somewhat by the tales of an empress's successful venture in the past. They answered the persistent call for female sovereignty from the believers in indigenous cults by raising Jingū to the exalted status of empress, appointed by no less an authority than a kami. Not content with having the same deity ordain a Korean campaign, they further endowed her with an ancestor who used to be a prince of Silla, thereby legitimating her claim on the Korean kingdom by right of descent. In attributing all the stories of belligerent foreign exploitation to Jingū, they mollified the real impact of Ōjin's emergence. By making him Jingū's son, they not only erased the obscurity of his origin but also put him in the bloodline of the imperial family.

The eighth-century scholars were hard put to reconcile two contradictory factors in their "history": the appearance of armed men who in reality seemed to have wrested suzerainty from the former supreme leader of the Yamato federation, and the theology that placed the female deity at the top of the national pantheon. They knew that matriarchy was a thing of the past in civilized China, and they wanted to make Japan appear as advanced as China in every way possible. Yet there existed undeniably strong vestiges of female worship among the indigenous population. The contending Japanese princes had come to terms with each other only when Suiko Tennō, a female sovereign, accepted the throne in the late sixth century. Half a century later, Japan had made much progress once again in consolidating the central government during the reign of the woman Jitō Tennō.

Nonroyal women had been holding high-ranking government posts in Japan. In 672, when Prince Ōama (later Emperor Temmu) rose against his nephew's administration, a woman called Komé performed divination for him and predicted his victory. The title given her was *kuni no miyatsuko* (magistrate). The gazetteer of Harima Province mentions another female kuni no miyatsuko by the name of Arasaka. Records show more women appointed as magistrates: Okura of Owari Province in 747; a high priestess of Kōzuke in 768; and a woman of Inaba in 771. It is significant that the Inaba woman's appointment took place during the reign of Emperor Kōnin (49th; r. 770–82). He had come to the throne ostensibly to rectify the country's ills allegedly caused by the controversial female tennō Kōken-Shōtoku (46th and 48th; r. 749–58 and 764–70). Historians have long contended that Kōken-Shōtoku was a highly irresponsible sovereign [for reasons that will be discussed in the Jitō chapter], and that her female failings led to the general conclusion that only males could be trusted with power. A simple entry in *Shoku nihongi* (Sequel to *Nihongi*, 793) reporting the appointment of a woman as the kuni no miyatsuko of Inaba at just such a time discredits these contentions.

Facts speak for themselves. Female worship, culminating in the belief in the Sun Goddess, defied any attempt by newcomers to conquer the Japanese population either by sword or by doctrine. It staunchly insisted on being recognized by each new community of settlers as the central force to be reckoned with. In their effort to reconcile the history of male rule and the tradition of female worship, the eighth-century scholars ingeniously created a composite character, Empress Jingū, by piecing together the known facts gleaned from the lives of real female sovereigns.

Suiko Tennō, for instance, was an effective ruler who achieved unity in the Yamato court and made Silla resume tributary relations with Japan. The expedition to Silla mentioned in the Jingū legend actually took place during Suiko's reign. Another model for Jingū is Kōgyoku-Saimei (35th and 37th; r. 642–45 and 655–61), who played an important role in Yamato politics by bringing otherwise contentious factions together to make peace. She was in Tsukushi readying her troops to fight combined Chinese and Korean forces when she died. And her granddaughter, Jitō Tennō, dressed in male attire and exhorted the soldiers when she was helping her husband bring off a successful coup to topple his nephew's government in the year 672. Quite revealing are the place names and local ceremonies at principal shrines mentioned in the Jingū legend. The appearance of various deities in her dreams and their demands for offerings seem to correspond to the coalition agreements reached between the Yamato court and local chieftains through the sacerdotal intermediary.

Just as intellectual empiricism questioned the creation myths in the Holy Bible in the West, the Japanese in the eighteenth and nineteenth centuries questioned the historicity of Jingū's reign. Reexamination started by Kamo Mabuchi was carried on by his disciple Motoori Norinaga (1730–1801), who relentlessly scrutinized the source materials on which the Nihongi compilers had relied in writing this empress's biography.

The precarious balance between fact and fiction tipped once again in the early twentieth century, as history repeated itself. Empress Jingū and her ancient Korean connection were played up in the official school textbooks as history, largely motivated by the national need to justify Japan's annexation of Korea in 1910. Then, at last, Jingū was reduced to a mythical figure in the aftermath of Japan's defeat in the Pacific War of 1941–45. Nevertheless, after all the rises and falls of her fortune, Jingū retains a place of great historical importance today.

As has been the case with the Homeric epics and Mediterranean mythologies, the dates in the Jingū legend are assigned arbitrarily or erroneously. Historical events that are known to have taken place over a long span of time are condensed into a month or some such short period. On the other hand, more than half a century attributed to her regency is hardly acceptable as historical fact. Yet, such poetic license, narrative expediency, and the ulterior motives of her creators notwithstanding, Jingū is a legendary woman of Japan with a considerable degree of historicity in her way. Not only does she embody certain real-life female leaders in particular, but also testifies to the sincere respect and the honored place commanded by Japanese women in general in ancient time, despite the active effort of the male-chauvinistic Neo-Confucian scholars in the feudal Tokugawa period (1600–1868) to ignore historical evidence and discredit women's social contributions in the past. The Jingū saga remains meaningful and relevant today as a vivid delineation of the state of women at the dawn of Japan's civilization.

Bibliography

Anesaki, Masaharu. *History of Japanese Religion with Special Reference to the Social and Moral Life of the Nation.* London: K. Trench, Trubner & Co., 1930.
———. "Japanese Mythology." In *The Mythology of All Races*, vol. 8, comp. C. J. A. MacCullock. Boston: Marshall, 1928.
Aoki, Michiko Y. *Ancient Myths and Early History of Japan.* New York. Exposition Press, 1974.
———. *Izumo fudoki.* Tokyo: Sophia University, 1971.
Aston, William George, trans. *Nihongi: Chronicles of Japan from the Earliest Times to A.D. 697.* Rutland, Vermont: Charles E. Tuttle, 1972.
Befu, Harumi. *Japan: An Anthropological Introduction.* San Francisco: Chandler, 1971.
Bock, Felicia Gressitt, trans. *Engi-shiki: Procedures of the Engi Era.* Tokyo: Sophia University, 1970.
Chamberlain, Basil H., trans. *Kojiki: Records of Ancient Matters.* Rutland, Vermont: Charles E. Tuttle, 1981.
Dioszegi, V., and M. Hoppal, eds. *Shamanism in Siberia.* Budapest: Akademiai Kiado, 1978.
Egami Namio. "Origin of the State in Japan." *Memoirs of the Tōyō Bunko* 23 (1964): 35–70.
Fairchild, William P. "Shamanism in Japan." *Folklore Studies* 21 (1962): 1–122.
Florenz, Karl. "Ancient Japanese Rituals." *Transactions of the Asiatic Society of Japan* 27, 1 (1900): 1–112.
"Fudoki." Translation of *Hitachi, Harima, Hizen,* and *Bungo Fudoki* by Michiko Y. Aoki. Ms.
Hall, John Whitney. *Japan: From Prehistory to Modern Times.* New York: Dell, 1971.
Harada Dairoku. *Jitsuzaishita shinwa.* Tokyo: Gakuseisha, 1966.
Hatada Takashi. *A History of Korea.* Trans. and ed. by Warren W. Smith, Jr. and Benjamin H. Hazard. Santa Barbara: American Bibliographical Center, 1969.
Henthorn, William E. *A History of Korea.* New York: Free Press, 1971.
Higuchi Takayasu, ed. *Tairiku bunka to seidōki.* Tokyo: Kōdansha, 1974.
Hora Tomio. *Nihon boken-sei no seiritsu.* Rev. ed. Tokyo: Waseda University Seikyō Shuppanbu, 1959.
Inoue Mitsusada. "Kodai no jotei." In *Nihon kodai kokka no kenkyū.* Tokyo: Iwanami Shoten, 1965.
Inoue Mitsusada et al., eds. *Wakoku no keisei to kofun bunka.* Tokyo: Gakuseisha, 1984.
Kadokawa Haruki. *Waga kokoro no Yamatai-koku: kodai-sen Yasei-go no chinkon-ka.* Tokyo: Tachikaze Shobō, 1976.
Kashiwara Institute of Archaeology, ed. *Sanseiki no Kyushu to Kinki.* Tokyo: Kawade Shobō Shinsha, 1986.
Kim, Jeong-hak. *The Prehistory of Korea.* Trans. by Richard and Kazue Pearson. Honolulu: University of Hawaii Press, 1978.
Kobayashi Yukio. *Kofun bunka ronkō.* Tokyo: Heibonsha, 1976.
Kondō Takaichi. *Sankaku-buchi shinjū-kyō.* Tokyo: University of Tokyo Press, 1988.

Kramer, Samuel Noah, ed. *Mythologies of the Ancient World*. New York: Doubleday, 1961.

Kuroita Katsumi, ed. "Shoku Nihongi." In *Kokushi taikei*, vol. 2. Tokyo: Yoshikawa Kōbunkan, 1932.

Ledyard, Gari. "Galloping Along with the Horseriders: Looking for the Founders of Japan." *The Journal of Japanese Studies* 1, 2 (Spring 1975): 217–54.

Miller, Alan Lee. "Chinese Influences on the Indigenous Folk Religion of Japan." Ph.D. diss., University of Chicago, 1968.

Miyazawa Akihisa and Yagiura Shun'ichi. "Shimane-ken Kōjindani Iseki no chōsa." *Kōkogaku zasshi* 7 (1986): 265–78.

Morris, Ivan. "Yamato Takeru, the Brave of Japan." *History Today* 21, 9 (September 1971): 642–49.

Nakamura Hajime. *A History of the Development of Japanese Thought from A.D. 592 to 1868*. Tokyo: Kokusai Bunka Shinkōkai, 1969.

Nakatsuka Akira. "Kindai Nihon shigaku-shi ni okeru Chōsen mondai." *Shisō*, no. 561 (1971): 346–63.

Origuchi Shinobu. "Jotei-ko." In *Origuchi Shinobu zenshu*, vol. 20. Tokyo: Chūō Kōronsha, 1956.

Pearson, Richard, et al., eds. *Windows on the Japanese Past*. Ann Arbor: Center for Japanese Studies, University of Michigan, 1986.

Philippi, Donald L., trans. *Kojiki*. Tokyo: University of Tokyo Press, 1968.

Piggott, Joan R. "Sacral Kingship and Confederacy in Early Izumo." *Monumenta Nipponica* 44 (Spring 1989): 45–74.

Reischauer, Robert K. *Early Japanese History*. Princeton: Princeton University Press, 1937; reprinted Glouster, Mass.: Peter Smith, 1967.

Saeki Arikiyo. [*Kenkyūshi*] *Yamataikoku*. Tokyo: Yoshikawa Kōbunkan, 1972.

———. *Shinsen shōjiroku no kenkyū*. Tokyo: Yoshikawa Kōbunkan, 1962.

Saitō Tadashi. *Nihon kodai iseki no kenkyū*. Tokyo: Yoshikawa Kōbunkan, 1968, 1971.

Sansom, Sir George Bailey. *A History of Japan to 1334*. Stanford: Stanford University Press, 1958.

Snellen, J. B., trans. "Shoku Nihongi, Chronicles of Japan." *Transactions of the Asiatic Society of Japan*, 2d series, 11 (1934): 151–240; 14 (1937): 210–78.

Suenaga, Masao. *Kogane-zuka*. Kyoto: Nihon Kōkogakkai, 1954.

Sunairi Tsuneo. *Yamato Takeru densetsu no kenkyū*. Tokyo: Kindai Bungeisha, 1983.

Takahashi Masakiyo. *Jingū Kōgō hakkutsu*. Tokyo: Sōbunsha, 1987.

Takamure Itsue. *Shōseikon no kenkyū*. Tokyo: Kōdansha, 1953.

Tsukaguchi Yoshinobu. *Jingū Kōgō densetsu no kenkyū: Nihon kodai shizoku denshō kenkyū*. Tokyo: Sōgensha, 1980.

Tsunoda, Ryūsaku, et al., eds. *Sources of Japanese Tradition*. New York: Columbia University Press, 1958.

Umehara Sueji. *Tsubai Ōtsukayama Kofun*. Kyoto: Kyoto Prefectural Board of Education, 1964.

Wheeler, Post. *The Sacred Scriptures of the Japanese*. New York: Schuman, 1952.

Yamagami Izumo. *Kodai Shintō no honshitsu*. Tokyo: Hōsei Daigaku Shuppankyoku, 1990.

Yokoyama Kōichi, ed. *Nihon minzoku bunka no ikusei*. Tokyo: Rokkō Shuppan, 1988.

Young, John. *The Location of Yamatai: A Case Study of Japanese Historiography*. Baltimore: Johns Hopkins University Press, 1958.

2

JITŌ TENNŌ
The Female Sovereign

MICHIKO Y. AOKI

FROM the late sixth to the late seventh century, a series of political reforms were enacted in Japan to strengthen the central government. The first of such efforts was led by Regent Prince Shōtoku (574–622) and Minister Soga no Umako (540?–626). Next came a far-reaching renovative period known as the Taika Reform, which began in 645 with a coup carried out by a daring and brilliant imperial prince (later Emperor Tenji, 38th, r. 668–72). Both events took place under the reigns of Japan's first and second female sovereigns.

Jitō Tennō (645–702; 41st; r. 690–97), daughter of Emperor Tenji, sat on the imperial throne in the last stage of a vibrant half-century and gave the finishing touches to the consolidation of the centralized imperial regime. Japanese historians have generally accepted A.D. 686 as the start of Jitō's rule as an acting sovereign and dowager empress, although it was not until 690 that she assumed the supreme title of Tennō. Her contemporaries knew her as Princess Uno, Sasara, or Hirono. "Jitō" is the posthumous formal appellation given her by the eighth-century historians. For the sake of clarity and consistency, however, she is referred to as Jitō throughout this chapter. The following account of her life and times is primarily based on the official history, *Nihongi* (720).

Family Vicissitudes

Jitō was the second daughter of Prince Naka no Ōe, who was to be Emperor Tenji. Early in 644, when the air at the court in Yamato was thick with hints of an imminent political clash, one of Umako's grandsons, Soga no Ishikawamaro, was approached by the Minister

Nakatomi no Kamatari, Prince Naka's mentor and strategist. Ishikawamaro not only pledged to support the prince's causes against the dangerously strong head of the Soga clan, Iruka, but also agreed, as a token of his good faith, to give his eldest daughter to Prince Naka in marriage. The night before the wedding, however, the bride-to-be disappeared. An immediate investigation revealed that Ishikawamaro's own half-brother Himuka had sent her into hiding to discredit him in the prince's eyes. But the evil scheme was foiled, for the anxious father's honor was saved by his second daughter, Ochi, who volunteered to take her sister's place and marry Prince Naka. Thus it was that Ochi came to bear the prince a daughter, who would etch her name in history as Jitō Tennō.

In midsummer of the following year (645), Prince Naka at last took a drastic step to change the balance of power at the Yamato court. He slew Iruka, virtually ending the mainline Soga's hold on the reins of government, which had lasted for nearly a century. Prince Naka became the heir apparent, and Ishikawamaro was appointed minister of the right. Jitō was born in 645—no historical source gives her exact birth date, but related entries in various records point to this first year of the Taika Reform.

Judging from the custom of the day, it is quite plausible that Jitō and her elder sister, who had been born in the previous year, spent their infancy at their grandfather's mansion in Naniwa, where he was known as an important financier. Their aunt, Ochi's younger sister, became a consort of Emperor Kōtoku (Naka's uncle; 36th; r. 645–54), and the capital was moved to Naniwa in 646. Three years later, Jitō and her sister would witness their grandfather Ishikawamaro's violent death.

The tragic chain of events began with the death of the minister of the left, Ishikawamaro's senior colleague. After a grand funeral, Soga no Himuka informed Prince Naka that his half-brother was planning to assassinate the prince. Naka reported the plot to his uncle the emperor, and an emissary was sent to question Ishikawamaro, but he declined to explain himself except directly to the emperor himself. As his residence was about to be surrounded, he fled to the family temple in Asuka. His son wanted to fight the palace guards, but Ishikawamaro refused to take up arms against the court and took his own life, followed by his wife and children. Ishikawamaro's loyalty was proven by documents found in his house and his innocence established, but not long afterward, Ochi (Ishikawamaro's daughter and Jitō's mother), who had borne her third child (a boy to live for a mere eight years), died of shock and grief over her family tragedy. Some time later, Prince Naka married Ochi's younger sister Nuhi and sired a girl who would be Japan's fourth female tennō, Gemmei (43d; r. 707–15).

Meanwhile, Ochi's children were given into the custody of their paternal grandmother, the retired woman emperor Kōgyoku (35th; r. 642–45). In 657, when Jitō was twelve years old, her father Naka arranged a marriage of political convenience between her and his own brother, Prince Ōama. The twenty-seven-year-old Ōama had been assisting his brother in carrying out a grand reform plan. Naka had already given him Jitō's elder sister as consort. Such in-breeding was a common practice in royal circles at the time.

In 660, ever powerful Tang China, which had been making friends with Silla, Paekche's neighbor and arch-rival, made a move to conquer the entire Korean Peninsula. Paekche had just fallen to them. Something must be done to prevent the Tang from trying to invade Japan next. Prince Naka was now the virtual ruler of Japan, except in spiritual matters belonging to the emperor's sacerdotal domain. He decided to set up his field headquarters in Kyushu, from which he would conduct his military campaign against the continental adversaries. Early in the following year, the Japanese fleet departed from Yamato for Kyushu. Families of prominent nobles sailed along. During the voyage, Jitō's older sister gave birth to a girl.

Jitō was seventeen years old. Bright but quiet and rather timid, always polite and thoughtful of others, she was a favorite among members of the court.

In Kyushu, during her second reign as Saimei Tennō (37th; 655–61), Jitō's grandmother died. Jitō's grief ran deep, for in this grandmother's care she had found love and security after her mother's premature death. The elderly tennō had not liked Kyushu and pleaded with her son Prince Naka to return to Yamato, but he had not complied. Her death convinced Jitō that her father was being too selfish in wishing to hold only the secular power over the Japanese state, shunning the title of emperor and the sacerdotal duties attendant to it.

Shortly thereafter, Jitō became pregnant. In 662 she gave birth to her only child, Prince Kusakabe. This was a real triumph over her sister, who only had a girl child as yet.

In 663 the Japanese Navy in Prince Naka's command arrived at the mouth of the Kum River on the southwestern side of the Korean Peninsula. On the following day they were reinforced by the Paekche Navy. Their combined forces engaged the Tang-Silla fleet, but the sea battle ended in a decisive victory for the latter. Prince Naka returned to Japan, taking along a considerable number of Paekche refugees. He gave them appropriate jobs and let them settle in various provinces. Fortunately, many of the refugees possessed craft skills and advanced technical knowledge that the Japanese found invaluable. Some were literate. Jitō, with her excellent mind and strong intellectual curiosity, learned about China from these knowledgeable people. She studied the Chinese classics and made herself acquainted with the history of China.

In 667, Jitō's father decided to move the government seat from Yamato to Ōmi, north of present Kyoto. The capital had been moved often before, and commoners, for whom the move meant more taxes and forced labor, remonstrated against the prince's decision. Many satirical comments appeared in folk ballads. In his new Ōtsu capital in Ōmi, Prince Naka at last ascended the throne to leave his name in history as Emperor Tenji (38th; r. 668–72).

The Ambitious Husband

In the meantime, a series of events had occurred to enhance the position of Jitō's husband, Ōama. When Tenji ascended the throne, he installed Ōama as his heir apparent. Had Tenji been more discreet in his choice of a successor, the course of Japanese history would have proved less tumultuous, and Jitō would not have come to occupy the imperial throne as a reigning and ruling sovereign in her own right. But there was a tragic key to the complicated turns of fortune—Jitō's half brother by a daughter of a local magistrate, Prince Ōtomo (648–72), whom Tenji loved dearly. Since Tenji made it increasingly obvious that he really wanted to have this son succeed him as the next tennō, the relationship between Tenji and Ōama became badly strained. Meanwhile, Prince Ōtomo had grown into an able statesman. Tenji appointed him his chief minister in 671 in what appeared to be his first move toward designating Ōtomo his successor. But his own brother Ōama had been legitimately declared the heir apparent. Inevitably, the appointment of Ōtomo as chief minister intensified friction among the nobles. The supporters of Ōama felt betrayed and indignant, while those in Ōtomo's faction vied for chances to promote their own positions and ranks at court.

When Tenji fell ill and lay near death, the atmosphere at court was so volatile that he called on Ōama after all to take charge of the affairs of state. Ōama, however, was well aware that his life would be in danger if he accepted. He not only declined but even asked for permission to retire from court service immediately, claiming that he felt a calling to take a Buddhist vow and dedicate his life to religious studies. Jitō was more than happy when her father gave his consent. Now well acquainted with Chinese history, Jitō considered it her destiny to emulate the wife of the First Emperor of Han China, who had assisted her husband to become a founder of his dynasty. Jitō decided it was time for her to leave her father's palace and join her husband. Ōama surrendered all the arms in his household to the court and had his head shaven in a Buddhist tonsure. Two days later, Ōama and Jitō departed for Yoshino, where they were to seclude themselves. After seeing them leave the capital, one man remarked that it was as though the sovereign had given tigers wings and let them loose.

The man's premonition proved right. Two months later, the emperor died. Within six months Ōama rose in revolt against Prince Ōtomo, who had succeeded his father. In fact, it was Ōtomo who provoked his uncle: he armed the workers who were assigned to build Tenji's tomb and attempted to block Ōama's access to the eastern provinces, the breadbasket of the Yamato-Yoshino region. Reading in his nephew's actions a clear signal of his intentions to eliminate his rival once and for all, Ōama decided to make his way to the eastern region before Ōtomo had the time to secure the support of the local powers in those areas. The situation was so urgent that Ōama could not wait for his palanquin to arrive. He started out on foot and then rode a saddle horse to continue his journey. Jitō followed her husband in a palanquin. After two days of hard traveling, they reached the residence of the district governor in Ise Province in midsummer of 672.

There Jitō addressed the assembled troops, proclaiming, "Heaven's mandate is with us." This indeed had a great effect on the men who had come to show their faith in her husband's cause. Thereafter she worked with Ōama on tactical plans for days. They deployed their most intrepid men to guard strategic posts in the key provinces. Special messengers were dispatched to recruit supporters from the remote provinces. Prince Ōama went to Ōmi to prepare an offensive against

Ōtomo. Jitō herself took command of the troops stationed in Ise. It was vital for Ōama to secure the Ise Shrine: the privilege to give offerings to the Sun Goddess enshrined there symbolized the legitimacy of the throne. Jitō volunteered to defend Ise.

The battle between Ōama and Ōtomo was over in thirty-two days, and the victor entered Yamato two months later. In 673, within seven months of Ōtomo's defeat and subsequent death, Ōama ascended the throne. He is known posthumously as Emperor Temmu (40th; r. 673–86). At the same time he installed Jitō as empress, making her one of the few women to receive the title *ōkisaki* (or *kōgō*) in premodern Japan. Wives of emperors were usually called *hime*, *kisaki*, *bunin*, or *chūgū*. The title Jitō received was the highest that could be given an imperial consort, and Jitō had indisputably earned it in her own right.

Joint Rule

As his posthumous name acknowledges, Tenji (Divine Wisdom) had been a brilliant monarch. Obviously inheriting some of his qualities, Jitō proved herself a woman of political astuteness fully capable of making cold calculations. Her husband Temmu (Divine Valor) was a great warrior but less of a statesman. He relied on her insight and sought her advice whenever he was faced with a difficult problem. In short, the successful rule under Emperor Temmu was made possible through the joint effort of two unusual talents: Temmu's great military acumen and Jitō's innate ability to grasp the significance of each given situation. Their alliance did much to further the aims of the Taika Reform initiated by Tenji: then continued expeditiously to carry out the reform measures, mostly designed to strengthen the central government.

The administration under Temmu and Jitō was blessed by a timely change in Tang China's attitude toward Japan. Now, ten years after Tenji's unsuccessful campaign against the Chinese and Silla navies, the Tang was no longer interested in waging war against Japan. With the possibility of foreign aggression thus removed, Temmu was able to move the capital back to the Yamato region, which had always been the favored location. After his victory over Prince Ōtomo, he rewarded various local magistrates who had been loyal to him with court ranks or posts in the central bureaucracy. By giving them opportunities to serve in such capacity, either in local areas or at the capital, Temmu had their activities under close observation. During the first nine years of his reign, most such appointments were made on an ad hoc basis, as were administrative rules and regulations. His energy was largely spent on his immediate concern, which was to stay in power. Realizing that one could not rule a country from horseback, he found his empress's political and administrative skills indispensable. Having educated herself in matters of law, Jitō willingly shouldered responsibilities in drafting rules and regulations.

Temmu fathered seventeen children in all, ten of whom were boys born to various mothers. The oldest was Prince Takechi, who had helped his father as one of the generals at the time of the rebellion. The second was Jitō's only child, Kusakabe. The third, however, was Ōtsu, born to Jitō's own sister and therefore a lineal equal to Kusakabe in the order of succession. According to the prevailing custom of the day, it was the mother's social status that determined the qualification of a candidate to the throne. Jitō pleaded with her husband to settle the matter of his successor. Temmu, nevertheless, was unwilling to make hasty decisions. Although he had been the victor in the rebellion, the existing practice still required a consensus of the nobles in such a grave issue as choosing the heir apparent.

In 679 Temmu took four of his sons and Tenji's two sons on a trip to Yoshino, the place of his exile before his uprising against the royal nephew. His intention was to have his sons and surviving nephews take oaths of loyalty before him and his empress in the Yoshino palace to forestall any contention over the succession. The princes all exchanged a vow of loyalty with each other, too, reciting, "We brothers and cousins will comply with the emperor's will, support each other, and avoid quarrels. If, from this time onward, any of us should fail to keep this vow, may he perish himself and his line become extinct." The oath was completed by the emperor and the empress, who each said, "If we go against this oath, may our bodies perish instantly." While it may very well have been Jitō's idea to stage this dramatic exhibition of family solidarity, keeping the children under oaths of loyalty to each other was a clever precaution that laid the way for harsh punishment in case of disloyalty.

Nevertheless, the necessity for each son and nephew to take a formal oath pledging his loyalty to his closest relatives only confirms the seriousness of the crosscurrents that must have existed at court. There was an acute need to have a duly installed heir apparent soon. The court nobles did reach a consensus, but their deliberation was stalled by an ill omen—a solar eclipse that occurred in 680. Such a natural phenomenon was believed to portend that misfortune would befall the nation if a decision as important as the choice of the imperial successor should be made at such a time.

Empress the Mother

There is no record left to tell if Temmu experienced any political and emotional dilemma such as the one that had plagued Tenji as monarch and father with a greater love for one candidate than for the other. General opinions at the court definitely favored Prince Ōtsu over Prince Kusakabe. Jitō's son was frail throughout his life, while Ōtsu, only one year younger, was a healthy and able man. A prefatory note in the anthology called *Kaifūsō* (Fond reminiscences, 751; a collection of Chinese poems composed by the contemporary Japanese literati) extols that Prince Ōtsu was noble and dignified, that his talents were infinite, and that since early childhood, he had been very fond of learning. Being an intellectual, he could write very well, excelling particularly in composing Chinese poems. Upon reaching adulthood, he worked hard at martial arts, acquiring great physical strength and skill. He was especially noted for his swordsmanship.

In the meantime, Jitō fell ill. If an illness was unavoidable, it could not have come at a more opportune time or ended on a happier note for the empress. For the court nobles, the prospect of her death portended a certain national crisis in the immediate future, for they were well aware how much Jitō's political talents had contributed to bringing stability to the nation and maintaining it. They were prepared to do everything in their power to aid her recovery. Temmu issued an edict requiring a temple to be built to house an image of Yakushi, the Healing Buddha. Temmu's call for this show of religious devotion also created a climate for favoring Jitō's son as the heir apparent. When the ill-omened year of the solar eclipse was over and the empress had recovered from her illness, the majority of the court nobles had agreed that Prince Kusakabe should be designated the successor.

His installation in the office of the heir apparent, however, did not put an end to the power struggle. As deep discontent spread among Ōtsu's supporters, the atmosphere at court became increasingly volatile. When Temmu sensed the approach of his own death, he entrusted the affairs of the government to his empress, Jitō, for she was the only one who had both the ability and political clout to cope with the situation. No one else could be relied upon to take correct and decisive steps in preventing disruptive political faction fights and carrying out provisions of the reform faithfully and effectively. Temmu died in 686.

Obviously the power struggle at court had already been intensifying while the emperor was on his deathbed. Anticipating the transfer of power to the empress, many nobles deserted Ōtsu's camp, leaving behind only a few die-hards. Most of them took a neutral stance, leaving the prince in an extremely awkward position. Less than a month after her husband's death, Jitō issued a warrant for the arrest of Ōtsu for alleged treason against the heir apparent, Kusakabe. Within days, the twenty-three-year-old Ōtsu was ordered to commit ritual suicide. Ōtsu's wife, Princess Yamabe, hastened to the site and joined him in death by taking her own life on the spot.

Four weeks after his death, Jitō decreed: "The Prince Ōtsu had been found guilty of treason. He had led officials and people astray. Therefore, there was no choice but to put him to death." By implicitly promising promotions to former supporters of Ōtsu, Jitō secured the favor of the court nobles for her son. There was no reliable evidence that Ōtsu had any deep scheme against Kusakabe or the empress, but perhaps, for Jitō, the very fact that Ōtsu had been popular was threat enough. In any event, Jitō's position at court became infinitely more secure thereafter. About thirty men who had sided with the prince were arrested, but she had twenty-eight of them released after Ōtsu's death, leaving only two men to receive light punishment. Jitō's daring move against Ōtsu served two immediate purposes. One was the removal of her son's rival for the throne. The other was to discourage the malcontent from rebelling by making an object lesson of the hapless prince. Jitō certainly succeeded in rendering the Yamato nobles docile for years to come.

Empress Dowager as Acting Sovereign

However strong-willed she might have been as a ruler, Jitō was also a woman of sensibility. When the dust settled after the disposal of Prince Ōtsu, she keenly felt the emptiness that the death of her husband left and was moved to compose a touching poem:

Even a flaming fire, I can grasp
    and hold it to keep—
Yet for this alone, I can do nothing,
    the passing of my Lord,
away from this world.

The poignant emotion of having lost her spouse, with whom she had shared joys and sorrows for twenty-nine years, is evident in another poem of hers:

Slowly trailing,
    clouds hang over the northern mountain
against the skies darkening
    away from the stars
and the moon.

Nevertheless, Jitō could not indulge in her private grief for too long, for she must tend to the pressing matter of easing the people's mind. After such a violent event as Ōtsu's forced suicide, the Yamato court had to find a way to restore the people's faith in Jitō. However treasonous Prince Ōtsu had been made to appear, it was difficult to erase the impression that the empress had had him eliminated to assure her son's enthronement. So in her effort to show that the event was inevitable, Jitō ordered an elaborate ritual in honor of the deceased prince. She had his sister, Vestal Princess Oku, preside at his memorial service. The ceremony would also benefit those who had switched sides by helping to allay their sense of guilt. And Kusakabe's faithful supporters could thank gods that they had escaped the tragic fate that would have been theirs and Kusakabe's, had the winner been Ōtsu instead.

Next, Jitō planned a series of memorial services for Emperor Temmu to remind his subjects of the importance of loyalty. Services for the dead were nothing new to the nobles in those days, because from early times the Japanese rulers had always emphasized rituals for the dead. Whenever a high official died, a series of memorial services would be held for the repose of his soul, until people felt assured that the spirit of the dead person was no longer restless and would not return to this world to do them harm. Jitō tried to use such a custom for more purposes than just the traditional one of appeasing the spirit of the deceased husband.

Her elaborate planning for the rituals had a fourfold purpose: first, to remind her subjects of the late emperor's glorious achievements and channel their grateful loyalty to her son Kusakabe; second, to demonstrate her regime's stability and convince people that by accepting her son as their next emperor, they could expect to receive benefits sanctioned by Temmu's spirit; third, to deify the imperial institution to the extent that it would be impossible for anyone other than the chosen heir of the former sovereign to aspire to the throne; and fourth, to set in motion the very process of establishing the divinity of tennō.

While Jitō waited for a propitious time to have her son enthroned, he suddenly died in 689, leaving behind a daughter (future Genshō Tennō) and a small son (Mommu) by Jitō's half-sister (Gemmei Tennō). His untimely death only strengthened Jitō in her lofty resolve. She still had a grandson whom she could groom for the throne. Since he was barely seven years old, he was not yet ready to be accepted as the heir apparent. To forestall power struggles in the court circles, Jitō decided it was necessary for her to assume the sovereignty herself. Thus it was that this astute woman with great political power and ability ascended the throne in 690. The fourth "female emperor" in Japan's history, she is designated as the forty-first tennō in a line originating in the mythological past.

The Ruling Tennō

Soon after her accession, Jitō appointed Prince Takechi, a famed general and the son of Emperor Temmu by another consort, as chief minister of the State Council. It seemed obvious to some people that this high post would naturally lead him to the office of the heir apparent, as had happened once before when Emperor Tenji appointed his favorite son Prince Ōtomo to the same post. Jitō's first official action, therefore, had a strong effect on Prince Takechi's supporters, who thought it advantageous to side with her. Being born of a woman of lesser lineage, this prince was not exactly qualified for the throne, so his chances for becoming heir were slim. Yet his appointment as chief councillor was a sound political move, satisfying to all parties. Jitō expected that Takechi would be loyal to her and her grandson as long as he received appropriate rewards for his services, one of the rewards in advance being the exalted title of his office and the privileges attendant to it, along with an increase in his land stipend.

Jitō made other strategic appointments in both central and local government offices. She had already distributed a volume of legal codes to all the local governments earlier in 689. She now decided to take a national census to update the family registry. The census had long been neglected because of administrative inefficiency and general social instability. Without accurate census records, the central government could neither assess nor collect reasonable tax levies. In 690 Jitō issued the order for all provincial offices to compile and submit family registries expeditiously. The entire population was required to register at their place of birth. Those who had left their villages and drifted into the cities were arrested and then returned to their original households to be disciplined or rehabilitated to become productive citizens. Also, Jitō formed the militia and drafted their training regulations and service codes.

After having implemented these new policies, Jitō ordered Prince Takechi to survey the site in Fujiwara for a new capital. What she envisioned was a permanent capital. Emperor Temmu had cherished a dream of building a capital in Fujiwara modeled after China's Chang'an. But the time being not quite ripe, he had had no choice but to leave the construction of a grandiose capital for his wife to carry out.

The administration under Jitō's leadership was bolstered by a curious mixture of two radically different groups. One consisted of the men well learned in Confucian philosophy who were sensitive to events taking place overseas, especially in China, whose civilization was more sophisticated than Japan's. The other group consisted of the persons not much interested in the outside world but staunchly holding the view that the nation should be governed by spiritual precepts rather than by formal legalistic concepts. The latter's belief that the sovereign was a direct descendant of the Sun Goddess helped Jitō in generating a consensus of opinion among her subjects. However irrational it might have seemed to the scholars of Chinese classics, it was the residual elements of shamanism that persuaded the Japanese majority to accept Jitō's plan and accorded the exclusive imperial succession right to her grandson.

In 692, Jitō announced her intention to visit Ise Province within a scant three weeks and asked the officials in charge to make preparations for the trip. Her journey had a tandem purpose. As a new tennō, she wanted to pay tribute to the Sun Goddess enshrined in Ise. At the same time, she felt it necessary to inspect areas along the route and make certain that the local magistrates' loyalty was dedicated to her and her descendants. Remonstration against her planned visit to Ise came from a middle councillor named Miwa, representing a group of learned men who wanted their sovereign to act in the Confucian way of a benevolent ruler. Now that agriculture had become the basic industry of the country, Miwa argued, the sovereign should be careful not to upset the farming schedule of the peasants by visiting them in the plowing season. His argument was legitimate and reasonable, but it did not succeed in getting Jitō to change her mind. She went ahead to name three councillors as her deputies to handle matters of state during her absence. Miwa then threatened to resign from his post, hoping that the gesture would provide sufficient weight to his protestations.

Miwa had been one of Temmu's loyal generals in the revolt and enjoyed much prestige and influence at the Yamato court. After Temmu's death, he had become an elder statesman in the position to offer counsel. Counting on his influence with Jitō, the Confucian scholars had urged him to present a formal protest. Jitō considered the matter, or at least appeared to do so, delaying her departure for three days, but she never yielded to his assertion. On the last day of the same month she left with her retinue for Ise. Councillor Miwa resigned immediately after the royal departure, but no other incident followed. It is apparent that the parties who opposed Jitō's travel plan simply advocated the Confucian teaching that the ideal king should not disturb farmers in a season important for agriculture.

Jitō's decision spelled the defeat of the faction that tried to use this issue as a leverage in forcing their political philosophy into practice. The failure of Miwa's protestation indicated that the dissemination of Chinese thoughts in Japan had not undermined the native religious tradition centering on the Sun Goddess. Jitō, as the direct descendant of Amaterasu, acted as she felt best, and this was accepted by the majority of the court nobles. Jitō took a calculated risk with her insistence on her own travel plans. She was, of course, aware of the importance of the plowing season, but she had a much larger plan in mind. Her husband's cherished dream was on its way to becoming reality at last. Now that she was fairly confident of her power as divine sovereign, she felt she could afford to take some risks in order to finish this new capital for herself and her descendants. She knew that the large-scale construction would mean heavier tax levies and extra labor on the part of the population living near the new capital. Her experience and political instinct warned her that she must take time to talk to the local people in person and thereby persuade them to provide building materials and manpower. In return, of course, they would be well paid through various relief projects and material compensations.

Why did she want to make her trip in the spring? Why not wait until winter when the peasants would be less busy? The answer seems simple: a winter tour would not be politically successful. People would not enjoy standing along the road to watch an imperial procession in the freezing weather. Who would leave his village to make a long journey just to see the sovereign when travel conditions were poor? The land of Ise usually had strong winds in the winter, which would discourage the crowds from participating in a feast. Those who did come would think of their discomfort instead of rejoicing at the sight of their sovereign and her court. Jitō's decision was consistent with the provision in the Yōrō Code of 718 (which is mostly a copy of the Taihō Code of 701), which instructs provincial officials to give peasants food and drink first to make certain they are feeling well-satisfied before reading a decree or message to them.

Plans for the construction of the new capital had already been drawn up. This was no time for Jitō to play the benevolent sovereign by postponing a grand tour, when a prompt departure would give her excellent opportunities to secure more solid political backing. Needless to say, the subjects whom Jitō wanted to see on this tour were not only of Ise but of all the neighboring provinces. Among them, Ōmi in particular was rich in timber. Japan, sitting on the volcanic belt, lacked proper kinds of native stone, and most buildings had to be made of wood. Large quantities of timber must be transported from Ōmi to Fujiwara via waterways. This project alone would require hundreds of willing workers mustered from local villages. Jitō intended to secure the loyalty of local chiefs by meeting them personally and regaling them with honors and rewards, which they could share with their people. Logistics required it, but this was a daring gamble that could have backfired. Jitō demonstrated the same kind of bold spirit in taking the risk as had her father Prince Naka half a century earlier in felling a powerful noble who had not been totally loyal to the imperial institution. Jitō's trip proved a twofold success: it expedited the construction of her new capital and augmented her power.

In 694 Jitō was able to move the seat of government to the completed city of Fujiwara. She shared a great sense of accomplishment with Temmu's loyal nobles. Kakinomoto Hitomaro, Jitō's laureate and Japan's greatest poet, paid a lofty tribute to the glorious sight of the new capital:

> *Our Sovereign, who rules earth's eight corners,*
> *   a goddess,*
> *with her august will*
> *has raised a towering palace here*
> *by the gushing water of Yoshino . . .*
>
> *The overlapping mountains,*
> *rising from the verdant walls,*
> *adorn themselves with blossoming flowers*
> *   in spring,*
> *and don the colored garments in the autumn*
> *   in many hues*
> *. . . these rivers and the mountains serve*
> *our Sovereign as one in will.*
> *'Tis truly the reign of divinity.*

Clearly, the very notion of the imperial institution is deified with a homage paid to the goddess-like charisma of Jitō. Here is an interesting recurrence of history. Queen Pimiko, the shamaness and first Japanese woman to be identified by name in history, had brought unity among the contending chieftains in third-century Japan, as mentioned in chapter 1. Now Jitō established political stability that her father Tenji had been unable to attain. Combined with the people's appreciation of Jitō as administrator, their high regard for the sacerdotal role of the tennō accorded her great advantages in accomplishing her goals. She was careful not to act aggressively or to give the impression that she wanted to be deified. She kept a relatively low profile as a caretaker sovereign after the deaths of her husband and son until her grandson's maturity, performing the role of a faithful executor administering plans that had been ostensibly entrusted to her by her husband but in fact were of her own making. (Her posthumous reign name, Jitō, means "to maintain the legitimate line.")

The Fujiwara capital marked the completion of the first stage of the reformation to consolidate the imperial institution in a manner of Tang China's. It was now time to proceed with the second stage to make it safe from any threat from within in the form of contenders for the throne. With remarkable astuteness, Jitō manipulated group sentiments in legitimizing the concept of Tennō until the sovereign stood with unshakable stature and power as the leader of both political and religious affairs.

The Ex-tennō

In 696 Prince Takechi died. Jitō's grandson, fourteen years old now, was already capable of performing many of the duties expected of a tennō. As the first step toward the throne, Jitō installed him as the heir apparent in early 697. Six months later she abdicated and became the first to use the supernumerary title of extraordinary significance, *dajō-tennō* (ex-emperor), which enabled her to continue wielding political power. At the same time she tutored, advised, and assisted the young Emperor Mommu (42d; r. 697–707) in the affairs of state, giving him "on-the-job" training. Mommu had been studying with Confucian scholars and had learned how an ideal sovereign should conduct himself in ruling his country. On the first day on his throne, Mommu announced 50 percent cuts in both land and labor taxes. This move was designed to assure his subjects that he would be a benevolent sovereign, as befitted a ruler following the precepts of Confucius.

Jitō's next project was to select the principal consort for her grandson. In searching for suitable candidates, she exercised utmost caution. Fearing, for example, that her late husband's other child or grandchild might wield influence in court politics as Mommu's father-in-law, she excluded women of royal blood from consideration. Another factor to contend with was a prevailing sentiment against primogeniture by male line. Her husband Temmu's ability to overthrow his nephew's government with the support of the majority of the nobles was proof enough that the succession right of the former tennō's younger brothers was still widely recognized. Jitō had no intention of giving other imperial princes sired by Temmu any chance to become part of Mommu's household and thereby acquire power. Her cautious attitude in selecting Mommu's principal wife effectively prevented any of his present, high-born consorts from being enthroned as empress.

The power map at the Yamato court had undergone changes in the last fifty years. Prominent now in the court power structure was

Fujiwara no Fuhito, the son of Nakatomi no Kamatari. The exact circumstances of his upbringing are not known, but he was adopted by a man called Tabe no Fuhito Ōsumi, who appears to have lived in Yamashina (present Kyoto). His adoptive father's court title, Fuhito (meaning "scribe"), became his first name. Jitō valued Fuhito's political insight and acumen just as her father Tenji had done Fuhito's father Kamatari's. Fuhito was twenty-seven years old in 686, when Jitō's husband died. Three years later Jitō made him a judge. This appointment brought him the privilege of entry into the Yamato court circles.

When a certain imperial prince became estranged from his wife, Fuhito wooed and married her. As the daughter of a man who had rendered meritorious service in Temmu's rebellion and as a former consort of royalty, Fuhito's new wife, known as Inukai Michiyo, commanded respect among the courtiers. Making great use of her popularity and influence at court, Fuhito succeeded in having his daughter by his first wife installed as a consort of Mommu. She gave birth to a male child, who was to become one of the strongest ruling monarchs in premodern Japan, Emperor Shōmu (45th; r. 724–49). During Mommu's reign, Fujiwara Fuhito was the most influential man at court, with yet another daughter of his (by Michiyo) betrothed to the future Emperor Shōmu. This daughter, known in history as Empress Kōmyō (701–60), the first Japanese woman of nonroyal birth to receive the exalted title, bore her husband a girl child who would ascend the throne twice under two separate reign-names: Kōken (46th; r. 739–58) and Shōtoku (48th; r. 764–70).

In the meantime, the Taihō Code was completed in 701 and promulgated the following year. It was based on the Ōmi Code, compiled in 668 during the reign of Jitō's father, Tenji. Her husband had planned to reissue it as the Kiyomihara Code, but it was under Jitō's leadership that detailed provisions were added to make it enforceable. The Taihō Code consisted of six volumes of penal laws and eleven volumes of administrative laws. The penal laws were primarily adopted from early Chinese models stipulating severe penalties. Contemporary documents suggest, however, that harsh punishments were meant as deterrent to serious crimes and rarely carried out in fact. The Japanese concept and practice of criminal law were considerably different from those in the West or in China. Administrative codes were also based on the Chinese examples, but a sizable portion of the civil laws derived from commonly accepted Japanese customs. By codifying them and making officials formally enforce them, Jitō-Mommu's government succeeded in providing the nation with a unified concept of law and order.

One of Jitō's great accomplishments that stands out in cultural history is her encouragement of literary arts, especially poetry. Narratives known as *norito* (Shinto prayers) and *kaki* (house histories) were often recited at Jitō's court for the purpose of promoting the prestige and power of certain families. Poetry, which used to be crude, repetitious incantations and quasi-narratives for the most part, became more refined in form and increasingly popular thanks to Jitō's interest and patronage. The fast-developing native poetry as well as such Chinese imports as the verses recounting the glorious achievements of the Six Dynasties period whetted the Japanese aesthetic taste, and poetic contributions to the frequently held literary competitions increased in number. Some poems known to have been composed by Jitō and her contemporaries are preserved in *Man'yōshū*, the oldest anthology of Japanese poetry, compiled in the mid-eighth century.

Jitō was fond of travels. Her favorite region was the Yoshino highlands, where she and her husband had once lived in exile. She visited the area more than thirty times. On many of these occasions, she encouraged her retinue to compete in poetry composition. She also loved to listen to storytellers. An old woman called Shii was her favorite. Jitō sent her a letter in the form of a poem playing on the word *shii*, which means "to insist" and also "to urge," and she received a reply in kind:

> *Though I say, "No More!"*
> *Shii insists on telling her stories.*
> *But when she indeed stops,*
> *and I do not hear them at all,*
> *I come to miss them greatly.*
>
>   Jitō Tennō

> *Though I say, "No more!"*
> *you urge me, "Go on, go on, tell me more."*
> *So I keep telling you my stories.*
> *And now, you are saying*
> *that Shii is insistent.*
>
>   Lady Shii

One of Jitō's literary trademarks was appreciation of nature, as seen in her poem rejoicing in the coming of summer:

> *Spring is gone,*
> *And summer must have arrived.*
> *Look how white robes are spread*
> *Over the heavenly Hill of Kagu!*

In the tenth month of 702, Jitō went on another tour of inspection through the eastern provinces, during which she bestowed gifts and even some court ranks on the local officials and leading farmers. She was on the road nearly seven weeks, returning in time for the anniversary of her father's death. Two weeks later Jitō fell ill, never to recover. She died on the twenty-first day of the first month in 703 at the age of fifty-eight. Her body was cremated in accord with Buddhist practice—it was the first cremation in the imperial household. Her ashes were interred in her husband's tomb.

Accomplishments

One major achievement of Jitō's reign was that the goals of the Taika Reform were attained: to end the tribal (kinship) system and place the state under a single sovereign instead of many chieftains. Japan needed a strong administration institutionalized through written codes and run by a permanent bureaucracy in order to have the country respected and taken seriously by its neighbors. The Chinese and Korean nationals who had emigrated to Japan during the early seventh and eighth centuries made great contributions by bringing with them political ideas that inspired the Japanese elite to outgrow traditional tribal practices. Making it a policy not to allow wealthy nobles and magistrates to turn them into their own servants or slaves, the government gave the refugees citizenship and utilized their knowledge and skills to the fullest for public benefit. Jitō endorsed this policy and saw to its enforcement.

What made Jitō so effective as a ruler? There is little doubt that it was much more than her political shrewdness. Her impeccable royal lineage as Emperor Tenji's daughter and Temmu's empress worked in her favor, as she strove to achieve consensus of opinion in the Yamato court. One thing that changed to give her an unexpected advantage was the international situation. Earlier in 663, Tang China had planned to subjugate or at least impress Japan with its might at the request of its proxy state, Silla. But since the initial aim had been partially attained through a victory over the Japanese Navy, China showed neither territorial ambition nor ideological aggressiveness, simply leaving Japan alone. Cessation of the military threat from abroad enabled Jitō to concentrate her efforts on consolidating Japan's own political and economic foundations. The succession struggle among her closest kin, such as she experienced twice in her lifetime, was indeed tragic, but her husband's victory and her elimination of a contender resulted in the growth of the Japanese central government. The memory of a national crisis once caused by the Tang alliance with Silla was not easily forgotten and served to sharpen the Japanese sense of patriotism, also to Jitō's advantage.

Buddhism, which had found its way to Japan from China via Korean kingdoms in the late sixth century, had permeated the leading class, and Jitō ardently supported the religion as her husband had done. She distributed ten thousand copies of the Golden Light Sutra to the provinces to be read aloud on every New Year's Day. She also made active proselytizing efforts to propagate Buddhism among the indigenous tribes on the frontiers of Kyushu in the south and Ezo (Hokkaido) in the north. Even as Buddhism became recognized by the local population as a universal syncretic faith, it did not eradicate or supplant the inherited native cults. By adopting local rituals at court, Jitō demonstrated tolerance of doctrinal differences.

She also made it a policy to promote and universalize diverse arts and useful customs of various localities so that they would be accepted by the majority of the people. Frequently giving banquets at court and staging performances by talented persons representing all regions, Jitō succeeded in reorienting the competitive impulse of local people. Her patronage of provincial arts and liturgies encouraged chieftains to give recognition and rewards to their native artists and performers. Martial arts, such as archery, horsemanship, fencing, and spearsmanship, also found their niche in the court rituals. In time, martial arts that had been in practical use became more ceremonial and aesthetic. Local chieftains who might have been bitter rivals to their neighbors were encouraged to demonstrate artistic excellence in cultural contests instead of physical prowess in armed confrontations.

All in all, Jitō is a brilliant exemplar testifying to the ability of Japanese women to occupy positions of power and shape the course of the nation's history.

Women Tennō of Japan

On August 15, 1945, ordinary Japanese citizens heard the voice of the emperor for the first time in their life. Over the heavily garbled radio, he stated that Japan had no choice but to surrender in the face of the invention of the atomic bomb and its deployment by the enemies, which could bring about not only the ultimate collapse of the Japanese nation but even the total extinction of the human race. Fighting stopped despite counterattempts by some militant elements, whose last effort was to jam the broadcast. Early in the following January, the emperor took to the radio again to announce that he was not a god but a human being, a historic proclamation denying his own divinity.

The Japanese view of the imperial institution as divine had been much emphasized in the mid-1800s, as the restoration movement gathered momentum to overthrow the Tokugawa Shogunate, a feudal samurai administration that had ruled Japan since 1603, and restore power to the imperial throne. After Japan established itself as a modern monarchy following the Meiji Restoration of 1868, the myth and the divine lineage of the imperial house were officially designated as national history and inculcated through school textbooks. By the 1940s the Japanese as a whole accepted the idea that their emperor was a living god. Hence, the denial of his divinity had to come from the emperor himself if it was to be believed by his people.

The Japanese emperor who sat on the throne for over sixty-two years, from 1926 to January 8, 1989, was the 124th *tennō*. This word is a Japanese reading of the Chinese term *tianhuang* (heavenly ruler), which means an exalted sovereign with Heaven's mandate, morally superior to a king. Western journalism referred to the late emperor as "Emperor Hirohito," his personal name. This common practice was not only highly irreverent by Japanese protocol, but also totally erroneous by historical convention. Unlike the kings and queens of other countries, who are normally called by their first names, Japanese tennō are historically known by their posthumously chosen formal or ritualistic appellations. Especially since Japan's modernization in 1868, the law stipulates that the emperor be called by the name of his reign only after his death. So the last emperor, who lived through the turbulent Shōwa period (1926–89), is recorded in history as Shōwa Tennō. In his lifetime he was simply referred to as "Tennō" or, if necessary, "Kinjō (current) Tennō,'' as his son will be through his new reign, which began in 1989 as Heisei 1.

What Is a Tennō?

In ancient times there was neither an emperor nor a living being considered to be a god in the Japanese islands. People believed that supernatural deities spoke to some mortals, who could then convey the message to the human community. Gods were thought to be endowed with both gentle and violent spirits. Unfavorable conditions, whether natural or otherwise, were supposedly caused by the violent spirit of one god or another. Therefore, the person who functioned as a medium between man and god was expected to discover whether any given deity was pleased and benign at a given time or so displeased about something as to unleash his violent nature. Experience had taught the elders that women seemed more attuned than men to divine the will of the gods. Consequently, most tribal federations were ruled by the joint leadership of a male administrator, called *kimi* (chief), handling the military and civil affairs and a shamaness (or high priestess) in charge of spiritual matters.

This mixed-double polity continued until immigrants from China's northeastern region settled in considerable number on the Japanese islands, bringing with them the sun worship of proto-Mongol peoples. They believed that the spirits of the Sun God would descend to the tree tops when a male shaman prayed to them. This belief gradually superseded the earlier Japanese practices, and in time the indigenous population came to accept the efficacy of the newly arrived male shamans. In various localities, however, the female shamans retained their superiority in spiritual matters. Eventually the new notion of sun worship became modified and transformed into deification of the sun as a goddess.

At this point in the religio-political evolution enters the first Japanese tennō, Jimmu. His existence is largely mythological, but according to ancient literature, Jimmu came from the southern island of Tsukushi (today's Kyushu). Pushing his way up the Main Island northeastward, he conquered the coastal areas along the Inland Sea and finally reached the Yamato plains, aided by a great raven which showed him the way and led him to triumph over the local oppositions. Probably deriving from a tale told by Finno-Ugric speaking peoples,

this raven episode suggests that those who came to dwell in the Yamato region may have been bearers of the north Eurasian cultures.
Jimmu is credited with adopting the Sun Goddess as the ancestral deity
of his people, but scholars consider the first nine reigns, including
Jimmu's in *Teiki* (Imperial genealogy) to be fictitious.

No tennō's presence is historically confirmable before Sujin (10th;
r. ca. 300). Prior to his emergence as the strongman in Yamato, there
seemed to have been as many sun goddesses worshipped as there were
political units. In other words, each tribal unit probably had its own sun
goddess served by her own high priestess. When the Japanese islands
were unified under Sujin's leadership, the sun goddesses of several
tribal units merged into one to be honored as the ancestral deity of the
entire island population. This perhaps represents the earliest stage of
the worship of Amaterasu, the Sun Goddess.

Sujin, possibly the first historical unifier of Japan, married into a
tribe that had traditionally had a female shaman as leader, and he
became the most powerful in the Yamato region. Sujin is said to have
had such reverence for the Sun Goddess that he was afraid to live in
her presence and erected a shrine for her away from his palace. He
revered not only the Sun Goddess but also many other deities, each of
whom he honored with a shrine and regular offerings. The real reason
for such a show of reverence was most likely his desire to separate
religion from state affairs and eliminate feminine influence from politics.

Interestingly, the myths seems quite emphatic in suggesting that the
spirit of the ancestral deity insisted on being worshipped within the
palace compound of the reigning sovereign rather than anywhere outside. Sujin's successor, therefore, set up a special dais in his residence
and consecrated it as a place of worship. The duty of giving offerings
to the goddess was reserved for female shamans. There were also male
shamans serving at court, but they often played the *koto* instrument to
entreat the Sun Goddess to manifest her will and to glorify other deities. The most important duties, however, such as offering daily meals
to the goddess and acting as the medium to receive her spirits, were
always performed by the highest female shaman.

Because of her importance, the high priestess of the Yamato court
was carefully chosen from the nobility. She was surrounded by a number of female shamans and protected against any advances by male
members of the court. She did not necessarily have to be a virgin, but
while serving as the high priestess, she was required to abstain from

physical involvement with the opposite sex. If there was a violation of this rule, the male was expelled from court and the priestess herself was removed from her office. The highest female shaman as supreme soothsayer was considered to be indispensable for the security and survival of the early Yamato court. On the other hand, the position of supreme political leader could possibly remain vacant for a time, for the community became vulnerable only when there was no one to hear the divine message. The people could solve problems as long as the words of the gods were delivered by the high priestess to persuade them.

In fact, the Yamato court was ruled solely by a shamaness named Princess Iitoyo (Rice in Abundance) from 484 to 485. The political factions at court had become contentious as Emperor Seinei (22d; r. 479–84) lay dying without naming a successor. Unless the nobles reconciled their differences, there would be clashes of interests as each man was left free to engage in his own selfish pursuit of profit-making activities in and out of the country. Upon Seinei's death, they chose their highest-ranking female shaman, Princess Iitoyo, as a consensus sovereign. A daughter of Emperor Richū (16th; r. 400–405) of Ōjin's blood line, the princess had been living at the palace of Katsuraki. Within Takaki (Tall Stockade) she dwelled, tending to the spiritual matters of the Yamato people. The princess declined to assume the supreme title but did consent to preside over the restless court until the children of her late brother could be brought back from exile.

The recorded existence of such a female leader is one proof that for a long time there remained in the Yamato court a strong vestige of ancient reverence for the shamaness with the ability to communicate with the higher beings and administrate secular affairs accordingly. But the high regard for female leadership or its sacredness would eventually fade as the continental forms and concepts of political institutions gradually gained acceptance in Japanese society. Nevertheless, until female-wary Buddhism and male-chauvinistic Confucianism really took root in Japanese soil in the late eighth century, female worship had persisted and occasionally even regained strength whenever the nation faced unusual situations. A traumatic event such as the death of a tennō with no son to succeed him would cause disputes among the council nobles. Time and again it was a woman of nobility and remarkable talents who would be asked to take over the leadership on such an occasion.

Through its history, Japan produced eight female tennō in all. Two of them served twice in their lifetime, so there have been ten imperial reigns under women. "Tennō" is not a gender-specific word like the English "emperor" (which is its common translation). Since their formal names are all auspicious and mostly gender-neutral, it is difficult to identify by name alone all the female tennō out of the list of 125 in the imperial genealogy. Some of the eight female sovereigns are well-known even to schoolchildren for their full, rich, or dramatic lives and impressive achievements, as can be deduced from the following brief accounts.

Suiko Tennō (554–628; 33d; r. 593–628)

Suiko Tennō, née Princess Kashikiya, was the first woman to hold this exalted position. Suiko came to the throne after a complex and prolonged power struggle that involved her maternal uncle, Soga no Umako (540?–626), who had been influential in Yamato politics. Because of her lineage as a daughter of Emperor Kimmei (29th; r. 539–71), widow of her own half-brother Emperor Bidatsu (30th; r. 572–85), and the full-blood sister of Emperor Yōmei (31st; r. 585–87), she was expected to bring about reconciliation of political factions. Beautiful in looks and progressive in thinking, as noted in *Nihongi*, she commanded the respect and affection of high councillors. She was well aware that her predecessor had been killed in a religious and political dispute fomented by her uncle. Umako patronized the Korean Buddhist priests who had brought advanced culture and technology to Japan, including the Chinese writing system and Buddhism. Emperor Sushun (32d; r. 587–92; Suiko's half-brother), who had sided with the faction critical of Umako's advocacy of the imported religion over the traditional worship of native gods (Shinto), is believed to have been assassinated by Umako's henchman. When the throne was offered to Suiko she declined to take it at first, until she was persuaded by many of the councillors.

As the installation of a female sovereign was unprecedented, so also was the title *sumeramikoto* ("the one who controls soothsaying") to designate her office. Until then the Japanese ruler had been selected by the aristocratic council from among well-qualified men known as *kimi* (chief, hence prince) to be called *ōkimi* (grand prince). When Suiko came to the office, the Chinese ideographs *tian* (heaven) and *huang* (emperor) were chosen and given the Japanese reading ''sumera-mikoto.'' Later in the eighth century those ideographs would acquire the Japanized reading of *tennō*, which is still in use today.

As the meaning of the new title indicates, Suiko's duties were mainly sacerdotal, including preparation of meals to offer to the ancestral gods. An ardent believer in the new religion of Buddhism, she nonetheless performed her imperial duties faithfully in serving the native Shinto deities. Most secular affairs were entrusted to her nephew Prince Shōtoku (571–622; Emperor Yōmei's son), whom she appointed regent and heir apparent in the year 600 after her own son's death. But she was obliged to handle such matters as mustering troops, sending an expedition (against Silla once), and dispatching emissaries to foreign countries that were bound to split the court nobles into bitterly contending factions. She had the knowledge and experience in international relations acquired in her days as Bidatsu's consort, when the court had received frequent visits by Korean envoys concerning, for example, possible recovery of the Japanese territory of Mimana on the peninsula.

Suiko's thirty-six-year reign, which saw what is now known as the Asuka Culture culminate in its aesthetic glory, was crowned with two significant institutional achievements. One was the establishment of a recruiting and promotion system for government officials similar to Chinese and Korean models. Called the cap-ranking system, it opened the door to government service for talented people not of noble blood to work in the expanding state machinery. The other was the promulgation in 604 of a set of moral injunctions to be observed by government officials entitled the Seventeen Article Constitution (rather malapropos in view of its nonlegal nature), which provided the newly organized bureaucracy with a definitive concept of administrative structure with the tennō at its apex.

Whenever the deliberative council was called to session, Suiko presided. On one occasion in 608, she spoke up and managed to get her word accepted as final. In the previous year the Japanese court had sent an emissary to Sui China to deliver a letter. On his way home this emissary, Ono no Imoko, was robbed while passing through the Korean state of Paekche and lost the Chinese emperor's reply. The councillors discussed the case in the presence of Suiko and decided that Ono deserved a harsh punishment for failing to consummate his mission. Suiko disagreed and pronounced Ono free from accountability. One thing that this episode illuminates is Suiko's ability to grasp the crux of an issue at hand instead of making too literal an interpretation of surface fact.

This view is borne out by some historians' theories speculating on the true nature of diplomatic relations between China and Japan at the time. It seems quite likely that Suiko surmised that the Chinese emperor was not pleased with the letter from Japan, which had been sent in her name but actually drafted by her regent, Prince Shōtoku. Its opening salutation went, "From the Scion of Heaven in the Land of the Rising Sun to the Scion of Heaven in the Land of the Setting Sun." If the Sui emperor had been offended by the possible political implications of the nature metaphor and responded with angry words, as Suiko suspected, Ono must have thought it best not to deliver the missive. One of a new breed of bureaucrats not of noble blood, he had risen from the pool of brilliant men produced through the newly instituted examination system. Ono acted upon his good judgment and prevaricated in order to save the Japanese sovereign from the embarrassing situation of receiving an impolite reply, which could possibly trigger hostility between the countries. As experienced in foreign affairs as she was, Suiko must have seen through Ono's explanation and intervened when the councillors decided summarily to punish him.

Suiko demonstrated her common sense and judicious insight in setting priority straight again in 624, when her uncle Umako demanded that a portion of the royal territory in the Nara basin be turned over to him as his private estate. His argument was that the *agata* (early royal territory) of Katsuraki had originally belonged to the Katsuraki tribe and, therefore, it should be returned to himself, the current head of a clan related to the Katsuraki. Umako aimed to gain more power and stature by increasing his wealth, taking it for granted that his niece would comply with his wishes. Suiko, however, had a mind of her own: she perceived her office to be the focal point of national cohesion and the royal territory to be the state property. She was certainly indebted to Umako, who had much to do with putting her where she was, but once in the supreme office she considered herself no longer a private person. Suiko answered Umako with a definite no, and he was unable to pursue the matter any further.

Early in 628 Suiko became ill. During a solar eclipse on the thirteenth day of the fourth month, she lost her eyesight completely and sensed that her end was near. She summoned two princes, each of whom might be her possible successor, and advised them how to conduct themselves as heads of state. Five days later she died at the age of seventy-four.

Kōgyoku-Saimei Tennō (594–661; 35th; r. 642–45;
and 37th; r. 655–61)

When Suiko's successor Jomei (34th; r. 629–41) died, the situation at the Yamato court reverted to a state of general unrest beset with power struggles quite like the time just before the accession of Suiko. The councillors again resorted to the choice of a female sovereign and installed Jomei's wife Princess Takara, to be known as Kōgyoku Tennō, for her first three-year reign. She had the traumatic experience of witnessing a violent event take place before her very eyes in the summer of 645, when her own son Prince Naka killed the overly ambitious minister Soga no Iruka (grandson of Umako), who had attacked Prince Shōtoku's son and drove him to suicide two years earlier. Having been kept in the dark about the plot, Kōgyoku was stunned and horrified when Iruka fell, critically injured. But she had the courage to question her son. Prince Naka explained that Iruka had committed treason in having used his official power for private gains. Kōgyoku left the scene of bloodshed without uttering another word. Two days later she abdicated in favor of her younger brother Kōtoku, since Naka himself opted for the position of heir apparent in order to carry out the reform as a secular leader and administrator. Nine years later, when Kōtoku died of an illness, Kōgyoku was called upon to take the throne for the second time. As the 37th tennō, called Saimei, she served until her death.

She made perhaps her greatest contributions to the imperial family and the nation as mother and grandmother. In addition to a son from her first marriage to Emperor Yōmei's grandson, she bore Jomei one daughter (consort of Emperor Kōtoku) and two sons (Naka, Emperor Tenji, and Ōama, Emperor Temmu) and then raised a granddaughter (Jitō). The latter three made significant contributions to the restructuring and consolidation of the imperial institution and laid the way for Japan to attain cultural maturity in the next century.

Jitō Tennō (645–702; 41st; r. 690–97)

The biography of Jitō Tennō appeared in the first section of this chapter.

Gemmei (or Gemmyō) Tennō (661–721; 43d; r. 707–715)

When Jitō's grandson Mommu died in 707, his heir, Prince Obito, was only six years old. To keep the imperial succession within the direct line of Emperor Temmu, Princess Ahe (Temmu's niece/daughter-in-law and Mommu's mother) agreed to serve as interim sovereign as requested by Mommu in his last will.

Emperor Tenji's daughter by Nuhi (the youngest of Soga no Ishikawamaro's daughters), Ahe, was the widow of Jitō's son Prince Kusakabe. Like her half-sister/mother-in-law, she steadfastly followed in the footsteps of Tenji and Temmu, keeping the reigns of government firmly in the imperial hand and strengthening the power of the centralized administration based on the legal codes and solidly institutionalized bureaucracy. Policies enforced to that end included proscription of runaway peasants and restriction on private ownership of mountain and field properties by nobles and Buddhist temples.

A number of ambitious projects were undertaken during Gemmei's reign. A new capital of Heijō was completed in Nara, on the grandest scale ever, which became the cultural center as well as the seat of government until 794. Progress in practical fields was promoted through such measures as the introduction of sophisticated new techniques for making brocade twills and dyeing; settlement of experimental dairy farmers in Yamashiro (near present Kyoto); and minting of what came to be known as the Wadō copper coins, in the first Japanese attempt to replace the barter system with currency.

Gemmei's most significant achievement was her gifts to cultural history—*Kojiki* (Record of ancient matters, 712), Japan's oldest extant document, and *fudoki* (local gazetteers). Until the Japanese adapted the Chinese writing system, they had preserved and transmitted tales about their forebears through *kataribe* (the office of reciters), whose hereditary job was to memorize records of official events and narrate stories of epic and lyrical nature. In 681, during the joint rule of Temmu and Jitō, a twenty-seven-year-old imperial attendant in a reciter clan by the name of Hieda no Aré was ordered to memorize *Teiki* (Imperial genealogy) and *Kuji* (Ancient tales), an attempt to formulate some sort of a Japanese history. It was Gemmei who carried this unprecedented literary project to completion by appointing a scholarly courtier, Ō no Yasumaro, in 711 to transcribe Aré's recitation phonetically using Chinese characters. One year later their joint effort crystallized into

Japan's first "history" book, *Kojiki*, the three volumes of which chronicled the rise of the imperial clan and aristocratic families from the mythological beginning of the universe down to the reign of the thirty-third tennō, Suiko.

In the following year, Gemmei ordered provincial governments to collect and compile local legends and orally inherited tales, as well as information about soil, products, weather, and geological features. The result was a large collection of local gazetters (*fudoki*), which are invaluable as virtually the sole sources of Japan's ancient traditions. Several of Gemmei's own poems are included in the *Man'yōshū*, a poetic anthology compiled in the mid-eighth century.

Gemmei continued to oversee the affairs of state until her death, even though she abdicated to Princess Hidaka, her daughter by Prince Kusakabe.

Genshō Tennō (680–748; 44th; r. 715–24)

Unlike the previous female sovereigns, Princess Hidaka (Genshō Tennō) had never been married. Her unexpected enthronement at the age of thirty-five came about because of her mother Gemmei's pro- longed illness while her nephew was still too young to assume the sacerdotal responsibilities of an emperor. One notable product of Genshō's reign was the Yōrō Code of 718, a faithful copy of the Taihō Code of 701. Recompilation of an earlier law code and its wide distri- bution throughout the country indicate that the jurisdiction of the cen- tral government had extended to every corner of the land, and that its administration was very effective.

The year 720 saw the completion of the second official "history," *Nihongi* (or *Nihonshoki*, Chronicle of Japan). Prince Toneri, Emperor Temmu's third son, had begun to compile it in 682 as editor-in-chief. Modeled on such Chinese books as the *Shih chi* (Historical records, ca. 90 B.C.) and *Han shu* (History of the Former Han dynasty, A.D. 90s), *Nihongi* was written entirely in Chinese with an excellent bibliographi- cal feature—parallel presentation of variant texts from such diverse sources as Korean and Chinese documents, government records, and house journals. While the episode-centered approach of *Kojiki* makes it richer in a sense of drama, *Nihongi* covers a longer historical period (including Jitō's reign) and assumes scholarly objectivity in tone, style, and chronological presentation when describing the same incidents.

After nine years on the throne, Genshō stepped down to make way for her nephew, now twenty-three years old, to become Emperor Shōmu (45th; r. 724–49).

Kōken-Shōtoku Tennō (718–70; 46th; r. 749–58; and 48th; r. 764–70)

Of the eight women who reigned in Japan, only Kōken went through the formal process of being officially designated the heir apparent. She is also the only tennō who forcibly deposed her own successor and reclaimed the throne. No interim sovereign, she ruled as well as reigned in her own right both times. Easily outrivaling most of her male counterparts in the abundance of dramatic episodes full of political intrigues, personal setbacks, and romance, she claims the distinction of being the only Japanese tennō to be featured as the protagonist in a modern Western novel (Shelley Mydans's *Vermillion Bridge*, Doubleday, 1980).

Granddaughter of Emperor Mommu and daughter of the famed Shōmu, Kōken was born Princess Abe. A more important genealogical connection, however, in light of the early eighth-century politics, lay in her maternal side—the Fujiwara, an aristocratic clan that would provide de facto rulers of Japan for the next two centuries. Kōken's mother, Lady Asuka (701–60), was the daughter of Fuhito, the powerful head of the Fujiwaras. Asuka's husband, Emperor Shōmu, was the son of her half-sister (Fuhito's daughter by his first wife). In early Japan, marriage between brothers and sisters was allowed as long as their mothers were different: Suiko had been married to her half-brother Bidatsu, and Jitō to her own paternal uncle Temmu. Asuka's marriage to her own nephew, therefore, was considered nothing unusual or improper.

In 727, when Princess Abe was nine years old, a brother was born of the same mother, but, to their father's great disappointment, he died within a year. In 729, Shōmu installed Abe's mother Asuka as Empress Kōmyō, setting a precedent for a woman not of the imperial bloodline to bear the supreme title. An ardent Buddhist, Kōmyō went on to become the best-known of Japanese imperial consorts, acclaimed even today for her social welfare work, which included the opening of two medical care clinics for the poor and for lepers, where she is said to have tended the sick in person. Even after her daughter was installed

as the first (and only) female heir apparent in 738, the empress continued to educate her until 740, when Kibi no Makibi (695–775), a brilliant scholar of institutional government who had studied in China
from 716 to 735, was appointed her official tutor to teach Chinese
classics and train her in statecraft.

In 746 Shōmu set out to construct the Tōdaiji (Eastern Great Temple) in Nara and ordered the casting of a great bronze statue of the
Cosmic Buddha Vairochana (also known as the Sun Buddha). Three
years later he abdicated, ostensibly to devote all his time to Buddhist
studies. In retrospect, however, there seems to have been an acute need
for a female sovereign to effect a compromise between political factions. Soon after the accession of Kōken, the Great God Hachiman of
Usa issued an oracle, which was reported by his high priestess. Kōken
erected a temporary shrine in front of the palace to receive the spirit of
the Usa Hachiman and invited the priestess to deliver the divine message: "With the consent of myriad deities of this land, I, the Great God
Hachiman of Usa, shall let you complete the erection of this great
Buddha image." Kōken was delighted, as was the cloistered ex-
emperor Shōmu. This divine endorsement lifted the morale of the people involved in the construction of the grandiose edifice. In 754 the
gigantic image of the Sun Buddha was completed in all its golden
splendor. Three years later, the Great Buddha Hall was finished to
house it. Standing thirty-two meters high, this building is still the largest wooden structure in Japan today.

Shōmu died in 756, naming one of the surviving grandchildren of
Emperor Temmu as Kōken's heir. The strong-willed daughter, however, ignored his wish and chose a prince of her own liking as successor when she abdicated two years later to dedicate her energy to the
propagation of Buddhism. Kōken did carry on her father's religious
projects by encouraging the casting of more Buddhist icons and the
printing of sutras to be distributed to Kokubunji (temples under imperial patronage, one to a province). Thanks principally to Kōken's efforts, Buddhism took root in Japan and flourished as the national
religion for centuries.

While retired in Hora Palace in Ōmi, Kōken fell ill. A Buddhist
priest with expert knowledge of medicine, Dōkyō (d. 772), served as
her physician and restored her to health. This experience led Kōken to
place excessive confidence in Dōkyō to the extent that rumors began to
run rampant. Legends have it that Dōkyō was an exceedingly hand-

some man pouring out Buddha's teaching from sensual lips in a sonorous voice. Kōken is said to have bewailed to her ladies-in-waiting: "A male tennō can marry at will, taking as many consorts as he wishes to have. Why is it that I alone, because I am a woman and tennō, cannot marry at all?" There is no historical record to substantiate such a legend, but Kōken's alleged complaint seems well founded. She must have realized that the majority of the nobles would never allow her to marry, and it would not do to violate the unwritten laws of long standing. In her predicament, an idea came to her—she appointed Dōkyō her official adviser and sought his counsel not only on religious matters but also on many important secular matters, which allowed the two to be together frequently without breaking protocol. But such open favoritism created friction among the court factions and eventually led to armed civil strife.

To complicate matters, Kōken's successor Junnin (47th; r. 758–64) seemed bent on waging war against the Korean state of Silla. Junnin was not pleased with Kōken's reliance on Dōkyō, and neither was his chief minister Fujiwara no Nakamaro (706–64), who had fostered his power at court in alliance with his aunt Empress Kōmyō and was now busy amassing a fortune on war materials. Junnin and Nakamaro were frustrated when Kōken announced that, as the ex-tennō, she would make decisions on such grave affairs of state as making war, giving rewards for meritorious service, and punishing transgressors. Nakamaro then raised an army to lead a revolt against Kōken, but the turn of events favored the latter. Learning of Nakamaro's plan in time, she managed to have her forces defeat him soundly in a fierce battle. Nakamaro fled to his home in Ōmi, only to be captured and killed. Before the month was out, Kōken sent her army to Junnin's residence with a decree announcing his retirement. She exiled him to Awaji Island with the title of the Duke of Awaji. On the same day, in 764, she ascended the throne for the second time to rule as Shōtoku Tennō. The Saidaiji (Western Great Temple) had been built in order for Kōken to seek divine help in quelling Nakamaro's coup d'état; after her victory, she had a million small stupas made to dedicate in thanksgiving.

Kōken-Shōtoku took strong measures to shore up the power of the throne in 765. She prohibited unauthorized persons from reclaiming public land for private purposes, and officials from keeping arms. She also installed Priest Dōkyō in the office of chief minister. She decreed that because she was an ordained Buddhist, her first duty was to serve

Buddha, but this would not interfere with her performance as the highest priestess of the land in making offerings to the ancestral Shinto deities. To avoid enmity between the followers of Buddha and those of native cults, Kōken-Shōtoku set the example of compatibility by erecting a Buddhist edifice in the Shinto sanctuary of Ise Shrine and calling it Ise-Dai-Jingūji, or Great Temple of Ise Shrine. Such conscious efforts to synthesize imported Buddhist teachings with the highly eclectic native Shinto beliefs would eventually lead Japanese Buddhism to make a decisive break from the type of Buddhism practiced in other East Asian countries.

In this atmosphere of religious eclecticism, Kōken-Shōtoku received another oracle from Usa Hachiman in 769, saying that the country would enjoy peace under Dōkyō as tennō. Even Kōken-Shōtoku questioned its authenticity, well aware that the supreme role should be handed down only to a direct descendant of the Sun Goddess, that is, a royal prince or princess in the bloodline of the imperial clan. She appointed a courtier, Wake no Kiyomaro (733–99), to go to Usa to ascertain the oracle. Kiyomaro returned with a new oracle denying the first one. Realizing that this emissary was part of the opposition faction, Dōkyō not only demoted Kiyomaro in rank but banished him and his sister to distant places, and similarly punished others suspected of trying to diminish his influence. This event did indeed hasten Dōkyō's downfall. Because the first oracle of Hachiman recommending him for tennō had made such a sensation, the countermanding of it stirred up equally impassioned reactions. Kōken-Shōtoku built a palace in Dōkyō's hometown in Kawachi Province and moved there with him, intending to stay until the situation in the capital was calmer. A member of the Fujiwara family was appointed governor of Kawachi, and Kōken-Shōtoku ran the country from this new palace until she contracted an illness. She returned to Nara and died on the first day of the ninth month in 770.

This remarkable female tennō, who lived through the height of Nara culture, has subsequently been the focus of a variety of romantic legends. One version portrays her as a Czarina Alexandra-like figure under the hypnotic influence of a Rasputinesque priest Dōkyō, who almost succeeded in undermining Japan's "sacred" imperial institution by threatening to contaminate it with nonroyal blood. Another popular version turns the entire incident into a romantic tragedy in the Hollywood tradition, in which Kōken-Shōtoku plays the role of her English counterpart, the Virgin Queen Elizabeth I, to Dōkyō's Earl of Essex—a female sovereign loves a younger, attractive, talented man but tearfully decides to thwart his ambition to take the crown, all out of her sense of royal responsibility and her love of her country.

In Japanese history, however, Kōken-Shōtoku was generally presented in a negative light prior to World War II. School children were taught that Kōken-Shōtoku's indiscreet behavior due to feminine failing was the primary reason for Japan's long-standing rule not to allow women to become tennō. At the time this explanation had a convincing ring, for it was reinforced by the prevailing neo-Confucian doctrine and the yin-yang theory that woman was inferior to man, hence wife to husband. It was difficult to argue that a woman could be the supreme sovereign when she would theoretically have someone superior to her the minute she married. It is certainly true that none of the eight female tennō was married while on the throne, and Kōken-Shōtoku was the only one who came even close to testing this unwritten law.

The problem of familial hierarchy was not limited to the male-female relationship. During the Heian period (794–1185), when the Fujiwara clan ruled Japan through the politics of marriage, controversies arose occasionally over the question of whether or not a reigning emperor's nonroyal maternal father was morally and socially superior to the tennō himself. In legal terms, nonetheless, the Statutes of the Imperial Household (Kōshitsu tempan), enacted in the late nineteenth century, specifically ruled out female succession rights. But in the meantime, two more female tennō were to come before Japan entered the modern era.

Meishō Tennō (1623–96; 109th; r. 1629–43)

Eight and a half centuries after Kōken-Shōtoku, a little girl became tennō because her father, Gomizunoo (108th; r. 1611–29), suddenly abdicated. Her mother's lineage was formidable enough: Kazuko (1607–78) was a daughter of the second Tokugawa shogun Hidetada (1579–1632; in office 1605–23). The marriage between Gomizunoo and Kazuko had been arranged as a gesture of political reconciliation between the declining imperial court and the all-powerful warrior administration, the Tokugawa Shogunate. The imperial house became wealthier on paper for Kazuko's vast dowry, but in reality all financial affairs were managed by the Shogunate officials, and Gomizunno had no funds at his disposal nor access to his wife's assets.

To augment the impoverished imperial purse, the emperor tried to "sell" certain social privileges. When he granted the prominent priest

Takuan (1573–1645) permission to wear the color purple for a fee, the issue was blown into what is known as the Purple Robe Incident, which resulted in the emperor being forbidden by the Shogunate to continue the practice of raising funds in such demeaning ways. Gomizunoo abdicated immediately in protest and put his six-year-old daughter, Princess Okiko, on the throne to embarrass the Shogunate. Although the shogun's family aspired to see a tennō of their own blood, they did not intend it to be a child, and a girl to boot.

In any event, the scholar-minister Fujiwara Kanetō served as Meishō's regent, and fourteen years later she was succeeded by her younger half-brother, Gokōmyō (110th; r. 1643–54). Meishō spent the rest of her life cloistered and died at the age of seventy-three.

Gosakuramachi Tennō (1740–1813; 117th; r. 1762–70)

Second daughter of Emperor Sakuramachi (115th; r. 1735–47) by his empress, Princess Toshiko found herself a tennō at the age of twenty-two, when her brother Momozono (116th; r. 1747–62) died leaving a four-year-old son. In 1768, when her nephew reached the age of ten, Gosakuramachi installed him as the heir apparent and stepped down two years later. Japan's last female tennō was learned in Chinese classics and accomplished in literary art to the extent that she personally tutored the child emperors Gomomozono (118th; r. 1771–79) and Kōkaku (119th; r. 1780–1817). Her scholarly and literary output includes *Annual Events of the Court*, which she compiled; nearly two thousand *waka* poems (in the thirty-one-syllable traditional form); and forty-one volumes of diary in her own hand covering the period between 1756 and 1780.

Bibliography

Bielenstein, Hans. "An Interpretation of the Portents in the Ts'ien-Han-shu," *Bulletin of the Museum of Far Eastern Antiquities* 26 (1959): 127–43.

Casal, V. A. *The Five Sacred Festivals of Ancient Japan.* Tokyo: Sophia University, 1967.

Crump, James I., Jr. "Borrowed T'ang Titles and Offices in the *Yōrō Code*," *Occasional Papers of the Center for Japanese Studies*, University of Michigan, no. 2 (1952): 25–38.

de Bary, Wm. Theodore, et al., eds. *Sources of Chinese Tradition.* New York: Columbia University Press, 1960.

Eberhard, Wolfram. *Settlement and Social Change in Asia*. Hong Kong: Hong Kong University Press, 1967.

Hall, John W. *Government and Local Power in Japan: 500–1700*. Princeton: Princeton University Press, 1966.

Hirai, Naofusa. "Japanese Shinto," *Understanding Japan*, no. 18 (1966): 1–76.

Holtom, Daniel C. *The Japanese Enthronement Ceremonies*. 2d ed. Tokyo: Sophia University, 1972.

Inoue Mitsusada. *Introduction to Japanese History before the Meiji Restoration*, rev. ed. Tokyo: Kokusai Bunka Shinkōkai, 1968.

Keiley, Cornelius J. "A Note on the Surnames of Immigrant Officials in Nara Japan," *Harvard Journal of Asiatic Studies* 29 (1969): 177–89.

Levy, Ian Hideo. *Hitomaro and the Birth of Japanese Lyricism*. Princeton: Princeton University Press, 1984.

Lewin, Bruno. *Aya und Hata: Bevolkerungsgruppen Altjapans Kontinentaler Herkunst*. Wiesbaden: O. Harrassowitz, 1962.

MacKenzie, Donald A. *Myths of China and Japan*. London: Gresham, 1923.

Muraoka Tsunetsugu. *Studies in Shinto Thought*, trans. Delmer M. Brown and James T. Araki. Tokyo: Japanese Committee for UNESCO, 1964.

Nakamura Hajime. *A History of the Development of Japanese Thought from A.D. 592 to 1868*. 2d ed. Tokyo: Kokusai Bunka Shinkōkai, 1969.

Philippi, Donald L. *Norito, A New Translation of the Ancient Japanese Ritual Prayers*. Tokyo: Institute for Japanese Culture and Classics, Kokugakuin University, 1959.

Reischauer, Edwin O., and John K. Fairbank. *East Asia: The Great Tradition*. Cambridge: Harvard University Press, 1960.

Roberts, Dorothy E. *A Scholar's Guide to Japan*. Rev. ed. Boston: Christopher Publishing House, 1969.

Sansom, Sir George Bailey. *A History of Japan*. Rev. ed. New York: Appleton-Century-Crofts, 1962.

Suematsu Yasukazu. "Japan's Relations with the Asian Continent and the Korean Peninsula (before A.D. 950)." *Cahier d'histoire Mondiale* 4 (1937): 671–87.

Tsuda Sachiko. *Jitō jotei no shōgai*. Tokyo: Gakuseisha, 1980.

Watson, Burton. *Ssu-ma Ch'ien: Grand Historian of China*. New York: Columbia University Press, 1958.

Webb, Herschel. *Research in Japanese Sources: A Guide*. New York: Columbia University Press, 1965.

Yamamoto Satoshi. *Jitō jotei no nazo*. Tokyo: Tachikaze Shobō, 1988.

Yoshino Hiroko. *Jitō Tennō: Nihon kodai teiō no jujutsu*. Tokyo: Jinbun Shoin, 1988.

The bibliography for chapter 1 should also be consulted.

3

MURASAKI SHIKIBU
The Court Lady

FELICE FISCHER

MURASAKI Shikibu's *Genji monogatari* (The tale of Genji, ca. 1000) is fiction of unprecedented richness and complexity written nearly one thousand years ago.[1] In its extant form *The Tale of Genji* consists of fifty-four chapters, covering about seventy-five years, and encompasses nearly five hundred characters and eight hundred poems. This work attained instant success during its author's lifetime, and it has inspired a vast body of creative and critical writings over the centuries, most analogous perhaps to Shakespeare's accomplishment in the English literary tradition in terms of impact and influence. In both cases, unique creative genius bequeathed the world literary masterpieces, yet the authors' personal lives pose many unanswered questions.

Writing a biography of Murasaki Shikibu is a bit like a firefly hunt. There are faint glows in the darkness of a thousand-year span, but they always seem to elude one's grasp. The only sources of information about her are those written by Murasaki herself: her collected poems, her diary, and *The Tale of Genji*.

It is thought that the poetry collection (*Murasaki Shikibu shū*) was originally compiled by Murasaki.[2] Arranged in chronological sequence, most of the poems have prose prefaces that give some information about the circumstances surrounding the composition of the verse. But these prefaces are vague about the exact identity of the recipients or subjects of the poems. Murasaki, for example, never directly mentions her husband, either in the prefaces or in the poems, although he was presumably the subject, recipient, or sender of 47 of the 128 verses included in Murasaki's collection.[3]

The *Murasaki Shikibu nikki*, or diary, is not so much an autobiography as an account of specific events at court and Murasaki's personal reflections and reminiscences during the years 1008–10. *The Tale of Genji* is one of the chief sources of information about the customs and atmosphere of the Heian period (794–1185), and some biographical material has been inferred from it as well. It is to these works that generations of Japanese scholars have turned for clues about the fortuitous harmony of biographical, psychological, and cultural conditions that produced the "magic synthesis" of creativity characteristic to the artistic and literary genius of Murasaki Shikibu in particular.

Scholarly Family

"Father, a most learned man, was always regretting the fact: 'Just my luck!' he would say. 'What a pity she was not born a man!' "[4] But if Murasaki had, in fact, been born a man, Japanese literature would most likely not include *The Tale of Genji*. The only reason to share Murasaki's father's regret is that had she been born a man, Murasaki would have held official posts and ranks, duly documented in the histories of the period. It is through public records about her male relations that Murasaki's genealogy, if not her personal life, can be traced.[5]

Her father was Fujiwara Tametoki. He was a fifth-generation descendant of the founder of the northern Fujiwara line, Fuyutsugu, through the latter's sixth son. This made Tametoki a kinsman of the most influential political figure of the early eleventh century, Fujiwara Michinaga (966–1027).[6] But the branch of the family to which Tametoki belonged was not in the mainstream of political power, and its members occupied positions in the middle and lower bureaucracy. Tametoki himself held only minor government posts and rank, including that of secretary in the Ministry of Ceremonial (Shikibu Shō). It was ten years before he received his next post as governor of Echizen in 966.[7] In 1011 he became governor of another province, Echigo, from which post he returned in 1014. Two years later he retired from public life, having reached only Junior Fifth Rank, Lower Grade.[8]

While of little or no political consequence, Tametoki's family was, nonetheless quite distinguished in the literary sphere. The most prominent literary ancestor of Murasaki was Tametoki's grandfather, Fujiwara Kanesuke (877–933). He was a friend of Ki no Tsurayuki, one of the compilers of the first imperially sponsored anthology of Japanese poetry, the *Kokinshū* (Collection of ancient and modern times, completed in 905). Kanesuke's poems were chosen for inclusion in the *Sanjū-rokunin shū* (Collection of thirty-six poets, ca. 1160), and many of his verses also appear in various episodes of the eleventh-century *Yamato monogatari* (Tales of Yamato).[9]

Tametoki himself was invited to submit poems to various poetry contests, and nine of his poems were included in the *Goshūishū* (Later collection of gleanings, completed 1086), as well as in several other anthologies of Japanese poetry compiled by imperial command. He was better known, however, for his poetry in Chinese. Thirteen of his Chinese verses were included in the anthology *Honchō reisō* of 1010. Legend has it that Tametoki's skill in Chinese poetry secured him the post as governor of Echizen: Tametoki reportedly sent a poem to the Emperor Ichijō, which so moved the emperor that he interceded on Tametoki's behalf for the Echizen post.[10]

Murasaki's mother, daughter of Fujiwara Tamenobu, was also descended from Fujiwara Fuyutsugu, through his eldest son. She and Tametoki had two daughters and one son; Murasaki was the second daughter. This raises the first of many unanswered questions about the life of Murasaki Shikibu: the date of her birth.

In her diary, Murasaki remarks in the year 1010, "The time too is ripe. If I get much older my eyesight will surely weaken to the point that I shall be unable to read the sutras, and my spirits will fall" (p. 141). It has been proposed that this was written by Murasaki in her thirty-seventh year, considered a milestone for women in Heian times.[11] In *The Tale of Genji*, for example, the hero Prince Genji's stepmother and lover, Empress Fujitsubo, dies in her thirty-seventh year, and his most beloved wife, Young Murasaki, almost dies. Prince Genji warns the latter to be especially on her guard during this year. By the traditional Japanese method of reckoning age, a person is one year old at birth. Thus, if Murasaki Shikibu were thirty-seven in 1010, it would mean that she was born in 974. Other scholars have argued for various other dates, ranging from 970 to 978.[12]

Sobriquets but No Personal Names for Women

The name by which the author of *The Tale of Genji* is now known is not the one she was given at birth, but probably dates to her service at court as a lady-in-waiting. Except for members of the imperial family and consorts, it was not customary to use, or at least to record the personal names of women of the aristocracy. In his diary, *Midō kampaku ki* (Record of the regent of the August Hall), Fujiwara Michinaga mentions some of the women in court service by their personal names. One of those names, given in an entry dated the first month, twenty-ninth day of Kankō (1007), is Fujiwara Takako (alternate readings could be "Kyōshi" or "Kaoriko"). It is possible that this is a reference to Murasaki Shikibu, but the question is still in dispute.[13]

Most women at court were called by sobriquets derived from a combination of their family name or a place name, and of the post or rank held by their father or husband. Thus, the "Shikibu" of Murasaki Shikibu refers to her father's post in the Shikibu shō, or Ministry of Ceremonial. In some sources, Murasaki is called Tō Shikibu. "Tō" is the Chinese reading of the first element of her family name, the "Fuji" of Fujiwara. "Fuji" means wisteria. The color of wisteria is purple, or *murasaki*. This may be the origin of the usage of "Murasaki" rather than "Tō."[14]

The more likely first usage of the name Murasaki has to do with *The Tale of Genji* and probably dates to an incident recorded in her diary. On the first day of the eleventh month of 1008, during the festivities celebrating the fiftieth day after the birth of Prince Atsuhira, Fujiwara Kintō, searching among the court ladies, asks, "Excuse me . . . , he said. Would our little Murasaki be in attendance by any chance?" The reply is, "I cannot see the likes of Genji here, so how could she be present?" (p. 91). This incident also marks Murasaki's first mention of the name of the hero of her tale. Fujiwara Kintō (966–1041) was one of the most celebrated literary figures of his time, so Murasaki Shikibu was no doubt pleased by his reference to her work and by the nickname he had bestowed on her.

Another entry in her diary tells of a nickname with which she was decidedly not pleased: She was dubbed "Our Lady of the Chronicles" (*Nihongi no tsubone*) by one Saemon no Naishi, "who, for some strange reason, took a dislike to me." The Emperor Ichijō, commenting on *The Tale of Genji*, had said of its author, "She must have read the *Chronicles of Japan*" (p. 137). The reason "Our Lady of the Chronicles" would have been less complimentary than "little Murasaki" is that it was considered unbecoming for a woman to know (or admit to knowing) Chinese, the language in which the imperially commissioned *Chronicles of Japan* (720) was written. As Murasaki says in the same section of her diary, "I realized that people were saying, 'It's bad enough when a man flaunts his learning; she will come to no good,' and ever since then I have avoided writing even the simplest character" (p. 139). Nevertheless, the fact that Murasaki recorded this nickname would perhaps indicate some false modesty about her knowledge of Chinese.

Stolen Education

In the same entry, Murasaki also quotes her father's regret over her not having been born a man. She recalls how, during her childhood, she would sit and listen while her brother Nobunori learned to read the *Shih chi* (Records of the grand historian), a Chinese history by Sima Qian. Murasaki proved the better student. But Chinese learning prepared one for a career in government service—a career not open to women—thus provoking Tametoki's lament.

This brief vignette of Murasaki at her brother's side learning Chinese from their father is the only vivid glimpse of Murasaki's childhood. It is significant for what it reveals of her youth and for her later development. This group portrait is unusual in several respects. First, it indicates that Murasaki grew up in her father's home. That is, in the polygamous Heian society, the norm would have been for Murasaki and her siblings by the same mother to live with their mother, who would have maintained a separate residence from Tametoki. Since Murasaki never mentions her mother and was raised in her father's residence, the mother probably died while Murasaki was an infant, perhaps during the birth of Nobunori.

Scholarly opinion is divided about where Tametoki's residence was, but he may have lived in the mansion built by his grandfather Kanesuke.[15] Located on the banks of the Kamo River in Kyoto, the mansion was a gathering place for Kanesuke's literary circle, including the most famous poet of his day, Ki no Tsurayuki. In her diary, Murasaki describes her quarters:

> So now my two kotos, one of thirteen strings and the other of six, stand in a miserable little closet blackened with soot, ready tuned but idle. Through neglect—I forgot, for example, to ask that the bridges be removed on rainy days—they have accumulated the dust and lean there now against a cupboard, their necks jammed between that and a pillar,

with a biwa standing on either side. There is also a large pair of cup-boards crammed full to bursting point. One is full of old poems and tales that have become the home for countless silverfish that scatter in such an unpleasant manner that no one cares to look at them any more; the other is full of Chinese books which have lain unattended ever since he who carefully collected them passed away. Whenever my loneliness threatens to overwhelm me I take out one or two of them to look at. (p. 133)

Not only in her own room, but certainly in her father's and brother's rooms, Murasaki would have been surrounded by books. Tametoki was a graduate of the literature course of the university, a noted poet of Chinese and Japanese verse, and a member of such societies as the Kangaku-kai (Encouragement of Learning Club). Scholars and literati such as Prince Tomohira probably gathered on occasion at Tametoki's residence.

In 986, with the end of the Emperor Kazan's reign, Tametoki re-signed his official post and had time to devote to the education of his son Nobunori, to prepare him for his university studies. Besides the histories, other Chinese texts they would have read include the *Wen Xuan* (Anthology of literature) of Xiao Tong (502–31), a compilation of pre-Tang poetry and prose. The most popular Chinese poet among the Heian literati was Bo Zhuyi (722–846), and his collected works, the *Bo shiwenji*, were assiduously studied. *The Sutra of the Golden Light* (Konkō myō saishō ō gyō) and the *Lotus Sutra* (Kokke kyō) were among the chief Buddhist texts to which Nobunori would have been exposed. Prose and poetry in Chinese written by Japanese au-thors, such as the *Chronicles of Japan*, were also required reading. So it was that Murasaki heard at her brother's side the first reading of the very chronicles for which she was to be nicknamed.

Because of her father's scholastic bent, Murasaki was probably ex-posed to an unusually broad range of Chinese literature. Tametoki would, however, also have encouraged his daughter in acquiring a more typically feminine education of the Heian aristocracy, including the reading of those volumes of ''old poems and tales'' in the cup-board in her room. It was also likely that during this time Murasaki learned to play the koto.

The poems in the *Murasaki Shikibu shū* have also been closely scanned by later scholars for further clues to her biography.[16] For example, verse 15 reads:

Send word
By the wild geese
flying north;
As often as they wing the clouds
Write constantly.

The preface to this poem begins: "My elder sister died. I met some-one whose younger sister had died and she suggested that we should think of each other as the lost relation. I wrote to her as such, and she to me. Both of us left for far-off lands" (p. 221). It is thought that this poem was written in 996, the year in which Tametoki, after ten years without an official government post, finally received the appointment to the governorship of Echizen Province.[17] Murasaki traveled there with her father, an unusual experience for high-ranking ladies of the time. It was a four- or five-day trip from Kyoto, first by land to Lake Biwa, from there by boat to Shiozu, and then again over land to the seat of the provincial office. Their route is partially recorded in a sequence of poems by Murasaki.[18]

A Brief Marriage

Murasaki did not stay in Echizen for the entire four-year term of her father's appointment. She returned to the capital in late 997 or early 998, possibly to accept the proposal of marriage from Fujiwara Nobutaka. Nobutaka was a distant relative, also descended from Fujiwara Fuyutsugu. Nobutaka was a fairly successful bureaucrat who served as secretary in the Ministry of Ceremonial and as governor of several provinces, including Chikuzen. *The Makura no sōshi* (Pillow book) of Sei Shōnagon relates an incident about Nobutaka when he made a pilgrimage to the shrine at Mitake with his son Takamitsu. Despite the usual custom of dressing conservatively on such a pilgrim-age, Nobutaka and his son appeared in gorgeous robes. Sei Shōnagon remarks that the gods must have approved of Nobutaka's choice of dress, for soon afterward he received his appointment as governor of Chikuzen.[19] Besides his elegant taste in clothes, Nobutaka seems to have had other talents, for in 988 he was chosen as one of the dancers for the Kamo Festival.[20] In that year he also returned to Kyoto from his post as governor of Yamashiro.

Although the exact date of his birth is not known, Nobutaka was in his mid-forties at the time of his marriage to Murasaki in late 998 or early 999. Murasaki herself, in her mid-twenties, was rather late in marrying by Heian standards. After the wedding, she probably continued to live in her father's house, to which Nobutaka would commute. Nobutaka already had several other wives by whom he had numerous offspring. His son Takamitsu was probably about the same age as Murasaki. Murasaki and Nobutaka had one child, a daughter named Kataiko (or Kenshi).

Fujiwara Nobutaka died on the twenty-fifth day of the fourth month of 1001, leaving Murasaki a widow after little more than two years of marriage. In her diary Murasaki recalls these years of her life:

> As I watched the rather drab scene at home, I felt depressed and confused. For some years I had existed from day to day in listless fashion, taking note of the flowers, the birds in song, the way the skies changed from season to season, the moon, the frost, and the snow, doing little more than registering the passage of time. How would it all turn out? The thought of my continuing loneliness was quite unbearable, and yet there had been those friends who would discuss trifling matters with me, and others of like mind with whom I could exchange my innermost thoughts. (p. 95)

Perhaps it was during this period that she wrote poem number 53 (pp. 233–34):

> My world was in confusion. I sent a morning glory to the same person with the poem:

> > *I know full well*
> > *The morning glory fades*
> > *As does the dew,*
> > *Yet still I mourn*
> > *This evanescence.*

Another poem (no. 48) laments the impermanence of this world while looking at a painting of Shiogama, a famous place in Mutsu (p. 232):

> > *The one I loved*
> > *Turned that evening into smoke;*
> > *And from then on*
> > *The name is full of memories,*
> > *Shiogama Bay.*

Murasaki's life, like that of most Heian women in her position, was quite uneventful—one day much like the next. With servants to look after her daughter and the household, she was left with ample leisure time. Besides writing and exchanging poems, Murasaki had her books, the "old poems and tales," to turn to for distraction and consolation. Among the books of poetry would have been the *Kokinshū*, the *Gosenshū* (Later collection, the second of the imperial anthologies, ordered compiled in 951), and many private collections by individual poets such as Lady Ise (flourished ca. 935).

Making of *The Tale of Genji*

Among the romances accessible to her were probably *Taketori monogatari* (Tale of the bamboo cutter) and *Ise monogatari* (Tales of Ise). In her diary she also mentions the most popular Chinese poet of the period, Bo Zhuyi. One of his best-loved works was "A Song of Unending Sorrow" (*Chang hen ge* in Chinese, *Chōgonka* in Japanese), a long narrative poem describing the love of the Xuanzong emperor (685–762) for his consort, Yang Guifei, and his grief at her death:

> But as waters of Shu are always green
> and its mountains always blue,
> So changeless was his majesty's love and deeper than days.
> He stared at the desolate moon from his temporary palace,
> He hears bell-notes in the evening rain, cutting at his breast.[21]

The beauty of Bo Zhuyi's lines not only helped console Murasaki in her grief, but perhaps inspired her to begin *The Tale of Genji* with the passage, "In a certain reign there was a lady not of the first rank whom the emperor loved more than any of the others" (p. 3). The name of Yang Guifei appears several sentences later, and there are nine quotations from "A Song of Unending Sorrow" in her first chapter, known by the title "The Paulownia Court" (*Kiritsubo*).[22]

Although "A Song of Unending Sorrow" may have provided Murasaki with the theme of an emperor's intense love for his consort and his grief at her death, Murasaki used the theme to create a different plot. The Xuanzong emperor's sorrow remains unending; the Japanese emperor's sorrow is assuaged by the presence of the son born to the lady of the Paulownia Court—Prince Genji, the Shining One, the hero of Murasaki's tale.

As she wrote successive chapters of *The Tale of Genji*, Murasaki probably shared her writings with her friends, who might have sent her back comments. They might have copied out chapters to pass along or to read later. There were, no doubt, many readers who felt as did the daughter of Takasue, who wrote in her diary, "I read some of the books about Lady Murasaki and longed to see the later parts. Since I was still new to the Capital and had no one to ask, it was impossible to find what I wanted. I was burning with impatience and curiosity, and in my prayers I used to say, 'Let me see the entire *Tale of Genji* from beginning to end!' "[23]

Life at Court

Murasaki's fame as the author of *The Tale of Genji* was probably one of the chief reasons for her being asked to enter court service with the Empress Shōshi (988–1074; also referred to as Akiko, another reading for the characters for her name). Shōshi was the eldest daughter of Fujiwara Michinaga and was married to the Emperor Ichijō (980–1011; r. 986–1011). Murasaki most likely began her service in Shōshi's retinue on the twenty-ninth day of the twelfth month of Kankō 3 (1006).[24] This period of her life is the best documented: her diary covers the years from mid-1008 to the fifteenth day of the first month of 1010.

The diary centers on the two most important events in Michinaga's continuing rise to power: the births of Shōshi's sons, through whom Michinaga would undisputably control Heian politics. Prince Atsuhira, born on the eleventh day of the ninth month of 1008, later reigned as Emperor Go-Ichijō (1016–36). On the twenty-fifth day of the eleventh month of 1009 Shōshi gave birth to her second son, Prince Atsuyoshi, the future Emperor Go-Suzaku (r. 1036–45).

Murasaki describes the events surrounding the births in great detail, and her diary is an important primary source from this aspect too. Both princes were born in their grandfather's mansion, known as the Tsuchimikado. The attire of the empress and her attendants as well as all the hangings and covers were white for the delivery. Buddhist and Shinto holy men were summoned to recite prayers. A lock of Shōshi's hair was cut, symbolizing the taking of Buddhist vows and thus assuring her salvation, in case she should die in childbirth.

After the safe delivery a series of ceremonies were held on the third, fifth, seventh, and ninth days after birth. The prince's father, Emperor Ichijō, had to wait until the sixteenth day of the month following Atsuhira's birth to visit Shōshi and their son. It was a grand occasion, with feasting, dancing, and musical entertainment. Murasaki recorded the gorgeous appearance of the ladies present in precise detail: "Saemon no Naishi carried the sword. She was wearing a plain yellow-green jacket, a train shaded darker at the hem, and a sash and waistbands with raised embroidery in orange and white checked silk. Her mantle had five cuffs of white lined with dark red, and her crimson gown was of beaten silk" (p. 77).

Yet despite the momentous events so closely observed and described, Murasaki herself does not seem completely happy with her new life. On the eve of the emperor's visit she writes:

> If only my appetites were more mundane, I might find more joy in life, regain perhaps a little youth, and face this mortal world with equanimity—seeing and hearing all these marvelous, auspicious things only served to strengthen my desires. How wretched I felt at the misery, the weariness of it all! "But why do I go on like this?" I asked myself. "Now surely is the time to forget. It does me no good to fret and, besides, it is quite wrong of me." As day dawned I looked outside and saw the ducks playing about on the lake as if they had not a care in the world:

> > *Birds on the water;*
> > *Can I look at them*
> > *Dispassionately?*
> > *I too am floating through*
> > *A sad uncertain world.*

Shōshi's court must have been a great change from Murasaki's days at her father's house in her widowhood. In her diary she repeatedly describes her efforts to avoid the many festivities, or to slip away as quickly as possible. One such occasion was the banquet on the fiftieth day after Prince Atsuhira's birth, when Fujiwara Kintō tried to lure her out with the nickname "little Murasaki."

Romantic Legends

Murasaki Shikibu was in her mid-thirties when she joined the entourage of the nineteen-year-old Shōshi, and scholars have wondered why she entered court service at all. Much of the speculation has centered on the relationship between Murasaki and Michinaga. The commentary by the fourteenth-century scholars accompanying the *Sompi bunmyaku* genealogy states that Murasaki was a consort of Michinaga.[25] This assessment may have been based on several sections of her diary that mention her encounters with Michinaga. His first appearance, for example, is in the opening pages of the diary (p. 45):

> I look out from my room at the head of the corridor into the light morning mist. There is still dew on the ground, but his Excellency [Michinaga] is already out in the garden ordering his attendants to clear the stream of some obstruction. Plucking a maiden-flower from a large cluster blossoming on the south side of the bridge, he tosses it into my room over the curtain frame. "And where is the reply?"
>
> So magnificent is he that I feel ashamed of my own rather dishevelled appearance and use it as an excuse to move over to where I keep my inkstone:

> > *Now I see*
> > *This lovely maiden-flower*
> > *In bloom,*
> > *I know for certain*
> > *That the dew discriminates.*

> "Quick, aren't we!" says he with a smile and asks for my brush:

> > *The morning dew*
> > *Does not discriminate;*
> > *The maiden-flower*
> > *Takes on the colors*
> > *That it pleases.*

In the first month of 1009, Murasaki records another episode. Michinaga had discovered *The Tale of Genji* in his daughter Shōshi's quarters. He was moved to send a verse in which he implies that the author of the amorous adventures of Genji might be an easy conquest herself. The section of the diary immediately following the above episode consists of another poetic exchange between Murasaki and someone who had knocked at her room the night before without gaining admittance.[26]

On the basis of these incidents, the compiler of the *Sompi bunmyaku* and some contemporary scholars have linked Murasaki and Michinaga in a romantic relationship. But such exchanges of poems were the norm among polite society of the Heian period, as depicted both in *The Tale of Genji* itself and in works of nonfiction such as Sei Shōnagon's *Pillow Book*. They did not necessarily imply anything other than that the senders were refined courtiers who could compose a poem appropriate to the occasion. It seems likely that Michinaga would have been more interested in Murasaki as a literary talent than as an amorous conquest.

Salons of the Empresses

Michinaga had had his daughter Shōshi installed in the palace as a secondary consort to Emperor Ichijō in 999, and the latter had named her empress the following year. This was an unprecedented event because it resulted in there being two empresses. The first was Fujiwara Teishi, the daughter of Michinaga's rival (and brother) Michitaka (953–95). The social and cultural life of Empress Teishi and her court had been immortalized in *The Pillow Book* of Sei Shōnagon. Emperor Ichijō himself is often depicted as an observer or participant in the activities at Teishi's salon.

Besides Teishi's coterie, there were other women of high rank who promoted cultural pursuits among the members of their entourages. The emperor's aunt, Princess Senshi (963–1035), for example, while serving as the Vestal of the Kamo Shrine presided over an elegant literary salon. With such precedents, Michinaga no doubt felt that Shōshi must have an even more stellar cluster of women at her court. As author of *The Tale of Genji* Murasaki would have been a desirable addition to Shōshi's entourage. For Murasaki, too, the opportunity to take part in life at court must have been tempting, both for the prestige attached to serving the empress and for the wider scope of experience and observation it would afford her.

Murasaki recorded some of these experiences in her diary. She is quite accurate in her descriptions of the public events, many of which are also mentioned in diaries by her male contemporaries. Many of these sections of Murasaki's diary form a sort of handbook of dress, etiquette, music, and dance of the period. Some of her experiences at court would also find their way into *The Tale of Genji*. One example might be the description of the visit of the fictional emperor to Genji's mansion at Rokujō in chapter 33. The model for this may have been the visit of Emperor Ichijō to Michinaga's mansion after the birth of Prince Atsuhira.

As noted above in connection with this imperial visit, Murasaki's diary is also interspersed with passages of personal commentary and musings. Most of these personal notes deal with her difficulty in adjusting to life at court:

> I returned to the Palace on the twenty-ninth of the twelfth month. Now I come to think of it, it was on this very night that I first entered service; and what a daze I was in then! But what an awful fate to have now become so blasé about life at court.
> It was very late. Her Majesty was in seclusion, so I did not go to see her but lay down to rest on my own. I could hear the ladies talking in the next room. "How different it is here in the Palace! At home everyone would be asleep, but here it's the constant footsteps that keep one awake!"

> > *As does the year*
> > *So my days draw to an end;*
> > *There is a coldness*
> > *In the voice*
> > *Of the night wind.* (p. 113)

Life at court afforded almost no privacy, since it centered around a small, exclusive group of people. Everyone knew everyone else's business, and one always had to be alert against the smallest misstep. Words of praise from the emperor might arouse jealousy, as Murasaki experienced when she was referred to as "Our Lady of the Chronicles" by one of her fellow ladies-in-waiting. Fortunately for Murasaki, the Lady Saemon apparently did not discover that Murasaki was secretly teaching the empress to read Chinese. It may be that one of Murasaki's roles at Shōshi's court was as a tutor; when Michinaga found out about their Chinese readings, he seemed tacitly to approve by sending his daughter other books of poetry which he had copied for her.[27]

Murasaki also on occasion composed Japanese poems on Shōshi's behalf.[28] It may have been because of her status as teacher to Shōshi that Murasaki also felt free to criticize her mistress. She comments on Shōshi's excessively high standards of personal behavior, which only resulted in the women of her court being considered haughty and reserved. It has indeed been suggested that Murasaki wrote her diary for Shōshi's benefit.[29] Murasaki does note, "Her Majesty has matured of late and now understands the ways of this world: that people have their good points and their bad, that they sometimes go to excess and sometimes make mistakes" (p. 127).

Literary Ladies and the Battle of Wit

Murasaki's comments about the Empress are found in the latter part of her diary, in a section devoted to commentaries on her women contemporaries. The portraits begin with those of her fellow ladies-in-waiting and consist chiefly of physical descriptions of their appearance and a brief note on their character. The longer and more interesting sections are about those women who were likewise to acquire a lasting name in Japanese literary history. The paragraph criticizing Shōshi for her conservatism, for example, is part of Murasaki's comments about Lady Chūjō, who was in the entourage of Princess Senshi. The latter was the Vestal Virgin of the Kamo Shrine and was admired for her elegant literary outings.[30] Murasaki seems a bit envious of the idle poetic life led by Princess Senshi and her ladies, and she is anxious to defend Shōshi and her women: the pressing demands of the social schedule of court life with the empress prevent her ladies from pursuing the elegance of Princess Senshi's world.

Murasaki next writes about an even more famous woman poet, Izumi Shikibu (ca. 970–ca. 1030), who was involved in scandalous affairs with two brothers, sons of the Emperor Reizei, the princes Tametaka and Atsumichi. Her romance with the latter is the subject of her poetic memoirs, *The Izumi Shikibu Diary*.[31] It may be this work that provoked the following comments by Murasaki:

> Now someone who did carry on a fascinating correspondence was Izumi Shikibu. She does have a rather unsavory side to her character but has a genius for tossing off letters with ease and can make the most banal statement sound special. Her poems are quite delightful. Although her knowledge of the canon and her judgments leave something to be desired, she can produce poems at will and always manages to include some clever phrase or other that catches the eye, and yet when it comes to criticizing or judging the work of others, well, she never really comes up to scratch; the sort of person who relies on a talent for extemporiza-

tion, one feels. I cannot think of her as a poet of the highest quality.
(p. 131)

Fujiwara Kintō, who had given Murasaki her nickname and was
ordered by the Emperor Kazan (968–1008) to compile the third of the
imperial poetry anthologies, the *Shūishū* (Collection of gleanings), apparently did not agree with Murasaki's assessment of Izumi's poems.
He included one of them in his anthology:

> *From darkness*
> *Into the path of darkness*
> *Must I enter;*
> *Shine upon me from afar,*
> *O moon above the mountain crest.*[32]

Izumi's poetry—mostly love poems—may have been too passionate
for Murasaki's tastes. Another well-known verse, "Sent to Someone
When She Was Ill," illustrates this passion:

> *This is a world*
> *Where I shall shortly be no more:*
> *If only you*
> *Would come to visit me just once*
> *For a remembrance of the afterlife!*[33]

Poems such as this may have led to Murasaki's critique of Izumi's
character and poetry. She was also probably envious of Izumi's literary
and personal popularity. Murasaki does not mention the fact that Izumi
also joined Shōshi's court, probably around 1009. It would seem that
Shōshi was willing to overlook Izumi's amorous past in exchange for
the prestige of adding such an illustrious poet to her coterie.

Another woman mentioned in Murasaki's diary is Akazome Emon
(c. 960–1041), the most praised of the literary figures. "She may not
be a genius but she has great poise and does not feel that she has to
compose a poem on everything she sees merely because she is a poet.
From what I have seen, her work is most accomplished, even her
occasional verse" (p. 131). Akazome was a lady-in-waiting to Empress Shōshi's mother, Rinshi (964–1053). She is best known as the
probable author of the *Eiga monogatari* (A tale of flowering fortunes),

a historical tale that glorifies the deeds of Shōshi's father, Michinaga.[34]
While Murasaki's praise of Akazome's poetry may have been less than
wholehearted, Akazome certainly admired Murasaki's prose. In her
Eiga monogatari, Akazome makes almost verbatim use of the sections
of Murasaki's diary describing the events of 1008 surrounding the
birth of Prince Atsuhira.[35]

Sei Shōnagon, the Arch Rival

Murasaki Shikibu reserves the harshest criticism in her diary for one
lady in particular:

> Sei Shōnagon, for instance, was dreadfully conceited. She thought
> herself so clever, and littered her writings with Chinese characters, but
> if you examined them closely, they left a great deal to be desired. Those
> who think themselves as being superior to everyone else in this way
> will inevitably suffer and come to a bad end, and people who have
> become so precious that they go out of their way to be sensitive in the
> most unpromising situations, trying to capture every moment of inter-
> est, however slight, are bound to look ridiculous and superficial. How
> can the future turn out well for them? (pp. 131–32)

Shōnagon was about ten years older than Murasaki. Her prose journal, *The Pillow Book*, was started in about 993 when she first entered
the court of Empress Teishi (976–1001) and completed sometime after
the death of Teishi. It may be that Murasaki and Shōnagon met while the
latter was in attendance on Teishi's son, Prince Atsuyasu (999–1019).[36]

Had they in fact met, it seems unlikely that they would have enjoyed
each other's company. Shōnagon, as she reveals herself in *The Pillow
Book*, seems quite different from Murasaki. The former is uninhibited,
gregarious, quick-witted, and unrestrained in her total devotion to her
empress. *The Pillow Book* is, in a way, a celebration of life at Teishi's
court. Since Teishi had been Ichijō's first empress and her cousin
Shōshi's predecessor, Murasaki was keenly aware of the comparisons
that would be made between the two. Perhaps her diary was partly an
attempt to glorify Shōshi and her court, and the remarks on Shōnagon
an attempt to discredit Teishi by vilifying her chronicler. Although
Murasaki never mentions *The Pillow Book*, it could not have escaped
the attention of such an avid reader as she. It has been suggested that
Murasaki bore a personal grudge against Sei Shōnagon because of

several specific episodes included in the latter's work. One such section might have been the description of Murasaki's husband Nobutaka on his pilgrimage to Mitake in his finest robes. *The Pillow Book* was one of the great prose works by a woman, and a standard by which others would be judged. Murasaki was perhaps hypersensitive to that possibility as she worked on her own *Tale of Genji*.

Murasaki makes special reference to the Chinese characters with which Sei littered her writings. This may again refer to a specific episode in which Shōnagon recounts how she amazed people by recognizing a Chinese poem and earning herself the nickname "Grass Hut" by virtue of her quick-witted reply.[37]

Self-Portrait for Daughter Kataiko

Following the sections about her contemporaries, Murasaki also writes about herself:

> So I seem to be misunderstood, and they think that I am shy. There have been times when I have been forced to sit in their company, and on such occasions I have tried to avoid their petty criticisms, not because I am particularly shy but because I consider it all so distasteful; as a result, I am now known as somewhat of a dullard.
>
> "Well, we never expected this!" they all say. "No one liked her. They all said she was pretentious, awkward, difficult to approach, prickly, too fond of her tales, haughty, prone to versifying, disdainful, cantankerous, and scornful. But when you meet her, she is strangely meek, a completely different person altogether!"
>
> How embarrassing! Do they really look upon me as such a dull thing, I wonder? But I am what I am and so act accordingly. Her Majesty too has often remarked that she had thought I was not the kind of person with whom she could ever relax, but that now I have become closer to her than any of the others. I am so perversely standoffish; if only I can avoid putting off those for whom I have genuine respect. (p. 135)

This description seems to fit the impression given by other parts of the diary that Murasaki was an introverted, reserved, egocentric, honest, and sensitive observer of life and human nature.

The format of Murasaki's diary—the mixture of description of public events with private commentary—has led to speculation that it was written as a handbook on court service to her daughter.[38] Kataiko would have been about twelve years old when the diary was completed, on the brink of womanhood, an appropriate time to receive advice about her life ahead.

If the diary was primarily intended for Kataiko, her mother's efforts were well rewarded. Kataiko did indeed enter court service. There she was known as "Echigo no Ben," probably owing to the fact that her grandfather Tametoki had been the governor of Echigo.[39] In about 1023 she became a consort of a nephew of Michinaga, Fujiwara Kanetaka (985–1053), whom she bore a child. In 1025 she was named *menoto* (nurse-guardian) to the newborn Prince Chikahito (1025–68).[40] His parents were the Crown Prince Atsuyoshi and his consort Kishi, a younger sister of Shōshi. Prince Chikahito ascended the throne in 1045 as the Emperor Go-Reizei.

In the 1030s Kataiko married Takashina Narinori, who was appointed senior assistant governor general (*daini*) of Kyushu in 1054 and was promoted to Third Rank (*sanmi*) the following year. Kataiko was subsequently known by the sobriquet "Daini no sanmi." She was also a poet of some repute, with an extant collection of her poems and thirty-seven verses in the imperial anthologies.[41] A prose work, the *Sagoromo monogatari*, has also been attributed to her, perhaps because of its resemblance to parts of *The Tale of Genji*, but this attribution is spurious. In any case, Murasaki would surely have been satisfied with her daughter's successful court and poetic career, which was also blessed by longevity. Kataiko died in the mid-1070s, well into her seventies.

Murasaki's Death

How long Murasaki herself lived is the final biographical puzzle still debated by scholars. The existing theories give a wide range for possible death dates, from 1014 to 1031.[42] Each theory is based on one clue from which an elaborate set of circumstantial evidence is inferred to substantiate that particular theory. All remain unproven and hampered by the fact that the need to know Murasaki's death date was not felt until the eighteenth century.

The first attempt to write a scholarly biography of Murasaki Shikibu was undertaken in 1703 by Andō Tameakira, entitled *Shika shichiron*. He refers to the passage in the *Eiga monogatari* that tells of Kataiko's promotion to the post of nurse to Prince Chikahito. This passage identifies Kataiko as the daughter of Murasaki Shikibu. From this it is inferred that Murasaki herself was still in court service at that date, 1025. Her name does not, however, appear in a 1031 list in the same source, where one would expect it, were she still alive. Thus the first theory about Murasaki's date of death proposed that she died sometime between the year 1025 and 1031. This theory remained unchallenged until 1928 when the poet-critic Yosano Akiko argued for the earlier date of 1015 or 1016, based on the fact that no poems by Murasaki after that date exist. Furthermore, her father Tametoki took Buddhist vows in 1016, most likely because Murasaki had preceded him in death. The date 1014 has also been proposed,[43] based chiefly on a poem by Fujiwara Yorimune, the preface of which refers to the death of "Shikibu no kimi." The preface of another poem, dated 1030, is used as the basis for the year 1031 as the year of Murasaki Shikibu's death. Another date recently proposed is 1019.[44]

These, then, are the facts and theories concerning the fairly unremarkable individual life of one Heian woman. What has fascinated scholars and lay readers about this particular life is, of course, that it culminated in the great prose masterpiece of all time, *The Tale of Genji.*

The Life of a Heian Noblewoman

The Tale of Genji is a pinnacle of Japanese prose literature, a work of astonishing complexity and psychological insight. The most recent English translation has almost 1,100 pages.[45] The hero of the novel is Prince Genji, "the shining one." Like the Buddha at the center of a great mandala, the character of Genji dominates the work. He is portrayed as the ideal Heian courtier, accomplished in the genteel arts of his age such as poetry, calligraphy, painting, music, dance, and, above all, the art of love. The plot revolves around Genji's emotional relationships with the many women in his life. The role of human attachment in all its manifestations and the effect of the passage of time form the binding themes of *The Tale of Genji.*

It is precisely this extraordinary heroic achievement that has made generations of readers want to know the details of the life of its creative genius, Murasaki Shikibu. Having gleaned everything possible about her from her diary and poetry, we must turn to *The Tale of Genji,* not so much for clues about the life of one particular Heian woman author as for an overview of the entire spectrum of female characters depicted. In the course of a famous lecture on literature, Murasaki's hero says: "I have been rude and unfair to your romances, haven't I? They have set down and preserved happenings from the age of the gods to our own. *The Chronicles of Japan* and the rest are a mere fragment of the whole truth. It is your romances that fill in the details'' (p. 437). Thus, both the realistic descriptions in the diaries of Murasaki and her contemporaries and the reflection and idealization of their world in *The Tale of Genji* can contribute to ''filling in the details'' of a picture portraying the life of a noblewoman in tenth- and eleventh-century Japan.

Birth Ceremonies

Imagine, then, what life would have been like for a female member of a prominent family of Heian Japan (794–1192). The scene of her birth would be filled with a profusion of sights and sounds—the ceaseless intonation of prayers chanted by the Buddhist priests in the neighboring chambers; the moans and cries of the female mediums employed to divert evil spirits from the mother, weakened as she would be by the process of giving birth.

One of the most chillingly memorable birth scenes in *The Tale of Genji* depicts the ''possession'' of Genji's wife Aoi during her labor. Thinking her near death, Genji goes to Aoi's side to hear her last words. She does speak a few words and a poem. ''It was not Aoi's voice, nor was the manner hers. Extraordinary—and then he knew that it was the voice of the Rokujō lady. He was aghast. He had dismissed the talk as vulgar and ignorant fabrication, and here before his eyes he had proof that such things actually did happen. He was horrified and repelled'' (p. 169). The Rokujō lady was a rival of Aoi's for Genji's affections. It seems that the intensity of Rokujō's jealousy was such that it could dispatch her spirit to possess Aoi during childbirth, and ultimately cause death. The prayers and mediums were not efficacious enough to protect Aoi in this instance.

Besides the prayers and chanting accompanying the birth, one's emergence into the world would also cause the constant bustle of women in attendance on the mother, as well as of the numerous messengers from various quarters inquiring after the progress of the birth. In contrast to this aural confusion, the immediate visual surroundings would be somewhat more serene. The mother would be confined behind her curtains on a raised platform, with only close family members and a few women in immediate attendance. The birth room, the robes of the mother and women, the hangings, curtains, and screens would all be ritualistically pure white. Since the process of giving birth was considered a ritual defilement, the birthing room would not be one in which someone would live or play later, as it would be specially built or set aside for this occasion.

In the care taken in preparations for and celebrations after birth, perhaps the most important aspect of Heian life was foreshadowed, namely, the primacy of adherence to form and ritual. The Japanese "rule of taste," as the British historian George Sansom so aptly dubbed it, was based on carefully codified and closely observed rituals, beginning with birth.

The first set of rituals were the bath ceremonies (*oyudono*), two on each of seven favorable days. The procedure began with the preparation of the bath water, drawn from a specially selected site. Suitable prayers were then said over the bath. The baby would be taken there, accompanied by several ladies dressed in white. One of the women might carry a sword to protect her from evil spirits. The birth was also celebrated by a series of lavish banquets on the third, fifth, seventh, and ninth nights, as fully described in Murasaki Shikibu's diary.

The importance of beginning life with proper adherence to ritual is not lost on Genji in Murasaki's tale, either. His only daughter is born to the Akashi lady, whom he had courted during his years of exile in a remote coastal area of Akashi. By the time the news of his daughter's birth reached him, he had already been called back to the capital, Heian Kyo, but Genji immediately dispatches a nurse and retinue to celebrate the infant's arrival properly. For while Murasaki Shikibu's father may have lamented that she was not born a boy, many Heian fathers rejoiced at the birth of a daughter more than at that of a son. Genji's great solicitude toward the Akashi lady and his newborn daughter may in part be ascribed to the prediction by a Korean fortune teller: that Genji would sire a daughter destined to become an empress.

Such an event would ensure a political power base, as proven by the Fujiwaras. The highpoint of this grand clan was reached with Michinaga. Four of his daughters, including Shōshi, whom Murasaki Shikibu served, married emperors; two emperors in the 1000s were Michinaga's nephews, and three his grandsons. By extension, "marriage politics" was also practiced by the rest of court society, as nobles vied to arrange advantageous matches for their daughters, either into the imperial family itself, or, if that was not possible, into another of the high-ranking families. So it was natural that fathers like Genji should show a great interest in every aspect of a daughter's life, from birth onward.

Despite his great concern Genji does not actually get to see his daughter until quite some time after her birth. In his case, it is partly owing to the physical distance between Akashi and the capital, but custom would have prevented him seeing her for over a month nonetheless. Heian women usually continued to live in their parental home after marriage, to which the husband could commute. Some women did live outside their parental home, as in the case of Empress Shōshi, who resided at her husband Ichijō's imperial palace, but they would normally return home for the birth of a child.

Therefore, the initial ceremonies of the baby's first bath and the banquets on the third, fifth, seventh, and ninth nights would have been held at the residence of the mother's parents. Not until the fiftieth day after the birth would the mother be considered sufficiently recovered and fit to resume normal activities. Only then could the father get his first glimpse of the baby. In *The Tale of Genji*, for example, Tamakazura's daughter returns home to give birth to her child but leaves for Emperor Reizei's palace after the fiftieth day in consideration of his eagerness to see his newborn daughter.

For the baby, the fiftieth day after birth would be marked by the first ritual feeding of solid food in the form of rice cakes. A grand banquet would be the occasion for the first meeting with the father. Genji's first meeting with his daughter is delayed due to physical distance, but the ceremonies are not.

> His daughter would be fifty days old on the fifth day of the Fifth Month. He longed more than ever to see her. What a splendid affair the fiftieth-day celebrations would be if they might take place in the city! Why had he allowed the child to be born in so unseemly a place? If it had been a boy he would not have been so concerned, but for a girl it was a very great disability not to be born in the city. And she seemed especially important because his unhappiness had so much to do with her destinies. He sent off messengers with the strictest orders to arrive on that day and no other. They took with them all the gifts which the most fertile imagination could have thought of for such an occasion, and practical supplies as well. (p. 277)

To a twentieth-century reader who might consider it quite desirable to raise a child in the fresh air of the countryside, Genji's regrets over having allowed the Akashi princess to be born in "so unseemly a place" might seem exaggerated. But Heian society would consider it a handicap to be born and reared in the provinces. The social, political, and cultural life of the Heian nobility was centered on the capital, and anyone from beyond its limits was considered uncouth and unworthy of serious attention. Any attention that was received would be as a target for ridicule, as happens to the hapless Lady from Ōmi in *The Tale of Genji.*

Even more important to a girl's future than the place of birth, though, was her lineage and breeding. The Akashi princess is virtually assured of a glorious future by the high social and political standing of her father. Her mother, however, as the daughter of a provincial governor, is not considered to be of sufficiently high rank. Genji solves this problem by bringing his daughter to the capital to live at his Nijō mansion, to be raised there by his childless but otherwise near-perfect consort Murasaki, the daughter of an imperial prince. Though the separation from her infant is painful and difficult, the Akashi lady accedes to Genji's wishes for the sake of their daughter's future. Having a higher-ranking consort adopt one's daughter by another woman was not without its historical precedents. Chancellor Fujiwara Kaneie had his consort adopt his daughter born of his other wife, as duly recorded by the former in her diary, *Kagerō nikki* (translated as *The Gossamer Years*).[46]

Adoption, nevertheless, was not the usual arrangement. A child born into a noble family living in the capital would be raised in the mother's home, which would probably be the residence of her parents. Genji's first son, Yūgiri, born to Aoi in her parent's home, grows up under the care of his maternal grandmother after Aoi's death. The most important person in a child's life besides her mother and grandmother was probably her nurse-guardian (*menoto*), carefully chosen since she would be influential throughout her charge's life. The nurse would be of fairly high rank and breeding herself, as is the woman selected by Genji to be the nurse for the Akashi princess. While her own mother remains behind in Akashi, the princess is entrusted to the nurse, who accompanies her to the capital and takes up residence with her (p. 334).

Prepuberty Rite and Education

In a child's third or fourth year, preparations would begin for the first in a series of rites of passage, the "Putting on of the Trousers" (*hakama-gi* or *chakko*).[47] The trousers (*hakama*) resembled a wide, divided skirt with openings at the side held in place by a cord fastened around the waist. This event was celebrated by both boys and girls at this age. Genji's *hakama-gi* ceremony is depicted as a very festive occasion (p. 4), as is that of his daughter the Akashi princess. The decorations for the rooms are especially made in miniature sizes, "as if for the finest doll's house in the world" (pp. 334–35). The trousers were put on the child and the waist cord tied by a respected senior member of the nobility. The rite was followed by a formal banquet and entertainment. The donning of the trousers marked the day when the child grew out of babyhood and her education for the life ahead began.

Sei Shōnagon illustrates what could be expected:

> In the reign of Emperor Murakami [in the mid-900s] there was a woman at Court known as the Imperial Lady of Senyō Palace. She was the daughter of the Minister of the Left who lived in the Smaller Palace of the First Ward, and of course you have all heard of her. When she was still a young girl, her father gave her this advice: "First you must study penmanship. Next you must learn to play the seven-string zither better than anyone else. And also you must memorize all the poems in the twenty volumes of the *Kokin Shu*."[48]

This quotation summarizes fairly well the spirit of women's education in Heian Japan. These three accomplishments—calligraphy, music, and poetry—formed the basis on which the success or failure of one's upbringing would be judged.

Calligraphy involved writing in the Japanese syllabary (*kana*). Since there was originally no native system of writing, the phonetic kana system was developed in the eighth and ninth centuries, using abbreviated forms of the Chinese characters, which had been introduced to Japan in the sixth century. Chinese characters and writing were part of every boy's education, as Murasaki Shikibu notes in her diary. Chinese characters were therefore referred to as "men's writing" (*otoko moji*). The kana system was called "women's letters" (*onna moji*), though men could also read and write it.

Calligraphy lessons would begin with the fifty kana syllables. The writing was done with brush and ink, so it was necessary to learn how to grind the ink stick and prepare the correct consistency of ink, and how to choose the appropriate type and color of writing papers. The latter depended on the occasion of the writing, the theme of the poem or letter, and the recipient. Samples of calligraphic styles were provided in the form of copybooks. When Genji's daughter, the Akashi princess, enters court service, Genji sends her off with a library of books and scrolls by master calligraphers of the past, to which he adds examples of his own and those of the best calligraphers at court (pp. 517–20). Since most forms of communication with people outside one's home would be in writing, calligraphy was one's most visible skill. Maturity, aesthetic judgment, and character were judged by one's handwriting, so many hours of practice had to be devoted to mastering various styles. One's better efforts as well as beautiful examples received from others were collected together for future references, especially during courtship.

Music also played a large role in Heian life. Learning to play a musical instrument helped instill a certain discipline. One learned to play not only for pleasure, but also to be able to participate in the many occasions for joint concerts. The choice of instruments for a girl was limited to stringed instruments: the lute (*biwa*) or one of the several types of Chinese and Japanese zithers (*koto*). In *The Tale of Genji*, the fathers teach their daughters how to play musical instruments: Genji's second formal wife, the Third Princess, had been taught the seven-stringed Chinese koto by her father, the Suzaku Emperor; the Eighth Prince, living in seclusion in the wilds of Uji, teaches his two daughters the lute and the thirteen-stringed koto; and Genji himself teaches the Akashi princess, his ward Tamakazura, as well as Murasaki. One of Genji's proudest moments is a gathering of his ladies, when three of his music students display their talents.

> The moon rose higher and the color and scent of the plum blossoms seemed to be higher and brighter too. The Akashi princess had a most engagingly girlish touch on the thirteen-stringed koto. The tremolo, bright and clear, had in it something of her mother's style. Murasaki's touch, strangely affecting, seemed quiet and solemn by comparison, and her cadenzas were superb. For the envoi there was a shift to a minor mode, somehow friendlier and more approachable. In "The Five Airs" the touch of the plectrum against the fifth and sixth strings of the seven-stringed koto is thought to present the supreme challenge, but the Third Princess had a fine sureness and lucidity. . . . Genji felt that he had won new honors as a teacher. (pp. 605–6)

The third essential ingredient in a girl's training was poetry. The role of poetry in Heian culture can hardly be exaggerated. Historically, the prestige of poetry in Chinese by Japanese poets helped promote the growth of the native tradition. In ninth-century Japan there were three imperially sponsored anthologies of poetry in the Chinese language. The *Kokinshū* (Collection of ancient and modern poems), compiled in 905, was the first imperial collection of Japanese verse, though it had two prefaces—one in Chinese, the more famous in Japanese. The Japanese preface, written in *kana* by the poet and compiler Ki no Tsurayuki, states:

> Japanese poetry has for its seed the human heart, and grows into countless leaves of words. In this life many things touch men: They seek then to express their feelings by images drawn from what they see or hear. Who among men does not compose poetry upon hearing the song of the nightingale among the flowers, or the cries of the frog who lives in the water? Poetry it is which, without effort, moves heaven and earth, and stirs to pity the invisible demons and gods; which makes sweet the ties between men and women; and which can comfort the hearts of fierce warriors.[49]

The verse form of this anthology, which every Heian boy and girl had to learn, was the thirty-one syllable poem (*waka*), written in five lines of 5, 7, 5, 7, and 7 syllables. As the poems were copied and memorized, one would learn the private, lyrical tone that reflected keen sensitivity to nature, to the perishability of beauty, and to the varieties of human emotions. One would also learn to use the two thousand or so words considered appropriate for poetic expression, as well as the rhetorical devices and allusions to poems of the past to expand the layers of meaning contained in the thirty-one-syllable format. The rules for poetic composition would be reinforced by poetry contests (*uta-awase*), which were recorded along with the commentary on the judgments of individual verses.

There was almost daily opportunity to write verses in the steady stream of correspondence, which was the main method of social communication. One of the chief functions of poetry mentioned by Ki no Tsurayuki in his preface was to make "sweet the ties between men and women." Genji scolds Murasaki for her choice of literature to read to the Akashi princess: "You must not read love stories to her. I doubt that clandestine affairs would arouse her unduly, but we would not want her to think of them as commonplace" (p. 348).

Two cosmetic practices characteristic of Heian women were to blacken the teeth and pluck the eyebrows. The most time and attention were paid to hair, which one let grow as long and thick as possible, for it was considered the most important aspect of personal beauty.

Puberty

At the age of twelve or thirteen, preparations began for the next important rite of passage, initiation into adulthood, or "Putting on of the Train" (*mogi* or *chakumo*). The *mo* was the long train of a woman's skirt worn on formal occasions. It was fastened with a thin cord that tied around the waist. The person chosen to fasten the cord of the train would be a prominent member of one's family or the court. The room where the ceremony took place would be redecorated with the most costly brocade hangings and cushions. Of the many gifts from relatives and well-wishers, some would be suitable for one's adult life: robes, combs, fans, and perfumes. Guests would receive commemorative gifts in turn. On the evening of the ceremony the guests would gather at the parents' home but the young woman whose adulthood was being celebrated would not be personally presented to most of them, as a woman did not show herself to anyone but her immediate family. The person who bestowed the train would be allowed behind the curtains for the brief ceremony; afterward, he or she would join the guests in the main chamber for the ensuing banquet and entertainments.

The train was the final element in a Heian woman's formal attire. It was made of figured silk—usually white, light lavender, or reddish brown. In summer it might be of a lighter weight gauze. The train was usually worn in conjunction with a short, jacket-like garment called *karaginu*, which was often made from sumptuous imported brocades. These were worn over a full-length lined robe (*uwagi*) of brocade or figured silk, with a plain silk lining that showed at the collar, sleeve, and hem. Under this was another robe of stiffer crimson silk (*uchiginu*). The set of robes worn under the *uchiginu* were the most important element of the ensemble and formed its aesthetic focus. These were called *uchigi* or *kasane-uchigi* and consisted of a series of five, seven, and sometimes more robes of varying colors. The robes were usually monochrome-colored silks and were only visible at the neckline, hem, and sleeves. The sleeves were broad open-cuffed, and the front of the robes were loosely crossed, so that the edges showed fully at the front and sides. Many of the robes were of sheer silk, which permitted the color of the layer beneath to show through. A glance at one's kimono sleeves instantly revealed one's sense of fashion refinement; the harmony and interplay of the layers of color was the key. The undermost robe closest to the body was a single, unlined robe with smaller sleeve openings, but a longer length of sleeve. The divided skirt, or *hakama*, usually scarlet in color, formed the final piece in one's attire.[50]

This elaborate series of robes was worn for ceremonial occasions. For less formal wear in one's own home, the *mo* and *karaginu* were replaced by a single full-length outer robe (*kouchiginu*), and sometimes the layers of the inner robes were abbreviated from full robes to false extra collars and sleeve bands. In summer, thinner silks and gauzes were often substituted for the heavier satins and damasks of winter. A Heian lady was a virtual prisoner of her own finery, forced into a sedentary existence. In what was known as the "twelve-robe" formal, she was just as encumbered as a Scarlett O'Hara in her crinolines, though freer to breathe without the corset or tight laces.

Discernment in color harmonies appropriate to the season and the occasion were advantageous as well in selecting the many gifts of robes and textiles that a Heian woman needed to give throughout the years. The focus on color meant that dyeing of textiles was an essential element of the progress. Thus, women acquired a knowledge of the roots and plants that were the sources for the dyes, such as indigo for blue or hawthorn for yellowish brown, and of dyeing techniques, such as resist or tie-dyeing, bleaching, and multiple dye baths. A woman had to be able to direct her staff or place precise orders with professional dyers.

The multiple layers of clothing worn even on informal occasions proved cumbersome at times, but they served to keep one warm in an age without central heating. The hangings and cushions that surrounded women in their quarters were also useful in providing protection from cold winter drafts. These textiles were often of brocades or gold-stamped silks, meant to please the eye as well. Soft, decoratively patterned hangings allowed a woman to see out without being seen, which gave protection from unwanted glances. Beyond the cloth hangings were thin bamboo blinds, allowing a view to the garden beyond. At night, wooden lattices gave additional protection.

A young woman's quarters would be in one of the wings (*tainoya*) of the house, set off from the central quarters (*moya*) inhabited by the father. Other wings, where other women members of the family or attendants lived, would be connected by corridors and form a horse-shoe-shaped plan that framed the courtyard and garden to the south. Gardens were planned to be beautiful in any season and were the focus of one's contact with nature and the changing seasons. The veranda surrounding the house and facing the garden was the setting for many of the music concerts and poetry exchanges described in Heian litera-ture. *The Tale of Genji* has a scene in the garden of Genji's mansion, where his son Yugiri and some of his friends are playing *kemari*, a sedate type of football. The following description conveys the ambi-ance of the age, the universal good cheer of young men, and the casual charm of a fateful moment.

Yes, there were many skills, and as one inning followed another a certain abandon was to be observed and the caps of state were pushed rather far back on noble foreheads. Yugiri could permit himself a spe-cial measure of abandon, and his youthful spirits and vigor were infec-tious. He had on a soft white robe lined with red. His trousers were gently taken in at the ankles, but by no means untidy. He seemed very much in control of himself despite the abandon, and cherry blossoms fell about him like a flurry of snow. He broke off a twig from a dipping branch and went to sit on the stairs.

"How quick they are to fall," said Kashiwagi, coming up behind him. "We must teach the wind to blow wide and clear."

He glanced over toward the Third Princess's rooms. They seemed to be in the usual clutter. The multicolored sleeves pouring from under the blinds and through openings between them were like an assortment of swatches to be presented to the goddess of spring. Only a few paces from him a woman had pushed her curtains carelessly aside and looked as if she might be in a mood to receive a gentlemen's addresses. A Chinese cat, very small and pretty, came running out with a large cat in pursuit. There was a noisy rustling of silk as several women pushed forward to catch it. On a long cord which had become badly tangled, it would not yet seem to have been fully tamed. As it sought to free itself the cord caught in a curtain, which was pulled back to reveal the women behind. No one, not even those nearest the veranda, seemed to notice. They were much too worried about the cat.

A lady in informal dress stood just inside the curtain beyond the second pillar to the west. Her robe seemed to be of red lined with lavender, and at the sleeves and throat the colors were as bright and varied as the book of paper samples. Her cloak was of white figured satin lined with red. Her hair fell as cleanly as sheaves of thread and fanned out towards the neatly trimmed edges some ten inches beyond her feet. In the rich billowing of her skirts the lady scarcely seemed present at all. The white profile framed by masses of black hair was pretty and elegant—though unfortunately the room was dark and he could not see her as well in the evening light as he would have wished. The women had been too delighted with the game, young gentlemen heedless of how they scattered the blossoms, to worry about blinds and concealment. The lady turned to look at the cat, which was mewing piteously, and in her face and figure was an abundance of quiet, unpretending young charm. (pp. 581–84)

This scene is one of the few instances in which a woman appears in such public views. Through her carelessness here, the Third Princess brings about serious and unhappy consequences for all, as discussed more fully later.

A Heian lady was thus expected to know that it was most inappropriate to allow anything more than the corner of her sleeves or a hem to be seen by any man other than her father or husband.

Courtship

The initiation ceremony at which a young woman first put on the train not only marked her debut into the adult world but also served to indicate that she was now considered to be of marriageable age. Heian society was polygamous, so a man could have more than one wife and any number of concubines, with varying degrees of formality and legality to the differing relationships.

A man's first marriage was almost always arranged. The woman he married at this time would be his principal and formal wife, and their children would be the heirs to the family property or rank. Naturally, parents tried to arrange for their daughter to become the principal wife of a man of equal, or, if possible, higher rank than herself. In *The Tale of Genji* there are several examples of this type of marriage, beginning with that of Aoi, the daughter of the minister of the left, to Genji, the son of the reigning emperor. This marriage is arranged by the two fathers in conjunction with Genji's coming-of-age ceremony (*gempuku*), the boy's equivalent to the girl's *mogi* ceremony. Genji is in his twelfth year at the time, and Aoi four years his senior. Years later,

Genji himself arranges for his daughter, the Akashi princess, to marry the crown prince. Since they are closer in age, the royal marriage takes place in conjunction with both their initiation ceremonies. The preparations for the princess's initiation are therefore very elaborate and include the blending of perfumes and sewing of covers and cushions for her trousseau. The Akashi princess leaves her father's mansion in a hand-drawn carriage to take up residence at the crown prince's palace.

Unless a girl was marrying an emperor or a crown prince, she would usually remain in her parental home, just as Aoi continues to reside at her parents' mansion after her marriage to Genji. Genji remains at his own residence and commutes to Aoi's, but a man might move in with his wife in her parental home. The Tsuchimikado mansion, for example, which was the residence of the Regent Michinaga described in Murasaki Shikibu's diary, belonged to his wife Rinshi. A third possibility would be for the wife to move into a residence provided by her husband, as is the case with Tamakazura who marries the future prime minister Higekuro in *The Tale of Genji*.[51] In the arrangements for marriage, one's family's economic, social, and political standing were of prime importance. On becoming a principal wife, the woman's parents supplied the residence and material goods, such as the costly robes and textiles used for the many festivals and ceremonies. The wife's father was expected to promote the political career of her husband as well. The ownership of parental property was nonetheless passed on to the wife or one of her sisters, rather than to her husband or brothers. A woman's marriageability thus depended in large part on her family's wealth and influence, and the rules of female inheritance of property applied even if she did not become a principal wife.

Even when a man already had a principal wife, he might court someone as a secondary wife. Such a match was not arranged by the parents, although they might encourage it, as the Akashi priest does Genji's suit of his daughter. The services of intermediaries were still essential, however, in the initial stages of courtship, because a woman was normally not visible or accessible to anyone outside her own household. The scene in which the Third Princess appears in full view on the veranda during the football match at Genji's mansion is memorable precisely because it is so exceptional. Usually, the most a man could hope for was a glimpse of a woman's sleeve from behind the blinds or a snatch of a tune from her koto heard outside her garden gate. A man's knowledge of a woman's very existence was often dependent on vague rumors from one of his attendants who had had contact with one of her ladies-in-waiting.

The Tale of Genji is filled with scenes of young noblemen catching their first look at a prospective conquest through a garden fence or sliding door. This is how Genji first discovers the child Murasaki and determines to raise her as his ideal wife (pp. 87–89). Genji's nominal son Kaoru's romantic interest in Ōgimi and her sister Nakanokimi is first piqued by the sounds of their lute playing. He manages to persuade one of the prince's guards at the Uji villa to let him have a peek at the sisters:

> A gate seemed to lead to the Princesses' rooms. Kaoru pushed it open a little. The blind had been half raised to give a view of the moon, more beautiful for the mist. A young girl, tiny and delicate, her soft robe somewhat rumpled, sat shivering at the veranda. With her was an older woman similarly dressed. The princesses were farther inside. Half hidden by a pillar, one had a lute before her and sat toying with the plectrum . . . the other, leaning against an armrest, had a koto before her. (p. 785)

Thus begins the web of complicated entanglements involving the sisters and Kaoru.

Once a man's interest was aroused, he began his overtures by sending a poem through the discreet offices of the same person who helped him gain his first inkling of a woman's existence. The verse was delivered by his contact in the woman's household, perhaps a nurse or a lady-in-waiting. The woman's impression of the would-be suitor was entirely dependent on the appearance and contents of his missive. The author of *The Gossamer Years* records her reaction to the letter from her future husband, the Chancellor Kaneie:

> It consisted of but one verse: "Sad am I, 'mid talk about the warbler. May I not too hear its voice?" The paper was rather unbecoming for such an occasion, I thought, and the handwriting was astonishingly bad. Having heard that he was a most accomplished penman, I wondered indeed whether he might not have had someone else write it. I was half-inclined not to answer, but my mother insisted that a letter from such a gentleman was not to be ignored, and finally I sent off a return poem: "Let no bird waste its song in a wilderness where it finds no answer." (pp. 33–34)

The man in turn would judge from the woman's verse and handwriting whether to continue his suit. His principal wife might also be anxious for a glance at the calligraphy, to determine how serious a rival for her husband's affections she might have. Genji's favorite wife, Murasaki, for example, realizes "why the Akashi lady had done so well" (p. 278) from a look at her handwriting, while the hand of his second principal wife, the Third Princess, is reassuringly bad (p. 558).

Sometimes the first few replies were actually written by an intermediary rather than by the woman herself. Especially during the initial stages of courtship, it was the trusted companion or lady-in-waiting who controlled the suitor's access to a woman. Genji gives his ward Tamakazura's attendant the following instructions about discriminating amongst the missives of prospective suitors: "You must rate them carefully and have her answer the ones that seem deserving. The dissolute gallants of our day are capable of anything, but sometimes they are not wholly to blame . . . you must judge each on his own merits. Some may be serious and some may not. The genuine should be recognized" (pp. 424–25).

Once a fairly regular correspondence was established, the suitor would naturally seek a personal interview. Here again, both the man and the woman were in the hands of the household attendants, who would either help or hinder the visit, sometimes even without the woman's knowledge or consent. On the first few visits, the couple would not speak directly, but through the intermediary. The woman's admirer would most likely be seated on the veranda under the moonlight, and the woman herself behind curtains and screens, so that mutual impressions remained tinged with an air of mystery. If the appearance and deportment of the man was considered proper and he was deemed a serious contender for the woman's attentions, the go-between would arrange to let him come inside the house and converse with her directly, exchanging poems about the seasons or the moon. Once the suitor managed to gain access to a woman's rooms, he considered his suit accepted, and it was only a matter of time and disposition until he was allowed behind the inner curtains and the vows were consummated. Even then, however, certain conventions had to be followed.

Nuptial Procedures and Marriage

The suitor had to leave before dawn. Once back in his quarters, before all else, he sat down and composed his "morning-after" poem for the woman. The sooner the messenger arrived at her residence with his letter, the more ardent his devotion. Although the messenger was supposed to deliver the letter in secret, the woman's family was by now aware of the suit and awaited the missive of the next morning as anxiously as she. Even in cases such as Genji's son Yugiri's marriage to Kumoinokari, after years of courtship with both fathers' tacit approval, the conventions of the "secret" visit and predawn departure were honored (pp. 528–29). As the messenger who brought the groom's letter waited for the reply, he was presented with gifts as a reward for his services. The same pattern was followed the next night and morning. The third night's visit was the most important, as it was the final one, which served to formalize the marriage. So it is that Genji's grandson Prince Niou risks his mother's ire as well as his own personal safety in setting out for the wilds of Uji on horseback to make his third night's visit to Nakanokimi (pp. 844–45). The atmosphere is quite different when he later marries Rokunokimi, for her father Yugiri prepares a lavish celebration for the third night: "The prescribed silver dishes were laid out most grandly on eight stands, and there were two smaller stands as well, and the ceremonial rice cakes were brought on trays with the festoon-shaped legs so much in style" (p. 903).

Unlike the usually ecstatic bride in Western love marriage, however, some Heian women might be caught unprepared and would react to the trauma of "the first night" in their inimitable ways, as tastefully described by Murasaki Shikibu. The following scene gives poignant insight into a girl's psychological state on the "morning after," with a full interplay of such emotions as surprise, embarrassment, distress, and resentment for what seems to be male betrayal of her trust. For nearly three years, Genji has been raising Murasaki like a surrogate father, but with a clear intention of grooming her into an ideal wife, which his true love the Empress Fujitsubo never could be. Now young Murasaki is thirteen years of age and Genji is twenty-one.

> What had happened? Her women had no way of knowing when the line had been crossed. One morning Genji was up early and Murasaki stayed on and on in bed. It was not at all like her to sleep so late. Might she be unwell? As he left for his own rooms, Genji pushed an inkstone inside her bed curtains.
>
> At length, when no one else was near, she raised herself from her pillow and saw beside it a tightly folded bit of paper. Listlessly she opened it. There was only this verse, in a casual hand:

> *"Many have been the nights we have spent together*
> *Purposelessly, these coverlets between us."*

She had not dreamed he had anything of the sort on his mind. What a fool she had been, to repose her whole confidence in so gross and unscrupulous a man.

It was almost noon when Genji returned. "They say you're not feeling well. What can be the trouble? I was hoping for a game of Go."

She pulled the covers over her head. Her women discreetly withdrew. He came up beside her.

"What a way to behave, what a very unpleasant way to behave. Try to imagine, please, what these women are thinking."

He drew back the covers. She was bathed in perspiration and the hair at her forehead was matted from weeping.

"Dear me. This does not augur well at all." He tried in every way he could think of to comfort her, but she seemed genuinely upset and did not offer so much as a word in reply.

"Very well. You will see no more of me. I do have my pride."

He opened her writing box but found no note inside. Very childish of her—and he had to smile at the childishness. He stayed with her the whole day, and thought the stubbornness with which she refused to be comforted most charming. (pp. 180–81)

The festivities on the third night served to introduce the new husband formally to the wife's family and to publicize the event to the world at large. The next morning he did not have to depart at daybreak, but could stay into the day. This was usually his first opportunity to see his wife in daylight, since previous meetings were clandestine and at night only. Thereafter he could come and go openly.

Married life, either as a principal or a secondary wife, allowed a woman to begin using the skills she had learned, such as the dyeing and sewing of her own and her husband's wardrobe. Proper preparations had to be made to receive visitors on the occasion of annual festivals and ceremonies; these evenings also tested one's musical and poetic talents after the feasting. A primary function of a woman was, of course, the bearing and raising of children. The birth of a child helped secure her position in her husband's affections and in the eyes of the world, as happens with the Akashi lady and Genji, or Nakanokimi with the birth of her first son by Prince Niou in *The Tale of Genji*. Needless to say, as a wife one was expected to remain faithful to her husband. As mentioned above, Genji's second principle wife, the Third Princess, is portrayed as flighty and careless when she allows herself to be seen by Kashiwagi during the football match in Genji's gardens. As a result of this ill-fated glimpse of her, Kashiwagi falls in love and finally succeeds in seducing her. A son, Kaoru, is born out of their affair, whom Genji allows the world to think his. Haunted by his own guilt, Kashiwagi wastes away and dies. But Genji himself cannot forgive his wife and her indiscretion and broods over it:

> And how was he to behave toward the princess? He understood rather better the reasons for her condition. He had come upon the truth himself, without the aid of informers. Was there to be no change in his manner? He would have preferred that there be none but feared that things could not be the same again. Even in affairs which he had not from the outset taken seriously, the smallest evidence that the lady might be interested in someone else had always been enough to kill his own interest; and here he had more, a good deal more. (p. 635)

Conversely, marriage did not guarantee a husband's faithfulness. The most a wife could hope to accomplish was to remain uppermost in her husband's affections. In *The Gossamer Years*, an older relative of Murasaki Shikibu known as Michitsuna's mother chronicles the history of her marriage to Kaneie, beset by a string of rivals for his attentions. Her description of the fate of one of her rivals and her reaction to that fate is unusually frank by Heian standards, and strikes us as distinctly modern:

> It began to appear that the lady in the alley had fallen from favor since the birth of her child. I had prayed, at the height of my unhappiness, that she would live to know what I was then suffering, and it seemed that my prayers were being answered. She was alone, and now her child was dead, the child that had been the cause of that unseemly racket. The lady was of frightfully bad birth—the unrecognized child of a rather odd prince, it was said. For a moment she had been able to use a person who was unaware of her shortcomings, and now she was abandoned. The pain must be even sharper than mine had been. I was satisfied. (p. 44)

The real-life "lady in the alley" mentioned in *The Gossamer Years* brings to mind the object of the youthful Genji's most passionate extramarital affairs, with Yūgao, the "lady of the evening face." She too was once a beloved of a high-ranking nobleman and Genji's best friend, Tō no Chūjō; having borne him a girl (Tamakazura), she was abandoned by him before Genji discovers her and falls in love with her. Even women of distinguished birth were sometimes abandoned by the world at large after their parents' death. The tangled garden and neglected appearance of the house of the "Safflower" lady (Suetsumuhana) reminds Genji of the late Yūgao. Hoping to find another woman like Yūgao, Genji pursues the occupant of this mansion, which is just as desolate as Yūgao's had been. The new lady turns out to be old-fashioned, untalented, and distinguished primarily by her long red nose, though unquestionably a princess by birth.

Before marriage, the romantic relationship could be terminated by either side—by the man through discontinuation of visits or letters, or by the woman in her refusal to see the man or answer his missives. The lack of formal acknowledgment did not, however, make a rupture any less difficult to bear. One of the most lyrical and moving episodes in *The Tale of Genji* is the parting of Genji and the Rokujō lady. Seven years his senior, she is the widow of the former crown prince, and Genji's first great love. But Genji's refusal to put their relationship on a formal footing makes Rokujō resolve to leave him and the capital by accompanying her daughter the Vestal Princess to Ise. Genji pays her a farewell visit before her departure.

> It was over a reed plain of melancholy beauty that he had his way to the shrine. The autumn flowers were gone and insects hummed in the wintry tangles. A wind whistling through the pines brought snatches of music to a most wonderful effect. . . . Gazing up into a sky even more beautiful now that the moon was setting, he poured forth all his pleas and complaints. . . . Now that she was with him again she found her resolve wavering. . . . Their feelings for each other, Genji's and the lady's, had run the whole range of sorrows and irritations, and no words could suffice for all they wanted to say to each other. The dawn sky was as if made for the occasion. Not wanting to go quite yet, Genji took her hand, very gently.

> *"A dawn farewell is always drenched in dew,*
> *But sad is the autumn sky as never before."*

> At length the lady replied:

> *"An autumn farewell needs nothing to make it sadder.*
> *Enough of your songs, O crickets on the moors!"*

No matter what type of relationship one entered into by choice or by chance, much of a woman's time was spent waiting for a visit or letter from her husband or lover. If she was a secondary wife, she might read with special sympathy and understanding the many passages in *The Gossamer Years*, in which the author describes her melancholy during the long nights spent alone waiting for the Chancellor Kaneie to come. It would have been little comfort to hear the perfectly rational explanations of ladies-in-waiting that he had other obligations (including his principle wife). Fear of abandonment, jealousy, and anger at one's husband for his neglect would still well up inside. Sometimes, as with Kaneie and Michitsuna's mother, the marriage would end in divorce.

The arrangements for divorce, unlike those for marriage, were not accompanied by any formal acknowledgment of the change in a woman's status. If she lived in a residence provided by her husband, she moved out of that house and back into her parents' as a final indication of separation. This is how Michitsuna's mother finalizes her divorce from Kaneie. In *The Tale of Genji*, Higekuro's first wife returns to her parental home, when he marries Genji's ward Tamakazura. In the latter instance, Tamakazura in effect supplants Higekuro's first wife as the principal wife. The financial independence of the Heian woman made divorce settlements relatively easy. If there were children, they stayed with the mother. The father might help his sons advance in the court hierarchy when they entered the ranks of the government bureaucracy. After the divorce, or if a woman was widowed, she could remarry if a suitable opportunity arose. Kashiwagi's widow, the Second Princess, for example, is successfully courted by his best friend, Yūgiri.

Career at Court

Another alternative open to a single woman, whether she was unmarried, divorced, or widowed, was entering court service. This option is highly recommended by one of the most outspoken women in Japan's history in her essay collection *Makura no sōshi* (*The Pillow Book of Sei Shōnagon*):

> When I make myself imagine what it is like to be one of those women who live at home, faithfully serving their husbands—women who have not a single exciting prospect in life yet who believe they are

perfectly happy—I am filled with scorn. Often they are of quite good birth, yet have had no opportunity to find out what the world is like. I wish they could live for a while in our society, even if it should mean taking service as Attendants, so that they might come to know the delights it has to offer.[52]

If a woman did take service as an attendant (or handmaid, *Naishi no Jō*), she would be among the lower-ranking female officials employed by the imperial court. Above her in ascending rank were four assistant handmaids and two principal handmaids. They were all in the employ of the Handmaids' Office (Naishi no Tsukasa), one of twelve offices originally created to oversee the management of the Women's Quarters (Kōkyū)[53] of the imperial palace. In which of the twelve buildings that comprised the Women's Quarters one lived depended upon one's position. Residents of the Women's Quarters included imperial consorts and concubines, the handmaids, and ladies-in-waiting. Among the ladies-in-waiting were many who did not hold official positions in the court bureaucracy but were on the private staff of the emperor or one of the high-ranking women of the palace. In *The Tale of Genji*, for example, when Genji's love Oborozukiyo is appointed principal handmaid, her new quarters are described as swarming with ladies-in-waiting who now attend her (p. 194). The imperial consorts had even larger numbers of ladies-in-waiting in their entourages. When the Rokujō lady's daughter Akikonomu becomes the consort of the Reizei Emperor, she brings with her the retinue of talented women in her service. The author of *The Tale of Genji* herself was at the court of the Empress Shōshi, as described earlier in this chapter, and Sei Shōnagon refers in *The Pillow Book* to her own life in the service of the Empress Teishi.

The annual round of ceremonies and festivals provided the nucleus for activities at court. Each month attendants were busy preparing foɪ one or another of these observances, each requiring the proper seasonal robes, hangings, food, dance, music, and poetry. In the first month, for example, were the New Year's celebrations; in the fifth, the Iris Festival; in the eighth, the Moon Viewing Festival; in the eleventh, the Gosechi Dances celebrating the rice harvest.[54] The most elaborate of the events on the calendar was the Kamo Festival in the middle of the fourth month. It celebrated the Shinto purification ritual carried out at the Kamo Shrines by the Vestal (*Sai-in*), who was usually chosen from among the imperial princesses. The Vestal set out for the shrines from the palace accompanied by an imperial procession. On the day of the festival the other women at court wore the full set of formal robes and rode in ox-drawn carriages. Along the route of the procession, the carriages of the ladies of the nobility vied for the best vantage points. One such "clash of carriages," between that of Genji's wife Aoi and that of the Rokujō lady, is vividly described in *The Tale of Genji*. The intensity of the rivalry and the humiliation suffered by the Rokujō lady in having to cede her place to Aoi's carriage causes the possession and death in childbirth of Aoi. In addition to the colorful procession during which the carriages and participants were decked out with garlands of hollyhock, there were court dance performances, archery contests, horse races, and banquets. On the next day a return procession escorted the Vestal back to her palace, with more banqueting and entertainments.

Besides the preparation for and participation in the official court events, days at court were accentuated by frequent outings to view the cherry blossoms or maple leaves during and after which participants were expected to produce elegant verses commemorating the event. There were also contests of various kinds, usually matches between two teams, the right and left; among the items matched were poems, fragrances, and paintings. Chapter 17 of *The Tale of Genji* describes the feverish preparations for a picture contest between two imperial consorts, and the judgments rendered as each picture scroll is presented by the opposing teams.

An attendant's other chief duty was to act as a companion to her mistress. Murasaki Shikibu records in her diary how she spent her time reading stories and poetry with Empress Shōshi, who was surrounded with a coterie of the most talented women writers of prose and poetry of the time.

Exciting as the days in the service of an empress or high noblewoman might have been, it also meant that one was constantly in the public eye. As described in Murasaki's diary, there was also a good deal of jealousy and rivalry among the ladies-in-waiting. Women were always under scrutiny, and the smallest mismatch of colors in robes could make them the object of derision and gossip. They were expected to be ready with an elegant poem at a moment's notice, and a constant worry was the embarrassment that might be felt if one could not come up with a quick poetic reply or failed to recognize a poetic allusion. Many of these verses were sent by courtiers and noblemen who expected women to be receptive to their advances as well. Murasaki Shikibu never seemed to have felt very comfortable with her life at court, but perhaps that was because she was already about thirty years old when she entered Shōshi's service.

Twilight Years

At thirty, a woman was already considered well along in years. The fortieth birthday was considered a milestone for both men and women and was celebrated with great pomp. The festivities for the celebration of Genji's fortieth birthday begin with his tasting of the new herbs, which are the symbols of renewal and longevity. As he receives his rounds of visitors, he is presented with forty baskets of fruit and forty boxes of food by forty courtiers led by his son Yūgiri. The feasting is followed by an informal concert. There are similar celebrations marking each successive decade after this initial acknowledgment of "old age."

Many of the women in Genji's life do not reach even their fortieth year. Yūgao dies at nineteen; Aoi is twenty-six when she succumbs in childbirth; the Rokujō lady is in her thirty-sixth year when she passes on. For women, the thirty-seventh year was considered a particularly dangerous one. Genji warns his beloved Murasaki to be especially cautious and have the proper prayers recited to help ward off illness. The very next night after Genji's warning to her, however, Murasaki is seized with severe chest pains and high fever which last many weeks. The principal recourse to effect a recovery is the standard one of the Heian period: Genji commissions prayers at Buddhist temples and summons priests to his residence to recite incantations and perform esoteric rituals. These were the same measures that had been taken when Genji's first wife Aoi was giving birth to their son. The basis for these actions is the belief that illness is due to the presence of an evil spirit (mono no ke) which has taken possession of the sick person. To cure her, this malignant presence must be exorcised, usually by transference to a female medium. If the evil spirit then identifies itself, the recovery of the patient can begin. So it is with Murasaki.

> The malign spirit suddenly yielded after so many tenacious weeks and passed from Murasaki to the little girl who was serving as medium,

and who now commenced to thresh and writhe and moan. To Genji's joy and terror Murasaki was breathing once more. (p. 617)

The spirit identifies itself as the same one that attacked Aoi many years before—the Rokujō lady. And the moving force is the fury of a lady scorned. I have gone on thinking you the cruelest of men. I heard you tell your lady what a difficult and unpleasant person you once found me, and the resentment was worse than when you insulted me to my face and finally abandoned me. I am dead, and hoped that you had forgiven me and would defend me against those who spoke ill of me and say that none of it was true. The hope was what twisted a twisted creature more cruelly and brought this horror . . . tell my child of my torments. Tell her that she is never to fall into rivalries with other ladies, never to be a victim of jealousy. (pp. 618–19)

While the lack of scientific knowledge about illness serves to remind us that the Heian period was nearly a millennium before our present age, some of the insights into the psychological factors contributing to health seem quite modern. Heian beliefs in possession, for example, acknowledged the role that emotional stress can play in causing sickness. In this polygamous society, a woman was not supposed to show any jealousy over her husband's or lover's other amorous interests. Genji is always chiding Murasaki for her mild displays of jealousy. Though she succeeds in remaining the most important woman in his life, the fear of being displaced by a rival in Genji's affections is always with her. Genji's marriage to the Third Princess occurs when the latter is about fourteen and Murasaki about thirty-two. The onset of Murasaki's chest pains five years later occurs one night when Genji is with the Third Princess. Murasaki's physical suffering is due to possession by the still intensely jealous spirit of the Rokujō lady, but its onset coincides with the occasion when Murasaki herself is in a state of great emotional anxiety over Genji's relationship with the Third Princess. It turns out that Murasaki's fears are unfounded, but that does not diminish their effect on her.

The Third Princess is about to give birth to the child fathered by her lover Kashiwagi. The delivery of the boy goes well, but the mother's recovery is very slow, and she feels herself near death. The psychological strain of the months since Genji's discovery of her infidelity leaves her vulnerable to possession by spirit. The cause of her weakness finally identifies itself as the spirit of the Rokujō lady. The Third Princess's recovery begins after she has taken Buddhist vows as a nun.

For a Heian woman, Buddhism as a religious institution was not a dominant element. Her exposure to Buddhism was primarily through the rituals performed at court ceremonies, or through an occasional outing to one of the temples near the capital. Nevertheless, Buddhist beliefs permeated Heian culture and constituted the basis for a person's outlook on art, nature, and life.

One dominant religio-aesthetic concept was *mono no aware* (pathos of things) deriving from the impermanence of life: the beauty of all things in this world is illusory and transient; the inevitable effect of the passage of time is to bring change and decay to natural phenomena and to human relationships. The realization that beauty is ineluctably bound to its perishability was transmuted by the Heian sensibility into a heightened appreciation of the poignancy of the scattering of cherry blossoms, of the falling of the autumn leaves, of the parting of lovers. It was this sensibility that produced the most evocative poetry and literature of the period.

Emotional attachment to this illusory, fleeting world was the cause of all suffering. Only by distancing oneself from the world, that is, by taking Buddhist vows and devoting oneself to prayer, meditation, and study of the Buddhist texts, could one attempt to decrease one's attachments. By such actions a person might be eventually be freed from the cycle of rebirth and enter Buddha's Nirvana Several of the characters in *The Tale of Genji* follow this path in search for salvation. When the Akashi lady's fate is auspiciously sealed by the birth of her daughter and her move to the capital, her father, the Akashi priest, retreats to the mountains. Likewise, Prince Hachi abandons the world and his two daughters at Uji. Their fate is not as happy as the Akashi lady's was, but Prince Hachi refuses all further communication with his family for fear it may rekindle his attachments to the mundane world.

To escape the chain of existence and attain Buddhahood, a woman first had to be reborn again as a man. That goal could be partially reached by taking the vows. This is perhaps the reason that so many of the women in *The Tale of Genji* request that the Buddhist vows be administered before they die. Such is the case with the Third Princess. Her father, the retired Suzaku Emperor, who has taken the vows, risks his own salvation by coming from his mountain retreat to see his daughter when she is so ill. The former emperor is present when his daughter takes her vows. Her long, thick hair is cut at shoulder length to symbolize her new religious status. She is moved out of Genji's mansion and into a residence inherited from her father. The Third Princess eventually recovers from her illness. In her case and others like it, the taking of vows perhaps effects a cure, because the process has relieved her of the great emotional stress of living under the same roof with Genji after her infidelity is known to him. It has also relieved Genji of the task of having to treat her as his wife, since there can no longer be any thought of intimacy between them.

Several of the other women in the novel who take Buddhist vows seem to be similarly motivated in part by a desire to escape intolerable emotional entanglements. But the women do not necessarily leave the world and its mundane beauty behind them. Genji's father's consort, Empress Fujitsubo, had, like the Third Princess, also once been unfaithful to her husband the emperor. She had been seduced by Genji and borne a son, thought by the world to be the emperor's. After the emperor's death Fujitsubo takes the vows, but she remains active in the political and cultural life at court. For her, too, becoming a nun serves to free her from Genji's further attentions and from the accompanying psychological stress over fear of the discovery of their secret liaison. This new freedom in turn allows her to mature and demonstrate her skills and wisdom in her later role as empress dowager. When she dies in her thirty-seventh year, Genji is at her side, and her last words express gratitude for his support of the Reizei Emperor, their son.

The other high-born woman who succeeds in severing her relationship with Genji is the Rokujō lady. With the accession of the new Reizei Emperor, a replacement for her daughter Akikonomu's position as Ise Vestal is appointed, and Rokujō accompanies her back to the capital. After her return the Rokujō lady resumes her former role as the cultural leader and presides over a literary salon. But she too takes Buddhist vows when she becomes seriously ill. When Genji comes to visit, she makes a final request and asks him to look after Akikonomu as a daughter.

> She will have no one to turn to when I am gone. Please do count her among those who are important to you . . . it is all so difficult. Even when a girl has a father to whom she can look with complete confidence, the worst thing is to lose her mother. Life can be dreadfully complicated when her guardian is found to have thoughts not becoming a parent. Unfortunate suspicions are sure to arise, and other women will see their chance to be ugly. These are distasteful forebodings, I know.

> But please do not let anything of the sort come into your relations with her. My life has been an object lesson in uncertainty, and my only hope now is that she be spared it all. (p. 285)

A week later, the Rokujō lady dies.

The Final Rite of Passage

A Heian lady would have had many occasions to witness the inevitable, final rite of passage. Priests would have been summoned to chant passages from the sutras over one's mortal remains. The final absolutions were performed and the body clothed in white before it was placed into the coffin. Funerals usually took place at night. The coffin was borne on a litter to the graveyard, preceded by torchbearers and priests and accompanied by a procession of mourners. The main graveyard was southeast of the capital, at a site called Toribe. Most funerals of the time followed the Buddhist practice of cremation. The funeral pyre was lit and allowed to burn until early morning when the embers were quenched with rice wine. The ashes were collected in an urn and taken to a temple. On the way back from the cremation grounds the mourners might have stopped at the Kamo River for a brief purification ceremony.

Special observances were held at fixed intervals after death. Every seventh day immediately afterward until the forty-ninth, special prayers and rituals were performed, and offerings of food and sutras made. It was believed that during these forty-nine days the next life of the departed could be influenced by the mourners' good deeds and prayers. On the forty-ninth day the ceremonies and offerings were especially elaborate.

Members of the family observed a period of ritual seclusion ranging from three days to one year. The length of seclusion depended on the closeness of relationship to the deceased, the longest being that of a child for a parent.[55] The husband was expected to remain in seclusion for twenty days. If he had died first, his wife would have observed a thirty-day period of seclusion. The term of mourning continued beyond the period of seclusion. During this time, mourning robes of shades of gray or black were worn, depending on the mourner's relationship to the deceased. After his first wife Aoi's death, Genji dons gray mourning robes, but he observes that hers would have been darker had he died first (p. 171). Memorial services are held on the hundredth day after death and on the annual anniversaries.

The chief quality that defined Genji as a hero to Heian readers was that he never abandons a woman he has loved. Many of the women whom he courts had been abandoned, either by a parent (Murasaki's father, for example, refused to acknowledge her), by a lover (Yūgao had been deserted by Tō no Chūjō, the father of their child Tamakazura), or by a husband's or parent's death (as, for example, the widow of the crown prince, the Rokujō lady).

As depicted by Murasaki Shikibu in *The Tale of Genji*, the great adventure in a female character's life is courtship and marriage. Each lady is defined by her relationship to Genji, or to his male descendants Kaoru and Niou. A woman's greatest fear is rejection, It is this fear that drives the Rokujō lady to leave Genji first, before he can abandon her. Her pride and the strength of her passion are depicted as negative elements, because they are extremes of emotion that cause the possessions of Aoi, Murasaki, and the Third Princess. Murasaki does succeed in remaining the woman whom Genji most loves, but she too is constantly haunted by the fear of being replaced by a rival.

> It was not kind of him, she thought, flushing, to have plans for leaving her. Such a difficult, constricted life as a woman is required to live! Moving things, amusing things, she must pretend to be unaffected by them. With whom was she to share the pleasure and beguile the tedium of this fleeting world? Since it chose to look upon women as useless, unfeeling creatures, should it not pity the fathers who went to such trouble rearing them? Like the mute prince who was always appearing in sad parables, a woman should be sensitive but silent. The balance was certainly difficult to maintain—and the little girl in her care, Genji's granddaughter, must face the same difficulties. (p. 699)

The most "successful" heroine in the novel, however, is perhaps the Akashi lady, who is a sort of Cinderella character. Though living in the provinces, she is courted by Genji and eventually brought to the capital where their daughter is raised to become the future empress. The Akashi lady's heroism consists in her perfect self-control and realistic attitude toward her own position. "She wanted to be what he wanted her to be, and she succeeded . . . she would count it her good fortune that he troubled himself to visit her occasionally, and ask no more" (p. 338).

After Genji's death, the world is a darker place, and the lack of a hero to replace him changes the nature of the possibilities in the lives of the female characters as well. In the post-Genji chapters the dominant characteristic of life is insecurity. The heroine of the last section is known as Ukifune (Floating Boat): she is able to understand that she must act in accordance with her own inner feelings, and she refuses to change her decision to search for spiritual enlightenment and devote her life to prayer and meditation as a nun.[56]

Another contemporary woman, the author of the *Sarashina Diary*, gave her point of view:

> How could I have let all those years slip by, instead of practicing my devotions and going on pilgrimages? I began to doubt whether any of my romantic fancies, even those that had seemed most plausible, had the slightest basis in fact. How could anyone as wonderful as Shining Genji or as beautiful as the girl whom Captain Kaoru kept hidden in Uji really exist in this world of ours? Oh, what a fool I had been to believe such nonsense![57]

The novel of which Genji is the hero does reflect many of the realities of a Heian woman's life. The fear of rejection in a polygamous society found in the fictional portrayals of Murasaki or the Rokujō lady is just as intensely etched in the *Gossamer Years*, by a real woman. The realities of life for a woman without male support such as Yūgao are described in the *Sarashina Diary* by the niece of the author of the *Gossamer Years*.

The sense of futility and abnegative self-image plaguing women are crystallized in a famous poem by Ono no Komachi, a superb poet of the early Heian period noted also for her beauty:[58]

Hana no iro wa	*The color of the flowers*
Utsurinikeri na	*Has faded away,*
Itazura ni	*In vain*
Waga mi yo ni furu	*I spent my days in this world*
Nagame seshi ma ni	*Gazing at the long rains falling*

In the Heian upper class, a woman was accorded much more freedom of choice than the women of succeeding ages. Not until modern times did men again talk with women on equal terms and share the pleasures of artistic pursuits. Despite the relative economic and legal independence of women, they were known only by appellations derived from the men in their lives: Michitsuna's mother, Takasue's daughter, Sei Shōnagon, Murasaki Shikibu. Yet they had the rare privilege and the precious means of achieving mastery over their world, if not through political power, then through their creative accomplishments.

It is the literary masterpieces produced by Heian women that make the capital, Heian Kyo, and its inhabitants come alive and matter to later generations. Their writings attest to their victory not only over the social limitations but even over death itself. Their self-reflection and observation of the life around them, stifling and constricting as it was, have made them immortal. Heian women succeeded, if unwittingly, in marking their individual identities in history even without personal names of their own.

Notes

1. Edward G. Seidensticker, trans. *The Tale of Genji* (New York: Alfred A. Knopf, 1979), copyright © 1976 by Edward G. Seidensticker. This is the most recent and complete translation. All quotations in this chapter are from this edition, reprinted by permission of Alfred A. Knopf, Inc. The translation by Arthur Waley, originally published in six volumes, 1925–33, is available as a one-volume edition (New York: Modern Library, 1960).

2. Richard Bowring, trans., *Murasaki Shikibu: Her Diary and Poetic Memoirs* (Princeton: Princeton University Press, 1982), pp. 217–55, copyright © 1982 by Princeton University Press. All quotations are from this complete translation, reprinted by permission of Princeton University Press. Nanba Hiroshi, *Murasaki Shikibu shū*, in *Genji monogatari kōza*, vol. 6, Sakka to jidai (Tokyo: Yūseidō, 1971), pp. 150–53.

3. Nanba, *Murasaki Shikibu shū*, p. 160. Cf. also Bowring's introduction in *Murasaki Shikibu*, pp. 209–16, for comments on the ambiguity of the poetry and the risk involved in using it as a biographical source.

4. Bowring, *Murasaki Shikibu*, pp. 42–155, gives a complete translation of the diary. All quotations are from this edition. For the original text, I consulted the following edition: Hagitani Boku, *Murasaki Shikibu nikki zen-chūshaku* (Tokyo: Kadokawa Shoten, 1971–73), vol. 2, sec. 71, p. 295.

5. The complete genealogy is given in *Sompi bunmyaku*, in *Shintei zōho Kokushi taikei* (Tokyo: Yoshikawa Kobunko, 1964), 2:53–54. This genealogy was compiled in the late fourteenth century. It lists Murasaki simply as "female child," with notes appended, according to premodern Japanese convention.

6. Ivan Morris, *The World of the Shining Prince* (Baltimore: Penguin Books, 1969), p. 312. Chart 1 shows the genealogical connections between Tametoki and Michinaga.

7. Hagitani, *Murasaki Shikibu*, 2:548–55, contains a complete chronology of

the years 845–1108 for events and people related to Murasaki.

8. Jean Reischauer and Robert Karl, *Early Japanese History* (Princeton: Princeton University Press, 1937) gives a complete listing of the Heian system of court ranks and posts.

9. Mildred Tahara, trans. *Tales of Yamato* (Honolulu: Hawaii University Press, 1980), pp. 21–22, 26, 41, 42–43, 82.

10. Robert H. Brower, *The Konzyaku Monogatari-syū: An Historical and Critical Introduction* (Ann Arbor: Michigan University Microfilms, 1974), part 2, pp. 546–47, recounts the entire incident. Morris, *Shining Prince*, p. 264 n. 5, also gives the poem.

11. Hagitani, *Murasaki Shikibu*, 2:486.

12. Itō Hiroshi, "Murasaki Shikibu-den no saibu," *Kokubungaku* 23 (July 1978): 116, gives a summary of these.

13. Tsunoda Bun'ei, *Murasaki Shikibu to sono jidai* (Tokyo: Kadokawa Shoten, 1966), pp. 7–37. Tsunoda originally proposed this thesis in "Murasaki Shikibu no hommyu," *Kodai bunka* 11, 1 (July 1963). This article is reprinted in *Genji monogatari*, in the series *Nihon bungaku kenkyū shiryō sōsho* (Tokyo: Yūseidō, 1970), 2:190–211. The same volume contains one of the refutations: Yamanaka Yutaka, "Murasaki Shikibu denki ko-Takako-sentsu Kentō," p. 212–22.

14. Oka Kazuo, *Genji monogatari no kiso-teki kenkyū* (Tokyo: Tokyodō Shuppan, 1966), pp. 128–32, quotes the primary sources for these theories. His detailed criticism of Tsunoda's "Takako" theory is on pp. 598–613.

15. Tsunoda, *Murasaki Shikibu*, pp. 98–120.

16. Shimizu Yoshiko, *Murasaki Shikibu* in *Iwanami Shinsho*, no. 854 (Tokyo: Iwanami Shoten, 1973). This work treats the poetry collection as an autobiography.

17. Tsunoda, *Murasaki Shikibu*, pp. 57, 74, for the poem, and 42–47 for a discussion of the chronology of the poems. A complete collation of the various texts of Murasaki's poetry collection is contained in Nanba Hiroshi, *Murasaki Shikibu-shū no kenkyū* (Tokyo: Kasama Shoin, 1971).

18. Tsunoda, *Murasaki Shikibu*, pp. 74–80, traces the exact route, based on poems 10–24.

19. Ivan Morris, trans. *The Pillow Book of Sei Shonagon* (New York: Columbia University Press, 1967), vol. 1, sec. 112, pp. 124–25, and vol. 2, pp. 100–101, n. 552.

20. Imai Gen'e, *Murasaki Shikibu* in *Jinbutsu gyōsho*, no. 131 (Tokyo: Yoshikawa Kobunkan, 1967), p. 84. A sample of Nobutaka's calligraphy appears on p. 85 of Imai's book.

21. Cyril Birch, comp., *Anthology of Chinese Literature* (New York: Grove Press, 1965), p. 267.

22. Cf. Maruyama Kiyoko, "Kanbungaku," in *Genji monogatari kōza*, vol. 8, *Genji monogatari no gensen* (Tokyo: Yūseidō, 1972), pp. 105–28.

23. Ivan Morris, trans., *As I Crossed the Bridge of Dreams* (New York: Harper & Row, 1973), pp. 54–55.

24. Hagitani, *Murasaki Shikibu*, 2:496. Imai, however, argues for 1005, *Murasaki Shikibu*, p. 138.

25. *Sompi bunmyaku*, p. 54. The poems also appear in *Murasaki Shikibu shū*, nos. 77 and 78.

26. Bowring, *Murasaki Shikibu*, p. 145. The same verses are also found in the poetic memoirs as nos. 75 and 76, as well as in the *Shinchokusenshū* as nos. 1021 and 1022. Only this last source identifies the caller by name as Michinaga.

27. Bowring, *Murasaki Shikibu*, p. 139.

28. Cf. poem 105 in the *Murasaki Shikibu shū*, sent on behalf of Shōshi, in reply to a verse from Ise no Tayū, poem 104.

29. Shimizu Yoshiko, "Murasaki Shikibu-ron," in *Genji monogatari, Nihon bungaku kenkyū shiryō sōsho*, 2:216–17.

30. Morris, *The Pillow Book of Sei Shonagon*, 1:86–87, records an exchange of poems and gifts between Senshi and Empress Teishi.

31. Edwin A. Cranston, *The Izumi Shikibu Diary: A Romance of the Heian Court* (Cambridge: Harvard University Press, 1969).

32. Ibid., p. 6; *Shūishū* no. 1342.

33. Robert H. Brower and Earl Miner, *Japanese Court Poetry* (Stanford: Stanford University Press, 1961), p. 227.

34. Bowring, *Murasaki Shikibu*, p. 131. For a sample of Akazome's poetry, see Cranston, *The Izumi Shikibu Diary*, p. 10. See also William H. McCullough and Helen Craig McCullough, *A Tale of Flowering Fortunes: Annals of Japanese Aristocratic Life in the Heian Period* (Stanford: Stanford University Press, 1980).

35. McCullough and McCullough, *A Tale of Flowering Fortunes*, 1:52–63, analyzes the use made of Murasaki's diary; the sections corresponding to the sections on Atsuhira's birth are translated on pp. 270–92.

36. Imai, *Murasaki Shikibu*, pp. 160–61. Imai estimates that this would have been in 1006.

37. Morris, *The Pillow Book*, 1:71–75; 2: notes 337 and 338.

38. Hagitani, *Murasaki Shikibu*, 2:508–28.

39. Oka, *Genji Monogatori*, pp. 138–43.

40. McCullough and McCullough, *A Tale of Flowering Fortunes*, 2:687.

41. Cf. Kenneth Rexroth and Ikuko Atsumi, trans., *The Burning Heart: Women Poets of Japan* (New York: Seabury Press, 1977), p. 27, reprints her best-known poem.

42. The summary of these theories follows that given by Tsunoda Bun'ei in his *Murasaki Shikibu to sono jidai*, pp. 177–97. Cf. Bowring, *Murasaki Shikibu*, pp. 13–15.

43. Oka, *Genji monogatori*, pp. 143–70.

44. Hagitani, *Murasaki Shikibu*, 2:503–8.

45. Seidensticker, trans., *The Tale of Genji*.

46. Edward G. Seidensticker, trans., *The Gossamer Years: The Diary of a Noblewoman of Heian Japan* (Tokyo and Rutland, Vermont: Charles E. Tuttle, 1964), pp. 126–29.

47. McCullough and McCullough, *A Tale of Flowering Fortunes: Annals of Japanese Aristocratic Life in the Heian Period* 1:393–94, n. 35. I have used the translations for the Japanese terminology of the various ceremonies given in this work. For a useful Japanese source, with line illustrations of costumes, furnishings, and architecture, see Shimizu Yoshiko, Mori Ichiro, and Yamamoto Ritatsu, *Genji monogatari tekagami* (Tokyo: Shinchōsha, 1975).

48. Ivan Morris, trans., *The Pillow Book of Sei Shonagon* (Middlesex, England: Penguin Books, 1970), p. 37.

49. Donald Keene, *Japanese Literature: An Introduction for Western Readers* (New York: Grove Press, 1955), pp. 150–52.

50. Hiromi Ichida, "A Brief History of Kimono," *Chanoyu Quarterly*, no. 21 (1978): 20, illustrates the full formal attire in color.

51. William H. McCullough, "Japanese Marriage Institutions in the Heian Period" *Harvard Journal of Asiatic Studies*, no. 27 (1967): 103–67, gives an exhaustive account of the marital arrangements, based on historical documents of the period.

52. Morris, trans., *The Pillow Book*, p. 39.

53. McCullough and McCullough, *A Tale of Flowering Fortunes*, 2:818–22, app. A, sec. 8, gives a complete analysis of the Kōkyū. I have used their terminology.

54. Morris, *Shining Prince*, pp. 167–78, gives a sampling of the annual events at court.

55. McCullough and McCullough, *A Tale of Flowering Fortunes*, 1:370, n. 9, gives a chart of the mourning and seclusion terms.

56. Andrew Pekarik, ed. *Ukifune: Love in The Tale of Genji* (New York: Columbia University Press, 1982). See especially pp. 63–81 and 113–38 for insights about the female hero in the last part of the novel.

57. Ivan Morris, trans., *As I Crossed a Bridge of Dreams: Recollections of a Woman in Eleventh-Century Japan* (New York: Harper & Row, 1973), p. 87.

58. Felice Fischer, "Ono no komachi: A Poetess of the Ninth Century Japan" (Ph.D. dissertation, Columbia University, 1972).

4

TOMOE
The Woman Warrior

ROYALL TYLER

JAPAN is famous in the West for its martial tradition, but not for martial women. But in fact, most daughters of the samurai class did take lessons in the martial arts, especially in the use of the short sword (*kodachi*) and the halberd (*naginata*). In the Tokugawa period (1600–1868), the security of the vast shogunal harem was entrusted to women skilled in the martial arts. As recently as World War II, grade school girls were taking mandatory lessons in the ritualistic wielding of the halberd, a weapon traditionally favored by nonsamurai such as young boys, women, and soldier monks. It is true, however, that few names of women warriors have come down to us from Japan's past.

The most famous woman warrior in the Japanese tradition is Tomoe. Tomoe's time was the turbulent second half of the twelfth century. The old chronicles picture her as formidable, and she is the title character of a later, but still medieval, play. This chapter reflects on Tomoe as a Japanese woman hero and tells all that can be known of her. It ends with a translation of the play.

First, however, I should make it clear that what follows is not history proper. No doubt Tomoe lived, but her story as we know it is probably romance. This account of her life is to be taken, therefore, as a passage from a historical novel. It is a tale at once stirring and sad.

All translations in these pages are my own.

Tomoe's Name, and a Preliminary Summary

The word *tomoe* designates a comma-shaped swirl pattern that has a long history in East Asia. As a name, the word is undoubtedly felicitous, and it is still used as a woman's name in modern Japan. If it were not, I might never have written this piece, for the subject would not have reminded me of the friend to whom it is dedicated: Tanaka Tomoe.

The whole of Tomoe's story is long and complicated enough to deserve a preliminary summary. Her deeds belong to one phase of the wars between the Taira and Minamoto clans in the twelfth century. Tomoe fought for her lord, the "Rising Sun General" (Asahi Shogun) Kiso Yoshinaka (1154–84). Although Yoshinaka was of the Minamoto clan, he was called Kiso because he came from a mountainous region by that name in central Japan. Two of Tomoe's brothers also fought for Yoshinaka. They were Imai no Shirō Kanehira and Higuchi no Jirō Kanemitsu.

Tomoe and Kanehira both won lasting fame in an episode that pitted not Minamoto against Taira, but Minamoto against Minamoto. Yoshinaka was engaged in a power struggle with his cousin Minamoto Yoritomo (1147–99), the chieftain who would emerge as the grand winner from all this turmoil to establish the Kamakura Shogunate, the first of its kind. It was Yoshinaka who drove the Taira from Kyoto, the capital, where he set himself up as a sort of dictator. Yoritomo then sent an army under two of his own brothers, Noriyori and Yoshitsune, to attack Yoshinaka. Yoshinaka was swiftly undone. He fled the imperial city, and Tomoe and Kanehira took part with extreme gallantry in the events of his last hours. Kanehira died just after his lord, and only Tomoe survived to live out her days. If the story of Yoshinaka's flight and death is true, it may be from Tomoe that we have it. Certainly no one else who rode with Yoshinaka lived to tell the tale.

Images of the Woman Warrior

How does one imagine a woman warrior? There is Diana of classical mythology, but she was a hunter. There is Judith of the Apocrypha, but she did not kill Holofernes in battle. There is Joan of Arc, but although she rode with the men, she herself did not fight. There are the legendary Amazons. A splendid example from Book II of the *Aeneid* is Camilla, beloved of Diana, and the Volscian queen. Resolutely unmarried and chaste, this fiery maiden rode with three women lieutenants and was the terror of all who encountered her on the field. After slaughtering many warriors, Camilla was brought down at last by a spear hurled through the breast she had bared for battle. Another medieval example is Madeleine de Saint-Nectaire, a lady from medieval Auvergne. She was beautiful and virtuous and, widowed young, customarily rode at the head of sixty mounted men. She took the Protestant side in the Wars of Religion and defeated the King's deputy, killing him with her own hand. Naturally, Camilla was a maiden, and Madeleine de Saint-Nectaire a virtuous widow. Both were at once fascinating and autonomous, outside the common order of things. They answered to no one, and especially to no man.

William Carlos Williams evoked this sort of sovereign woman in his essay "Jacataqua," included in *In the American Grain*. Williams described the arrival, at a fort on the way, of a force of "soldiers who go fight the English at Quebec under Arnold." Among those present for the event were some twenty Abenaki Indian warriors. One among them was struck by the glance of an arriving American officer. The officer was equally struck:

> "That [asked the warrior of a white man standing by], that Anglese! Who?"
> "Thet? Thet's young Burr, the one Cushing said got off a sickbed to come."
> Startled, she stepped back among her people.
> Young Burr but waited to gain his genial host's attention to ask excitedly:
> "What is that beauty?"
> "Jacataqua, Sachem of the Indians of Swan Island; you passed the wigwams of her people on the way up the river."
> In a moment Burr was standing before the Indian princess, for the first and last time at a loss before a woman.
> Primitive and direct, it was she who opened the conversation and opened it with a challenge:
> "These," with a wave of her brown hand toward Howard and the group of officers, "these need meat. You hunt with me? I win."

Thus Williams wrote of Jacataqua as a sort of Indian Artemis, quick, proud, and free as the wind.

Tomoe, however, was no Jacataqua. She may well have been quick and proud, but one cannot say of her that she answered to no man. The word "samurai" comes from a verb meaning "to serve," and a samurai was normally in the service of a lord. As a samurai, Tomoe answered to Yoshinaka, as did her two brothers. She rode with Yoshinaka in every battle, and she fought brilliantly. But when Yoshinaka knew himself lost he ordered Tomoe to leave him, for he did not want it said of him that he had gone to face a warrior's death in the company of a woman. Tomoe wept but obeyed.

An American writer named Jessica Amanda Salmonson has recently published two books of a fantasy series billed as "The Tomoe Gozen Saga." The title of the first book is *Tomoe Gozen* (Ace Books, 1980), and the second *The Golden Naginata* (1982). Both are set not in Nippon (Japan) but in Naipon, a parallel world that is at no point obliged to be identical with historical Japan. The plot of *The Golden Naginata* is recognizably derived from the story of Tomoe and Kiso Yoshinaka. In the Naipon version of the tale, Tomoe is still Tomoe, at least in name, but Kiso Yoshinaka turns into Kiso Yoshinake, and Imai Kanehira into Imai Kanchira. Other names are variously transmogrified or invented. The book is an example of the integration of genuinely Japanese motifs into contemporary American fantasy.

In the matter of Yoshinaka's flight and death, Salmonson clearly kept the original story in mind. Yoshinake, like Yoshinaka, tries to send Tomoe away. But the Tomoe of *The Golden Naginata* does not obey. Although married to Yoshinake (Tomoe was *not* in any modern sense married to Yoshinaka), she remains irreducibly her own woman and refuses to leave. She does not, however, commit suicide with him. (Yoshinaka commits suicide only in the play *Tomoe*, but not, as will be seen, in the earlier chronicles.) Her reason is not that he has forbidden her to do so, but rather that since he has forbidden her to do so, his soul would reject the company of hers after death, and the gesture would therefore be useless. Having seen this, the Tomoe of Naipon decides quite rationally to remain alive; and she oversees with heroic detachment the suicide not only of Yoshinake but of his whole band. (The Yoshinaka of the chronicles died alone.) By this time in the novel it is clear that the Tomoe of Naipon and the Tomoe of Nippon are not, after all, the same person. Naipon's heroine is as free as Jacataqua, if less lighthearted. Though married, she keeps her own name and her own public sovereignty. On that score alone, Salmonson's Tomoe is a woman hero unimaginable in Japanese song or story.

Tomoe "Gozen": Male and Female in Medieval
Japanese Romance

"Gozen" is a title whose rough equivalent in English might be "mistress." It is not applied to Tomoe in the chronicles, but by the time of the play *Tomoe*, in the fifteenth century, it seems to have become customary to speak of "Tomoe Gozen."

"Gozen" means literally "one who is in attendance before an august person." The title could be applied to a lady of good family—the head of the family being of course male—or, equally well, to a singing girl. Thus Shizuka, a dancer who became exceedingly famous as the concubine of Minamoto Yoshitsune (Yoritomo's brother), was commonly called Shizuka Gozen. In Tomoe's case there is a theory that her story came to be told professionally by a line of woman reciters who were all "Gozen," and who took the heroine's name as their own. Therefore, "Tomoe Gozen" may at one time have meant a woman storyteller. If so, then perhaps that is how the "Gozen," by a reverse process, came later to be associated with Tomoe herself. The association would have sounded quite plausible.

Certain clichés about women appear in the ethical and religious literature of premodern Japan. They probably do not describe the actual position or powers of women in Tomoe's time, but even as a kind of public fiction they are significant; and I do not think they were entirely without effect upon the lives and thoughts of actual people. Their existence certainly may be detected often enough in tales, in plays, and (I believe) in the present story.

The gist of these clichés is that men stand higher than women. Mahayana Buddhism taught quite plainly that men were less subject to the passions and thus closer to enlightenment—although under the influence of ideals of universal salvation, it also proposed various ways around this problem. Other modes of thought with which Buddhism was then integrated led to the same conclusions. Yin-yang ideas (originally Chinese) were widespread and identified "heaven" (the sky, "up") with the male and yang, and "earth" ("down") with the female or yin. Thus the lowliness of women in Buddhist thought was confirmed by the place of the feminine in the yin-yang cosmos. This pattern was even projected onto the landscape. Mountaintops (yang, male) were associated with ideas of paradise, purity, wisdom, and spiritual perfection, while the lowlands (yin, female) were the realm of "this world" with all its foolishness and delusion. This way of thinking did not acknowledge for women any place in the councils of the wise.

It was certainly unusual for Tomoe to ride into battle with the best; and in the above frame of reference, it was perfectly natural for Yoshinaka at last to send her away. A lord might kill himself in the company of his official wife, but not on the field; and in any case, Tomoe was not Yoshinaka's official wife. For all her prowess, Tomoe the warrior was tainted by her feminine sex; faced with death in war, Yoshinaka could abide no taint. No Japanese knight ever swore fealty to a lady, however brave or beautiful. The world of the warrior was entirely for men. Tomoe's place was at home, and that is where Yoshinaka sent her. To have sent a man home under the circumstances would have been an indescribable insult, and Tomoe herself took Yoshinaka's words rather hard. There may have been warmth and affection between them also, however. In the presence of death Yoshinaka had to say what he did, but perhaps he was glad as he spoke to be able at least to save Tomoe's life.

It was normal for a man of rank to have several women, while it was mandatory for a woman to have only one man at a time. Yoshinaka had more than one woman. He had a wife in his home province of Shinano but, according to *Heike monogatari*, "Lord Kiso set out from Shinano with two beautiful women named Tomoe and Yamabuki." He also fell in love with a high-ranking Kyoto lady, and *Gempei jōsui ki* mentions a woman named Aoi as one of two women commanders under Lord Kiso—the other being Tomoe. Yamabuki, one reads, was ill and remained in the capital when Yoshinaka fled; Aoi had been killed previously in battle.

Yamabuki and Aoi were not necessarily Yoshinaka's concubines, though one perhaps too easily assumes that they were. Tomoe's own upbringing gave her ample reason for devotion to Yoshinaka, as I will explain in more detail below, and one may imagine her at once fierce in loyalty and fastidiously reserved in private conduct. But *Gempei jōsui ki* mentions an intimate relationship between her and Yoshinaka, and later writers have not questioned the idea. Her devotion to Yoshinaka is explained here as being in large part that of a lover. That is quite plausible, and moreover it makes a more appealing story—one in which Yoshinaka retains more easily the position of honor. Yoshinaka, for his part, appears especially in *Gempei jōsui ki* as thoroughly susceptible to feminine charms. People in the polygamous Japanese society of premodern times seem to have liked the image of the hero with multiple loves. Yoshinaka's famous cousin Yoshitsune is reported in an utterly extravagant account of his deeds in *Gikei-ki* (The Chronicle of Yoshitsune) to have fled from Kyoto with a whole train of ladies, none of whom could bear to be left behind. At any rate, the relative prominence of disinterested affection in the accounts of Tomoe and Yoshinaka, and a counterpart stress on such simple and heroic motives as bravery and honor, constitute one way in which these accounts betray themselves as romance rather than history.

Sources of the Tomoe Legend

I have spoken of chronicles entitled *Heike monogatari* and *Gempei jōsui ki*. *Heike monogatari* means "Tale of the House of Taira," while *Gempei jōsui ki* means "Record of the Prosperity and Decline of Minamoto and Taira." Both tell the tale of the Minamoto and Taira wars. There are various versions of each, but they date roughly from the thirteenth to early fourteenth centuries. *Heike monogatari* is particularly well told. *Gempei jōsui ki* tends toward an excess of incident and detail. Each gives a slightly different account of Tomoe and of Yoshinaka's death. There is a much more formal history of the Minamoto rise to power, written in Chinese and entitled *Azuma kagami* (Mirror of the East); but although this document has much to say about Yoshinaka, it does not describe his death, and it does not even mention Tomoe. As for the play *Tomoe*, it cannot be considered a source of new information, although it is a moving expression of continued interest in her story.

I have already mentioned reciters who may have specialized in telling the story of Tomoe. Medieval Japan was full of traveling reciters and storytellers of one kind or another. Some specialized in religious topics, while others told the epics. *Heike monogatari* in particular was not normally read but heard. It was recited to the accompaniment of the *biwa*, a sort of lute, and was exceedingly popular. The play *Tomoe* is based on the *Heike monogatari* account, with key revisions apparently by the playwright himself.

Yoshinaka's Career in the Minamoto-Taira Wars

Kiso Yoshinaka was born in 1154. At his death in the first moon of 1184 (roughly February) he was only in his thirtieth year. He died only ten days after being named by the retired emperor to the highest possible military post in the land, sei-i taishōgun (shogun in present English usage), or "Great General Who Subdues the Barbarian." He had captured the capital and begun to make his bid for this magnificent appointment in the seventh moon (roughly August) of 1183. His rise and fall were swift indeed.

The Taira-Minamoto wars, in which Yoshinaka played a prominent part, shook late twelfth-century Japan. Both clans were great forces in the provinces. The Taira were based largely in the south and west of Japan, and the Minamoto were strong in the east and north. Yoshinaka was an eastern warrior. He and Tomoe grew up in Shinano (now Nagano Prefecture), a province in the mountains of central Japan, far to the east of the capital.

Both clans had traditionally ranked somewhat below the court nobility proper, the vast clan of the Fujiwara. The Fujiwara, however, not being warriors, usually left military matters to the Minamoto and Taira, and this practice eventually caused them serious trouble. In 1156 the first of a series of clashes occurred between the warlike Taira and Minamoto in the streets of the capital itself. The Taira won the initial round of skirmishes and took over almost all effective political power. Their clan leader, Taira no Kiyomori, became a virtual dictator. Minamoto chieftains were killed, and only a few of their children were allowed to survive in distant exile.

Taira glory lasted only one generation, however. In 1180 the Minamoto forces began to move again, and to press the Taira hard. The call for a Minamoto uprising went out from Minamoto Yoritomo, who as a boy had been exiled to the Izu Peninsula, not far from today's Tokyo. The Taira army sent to oppose him in the summer of 1180 suffered an ignominious defeat near Mt. Fuji. Yoritomo saw far ahead, however, and for the moment disdained to march further west toward the capital. Instead he established an autonomous government in the eastern seacoast town of Kamakura.

Meanwhile Yoshinaka, in the central mountains, was not fully prepared to accept Yoritomo's leadership. He extended the area of his own control, and he too began acting like an independent ruler. Thus he set himself up as Yoritomo's rival.

In the spring of 1183 the Taira advanced against Yoshinaka and had some initial success. But at Tonamiyama (at the base of the Noto Peninsula), on the eleventh day of the sixth moon, Yoshinaka inflicted upon the Taira army a resounding defeat. Tomoe was with him, and she personally commanded a force of one thousand mounted warriors. Then, at Shinohara, Yoshinaka triumphed again. His advance after that was swift, and by the middle of the seventh moon of 1183 he was approaching the capital.

The Taira were unable to muster any resistance. They fled toward the west and south, leaving the capital burning behind them. On the twenty-eighth day of the seventh moon, Yoshinaka swept into Kyoto. The Taira had absconded with the reigning emperor, a little boy who by his mother was the grandson of Kiyomori. But the retired emperor was still in Kyoto, and he immediately conferred various lofty titles upon the newcomer. He also insisted that Yoshinaka pursue the Taira. This Yoshinaka did reluctantly and without success. He was much more concerned about Yoritomo, who, he felt sure, would soon be pursuing *him*.

Yoshinaka therefore sought from the retired emperor an imperial mandate to destroy Yoritomo. Such a mandate was essential to the legitimacy of the campaign, and to Yoshinaka's ultimate ambition: to be appointed as, so to speak, the Defender of the Throne. Despite threats and even acts of force, however, the retired emperor consistently refused.

Gempei jōsui ki describes Yoshinaka as *ara-ebisu*, a "wild barbarian." That seems a fair enough assessment although Yoshinaka certainly was a great soldier. He intervened brutally in the affairs of the court and committed various outrages that did not endear him to anyone in the imperial city. In the eleventh moon of 1183, for example, he attacked and burned one of the retired emperor's residences, publicly displayed some one hundred heads of the defenders, and extorted from the retired emperor the dismissal of about fifty high court officials. Yet the retired emperor still would not grant him his mandate. Moreover, his violence in Kyoto did not prevent the Taira from making considerable headway that same month in their drive back toward the capital. Yoshinaka even approached the Taira about a joint campaign against Yoritomo. The Taira, however, declined.

At last, in the twelfth moon, the retired emperor gave in. Yoshinaka got his mandate to attack Yoritomo. In the final days of that moon, and of the year, before Yoshinaka could act, Yoritomo sent Noriyori and Yoshitsune to suppress him.

It was on the tenth day of the first moon of 1184 that Yoshinaka was appointed shogun. He was only the third man in Japanese history to have held the title, though he was by no means the last. The honor was hollow, however. Yoshinaka was almost finished, his luck all but run out.

Noriyori and Yoshitsune moved with great dispatch and reached the approaches to Kyoto by the nineteenth of the first moon. Noriyori aimed for Seta, where there was a bridge over the river that flows from the south end of Lake Biwa, east of the capital, while Yoshitsune went for the bridge over the Uji River to the south. Both crossings were thought to be next to impossible if the bridges were destroyed. Accordingly, Yoshinaka, likewise on the nineteenth, sent a force under his uncle Shida Yoshihiro to hold the crossing at Uji, and he sent Imai Kanehira with eight hundred men to hold Seta. Both commanders rendered their bridges unusable and hoped thus to have stopped the enemy. On the same day Yoshinaka sent yet another force under Higuchi Kanemitsu, Tomoe's other brother, to chastise a rebellious confederate in the province of Kawachi (roughly modern Osaka). Thus he had only a handful of troops left with him in Kyoto.

Alas, with great daring and with complete success Yoshitsune had his troops, on horseback, swim the Uji river anyway, and Noriyori found a ford. Both forces immediately overwhelmed their woefully inadequate opposition. On the twentieth, Noriyori and Yoshitsune stormed into Kyoto.

Tomoe

Tomoe had grown up with Yoshinaka. It was the custom in premodern Japan for children of rank to be suckled by a *menoto* (wet nurse), who normally was a woman of respectable social standing. Tomoe, Imai Kanehira, and Higuchi Kanemitsu were all the children of Yoshinaka's menoto. Their father was a warrior named Nakahara Kaneto. Thus Tomoe was Yoshinaka's foster sister.

The position of menoto was an honor usually bestowed as a reward for service. The menoto and her family played an essential role in bringing up and educating the child entrusted to them, and they identified their interests completely with the child's. In return, they could normally expect to wield great influence behind the scenes when the boy grew up and assumed high station. Thus, there naturally developed between Yoshinaka and his foster siblings a closer relationship than any he might have enjoyed with blood brothers and sisters, who would be potential rivals in succession disputes. Tomoe, Kanehira, and Kanemitsu were not Yoshinaka's rivals. For them, Yoshinaka was both lord and oldest friend. It is touching and revealing that they were all Yoshinaka had to fall back on in the hour of his greatest need.

Moreover, it was common for menoto families to "marry" one of their daughters to their charge. This was not a permanent marriage in the modern sense, but a sensible arrangement such as the late anthropologist Margaret Mead would have approved. Later the young man would, so to speak, outgrow it; often he would arrange a suitable marriage for his foster sister/"wife" to ensure her a secure life. He himself would enter into relationships with the daughters of more powerful families and would acquire an official wife of a standing commensurate with his own. Tomoe had probably had this kind of family-sponsored intimacy with Yoshinaka. *Heike monogatari* describes her as being beautiful as well as valiant:

> Tomoe was of very light complexion and her hair was long. Her face was quite lovely. She was an archer of rare strength and skill, a mighty warrior who could stand alone against a thousand and who with bow and arrow or the sword was a match for any god or demon. She could break the wildest steed and ride him headlong down the roughest slope. In battle she wore resplendent armor and bore a great bow and a long sword, and commanded large forces of men. So great was her renown, won in many a fight, that none could equal her.

This is dramatic language, but Tomoe was certainly an expert at arms. She came through the battle of Tonamiyama unscathed, and no enemy hurt her during Yoshinaka's flight from Kyoto even though she was in the thick of a dozen fights.

It is hard to say how Tomoe became, or was allowed to become, such a warrior. A woman warrior was rare. *Gempei jōsui ki* does speak of one Hangaku Gozen, who was a tremendous archer. When her side was besieged in a fortress in 1201, Hangaku slew countless of the enemy from a tower above the fortifications. But there is no mention of Hangaku ever having ridden in battle, commanded troops, or wielded the sword.

Yoshinaka's Farewells

When Yoshinaka learned that the enemy was nearly upon him, he rushed to the retired emperor's residence. *Heike monogatari* says that he wished only to say good-bye, but *Gempei jōsui ki* alleges that he planned to carry off the retired emperor as hostage if he could. At any rate, it was too late. Further word reached Yoshinaka that the enemy was in the city itself. At the retired emperor's gate he gave up and hastened (if *Gempei jōsui ki* is to be believed) on a far more personal errand.

It appears that Yoshinaka was in love with the sixteen-year-old daughter of the imperial regent. It was Yoshinaka himself who not long before had engineered the gentleman's appointment to this lofty post, and Yoshinaka now went to the lady for the last time, lingering long. Perhaps he had largely political motives for doing so (if he did so at all), but the account in this chronicle evokes only infatuation. He lingered so long that one of his men finally resorted to the sternest rebuke a retainer could address to his lord: admonitory suicide. Yet Yoshinaka still could not tear himself away. Then another retainer, desperate that his lord's honor was all but lost, likewise cut his belly, and at a far less decorous distance from the curtains behind which Yoshinaka and the lady were hidden. Only then did Yoshinaka come forth and ride.

He did not flee quite yet, however. *Gempei jōsui ki* says that he left the regent's residence with one hundred mounted men and was soon joined by two hundred more. Tomoe might have been among these, but all we know is that she rode with Yoshinaka out of Kyoto. Meanwhile, white banners, the emblems of Yoritomo's army, were everywhere. Yoshinaka was challenged by wave after wave of attackers. Each time he slashed his way through, but not without losses. At last he encountered Yoshitsune himself at the head of some three hundred horsemen. Yoshinaka charged. Yoshitsune's men simply parted to either side and showered arrows upon him, two of which lodged in his armor. Yoshinaka broke them off and galloped once more toward the residence of the retired emperor. Whatever his intention may have been this time, however, the gate was secured by a chain.

By now Yoshinaka had only seventy or eighty horsemen left. He would normally have headed roughly north toward his old stronghold in the mountains of Shinano. Instead he, Tomoe, and the rest galloped east toward Seta. This was not the way to escape the forces of Yoritomo. Yoshinaka was desperate to rejoin Imai Kanehira, Tomoe's brother, whom he had sent to defend Seta the day before.

As Yoshinaka fled toward Seta the enemy followed. There were more clashes, and the band continued to dwindle. Shouts taunted Yoshinaka from behind, challenging him to stand and fight, and reminding him how his name would suffer if he showed only his back to his foe. Skirmish followed skirmish. Yoshinaka's band soon numbered only about a dozen.

Tomoe's Exploit and Dismissal

Up to this point the two sources do not contradict one another, though *Gempei jōsui ki* is richer in incident; nor do they disagree on Yoshinaka's end. But while *Gempei jōsui ki* places Tomoe's display of valor before Yoshinaka's reunion with Imai Kanehira, *Heike monogatari* places it after. Moreover, the two accounts attribute different adversaries to Tomoe. The *Gempei jōsui ki* account goes as follows:

> Now there sallied forth from Kiso's band a warrior in armor bound with pale yellow-green cord, bearing a quiver with a few last hawk-feathered arrows and a rattan-wrapped bow; and riding a powerful roan whose saddle was dotted with *tomoe* patterns. The warrior was a lethal archer and mighty swordsman, and charged time and time again until Hatakeyama, for all his high renown, fell back in haste to the river bank.
>
> There he summoned Hanzawa Narikiyo. "Well, Narikiyo?" he said. "I have never seen anyone attack so fiercely, though I have been fighting battles since I was sixteen. Kiso has Imai, Higuchi, Tate, and Nenoi, and they are the ones who are called the Four Guardian Kings. But that is not Imai or Higuchi. Who can it possibly be?"
>
> "That," replied Narikiyo, "is the daughter of Nakahara Kaneto, whose wife was Kiso's wet nurse. She is a splendid archer and a tremendous rider; and she is at once his foster sister and his mistress. He treats her with the greatest consideration. In battle she commands large forces for him. There is not a stain on her name. Imai and Higuchi are her brothers, and she is a formidable warrior."
>
> "Then what would be best to do?" asked Hatakeyama. "It is galling to be forced back by a woman, but if I attack her and then make a slip, I

will be dishonored forever. Of all the warriors I could have met, it was bad luck to run into this woman Tomoe. Still, if she is Kiso's mistress, I want her. So I will have Tomoe for my prize today. I will fight her and take her prisoner. Beat them back, men, beat them back.''

Hatakeyama's warriors beat back Kiso's band and surrounded them, and Hatakeyama made straight for Tomoe. He charged in and out and around, trying to get at her, but Kiso did not wish her to fight him, and kept galloping in between. At last, after circling two or three times, Hatakeyama managed after all to get close, and thought he saw his chance. He urged his horse on faster and seized the left sleeve of Tomoe's armor. Tomoe knew her peril. Now, her steed was Harukaze [Spring Wind], the best in all of Shinano. At a touch of the whip he sprang forward, the sleeve of her armor suddenly tore away, and she put many yards between herself and her attacker.

"This is no woman," thought Hatakeyama to himself, "this is a demon at work. To take a single arrow from such a being would mean eternal shame. I must not let that happen. I had better withdraw." So he withdrew westward from the river, and returned to the retired emperor's palace.

Thus Yoshinaka's band moved past the Kamo River on the way out of Kyoto, but now they numbered only seven. They crossed Ausaka Pass, which separates Kyoto from Lake Biwa and the east, and headed for Awazu. It was on this stretch of the southernmost shore of Lake Biwa that they were to find Imai Kanehira at last.

Now Tomoe took off her helmet and let her black hair, "longer than she was tall," fly behind her. On her forehead she placed an ornamental fillet, and on her head an elegant white hat. Looking very striking, she rode ahead of the band.

Then she encountered one Uchida no Saburō Ieyoshi leading some thirty-five riders. Uchida was astonished to see a woman warrior, but he had heard of Tomoe and realized that this must be she. He feared Tomoe's exceptional prowess. He also recalled an order from Lord Yoritomo in Kamakura that Tomoe should be captured and brought back to him alive. Uchida was not sure how to meet this challenge.

"Well," said he to his warriors, "she cannot outfight a hundred, however strong she may be. I myself am worth sixty men, and there are over forty of you. That is more than a hundred already. Split up, then, and take Tomoe from either side, while I come at her head-on. That way we cannot miss her."

On further reflection, however, Uchida decided that this excessively cautious plan did him little credit. He determined to take on Tomoe alone. His men, *Gempei jōsui ki* says, were relieved to be spared so dangerous an encounter.

Tomoe saw him coming. "Ah!" she cried, "a gallant warrior! . . . What is your name? I who ask am the woman Tomoe, the foster sister of Lord Kiso and the daughter of Nakahara Kaneto." Uchida flung out his name and titles, and she advanced on him, "eager to hew off that head of his and offer it to the God of War."

Since Uchida made no move to ready his bow, Tomoe did not touch hers; likewise no sword was drawn. They came next to each other, exchanged glares stirrup to stirrup, and grappled with a yell. Their mounts could only stand stock-still.

Uchida got a good grip on Tomoe's hair and drew his dagger to behead her. Tomoe understood. "You called yourself Uchida Saburō," she said, "but I do not think much of your manners. You are not Uchida. Are you one of his underlings?"

"I command," retorted Uchida, "I am no underling. What is wrong with my manners?"

Tomoe answered: "Does a man good enough to close with a woman draw his dagger as they fight and let her see it? Uchida, you know nothing of the old ways."

Then she clenched her fist and struck him hard in the elbow of his dagger arm. The blow was so powerful that the dagger fell out of his hand. "See, Ieyoshi," she cried, "I am from a mountain village in Kiso, acknowledged the best in the land. I am the combat instructor you need!" And she stretched out her left hand, seized Uchida's faceplate, and forced his head down onto the pommel of her saddle; then she slipped her hand under the faceplate, drew her own dagger, wrenched the head round, and struck it off. The dagger was a marvelous blade and went through flesh and bone more easily than through water. Tomoe straightened in her saddle and urged her horse forward a little, whereupon the corpse tumbled to the ground. She lifted the head and displayed it to Lord Kiso.

"Poor man!" Lord Kiso cried. "Poor man, brave and handsome as he was, and famous throughout the Eight Provinces of the East, to have been killed! He must have been out of luck, to be struck down thus by you! Well, my luck is gone too, and I will soon be dying a dog's death by someone or other's hand. This armor I never gave a thought to before now burdens my shoulders. Once I am killed, everything will be over.

And I am ashamed that people will tell of me how at last I had a woman precede me in battle. I release you from your duty. Go now, quickly, leave."

Tomoe spoke. "My lord," she said, "I have served you ever since you and I were children. I am resolved that your way shall be mine to the end of the farthest plain, to the innermost fastnesses of the mountains. It hurts me now to hear you speak so. Wherever you fall, my lord, I would lay my head beside yours."

So she sought to change his mind. Lord Kiso replied: "That is my own wish. But last year when we rode from Shinano I left my wife and children behind, and now I must be parted from them forever, and never see them again. This fills me with grief. Rather than have you with me to the last, I wish you to go now and carry the news of my death, and pray for my afterlife. Quickly, escape from here and go back to Shinano. Tell those there what has happened. I see the enemy everywhere. Hurry, hurry."

Although deeply distressed, Tomoe obeyed. Wiping the tears from her eyes, she stole to the top of a hill that overlooked the field. When the battle of Awazu was over she cast off her armor and, dressed in a simple robe, returned to Shinano. There she told her lord's wife and family all that had happened, and teller and listeners together wrung the tears from their sleeves.

According to *Gempei jōsui ki,* it was only after all this that Yoshinaka and Kanehira found each other. But *Heike monogatari* gives them a moving reunion before Tomoe's last fight and departure. Here, then, is the *Heike monogatari* account from the point at which Yoshinaka and Kanehira sight each other from afar:

Yoshinaka was so worried about what might have happened to Imai that he fled toward Seta. Imai no Shiro Kanehira himself, meanwhile, had defended Seta with some eight hundred horsemen, until his force was reduced to about fifty. He then furled his banners and, worried about his lord, turned back toward the capital. He and Lord Kiso met on the beach of Uchide at Otsu. Lord and vassal knew each other a hundred yards off, and galloped to their reunion.

Lord Kiso took Imai's hands in his. "I should have died," he said, "there on the riverbank [on the way out of Kyoto]. But rather than die in some random place, I preferred to be with you at the end. That is why I showed my back to so many of the enemy, and came all this way to find you. And you?"

"My lord," replied Imai, "your kindness overwhelms me. I myself should have died at Seta, but I was so concerned about you that I escaped all this way to find *you*."

"Well then," said Lord Kiso, "our friendship is not over yet. My men have scattered into the hills and woods, and they are probably lurking somewhere about. Have the banners you furled raised again."

Imai raised his banners, and some three hundred men galloped to them. Whether they had retreated from the capital or from Seta one could not tell. Lord Kiso was very pleased. "With a force this size," he said, "we can put up a good last fight. Whose are those men I see yonder?"

"I understand, my lord, that they are commanded by Lord Ichijō no Jirō of Kai."

"About how many are they?"

"Six thousand, my lord, I believe."

"Excellent, then they will make a fine adversary for us, and we for them. We are sure to die anyway, but I would rather meet a worthy adversary and die in the thick of a good fight." And with these words Lord Kiso rode straight ahead.

Lord Kiso, Captain of the Left Imperial Stables [one of Yoshinaka's court titles], was wearing that day a red brocade jacket under armor laced with Chinese patterned silk cord. His sword handle and scabbard were of bold design, and from his helmet curved golden horns. A few of the two dozen splendid arrows he started out with that day were still left, and he displayed these high in his quiver, and gripped the center of his rattan-wrapped bow. His saddle was gilded, and he rode the steed known as Kiso no Oni-Ashige, "The Demon Roan of Kiso." Rising in his stirrups Lord Kiso shouted in a great voice:

"You will have heard of the Lord of Kiso. Now you see him before you. I am the Captain of the Left Imperial Stables and the Governor of Iyo [another court title], the Rising Sun General, Minamoto no Yoshinaka. He who has the heart to try, come, let him slay Yoshinaka and show off his head to Yoritomo!" And he charged.

"The one you heard," cried Ichijō no Jirō, "is their great commander! Do not let him pass you by, my men, do not let him get away! Cut him down!" And he and his men surrounded Yoshinaka, each eager to strike.

Lord Kiso's three hundred men charged in among the six thousand, and cut and slashed their way right through. But only fifty of them emerged. As they came forth, Toi no Jirō Sanehira blocked their path with two thousand men. Again they broke through. On through wave after wave they charged, and each was of several hundred men; until at last their number had shrunk to only five.

Among these five, Tomoe alone was unwounded. Lord Kiso summoned her.

"You are a woman," he said. "Get away from here now, quickly, and go wherever you will. I am going to die in battle; or, if I am not killed by another, I will take my own life. It would be too bad if they were to say of me that at my last encounter I had a woman with me. Leave now, quickly."

Tomoe made no move to go. But Yoshinaka insisted until at last she said: "At least I would like a worthy opponent. I would like to show you, my Lord Kiso, my last combat in your service."

So she lay in wait for an enemy. And there approached one famous for his strength throughout the province of Musashi, Onda no Hachirō Moroshige, with thirty horsemen. Tomoe charged in among them, went straight to Onda no Hachirō, fiercely seized him and pinned his head on the pommel of her saddle, then wrenched it around, cut if off, and tossed it away. After that she removed her armor and escaped toward the East.

The Death of Yoshinaka

Yoshinaka's end was sad, and the last gesture of Kanehira truly heroic. It was a dishonor to be killed by one of unworthy standing, and it was highly honorable to take one's own life to avoid such a fate or, even worse, capture. Kanehira tried to spare his lord ignominy. Fortune, however, was not with Yoshinaka. I pick up the *Heike monogatari* account once more.

Meanwhile Lord Kiso galloped all alone toward the Pine Wood of Awazu. It was the twenty-first day of the first moon, and twilight was falling. The ground was covered by a thin sheet of ice. He had no idea that a sunken field lay before him, and when he urged his horse forward into it, the animal's very head vanished. Lord Kiso desperately applied spur and whip, but the horse did not move. He then turned round to see what had become of Imai. As he did so Ishida no Jirō Tamehisa of Miura caught up with him and let fly; and the arrow went in under his helmet. Lord Kiso suffered a terrible wound. He collapsed face forward onto his horse's neck and lay still. Two henchmen of Ishida's dashed up to him and took his head. Ishida lifted it high on the point of his sword and shouted in a great voice: "I, Ishida no Jirō Tamehisa of Miura, have slain Lord Kiso, so lately renowned throughout the land of Japan!"

Imai Kanehira was still fighting. When he heard this, however, he said: "I have no one now left to protect. See, you men from the East, the greatest brave in all the land show you how a warrior takes his life!" And he took the point of his sword in his mouth, hurled himself headlong from his mount, and died transfixed. So ended the battle of Awazu.

Tomoe's older brother, Higuchi no Jirō Kanemitsu, had been dispatched by Yoshinaka toward the southwest to suppress a rebellious confederate. He heard that there was fighting in the capital and encountered one of Imai's men, who told him that both Imai and Yoshinaka were dead. Kanemitsu announced to his warriors that all who had loved Yoshinaka should disperse and survive however they might, even by begging, so as to pray unceasingly for their departed lord. "I," he cried, "will go up to the capital and die in battle there, in order to wait upon my lord in the afterworld and to rejoin Imai Kanehira." Alas, Kanemitsu was captured alive and, on the twenty-seventh of the first moon, beheaded.

Tomoe after Yoshinaka

Several approximate contemporaries of Tomoe came to be celebrated as she was, and even more than she, in song and story. But all these women were known for a single incident, or for a single passage in their lives. They flared up for a moment like flames, then sank again into obscurity. It was that way with Shizuka, Yoshitsune's famous love, whose documented existence is confined to a brief span. As far as the records go, she appeared from nowhere and vanished into nowhere. Nothing definite is known of what became of her.

What became of Tomoe is only a matter of legend. *Gempei jōsui ki* says that Yoritomo commanded her to appear in Kamakura, and that she complied. Yoritomo and his lieutenants seem to have been perplexed as to what to do with her. On the one hand she was a woman, but on the other hand she was an enemy warrior. A woman would not normally have been executed, but Tomoe was a commander for the other side. In the end she was placed in the custody of one Mori no Gorō in preparation for her execution.

At this point, however, one of Yoritomo's officers, Wada no Kotarō Yoshimori, conceived the thought that so valiant a woman as Tomoe would surely bear him valiant sons. He therefore asked Yoritomo to give him Tomoe. Yoritomo, taking full account of Tomoe's exploits, at first refused. But Miura no Osuke Yoshiakira interceded, reminding Yoritomo that one warrior alone could do no harm, and that her progeny might accomplish great things in the service of Yoritomo and his successors. At last Yoritomo relented.

Thus (so this story runs) Tomoe had a son by Yoshimori. His name was Asahina no Saburō Yoshihide, and he became a legend for his colossal strength. Later on, Wada Yoshimori, Asahina Yoshihide, and all their confederates were killed in battle. Tomoe is said to have left the world and become a nun, and to have devoted her remaining life to praying for the souls of Yoshinaka and of Asahina Yoshihide. Unfortunately, the story is implausible. Chronology makes it unlikely that Asahina was Tomoe's son. Whether she did nonetheless marry Wada Yoshimori, we will never know.

It is quite possible that Tomoe eventually became a nun, even if she was not Asahina Yoshihide's mother. Both men and women could retire in this fashion after their active life was over, and a woman who had lost her place in the world had almost no other option. After the annihilation of the Taira clan, Taira Kiyomori's daughter also became a nun. Empress and mother of a young emperor, she had been an exalted lady indeed, but now she had nowhere else to go. Becoming a nun, however, did not necessarily mean confining oneself to a cloister. The nun Tomoe (she would have taken a religious name) might have lived quite independently and moved about at will, especially on pilgrimage to the holy places which are so numerous up and down Japan. At any rate, *Gempei jōsui ki* says that Tomoe finally died at the age of ninety in Etchū, a province that borders the Japan Sea.

The Noh Play

The play *Tomoe* belongs to the classical genre of theater known as Noh, which culminated in the fourteenth century under the patronage of the Ashikaga shoguns and samurai aristocracy. The magnificently accomplished tradition is still a living art, and one may see *Tomoe* performed even today. One may also see *Kanehira*, for Imai Kanehira's death also inspired a play. Both are "warrior plays," the smallest of the five categories distinguished by the Noh tradition. There are about eighteen warrior plays out of the more than two hundred in the present repertoire, and *Tomoe* is the only one about a woman.

The text of *Tomoe* is not long, but on stage the play takes over an hour. The language is both verse and prose, and the verse passages are often difficult, being at once condensed in meaning and highly ornamented. This translation preserves a little of their quality. The reader will find in occasional repetitions of lines a reminder that the verse is not spoken but sung.

In Noh plays, the characters are conventionally designated not by name but by type role. Thus the typical *waki*, or witness, is a traveler—often, as in *Tomoe*, a wandering monk—who comes to a certain place. There he encounters the *shite*, or actor in the original sense of the word. The shite at first seems ordinary but turns out to be the phantom of some well-known figure from the past who has a connection with the place. Thus the shite in *Tomoe* is Tomoe herself, and the place is Awazu, where Yoshinaka died. There is also a chorus, which has no particular identity of its own, but which often sings in place of the shite or the waki, mostly while the actor is dancing or moving. Finally there is a *kyōgen*, often a local commoner, a genuinely ordinary inhabitant of the place. The kyōgen is of lower standing than the waki or shite and speaks a more commonplace sort of language. He is, however, essential to the dramatic structure.

In *Tomoe*, Yoshinaka's spirit has been enshrined as a god in a Shinto shrine set up on the spot where he died. This seems to be an invention of the playwright, although such a thing could in principle have happened. Moreover, the spot where Yoshinaka died is in this case the one defined only by this play, not by the older sources. For according to *Tomoe*, Yoshinaka did manage to take his own life, as Kanehira had urged him to do, in the Pine Wood of Awazu. He did so with Tomoe's help, implausible though this may seem in light of the older accounts. The net effect of these changes is to preserve Yoshinaka's honor after all, and greatly raise him in dignity. In fact, Yoshinaka as a deity is identified as being analogous with Hachiman, an important god in Japan, and the patron of the Minamoto clan. When the waki (a monk from Kiso) asks the shite (Tomoe) why she weeps before Yoshinaka's shrine, she reminds him of a monk of old whose tears before the shrine of Hachiman in Kyushu moved that great god to come and inhabit a hill near Kyoto, whence he mounted guard over the capital itself. Thus the shite conceals her personal grief but affirms the exalted state of Yoshinaka's spirit.

Yoshinaka's ignominious death, as described in the chronicles, destroyed his personal superiority over Tomoe. In the play *Tomoe* this superiority is restored. Yoshinaka has become a pure and lofty being, and an uncharacteristically benevolent one as well. He is free from all earthly taint. Tomoe, on the other hand, even as a phantom, clings to the earth (Awazu) because of her bitterness at having been ordered by Yoshinaka to leave him. Thus she is stained and, in an important sense, humbled. In this manner the play restores proper harmony to a story that, although stirring, had ended in disarray. Even as it celebrates Tomoe's valor, it confirms the fittingness of Yoshinaka's order. Now Tomoe—in the play—must seek the monk's prayers and his recitation of "the Sutra" (the *Lotus Sutra*) in order to achieve liberation.

Bibliography

Jones, Stanleigh H. Jr., trans. *Kanehira*. In *Twenty Plays of the No Theatre*, ed. Donald Keene (New York: Columbia University Press, 1970).

Kasahara Kazuo et al., eds. *Gekidō no yō to onna no aikan* (Tokyo: Hyoronsha, 1971).

Kitagawa, Hiroshi, and Bruce T. Tsuchida, trans. *The Tale of the Heike* (Tokyo: University of Tokyo Press, 1975; paperback ed. in 2 vols., 1977).

Kokusho Kankō Kai, ed. *Azuma kagami*. Vol. 1 (Tokyo: Meicho Kankō Kai, 1968).

Mass, Jeffrey P. *Warrior Government in Early Japan* (New Haven: Yale University Press, 1974).

Sanari Kentarō, ed. *Tomoe*. In *Yōkyoku taikan*. Vol. 4 (Tokyo: Meiji Shoin, 1964).

Shimode, Sekiyo. *Kiso Yoshinaka* (Tokyo: Jimbutsu Ōrai Sha, 1966).

Shinoda, Minoru. *The Founding of the Kamakura Shogunate* (New York: Columbia University Press, 1960).

Tomikura, Tokujirō. *Heike monogatari zenchūshaku* (Tokyo: Kadokawa, 1967).

Tsukamoto Tetsuzō, ed. *Gempei jōsui ki* (Tokyo: Yūhōdō, 1917).

THE NOH PLAY: *TOMOE*

AUTHOR: UNKNOWN

DATE: FOURTEENTH CENTURY

Waki: a monk from Kiso in Shinano province
Shite: a village woman, revealed as the ghost of Tomoe
Kyōgen: a man of the place
Place: Awazu Plain in the province of Ōmi along the southern shore of Lake Biwa
Time: the first moon (approx. February)

Monk enters, carrying a rosary. He stands upstage left.

Part One

MONK: With each step the high ranges
drop, and down the rough
with each step the high ranges
drop, and down the rough
Kiso Road this day
I will be roaming.

I am a monk from a mountain village in Kiso. Having never yet seen the capital, I am setting out today on a journey there.

So does my travel wear
long up the Great Col
of Kiso bound
long up the Great Col
of Kiso bound
the path threads on
through Mino and Owari
whose names mean "we pass"
from inn to strange inn
nightfall by nightfall
the count of days
grows till now
here is Lake Biwa

and the Ōmi Way
here is Lake Biwa
and the Ōmi Way.

During this "song of travel" he steps forward to indicate travel, then returns to where he was.

I have come so fast that I have already reached Awazu Plain, or so I believe it is called, in the province of Ōmi. I think I will rest here a while.

He sits downstage right. Woman enters and stands upstage left. She wears the zō mask, the face of a young woman.

WOMAN: Magnificent!
Waves lap quietly
the shore of the broad lake,
while under the pines
of Awazu Plain
the God is duly honored
with rites of a happy reign,
and gives us blessings
most worthy of trust!

She weeps. Monk stands and faces her.

MONK: How strange! I see a woman go before the God, and she is weeping. What is it, I wonder, that troubles her so?

WOMAN: Are you speaking of me, O monk?

MONK: Indeed I am. I wonder that you should go before the God with so many tears.

WOMAN: Your perplexity betrays your ignorance.
For I have heard
that when the Venerable Gyōkyō
stood at Usa
before the God Hachiman
he spoke this verse:
"What you are,
O Great One,
I do not know,

but my tears flow
in thanks for your grace.''
Such was the poem
that noble monk made,
and the God, it seems,
was moved to answer,
for the monk's sleeve shone
with the Divine Face.
It was then that the God
hallowed Otokoyama
whence he guards
the peace of the Realm.
Your wonder, sir,
does not flatter you.

MONK: O gentle reply!
Woman you may be,
but this hamlet of yours
is so near the Capital
that true distinction shows
in each gentle word!

WOMAN: And you, your reverence,
where do you live?
What province are you from?

MONK: I am from the province of Shinano, from a mountain village
in Kiso.

WOMAN: From a mountain village
in Kiso? Why then,
unless you asked
the name of the God
of Awazu Plain,
you certainly
could hardly know it!
Here dwells in state
one from your own home,
Kiso Yoshinaka.
Here he is enshrined.
Bow your head before him,

O wayfarer!

MONK: Astonishing!
Then Yoshinaka
revealed himself a god
and made this place his.
A wondrous thing!
I come before the Presence,
palms pressed together:

CHORUS: In a time now past
he was my lord
and his name still
he was my lord
and his name still
lives on like the moon at dawn
for Yoshinaka
is revealed a Buddha,
is changed to a God,
and has made a vow
to protect all the world.
O wondrous blessing!
Know O traveler
that even two who pause
under one tree
share a link from past lives.
Break your journey then
beneath this pine,
and through the night
read aloud the holy Sutra
for the comfort of the god!
O the precious
and blessed encounter!
O truly the precious
and blessed encounter!

Woman moves to stage center and sits. Monk sits downstage right.

CHORUS: All the while
the westering sun
sinks below the mountains' rim,

the bell of evening
tolls across the waves of the shore,
each ushering in
an eerie twilight time.

Woman rises.

Yes, I have come
who am not of the living.
If you fail to know me,
then ask of those
who inhabit this village,
she says as light fades
into the glimmering grasses
she sinks and is gone
into the glimmering grasses
she sinks and is gone.

Woman exits. Local enters and stands upstage left.

Interlude

LOCAL: I am an inhabitant of Awazu Plain. I have a mind to visit our Shrine, for today a rite is to be performed there.
Ah, there is a monk whom I have not seen before. Where are you visiting from, your reverence?

MONK: I am a monk from a mountain village in Kiso. And you, are you from nearby?

LOCAL: Indeed, your reverence, I am.

MONK: Then please come closer. There is something I would like to ask you.

LOCAL: Certainly, your reverence.

Local sits at stage center.

Now, your reverence, what is it you wish to know?

MONK: It is an odd thing to ask, but please tell me all you can about Kiso Yoshinaka and about the woman warrior Tomoe.

LOCAL: You do indeed ask something most unexpected. But al-

though I have no particular knowledge of them, I will tell
you what I have heard.

MONK: I will be very grateful.

LOCAL: It was summer in the second year of Juei [1183] when Lord
Kiso gathered fifty thousand horsemen and set out from the
province of Shinano. Two women warriors, Tomoe and
Yamabuki, were with him as he made his way toward the
capital. Yamabuki was killed in the battle of Tonamiyama. As
for Tomoe, she was a very beautiful woman, and immensely
strong. She could ride the most powerful horse, and was so
fine a swordsman that she was given command of large forces.
Many had been struck down and killed in this battle or that,
but Tomoe had not even been wounded. She stayed by
Yoshinaka until his whole band had been reduced to seven.
Lord Kiso said to her: "Flee now, for you are a woman. I
myself mean to die fighting. I would not have it said that Kiso
took a woman with him into his last battle, for the shame of it
would last eternally. Go back to our home and tell them what
happened, and I myself will let my companions in death know
why you have gone." That was the order he gave Tomoe, and
she could only obey. She wished for a worthy opponent, however, so that she could show Lord Kiso one last fight. And as
she waited for one, Uchida no Saburō came charging up at the
head of thirty horsemen. He was from the province of Tōtōmi,
and famed for his great strength. He went straight for Tomoe.
She, of course, was ready for him. She charged in among his
men, dashed his head down onto the pommel of her saddle,
wrenched it round and struck it off, and displayed it for Lord
Kiso to see. Then she took off her armor, left it there, and
disappeared. Yes, she was a woman, and in managing to stay
by Lord Kiso until the end she proved herself better than a
man, or so people say now. Anyway, since Lord Kiso died on
this spot, the people here came together to build him a
shrine—this very one—where they celebrate him as a god.
And today there is to be a rite here. That really is all I know.
But why did you ask? I am puzzled.

MONK: Thank you for all you have told me. This is why I questioned you. Before you came, a woman appeared as it were from nowhere. She said she had come for the rite at the shrine here on Awazu Plain, and she was weeping. I thought it strange. She told me all about Yoshinaka. Then in the most curious manner she seemed to sink into the grasses here, and vanish.

LOCAL: That is indeed an amazing tale you tell. I believe that Tomoe's ghost must have appeared and spoken with you. Do please stay here a while and comfort her before you pass on.

MONK: Then I will stay a while and read the most holy Sutra, and comfort as well as I can the ghost of that lady.

LOCAL: If your reverence will stay, then please accept my hospitality.

MONK: Thank you very much indeed.

LOCAL: You are most welcome.

Local exits.

Part Two

MONK: Ah, the dews that moisten
the wayfarer's pillow!
Ah, the dews that moisten
the wayfarer's pillow!
The day is done
and now night has fallen
upon all the sorrows
of Awazu Plain.
Come, let me comfort
the ghost of the dead.
Come, let me comfort
the ghost of the dead.

Tomoe enters, again wearing the zō mask. She is girded with a sword, and carries a halberd. She stands upstage left.

TOMOE: The falling flower tastes vanity;

and flowing water
of itself, without thought,
clears: so the mind.

CHORUS: For where I suffered
seed and fruit of retribution
now, by the power of the Teaching,
I shall rise.
By that power plants, trees,
and land are enlightened;
still more so I
for whom the comforting Sutra
traces a straight way.
No, all doubting is past,
and my faith is sure,
yes, my faith is sure.
O monk, I thank you!

MONK: O vision most strange!
To the wayfarer's pillow
on Awazu Plain
comes the woman last seen,
but now clad in armor:
a strange sight indeed!

TOMOE: You are not mistaken:
the woman warrior
called Tomoe,
in grief and anger
that for being a woman
she was forbidden
to die by his side,

MONK: and filled with bitterness,
to this day

TOMOE: spends herself
in her Lord's service;

MONK: yet her anger still

TOMOE: lingers as rough waves

CHORUS: pound Awazu shore.
Unto death in battle
I would have stood by him,
but I was a woman,
and at the last
he cast me from him.
It is bitter, bitter!
"All you have for your lord,
and your life for the right,"
they say, as all know
who wielded the bow;
and who of these
will not at the last
be jealous of his good name?

Stage assistant takes her halberd. She sits on a stool at stage center.

CHORUS: Now when Yoshinaka set forth from Shinano, fifty thousand rode with him, bit by bridle, toward the capital, on the attack. At Tonamiyama, at Kurikara and Shio he gave battle, and there he and his men did mighty deeds, and won great glory;
nor did each measure
who might surpass him,
whom he might best,
but kept only in mind
what tales might be told of him
after his death.

TOMOE: But now his time was come,

CHORUS: his fortune over,
his bow of no use;
from the wave-washed shore
of Awazu Plain
he was gone from the grass.
O reverend monk,
this was the place.
You who are from his home,
comfort him, comfort him
as one of your own.

CHORUS: Tell then how he died,
          Yoshinaka,
          who was killed in battle
          upon this plain.

During narration below Tomoe moves about stage miming the actions described, both hers and Yoshinaka's.

TOMOE: It was the first moon.

CHORUS: Snow still lay in broad patches on the ground. He let his mount run down the shore, until he galloped into a sunken, mud-filled field thinly sheeted with ice. The horse sank in past the stirrups. Without footing he could not dismount, and though he clung to the reins and applied the whip, he was trapped. He simply sat there, helpless. It was then that I galloped up and saw him. He had sustained a dreadful wound. I had him change horses, and brought him here to this grove of pines. "Die here, my Lord, by your own hand," I told him; "I will die with you." But Yoshinaka said: "You are a woman. You will be able to get away. Take my amulet bag and my robe back to Kiso. If you refuse I will sunder the bond that for three lifetimes joins vassal to lord; I will disavow you forever." I could only obey; but I paused there, speechless with weeping. So I left my lord, and saw a strong enemy force approaching. "Is that Tomoe," they cried, "the woman warrior? Do not let her get by you!" They all charged me, and I knew I could not evade them. "Well then," I thought, "I will enjoy a good fight!" And very calmly, just to get them close, I held my halberd in and low, as though afraid. They thought they had me, and came slashing at me. Then I thrust out the halberd full length, and swept it round. That circle of men fell like autumn leaves, like a rain of petals torn loose by storm winds. Such was my fight, and all the warriors, sorely wounded,
          fell far back
          till I saw them no more
          fell far back
          till I saw them no more.

TOMOE: "It is all over now," I thought,

CHORUS: and returned to my Lord. But alas! He had already taken his life, and lay here beneath this pine. By his head he had left the robe and the amulet bag.

Narration now shifts to third person, but Tomoe continues to mime action.

Weeping, Tomoe took them, bid her Lord a last farewell, and set off. But in her grief she could hardly go forward. "Oh what am I to do with these, my Lord's keepsakes?" she wondered, but remembered her Lord's last injunction. Yet in her sorrow she went to the beach of Awazu. There she cut the cord, and took off her armor, and quietly laid it by her. Her helmet too she removed, and laid down. Then she dressed in the robe, and hid beneath it the dagger which hitherto she had always paired with her sword. At last, wearing a villager's hat, Tomoe set her face toward Kiso and left this place all alone, lost in weeping. Alas for her bitter regrets!
O comfort her
in her sorrowful clinging
O comfort her
in her sorrowful clinging!

Tomoe stops with palms pressed together in supplication, facing Monk.

5

HŌJŌ MASAKO
The Dowager Shōgun

MARGARET FUKAZAWA BENTON

Hōjō Masako (1157–1225) exerted a major influence on Japanese history, first as the wife of the founder of the Kamakura Shogunate, Minamoto no Yoritomo, next as the mother of two shoguns, and finally as "dowager shogun" (*ama shōgun*) during the reigns of Hōjō regents. She outlived not only her husband but all four of her children. Her life contains the stuff of legend. A passionate and proud woman, she was so jealous of her husband's interest in other women that she sent an army to destroy the house of one of his lovers. She was also staunch and astute. Faced with the incompetence of her eldest son Yoriie, Masako maneuvered to remove him from his supreme position as second Kamakura shogun after her father and brothers caused the deaths of his wife and son.[1]

The few sources that deal with Hōjō give an incomplete view of her life, but a vast body of legends has proliferated on scant historical facts. If anything, she has been a notorious heroine. Four centuries after her time, storytellers played up the streak of jealousy in her character, portraying her as being so furious at Yoritomo's philandery that her anger materialized in the form of a vengeful spirit who killed him. Another popular view of Masako holds her to have been power hungry, marrying Yoritomo in order to fulfill this need, and after his death ruling indirectly but firmly through her shogun sons and her regent father and brothers.

Novelist Nagai Michiko (b. 1925) presents the first balanced study of Masako in her novel, *Hōjō Masako* (1969). A noted figure in the genre of the historical novel, Nagai does more than merely elaborate upon known facts of history in her fiction. She bases her novels on thorough research into primary sources of the period, always taking into account the possible biases in these sources. In all the historical material she has worked on, she has uncovered blind spots, errors, and weaknesses in previous interpretations. Her critical analysis of so-called historical consensus is highly regarded even by academic historians. For one thing, she is married to the scholar son of the prominent historian Kuroita Katsumi and can make full use of the formidable family library. For another, she contributes fresh insight gained from the vantage point of female perspective, so rare in Japanese scholarship until today. She has done much to enlighten us about the position of women in Japanese history. More recently, her research has rectified our knowledge of Hōjō Masako and her period.

In 1982, Nagai Michiko became the twenty-first recipient of the coveted Women Writers Literary Award (*Joryū bungaku shō*) for her two volume novel *Hyōrin* (Icy Moon, 1981), which deals with the life of the blind Chinese priest Ganjin in ninth-century Japan. But Nagai is at her best when she recreates the lives of women who shaped history. She has written nonfiction works on Western women famous as great rulers and paragons of virtue, infamous as villainesses and femmes fatales, or spectacular as victims and martyrs. Not coincidentally, Nagai has concentrated her major efforts on prominent female figures of premodern Japan: the reigning "virgin emperor" Kōken-Shōtoku of the ninth century, the only woman in Japan's imperial genealogy to become a *tennō* (emperor) in her own right [cf. chapter 2]; Hino Tomiko (1440–96), whose machinations in the succession dispute as wife of the eighth Ashikaga shogun Yorimasa helped cause the devastating Ōnin War; Lady Oichi (1547–83), who was married off twice only to lose both daimyo husbands and take her own life in the power game won first by her own brother Oda Nobunaga and then his successor Toyotomi Hideyoshi, who coveted her; and Hōjō Masako. Nagai's novels on Lady Oichi and Masako were made into year-long prime-time television serials by NHK, Japan's public broadcasting corporation. The programs were very popular, and her novels became best sellers.

Nagai Michiko began her literary career with the publication of *Enkan* (Ring of flames, 1962), a novel about four twelfth-century men close to Minamoto Yoritimo, Masako's husband. In 1964 this novel won the Naoki Prize, the most respected award given to popular novelists. Nagai has demonstrated a sustained fascination with this particular historical period, publishing four other major works set in this age: *Emaki* (Picture scroll, 1966), *Sagami no Mononofu-tachi* (Warriors of Sagami, 1970), *Tsuwamono no Fu* (Song of warriors, 1978), and *Minamoto no Yoritomo no Sekai* (The world of Minamoto Yoritomo, 1979). A perusal of these books confirms how thoroughly Nagai has researched the period. She was writing a novel about Kugyō, Masako's grandson who assassinated her son, Shogun Sanetomo, when I had the opportunity to interview her.

On May 29, 1981, I sat with Nagai Michiko for five hours and talked at length about her interpretation of Hōjō Masako. Nagai has rectified our view of Masako, as her comments below indicate. Some of the famous episodes about Masako's life, interesting as they are, can no longer be considered true, for Nagai has replaced the legends with concrete evidence in tracing the ways in which Masako and other women of her age did indeed help shape history.

Marriage to a Political Exile

Hōjō Masako was born in 1157 as the second child and oldest daughter of Hōjō Tokimasa, the lord of a relatively small domain located on the Izu Peninsula south of present-day Tokyo. The Hōjō family did not rank in size with larger landowners of the region or in strength and number of warriors with powerful clans like the Miura, situated on the Miura Peninsula. Nagai Michiko was one of the first historians to point out that the Hōjōs were not as influential in the Kantō area (today's Tokyo-Izu region) as had been formerly assumed.[2] The phenomenal rise to power of the Hōjō clan was intimately connected with Minamoto Yoritomo (1147–99). Had Masako not married Yoritomo, her own life might have been far from remarkable, and she and her family would have left no trace in history.

The Hōjō landholdings and number of warrior retainers were too small to give the clan any distinction. Moreover, the family itself was not of distinguished lineage. They claimed Taira descent, as did a number of warrior families in the Kantō area,[3] but their lineage was probably too insignificant to yield well-documented proof. At the time of Masako's birth, Izu itself was a proprietary province of the ruling Taira clan, and the governor was appointed from Kyoto. But Hōjō Tokimasa, Masako's father, had few political ties in the capital and was not among those who were entrusted with this position.

Masako's mother had died from complications following childbirth when the girl was still in her teens. To Masako fell the task of taking over her mother's duties. It is difficult to know exactly what this entailed, but as oldest daughter she probably had to care for her baby brother Gorō, the fifth son of the family, and supervise daily household affairs with only her younger sister to help her. Masako married late by the standards of the time, and no doubt it was these responsibilities that prevented her from marrying earlier.

Masako was three years old in 1160, when Yoritomo, the heir of the Minamoto chieftain, was exiled to Izu. His father Yoshitomo had led an unsuccessful revolt known as the Heiji Disturbance in 1159 against Chancellor Taira no Kiyomori, the head of the rival military clan then in power. Yoshitomo was killed by a treacherous retainer, and his allies and their descendants were executed. Kiyomori, however, showed special leniency to Yoshitomo's surviving sons, who would have been summarily executed according to the prevalent custom of the day. Kiyomori's stepmother, known as the Nun of the Pond, is said to have pleaded for mercy on behalf of the eldest, Yoritomo, because he resembled her son who had died as a boy. Yoritomo's three half-brothers, Zenjō, Yoshitsune, and Gien, were consigned to monasteries when their mother Lady Tokiwa interceded with Kiyomori. Daughter of the chief priest at Ise Shrine, Lady Tokiwa is counted among Japan's femmes fatales, for Kiyomori's love for this beautiful widow is believed to have proved one cause in the chain of events that eventually led to the downfall of his mighty clan. Yoritomo was but thirteen years old when he was exiled to Izu.

His father had taken up residence in Sagami Province in eastern Japan after 1140 with the hope of ultimately gaining control of four provinces in the east known as the Kantō region.[4] To exile the heir of such an ambitious Minamoto leader to the Kantō was a fatal mistake on Taira's part. Twenty years later Yoritomo and the eastern warriors would take up arms against the Taira. No one in Kyoto, however, could have properly assessed the military potential seething in the Kantō at the time. To the ruling class in the capital, the eastern region meant underdeveloped hinterlands. Historically, eastern Japan had not been much more than this, but as farmers with better tools cleared new lands, new crops were grown to support a larger population. Quarrels over land boundaries between neighboring holdings became frequent, giving birth to various coalitions of farmers who depended upon a landlord for defense. Powerful landlords with control over large groups of dauntless warriors, who were also practicing farmers, came to hold reign over larger and larger areas. This sort of development soon transformed the eastern hinterlands into a potential base of independent economic power, fortified with trained warriors able to protect what was theirs. Nagai Michiko argues that Yoritomo's rise to power should not be viewed as his own personal history but rather as an inevitable result of economic development in the Kantō, a phenomenon that Kiyomori and his urbanized compatriots in the capital failed to notice. Yoritomo's credentials as the Minamoto heir made him a good rallying point for the Kantō warrior landlords. But, Nagai argues, had Yoritomo not been in Izu at the time, the Kantō of necessity would have given birth to another shogun anyway.

Masako's father Hōjō Tokimasa and other Taira lords in the area took turns serving guard duty in the capital, for which they provided their own warriors, arms, and provisions. The eastern lords made excellent guards, but they were held in contempt in Kyoto for their cultural backwardness. When Masako was in her late teens, Tokimasa left home for a three-year term of guard duty. During his stay in Kyoto, he met and married his second wife, known as Lady Maki, a sister of the steward of the manor owned by one of Kiyomori's half-brothers. This woman, whose sobriquet indicates that she was related in some way to a manorized horse ranch (*maki*), took pride in the fact that she knew something of Kyoto. The still unmarried Masako found to her chagrin that her father's new wife was of the same age as she was—twenty years old. Their different upbringing and proximity in age would breed disharmony and prevent any intimacy in their relationship. Lady Maki went on to give birth to several daughters. Hostility between Masako and her half-siblings would eventually cause the downfall of their father.

It was during Tokimasa's absence on the same tour of duty at the capital that Masako began her liaison with Yoritomo. When her father returned home and learned of their relationship he was furious. His strong objections to their union were not unfounded. First and foremost, he did not want to ally his family with a Minamoto, archenemy of the ruling Taira, for to do so would put the connections he had cemented through his marriage to Lady Maki in jeopardy. Yoritomo, furthermore, had already fathered a child by the daughter of Itō Sukechika, a local lord more powerful than Tokimasa. Sukechika had killed the baby in order to sever his daughter's liaison with a potential exile and protect the family's Taira connections. Tokimasa presumably had no intention of allowing his daughter to make a match that could have dangerous consequences for him and his entire family.

Masako knew her own mind even as a young woman. She also must have loved Yoritomo deeply, for in the face of her father's opposition, she ran away from home one dark, rainy night. With the help of a brother, she hurried on foot over muddy mountain roads to Yoritomo's side. They went into hiding at a mountain temple until Tokimasa's anger cooled and he grudgingly consented to the marriage.

According to a well-known legend concerning the romance, Tokimasa, upon learning of Masako's interest in Yoritomo, quickly arranged for her to marry Yamaki Kanetaka, the governor and top representative of the Kyoto government in Izu. Masako initially agreed to the match, but as the date of the marriage approached, she began to have second thoughts. It was on the evening of the wedding ceremony that she ran away from home to join Yoritomo.[5] It would turn out that Yoritomo's first act of rebellion when he took up arms in 1180 was to kill Kanetaka. In my interview with Nagai Michiko, I sought to clarify episodes relating to Masako's marriage.[6]

BENTON. Would you care to comment on this particular legend concerning the possible love triangle?

NAGAI. This is a very famous story, but pure fabrication. *Azuma kagami* [Eastern mirror, the chronological record of the Kamakura Shogunate from 1180 to 1266 compiled during the mid-thirteenth and early fourteenth centuries] gives Yoritomo's reason for the attack against Kanetaka as "revenge." Revenge here does not necessarily mean, as everyone likes to think, that he was retaliating against a former rival for Masako. The legend first appears in *Soga monogatari* [Revenge of the Soga brothers], a heroic tale set in Yoritomo's time but completed sometime during the fourteenth century. This proves that it was a later interpolation. We know for certain that Kanetaka was indeed assigned to Izu, but by the time he arrived, Masako and Yoritomo were already married and had one child. The love triangle story is so well known that anyone who writes about Masako invariably includes it. Now I wonder sometimes whether I should have omitted it from my novel, but the legend was too appealing to leave out at the time.

BENTON. There are other legends concerning their marriage that you did not use in your novel. Would you mind discussing them?

NAGAI. According to a famous episode, also found in *Soga monogatari*, Yoritomo entrusted a retainer to deliver his first love letter, meant not for Masako but for her younger sister. After the letter was mistakenly handed to Masako, she learned that her sister had had an auspicious dream. Masako promptly purchased the dream from the sister, thereby procuring for herself Yoritomo and her later fame as wife of the founder of the Kamakura Shogunate. This legend has another version: Yoritomo did not want to form a liaison with a motherless girl lacking the protection of a female guardian, and for this reason he set his affections on her younger half-sister instead; but Yoritomo's retainer favored Masako and saw to it that the love letter found its way into her hands. My research has convinced me that this story is also fiction. Masako had another younger sister but of the same mother. Lady Maki's daughters were too young at this time to have been objects of Yoritomo's attention. So this story has no factual basis. I have used neither of these two famous versions in my novel.

BENTON. What is your opinion on the marriage of Yoritomo and Masako?

NAGAI. Masako's love for Yoritomo was intense. All her emotions were intense. Her love did not permit Yoritomo to show affection for other women. Traditional accounts portray Masako as the epitome of the ambitious woman, so greedy for power that she had her heart set on becoming the wife of a shogun and married Yoritomo for that reason alone. The Hōjō family also supported Yoritomo on the battlefield to gain personal power. When Yoritomo and Masako married, however, there was no indication that the Taira hold on political power could do anything but increase. Yoritomo's future, on the other hand, looked bleak. I believe Masako loved him. It did not matter to her, therefore, that he had no hope of changing his status as an exile. Yoritomo was already in his thirties, no longer a young man by the standards of the day. Masako thus chose to marry a middle-aged exile, a man with no prospects of his own, a man with no hope of attaining any position in the capital. Her motive must have been love.

Rise to Power

In early 1180 Prince Mochihito, a disaffected member of the imperial clan, was persuaded by a group of courtiers to issue a clandestine decree calling on Minamoto supporters to overthrow Kiyomori and his government. Yoritomo's attack on Yamaki Kanetaka was a response to this august mandate. Historical sources document other attacks upon government officials by local warrior families, who used the mandate as a pretext for disposing of unpopular officials. By the following month, however, the Taira regime recognized the uprising for the plot it was and executed Prince Mochihito and others directly involved in its planning. By then, Yoritomo had already succeeded in rallying the former Minamoto forces in the eastern provinces, including the families who had supported his father in the Heiji Disturbance twenty years earlier. He had irrevocably committed himself by the time he received word of the executions in the capital from a messenger sent by the nephew of his nurse.[7]

How did Masako view this situation? In the absence of her own writings, it is impossible to know what was going on in her mind. To what extent did she understand her husband's predicament? If Yoritomo should rise up against the Taira and lose, he would be killed. Her natal family, furthermore, would be punished if they supported him—their lands confiscated, her father and brothers executed. On the other hand, if Yoritomo fled to the north, he might save his skin; but if Masako and her daughter should accompany him, this act alone would implicate her natal family, who until this point had unquestionably supported the Taira.

The initial response to Yoritomo's appeal for help in attacking Yamaki Kanetaka was not overwhelming, to say the least. Only thirty to forty men participated in the surprise nighttime attack, but they did accomplish their purpose. Three days later, however, a numerically superior force engaged Yoritomo at Ishibashi Mountain and soundly defeated him. Yoritomo's supporters had increased to three hundred men including the Hōjōs, but they were outnumbered by the three thousand Taira loyalists, according to *Azuma kagami*.[8]

Before the fighting began, Lady Maki had returned to Kyoto. Masako, her little daughter, and her sisters took refuge at Izuyama Gongen, a Buddhist temple in the Izu Mountains sympathetic to Yoritomo. During this period, temples had an independent status: not only were they exempt from taxes, but they retained large forces of warrior monks. Government officials were prohibited from entering the sacred precincts. The Izu temple offered an ideal place of refuge. Masako stayed there until she learned of Yoritomo's defeat at Ishibashi Mountain. Afraid that the victorious Taira troops would come in force to take her group hostage, she resolved to go into hiding. The monks at Izuyama Gongen did not request her group to leave. Masako and Yoritomo had spent the early days of their marriage at this temple, and the monks were pro-Minamoto. If Masako had not left the temple when she did, warrior monks probably would have fought against the Taira troops to protect their guests. But they were no match for a veteran army, and Masako's decision to leave the temple was sensible.

Masako and her group fled to the small fishing village of Akido, where the city of Atami is now located. The village was only a day's walk away and offered the further advantage of an escape route by sea. A few days later, a messenger arrived to report that her father and brothers were alive, but her husband's whereabouts were uncertain. There was a strong possibility that Yoritomo had died in battle or, even worse, been captured. A weaker woman would have been overcome by despair; Masako, however, remained resolute. Her mettle is often attributed to her upbringing in eastern Japan. Women raised in the Bandō area, literally the provinces east of the Ashigara Barrier and the Usui Pass, were known to display resoluteness and tenacity born of necessity. Frequent military struggles for land rights produced competent warriors and steadfast women. Compared to their more urbane counterparts in Kyoto, for example, they may have lacked certain cultural finesse, but they more than made up for this by their strength of character.

One week passed before Masako heard news of her husband. When defeat had seemed certain, Yoritomo had retreated into the mountains and made his way through the underbrush to Hakone Gongen Temple, whose head priest had been an ally of his father's. Eventually, Yoritomo made his way to Kamakura, the site he chose for his military headquarters, some thirty miles southwest of present Tokyo. There he regrouped and the rebellion rapidly gained momentum. One reason for this seemingly miraculous comeback was Yoritomo's "willingness—in fact, his eagerness—to embrace his former enemies."[9] Another reason, even more important, was the new system of political organization he had begun to establish. In return for oaths of allegiance, Yoritomo pledged to confirm his vassals in whatever land rights they considered rightfully theirs. In doing so, he bypassed existing Taira administrative organs in Kyoto, in effect leading the eastern provinces in their secession from the central government.

Yoritomo arrived in Kamakura less than two months after he began his rebellion. Five days later, Masako and her daughter joined him. To her surprise, the messenger sent to meet her referred to her husband as "Gosho-sama" (My Lordship), and to Masako herself as "Midaidokoro-sama" (My Ladyship), terms of utmost respect reserved for members of the imperial family, ministers, generals, and their consorts. The new designation not only symbolized Yoritomo's sudden rise in status but was also one way of giving legitimacy to the rebellion he headed—a legitimacy that had not yet been accorded through imperial sanction. As far as the court was concerned, Yoritomo was still an outlaw. Two weeks after his attack on the governor of Izu, the court issued a pronouncement declaring Yoritomo the enemy and authorizing his capture. Undaunted, Yoritomo ordered construction of his headquarters to house himself and his family as well as administrative offices on a scale that would give notice of his importance.

Two months after his victory at the Battle of Fuji River over a large Taira army, Yoritomo moved into his new Kamakura residence, in which family living quarters adjoined eighteen rooms assigned to the *samurai-dokoro*, a bureaucratic organ set up barely a month earlier to assist him in administration. His closest vassals, 318 men, gathered for the ceremonies to open the new headquarters.[10] Yoritomo's vassals competed with one another in building their own residences in Kamakura, quickly transforming the secluded village into a bustling city. By spring of 1181, Yoritomo had succeeded in unifying the east under his control.

The *Menoto* System

The three years from 1181 to 1183 saw a virtual suspension of hostilities. The Taira leader Kiyomori had died of fever in the spring of 1181. On his deathbed he had made his son vow to destroy the Minamoto, but a severe famine due to widespread crop failure plagued the country, making it impossible for either side to mobilize troops. Masako and Yoritomo were safely settled in their new residence. Yoritomo turned his attention to the civil affairs of governing his vassals.

One important event in 1181 was the birth of Yoriie, Masako and Yoritomo's first son. Two months earlier, in preparation for the birth, Masako had moved to a separate dwelling in accordance with the customs of the day. The honor of housing Masako during her confinement was granted to Hiki Yoshikazu and his family. Yoshikazu was the head of a wealthy warrior family in Musashi province and the son-in-law of the Nun Hiki, one of Yoritomo's nurses, and as such had been a reliable liegeman to Yoritomo. During Yoritomo's twenty years of exile in Izu, the family of this particular wet nurse had been the main provider of financial support for Yoritomo. Adachi Morinaga, the husband of the Nun Hiki's third daughter, had served as Yoritomo's trusted adviser in Izu. It was Adachi who had acted as messenger between Yoritomo and Masako in their romance. The Nun Hiki's second daughter, married to a lord from Musashi by the name of Kawagoe Shigeyori, was given the honor of serving as wet nurse for Yoritomo's newborn heir, Yoriie.

Yoritomo assigned various important vassals to perform other ceremonial duties following the birth of his son, but chose the wet nurse from the family of his own nurse. When the heir reached maturity and assumed his political responsibilities, the family of his nurse would stand to gain tremendous power and influence, which could easily be misused in wrong hands. To give such a crucial position to the family of a vassal could conceivably prove dangerous to the balance of power among vassals. Considerations of this sort prompted Yoritomo to look to the family of the Nun Hiki. The choice would later prove to have been a poor one.

One of Nagai Michiko's major contributions to our understanding of the Kamakura period is her research on the subject of *menoto*. The term is often translated as wet nurse or nurse, and in a strict sense it does refer to the woman chosen to suckle the child of a person in high position. More frequently, however, it designated her husband and family in their position as influential supporters of the child after he had reached adulthood. Three Chinese characters meaning "milk," "mother," and "husband" were made into a compound word implying "nurse's husband" and given the phonetic reading of *menoto* during this period. The term therefore refers to the nurse herself, her husband, and, in a wider sense, her extended family and its associates. Curiously enough, Nagai Michiko has found evidence that some menoto did not actually suckle their charges.

Women in Masako's position did not bring up their own children. Soon after birth, the baby was entrusted to the menoto family. Their responsibilities did not end when the child was weaned, but lasted throughout his lifetime. Their duties were wider in scope than just providing nourishment. They educated the child, arranged important ceremonies marking his growth, and supported his ambitions for social advancement. The influence such a family could wield corresponded to the position their charge assumed as an adult. If he became shogun, for example, the head of the menoto family, his sons, and relatives could assume untold power. After the death of Yoritomo the second shogun retained authority (*ken'i*) but exercised little real power (*kenryoku*), a distinction Nagai Michiko is fond of making. So for the remainder of the Kamakura period, political clout rested in the hands of those surrounding a figurehead shogun and acting in his name. Needless to say, the menoto family and associates constituted the most influential clique.

Despite an appearance of political stability, factional in-fighting within the Kamakura shogunate was fierce at crucial points of power transition. Nagai has shown that much of the in-fighting has been misinterpreted because historians have ignored menoto relationships. Most ambitious warrior leaders aspired to gain positions of power by serving as menoto, much as their aristocratic counterparts in the imperial court tried by marrying their daughters to emperors. Menoto families used all means at their command—even resorting to murder—to secure or protect the succession right of their charge. Whether successful or not in their ambitions, menoto proved an undeniably influential force in Kamakura politics.

Chosen by Yoritomo as wet nurse for Yoriie, the wife of Kawagoe Shigeyori actually suckled the child. Three or perhaps four other families were also named menoto. Hiki Yoshikazu and Adachi Morinaga, like Shigeyori, were the husbands of the Nun Hiki's daughters. The Hiki, Yoshikazu in particular, wielded the most influence among the menoto families, outshining Kajiwara Kagetoki, Yoritomo's most trusted staff general, who was also given the honor. At this point, or more likely sometime later, Hiraga was also added to the group. The Hiraga were a respected Minamoto family, but it was as a representative of Hōjō interests (his wife was Masako's half-sister) that he became menoto.

When Yoritomo assumed leadership in Kamakura, Masako's position was suddenly elevated from being the wife of a forgotten exile to being the wife of the most powerful man in eastern Japan. Brought up as the daughter of a local warrior lord, she was poorly prepared for such a sudden rise in status. Different levels of society had different customs concerning raising children. She already had one daughter, ōhime, whom she was bringing up herself. Nagai's comments are an aid in understanding how the menoto system worked.

NAGAI. Tokimasa was the warrior lord of a small domain, and therefore the Hōjō probably had not given their children over to menoto to be brought up.

BENTON. Is there any evidence that Masako's brothers were brought up by menoto?

NAGAI. No, there is none. Her younger brothers later became important political figures as regents for the shogun so that their menoto would have been known, had there been any. But no mention of such has been found in historical documents.

BENTON. Could this be due to a difference of custom between eastern Japan and the capital region?

NAGAI. No, I don't think so. It seems to have to do with a class difference. The aristocracy appointed menoto; other classes did not. A small warrior family like the Hōjō had no experience with menoto. Of course they employed wet nurses and women servants to help care for the children. They did not, however, give their children over to a woman of high birth to be raised and educated by her family. Given these differences, it is my opinion that Masako probably found it very difficult to accept the idea of giving up her Yoriie to a menoto. On the other hand, the fact that menoto were chosen for him showed that the family had attained a high status in society. Masako, I believe, knew of the menoto system itself, for we have records of powerful vassals in the east being appointed menoto for the children of the Kyoto aristocracy. For example, Yoritomo's father had a menoto from the east. Masako knew of the system and approved of it to the extent that adopting it demonstrated her family's new aristocratic status. However, deep in her heart, she must have had difficulty accepting it.

The menoto system had by this period existed for several hundred years in the capital. Women in the court felt no compunction about turning over their babies to other families to be raised. It was accepted as the proper way to do things. The present Empress Nagako did not bring up her own children. As soon as they were born, each was entrusted to a wet nurse and taken away to be brought up separately. But Crown Princess Michiko is raising her own children—the first instance of this in the history of the imperial family—and Crown Prince Akihito and the Princess [they became emperor and empress in 1989] are living together with their children, away from the Imperial Palace. Up until the present, imperial parents and children never lived as a unit. The menoto system lasted longest within the imperial family—evidence that it was mainly practiced among the cream of the aristocracy.

Recent research has indicated to me that in areas where ancient matriarchal customs still prevailed, ties between mother and child were very strong. In Kyoto, the menoto system served to loosen these ties; but in the rustic east, older patterns of child raising were naturally still prevalent. In this sense, Masako probably believed that her children should obey her, above all others.

BENTON. She was personally raising Ōhime. Therefore, she understood a mother's role. Can we not presume that she felt emotional conflict when she found that she would not be allowed to take part in raising her first-born son?

NAGAI. Yes, I do agree. Throughout Japanese history—even today this is true—Japanese women have tended to view children as their possessions. When a son grows up, the ties between mother and son inevitably become distant, despite the fact that the mother has devoted herself to him. The mother resents this; she resents the grown son's loyalty to his wife.

BENTON. This pattern is very Japanese. In the West, mothers take pride when children show early signs of independence.

NAGAI. Yes. This is a very Japanese way of viewing children, to see them as one's possessions. I believe that Masako shared these feelings. In addition, she was not brought up to be the wife of a political leader. Emotional conflict due to these factors would influence her relationship with Yoriie.

Revenge Rights of a Wronged Wife

When Masako presented Yoritomo with a son, it confirmed her position as his formal consort and called for rejoicing in Kamakura. Vassals vied to offer presents: swords and over two hundred horses were given to commemorate the auspicious event.[11] Five weeks after the birth, Masako and her son returned to Yoritomo's mansion in full procession.

Masako's joy, however, was not destined to last long. Hardly a month after her return, her father's wife Lady Maki disclosed a matter that would give her much concern. During Masako's confinement,

Yoritomo had been making regular visits to Lady Kame,[12] a woman with whom he had had a liaison in Izu before his marriage to Masako. In fact, he had installed Lady Kame in a house in Kamakura. The matter was a public secret, known to everyone but Masako. Lady Maki's motives in informing Masako were questionable. As could be expected, Masako was furious. Lady Maki offered her brother Munechika's services, and under Masako's orders he led a small army of men to destroy the residence of the retainer housing Lady Kame. Kame and the retainer somehow managed to escape.

Yoritomo's ire matched Masako's. Two days later, under the pretext of going on an outing, he ordered Munechika and several others to accompany him. At the destination, which was near the destroyed house, he interrogated Munechika, who prostrated himself in abject apology. Yoritomo rebuked him and cut off his top-knot—a humiliation that would prevent Munechika from appearing in public until his hair grew back. That night Yoritomo stayed away from home.

Masako's father Tokimasa was equally furious at what he viewed as an affront to Hōjō's honor. In protest, he announced his intention of leaving Kamakura for Izu. Conscious of the gravity of losing Tokimasa's support, Yoritomo immediately returned home, but not in time to prevent Tokimasa and his retinue from departing. To be deserted by the Hōjō was a serious matter. Masako's brother Yoshitoki had the wisdom to stay behind, however. After some time passed, Tokimasa did return to Kamakura, and Masako forgave Yoritomo. Yoritomo continued his visits to Lady Kame, albeit in a somewhat more discreet manner.

This famous incident is the basis for Masako's reputation as a jealous wife. Yoritomo's interest in other women would continue to infuriate Masako throughout their life together. It was a custom of those polygamous days for men to visit other women, although in defense of Masako it can be said that this custom was more ardently observed in aristocratic circles in Kyoto, where Yoritomo had spent his youth, than in samurai families in Masako's own eastern region. Even today, Japanese opinion, both male and female, tends to hold Masako at fault for overreacting in her retaliation.[13] Did most Kamakura women complacently condone the philanderings of their mates in the name of the time-honored polygamous system? Was Masako the only jealous woman of the day? Masako may have been jealous, but she was not alone in her feelings. Nagai Michiko has found evidence that Masako's retaliation for Yoritomo's attentions to Lady Kame followed the familiar pattern of a custom known as *uwanari-uchi*.

Marriage in Kamakura times was still a vague concept for all but the highest levels of society. A man visited many women. At some point, his attention would settle on one particular woman, and she would bear him children. Often the man would join the woman's family, who would give him material support. This woman would then be considered his "wife," although no ceremony marked her change of status. The "marriage," if it may be called that, did not prevent the man from visiting other women. But a problem arose if he began to prefer a new lover to his "wife." When such a situation arose, the term *konami* (literally, old wave) was used to refer to his "wife," and *uwanari* (later wife) to the new lover. The terms are so ancient that their etymology is uncertain, but one theory, rather forced, holds that these are metaphorical expressions comparing the women to waves: if the wife is an "old wave," then the new lover is a "ripple" disturbing the surface of the water, the word *uwanari* being a corruption of *uwanami* (ripple). Custom allowed the wife in this situation to vent her anger on the newcomer for stealing her husband's affections. Her revenge was known as *uwanari-uchi* (getting even with a later wife), and most often took the form of attacking her rival's house. As early as the Heian period, diaries give frequent references to actual incidents in which the "wife" exercised her right to revenge. Kamakura society sanctioned this practice.

When Masako took revenge on Lady Kame by destroying her dwelling, she was acting in a socially acceptable fashion. Likewise, Lady Kame had the right to defend herself and her property by means of arms if necessary. Some cases of uwanari-uchi ended in the victory of the "later wife" and humiliation for the "old wave." Traditional interpretations also condemn Masako's stepmother Lady Maki for instigating her, taking the incident as proof of their unsettled relationship. It is more likely, however, that Lady Maki was acting to protect the Hōjō family interests in supporting Masako in her revenge. Masako was not only jealous; she no doubt feared that Yoritomo might sire another son, who would be a threat to Yoriie's succession right. Rather than leaving it up to fate, she took measures to see that Yoritomo's relationship with Lady Kame would not jeopardize her own position as his main wife and mother of his only heir.

NAGAI. Uwanari-uchi lasted as an acceptable social custom until the early sixteenth century. It is related of course to the prevalent marriage pattern of the day. At the beginning of a relationship, a man and his woman lived separately. The man visited the woman, but they were economically independent of each other. When their relationship progressed to the level of considering themselves man and wife, the man left his own family and joined the woman's. He received economic support from her family. The family had clothes made for him, for example.

BENTON. The woman's family had economic power; therefore, they were in a strong position.

NAGAI. Yes. They were the ones who held the purse strings. The family pattern took many forms, of course. But in essence, the income of the family passed through the hands of daughters to the daughters' husbands. Therefore, when the husband of a daughter whom the family was supporting began to concentrate his attentions on another woman, the family suffered possible loss of economic investment, so to speak. This gave them the right, by social custom, to take revenge or protect their interests.

BENTON. You do not mention this custom in your novel or *Tsuwamono no fu*. Why not?

NAGAI. At the time I wrote those books, I was not aware of the custom of uwanari-uchi. Therefore, I followed common interpretations of the Kame incident and presented Masako's behavior as due to jealousy. A fair historical portrayal of Masako must, of course, take account of the family system, the economics of marriage, and customs of the day, including uwanari-uchi.

Ill-Starred Princess

By the spring of 1183, Kiso Yoshinaka, Yoritomo's cousin and a powerful Minamoto leader, had established an unchallenged position in north central Japan. Sensing a threat to Kyoto, Taira leaders sent out a large force to subdue him. Yoshinaka routed them and relentlessly pursued the Taira army toward Kyoto as far as Ōmi province. Prior to attacking Kyoto, he had exchanged an agreement with Yoritomo and, as a sign of goodwill, sent his oldest son Shimizu Yoshitaka to Kamakura.

Early marriages were common at the time, particularly among the aristocracy to cement political ties. Yoshitaka was only eleven years old, but his father already entertained hopes of marrying him to Yoritomo's oldest child, the five-year-old Ōhime (literally, Eldest Princess). Ōhime adored Yoshitaka, and in Masako's eyes the two children seemed perfectly matched.[14] As far as Yoritomo was concerned, however, Yoshitaka was a hostage, to be detained in Kamakura to ensure that his father would remain loyal.

Yoshitaka's position at Yoritomo's residence did become precarious several months after his father succeeded in seizing Kyoto. There was little doubt in anyone's mind that with this move, Yoshinaka was challenging Yoritomo for Minamoto leadership. Yoritomo responded by ordering his brothers, Noriyori and the famed hero Yoshitsune, to proceed to Kyoto. Within a month, Yoritomo's armies entered Kyoto and drove Yoshinaka to his death. Yoshitsune went on to pursue the Taira to Ichinotani by the shore of the Inland Sea and soundly defeated them. The mandates issued by the court at this time finally acknowledged Yoritomo's position as military head and leader of government troops (*kangun*).

In the meantime, Masako and Ōhime had grown fond of the young hostage Yoshitaka. In spite of Yoshinaka's seeming disloyalty, Masako hoped to convince Yoritomo to pardon his son. Yoritomo, however, resolved to have him killed. His reasons can be easily inferred. Yoritomo himself had been only thirteen years old when his father had died in revolt against the Taira. Kiyomori's leniency in allowing him to go into exile rather than killing him had led to the Taira downfall. Mercy to Yoshinaka's son could, he reasoned, eventually lead to a similar fate for his own direct line. As soon as Masako fathomed Yoritomo's intentions, however, she made her own plans to help the boy escape. Early one morning Yoshitaka slipped out of the residence with a group of Masako's women attendants, disguised as one of them. At an appointed place a horse was waiting. Yoshitaka's close retainer stayed behind impersonating his master to give him time. But that night Yoritomo's men discovered the scheme. Five days later, a retainer of one of Yoritomo's vassals captured and killed the boy. Masako, Ōhime, and many men and women in the palace mourned his pathetic fate.

Ōhime suffered the worst. Following Yoshitaka's death, she became seriously ill. She blamed her parents for causing the death of the young man she had adored. Masako was in turn furious with Yoritomo for not showing more leniency with the youth, who was after all so close to their daughter. Ōhime's illness, she argued, was directly caused by grief, and for this she blamed her husband. Her anger caused Yoritomo to take a drastic measure: he had the samurai who had killed Yoshitaka decapitated. A year later Masako would try to atone for the incident by adopting Yoshitaka's sister, whom Yoritomo would grant land rights and a stipend.

In retelling this incident, Nagai Michiko departs from the traditional interpretation based on *Azuma kagami*, which gives Ōhime, not Masako, the main role in helping Yoshitaka escape. *Azuma kagami* also refers to Yoshitaka as Ōhime's husband. But in addition to the absence of Yoritomo's sanction, the two children's ages—five and eleven—make their marriage implausible. Ōhime's tender age also means that she could not have played a major role in the escape plan. Nagai believes that *Azuma kagami* tries to downplay Masako's role in what amounts to a subversive plot.

BENTON. Is there any evidence in the sources for your interpretation?

NAGAI. No, not any direct evidence, but if we read between the lines, I believe that we can find proof that Masako planned the whole thing. When Ōhime gets sick, it is Masako who blames Yoritomo for killing the boy and causing Ōhime's illness, according to *Azuma kagami*. Why should she blame him if she knew all along that Yoritomo intended to kill the hostage? One can imagine various scenes: for example, at first perhaps Yoritomo may have agreed to Masako's plan to let Yoshitaka escape, but then changed his mind.

BENTON. Another possible interpretation is that Yoritomo used Masako and Ōhime to persuade Yoshitaka to try and make an escape, for it would be difficult to kill him while he was still living at Yoritomo's residence.

NAGAI. Yes, that is also feasible. In any case, we do have evidence that Masako blamed Yoritomo for Ōhime's illness. In addition, when Masako learned of Yoshitaka's death, she immediately accused the retainer involved. Yoritomo then had the man who killed the boy executed. These events are reported in *Azuma kagami*. I can only conclude that Masako must have been involved very deeply from the beginning. *Azuma kagami* describes the incident as Ōhime's doing, but it was Masako who was working behind the scenes.

In any case, it is true that Yoritomo and Masako did not agree about Shimizu Yoshitaka. Yoritomo was placed in an awkward position. It is not clear whether he agreed to Masako's plan and then tergiversated or whether he opposed it from the start. Executing the man who killed Yoshitaka may seem a strange way of vindicating himself, but it is not surprising in view of Yoritomo's later harsh treatment of his own younger brothers, who had done most in defeating his enemies.

Yoritomo and Masako's third child, a girl named Sanman, was born around this time. *Azuma kagami* does not report Sanman's birth, but later entries prove that she did exist. There are several theories concerning the date of her birth, but I will follow Nagai in placing the date in 1185. We also know that Sanman had a menoto, Nakahara Chikayoshi, who was an important member of Yoritomo's government. Nevertheless, the facts that she had only one menoto and that records omitted even the slightest mention of her birth indicate that girl children were not considered as important as male offspring.

Disappointed at not having borne her husband another son, Masako returned from her confinement to new evidence of her husband's infidelity. This time the object of his affections was a lady-in-waiting to whom Nagai gives the name Nohagi (Wild Bush Clover) in her novel. She was the daughter of one Hitachi-no-suke Tokinaga, but her real name is not known. The sources refer to her as Daishin no Tsubone, a title indicating that she was occupying a fairly high position. Irate and unrelenting, Masako confronted Yoritomo, and he, in an atypical move, offered to dismiss Nohagi from service. The dismissal of Nohagi was, however, not done simply to placate Masako but to protect Nohagi, who was pregnant. She later bore Yoritomo a son. Masako's father Tokimasa and Yoriie's menoto Hiki Yoshikazu responded to the unexpected crisis by making secret plans to dispose of the baby, who posed a threat to Yoriie's prospects. Nohagi fled Kamakura and went into hiding.[15] The incident is often cited as proof of Masako's jealousy: she was not content at merely having Nohagi dismissed, she had to have her rival run out of Kamakura. In fact, this is probably another example of uwanari-uchi, in which the family of the "old wave" succeeded in safeguarding their political interests.

Shizuka the Tragic Heroine

Masako's period produced one mistress who earned more fame than the wife, richly deserved for her courage and loyalty as well as for her tragic fate.

By early 1184, Yoritomo had extended his control as far as Kyoto. His brother Yoshitsune's spectacular victory at Ichinotani had forced the Taira to flee to Shikoku Island. Yoritomo sent a memorial to Go-Shirakawa requesting, among other items, that Yoshitsune be placed in command of all military matters in areas near Kyoto, but that rewards for his warriors be withheld until Yoritomo himself decided how to distribute them. The significance of this request was enormous. Under Yoritomo's new system of law and order, all military vassals owed their allegiance exclusively and directly to him, in return for which he would distribute land rights and other honors. This was a fundamental rule of Yoritomo's feudal government.

Inevitably, Yoshitsune soon violated the cardinal rule of vassalage by accepting certain titles and honors from the court without Yoritomo's permission. Yoshitsune had already acquired fame as a great general. If he could command enough of a following and secure the support of the court, he could conceivably go on to claim leadership of the Minamoto.

Nevertheless, Yoritomo did make one attempt at appeasement. He arranged for Kawagoe Shigeyori, the son-in-law of the Nun Hiki and Yoriie's menoto, to give his daughter Kogiku (so named by Nagai for narrative convenience) in marriage to Yoshitsune. In 1184, Kogiku went to join Yoshitsune in Kyoto. Yoritomo would not have arranged Yoshitsune's marriage to the daughter of such a close vassal had he given up hope of reconciling their differences. An alliance with a vassal like Shigeyori would help cement Yoshitsune's connections with Kamakura, or so Yoritomo and Masako hoped. If Yoshitsune could be persuaded to give up his court appointments and show loyalty to Kamakura, Yoritomo was no doubt prepared to forgive him.

At the end of 1184 Yoritomo was forced to call upon Yoshitsune for services again. Yoshitsune met the Taira fleet at Dannoura, the narrow channel separating Kyushu from the main island of Honshu. When the spectacular and tragic sea battle ended in the destruction of the Taira ships, Kiyomori's widow leapt to her death, drowning with her grandson, the seven-year-old Emperor Antoku, in her arms. The Minamoto under Yoritomo were now the undisputed military power in Japan. Yoshitsune had performed brilliantly on the battlefield. One ironic outcome of the Taira downfall, however, was that Yoshitsune had eliminated his own raison d'être. Yoritomo no longer needed him.

Yoritomo had always counted on eventual victory; from the outset he had concentrated his efforts on establishing a political system of law and order under his command. His greatest fear was not defeat at the swords of the Taira, but that relatives like Yoshinaka or Yoshitsune might through influence at the court usurp his own position as head of the Minamoto clan. Legendary accounts describe Yoritomo as a suspicious man whose "character was flawed by a streak of cruel perversity which he directed at members of his own family."[16] His ire at Yoshitsune, they claim, was due to jealousy of his dazzling military successes and the admiration he enjoyed in court circles. The fact that Yoshitsune was Yoritomo's brother makes his ultimate betrayal of Yoshitsune more puzzling. It must be remembered, however, that the two brothers had different mothers, and they did not grow up together. It seems unlikely that they ever met in person during their adult life.

Before long, Yoritomo confiscated his brother's lands, in effect dropping him from the ranks of his followers. In 1185, Yoshitsune succeeded in procuring a mandate from the ex-emperor Go-Shirakawa authorizing him to "chastise" Yoritomo. In self-defense, Yoritomo dispatched his forces to Kyoto. Unable to gather enough support to confront this army, Yoshitsune fled to the west, hoping to find new connections. But his luck had run out. Yoritomo now sent a larger army to Kyoto under the leadership of Masako's father Tokimasa. Go-Shirakawa immediately reversed his position and issued a mandate to capture Yoshitsune. Soon he issued another mandate declaring Yoshitsune a rebel. Yoshitsune fled for his life, hiding out until he reached Mount Yoshino.

The rich legend that grew later to make Yoshitsune the most beloved hero in Japan, as invincible in battle as irresistible to women, had at least one solid basis to build on. In his company during the precarious flight was a young woman. She was not his wife Kogiku, nor his formal consort who was the daughter of Taira Tokitada, but Shizuka, a beautiful young dancer from the capital. Yoshitsune eventually managed to elude the pursuing Kamakura forces thanks to self-sacrifices by his dedicated vassals. He headed northeast to the Ōshū fief of Fujiwara Hidehira. Shizuka, however, was captured. Yoritomo ordered that she be brought to Kamakura. She arrived in the company of her mother, a nun.

Shizuka enjoyed great renown in Kyoto as a dancer in the *shirabyōshi* style, which was in vogue in the capital. The term derives from the dancer's attire: a white robe and black cap usually worn by men. Shizuka had probably danced for the aristocracy; legends attest to her beauty and talent. Reserved in character, she did not display the ostentatiousness typical of her profession. As soon as she was captured at Mount Yoshino she was interrogated about Yoshitsune's whereabouts, but there was no reason to expect that she would reveal anything, if she did in fact know at all. Yoritomo wished to see her for himself, however; calling her to Kamakura could very well have been a pretext for his own designs on her. When he discovered that she was pregnant with Yoshitsune's child, he was forced to settle for less: a request that she dance at the Tsurugaoka Hachiman Shrine, not in public but in the innermost sanctuary as an offering to the deities. Yoritomo and select vassals came to view the dance. Yoritomo, it has been suggested, was considering giving her full pardon when she finished her dancing.

How did Masako feel about Shizuka? We can presume that at least initially she probably did not like her. Yoritomo's habitual philandering may have made her wary about his motives toward Shizuka. She was also probably sympathetic to the plight of Yoshitsune's wife Kogiku, a girl raised like herself in the east. Yoshitsune had shown absolutely no interest in Kogiku and instead flagrantly dallied with other women. After Yoshitsune fell out of grace with his brother, Kogiku had been sent for by her father, but with an obstinacy characteristic of women born in the east, she had refused to return and remained in Kyoto. Her father was punished for her disobedience. Because Kawagoe Shigeyori happened to be one of Yoritomo's most trusted retainers and one of his only son's menoto, and because he had given his daughter in marriage to Yoshitsune at Yoritomo's command, the punishment was a token one: Yoritomo confiscated his lands, only to award them to his mother-in-law, the Nun Hiki.

At any rate, if Yoritomo had intended to show leniency to Shizuka, his intentions were thwarted by Masako's unexpected appearance at the shrine and Shizuka's less than cooperative behavior. The assembled company listened aghast as Shizuka began to sing in self-accompaniment to the dance. Dauntlessly she sang of her love for the fugitive lover, of parting with him at Mount Yoshino, and of longing for the happy times they had shared:

> *One day some time ago*
> *He walked into the white snows*

Of the ancient and honorable Mount Yoshino.
How my heart yearns after him!

Humbly and silently
The spool of linen yarn keeps turning.
Would that I could find the ways
To bring back the past![17]

Shizuka's song was a deliberate insult to Yoritomo, and he immediately rose and left the gathering in anger. To expect the mistress of his declared enemy to sing praises of his own regime had been a serious miscalculation on his part. On the other hand, had Shizuka been a more devious or tactful woman, she might have played along with him in hopes of appeasing his anger on her lover's behalf.

Masako's reaction differed from Yoritomo's. Even if she had at first disliked Shizuka, she could not help but admire her unwavering loyalty to her love, realizing all too well the consequences of her daring move. Had Masako been put in a similar situation, she would have acted in a similar manner, rather than bow to the demands of a declared enemy. (*Azuma kagami* contains a famous passage in which she justifies Shizuka's behavior to Yoritomo by recalling how her own love for him had given her the strength to defy her father and make her way through the rain to his side, and to wait in Izu when he went off to the Battle of Ishibashi Mountain.) The next day Masako paid a visit to Shizuka. Regardless of whether Yoritomo would agree to overlook Shizuka's defiance, Masako wished to express her sympathy for Shizuka's plight.

Shizuka had one more supporter, Ōhime. Since Yoshitaka had died, Ōhime had not been well. Masako was having prayers said for her recovery. The priest urged Masako to have Ōhime come to the temple for a retreat. Ōhime, who had declined all of her mother's well-meaning suggestions, agreed this once to the retreat. From the temple, she sent for Shizuka with a request for her to dance. Yoshitaka had been killed at Yoritomo's orders, and Ōhime, perhaps more than anyone else, felt a strong empathy for Shizuka. She offered to help Shizuka escape from Kamakura. Pretending that Shizuka was on retreat with her at the temple would give her enough time to flee to safety before the soldiers were sent out in pursuit. But Shizuka declined to accept the offer. Before she had agreed to dance in Yoritomo's presence, she had resolved to die, and her resolve was not to be shaken.

Yoritomo did not have Shizuka killed. He ordered that she be permitted to return to Kyoto after her baby was born. If the baby was a girl, Shizuka would be allowed to bring her up. But if it was a boy, the baby would be killed. This decree was relatively merciful. Masako's support for Shizuka is said to have influenced Yoritomo's decision. Unfortunately, Shizuka had a baby boy, and he was taken from her right after birth and killed. Shizuka returned to Kyoto, where she took orders as a nun. She died a year later, to be immortalized as one of Japan's legendary heroines. Ivan Morris, in his study of the Japanese hero type entitled *The Nobility of Failure*, notes that Shizuka is "the great romantic figure in the Yoshitsune cycle of legends." He regards her as "the first (and one of the very few) of Japan's failed heroines" (p. 95). Shizuka later was made the subject of two Noh plays, *Yoshino Shizuka* (Shizuka at Yoshino) and *Futari Shizuka* (Two Shizukas). My description of the Shizuka legend follows Nagai Michiko's, which is based on *Azuma kagami*. The version in the narrative romance *Gikeiki* (Chronicle of Yoshitsune, fourteenth or fifteenth century) is similar except that the dance follows the birth of the son.

Could Masako and Ōhime have had their way, they would have saved Shizuka's baby. Yoritomo, however, stood firm. As head of the government and leader of countless warriors, he could not allow Yoshitsune's son to live, for to do so would be to set up conditions that could jeopardize the future of his regime. Yoritomo may appear heartless, but he had little choice. The famous story of how Masako interceded on behalf of Shizuka is based on *Azuma kagami*, which reports that it was Masako who soothed Yoritomo and helped him get over his anger at Shizuka's song. However, since there is no other source to corroborate the statement, we cannot be sure that it really happened. Nagai's comments shed light on the background of this incident.

> NAGAI. The compilation of *Azuma kagami* was commissioned by the Hōjō. This incident may have been fabricated to show Masako in a favorable light. What does sound real in the report is Masako's speech about how she loved Yoritomo so deeply that she defied her father to flee to him on a dark, rainy night. This does seem to be based on fact.
>
> On the other hand, even if Masako had not spoken up for Shizuka, she would have been spared, for she was not Yoshitsune's main wife. Yoritomo's reason for decreeing that Shizuka's baby be killed if it were a boy and not killed if a girl was not his jealousy of Yoshitsune or his fear that Yoshitsune's son would grow up and try to kill him some day.

Rather, it was related to a custom with a long history in Japan. According to this custom, male children belonged to the father and female
children to the mother. This unwritten law existed during the Kamakura
period and probably earlier. We do not know when it first took root.
However, evidence is found in the Jōei Code of 1232, a set of laws
compiled by order of the Hōjō. The section concerning slaves stipulates
that the male offspring of a union between two slaves of different
masters is the property of the father's master, and females that of the
mother's master. Over three centuries earlier, the Nara period codes had
differed on this matter in giving all the children to the mother.

When they compiled the Jōei Code, the Hōjō did not write new laws
but rather put into written form practices that were already in existence.
The custom of dividing children by sex was probably common not just
among slaves but throughout Japanese society of the period. Therefore,
it would be wrong to conclude that Yoritomo was acting cruelly when
he had Shizuka's baby killed. The boy baby belonged not to her but to
Yoshitsune. Yoshitsune had been declared an enemy of the state by the
ex-emperor, and his son was killed for that reason. Had it been a girl,
she would have belonged to Shizuka and been allowed to live. The fate
of Shizuka's baby was determined by custom. Even if Masako had not
pleaded on Shizuka's behalf with Yoritomo, the outcome would have
been the same, I believe.

Sons and Daughters

After the death of Yoshitaka, Ōhime's relationship with her mother
was strained, and Yoritomo's treatment of Shizuka did not help
matters. Masako's relationship with Yoriie was no better. She had
too few opportunities to see her son, and when she did, the presence
of menoto allowed no intimacy. Besides Kawagoe Shigeyori's wife,
who had actually suckled the child, there were the wives of Hiki
Yoshikazu, Adachi Morinaga, Hiraga Yoshinobu, and Kajiwara
Kagetoki. They vied for the child's affections, indulging his every
whim in the hopes of gaining easy access to power when he came of
age. The Hiki family, who had custody of the boy, already enjoyed a
prominent position among the menoto families. There are no credible sources to tell us of Yoriie's boyhood, but it is not far-fetched to
assume that he was spoiled by his menoto attendants, and that this
disturbed Masako. Nagai describes him as a petulant child, who
grew angry when Masako attempted to discipline him. What we do

know of his character as an adult would support this view.

In fact, mothers of that period were accorded little power and few rights over their sons, especially those of noble lineage. In July 1188, the six-year-old Yoriie was installed as official heir to Yoritomo in an elaborate ceremony. Selected vassals, with his menoto Hiki leading, took turns in outfitting the boy with armor, helmet, sword, bow, and arrows. Seated on a horse, the little warrior general was paraded around the large front garden of the Shogunate before his father's vassals. Custom forbade Masako, or any woman, from attending such ceremonies marking her son's rites of passage.

Yoritomo soon turned his attention from military matters to his relations with the court. In 1190 he returned to Kyoto in glory with an impressively large retinue, for the first time since his exile to the east some thirty years ago. He was awarded several prestigious court titles, each of which he resigned immediately to signify his independence. The one office he did desire—that of Seii Taishogun (literally, Commander-in-Chief of Expeditionary Forces Against Barbarians)—was offered to him only after the death of Go-Shirakawa in 1192. He was not the first to hold this title, but he was the first to establish and head an administrative institution known as the shogunate.

In the same year Masako and Yoritomo's fourth child and second son, Sanetomo, was born. This time only one menoto family was chosen, and not from among Yoritomo's close retainers or from the Nun Hiki's family. Masako's sister Lady Awa and her husband Zenjō, Yoritomo's half-brother, were given the honor. The choice reflected Masako's opinion, it is believed. By giving Sanetomo over to the charge of her own sister, Masako would be able to oversee his upbringing. The Hiki family had not only overindulged her eldest son, they had grown arrogant in their assumption of power. As the menoto family for Yoritomo's second son, Zenjō and Lady Awa would provide a check upon Hiki influence and prove more pliable to Masako and Yoritomo's wishes.

In 1193, Yoritomo led his vassals in several large hunting expeditions. In years past, he had used hunts as a pretext for visiting his concubine Lady Kame. But the expeditions this time were meant to be military exercises for his troops and demonstrations of his power. The eleven-year-old Yoriie accompanied him. On one expedition at the foothills of Mt. Fuji, he killed his first deer. The proud father sent a messenger to report it to Masako, but she showed no signs of sharing his exuberance. Trained by a famous archer and aided by his father's retainers, Yoriie probably had little trouble in shooting a deer. The messenger returned to the hunt astounded by Masako's indifference and not a little disappointed at receiving no reward for his efforts. This incident is often cited as proof that Yoritomo was a doting father and Masako a cool and unsatisfactory mother. Masako's indifference does suggest a lack of intimacy in her relationship with Yoriie, but it is also true that Yoriie's deer could not be credited entirely to his own abilities. It was probably difficult for Masako to feel joy at seeing her son being manipulated by Yoritomo's vassals. One other common interpretation is that Masako was out of sorts because she knew that her husband was enjoying the company of other women every evening during the expedition.[18]

Twelve days later, fighting broke out at the Mt. Fuji camp in the middle of a rainy night. The incident would later be known as the "Sogas' Night Attack," and the two Soga brothers would be held up as models of filial piety for avenging their father's murder over a land dispute. There was much bloodshed, and rumors reached Kamakura that Yoritomo had been assassinated together with his son and some member of the Hōjō family. Masako was weeping in anguish at the unexpected turn of fate when Yoritomo's brother Noriyori came to console her and offered to take care of everything. The rumors proved false, however, and Yoritomo, Yoriie, and the Hōjō all returned from Mt. Fuji alive and well.

Historians have only recently begun to doubt the revenge story as put forth by *Azuma kagami*. Nagai Michiko, for instance, views the incident as an uprising by certain Izu families jealous of the Hōjō, who had been but a minor influence before Yoritomo's rise to power. As luck would have it, the Hōjō father and sons were not found where they were presumed to be, and the Soga brothers proved to be the only ones who accomplished their objective, a private revenge. It seems that behind the scenes, Noriyori supported the Izu lords in the hopes of usurping Yoritomo's position. A possible insurrection was snipped in the bud, to Masako's great relief, we may presume. Both Soga brothers ended up dead; Noriyori, ostensibly for his premature gesture of assuming responsibility of clan leadership, was exiled to Izu, where he was later murdered.

In 1194, Masako, with Yoritomo's support, carried forward plans to marry her frail and still despondent daughter Ōhime to a cousin, Ichijō

Takayoshi, the son of Yoritomo's older sister and the court noble Ichijō Yoshiyasu. To help cement the relationship, the two families traveled together to the Miura Peninsula. But Ōhime flatly refused to marry Takayoshi, going so far as to threaten suicide if pressed. Memories of Yoshitaka seem to have taken away from her any desire to form new relationships. Masako had no choice but to agree to cancel the plans.

Yoritomo made his second visit to Kyoto in 1195, ostensibly to participate in the dedication ceremonies marking the reconstruction of Tōdaiji Temple, made possible in great part by his contributions. This time, Masako, Ōhime, and their other three children accompanied him. Masako had received a letter from Lady Tango, a favorite of the late emperor Go-Shirakawa, indicating interest in having Ōhime brought to the court as a consort for the present emperor. After Go-Shirakawa died, Fujiwara Kanezane, the regent for the fifteen-year-old emperor Go-Toba, had gained new influence. If Ōhime were accepted as Go-Toba's consort and bore him a son, Yoritomo could acquire the powerful position of regent for himself, and maybe even the supreme honor of being the grandfather of an emperor. Lady Tango, who had her own reasons for promoting the match, received Masako and Ōhime more than cordially during their three-month stay, offering every assurance that Ōhime would be accepted as imperial consort.

Masako and Yoritomo returned to Kamakura in high spirits. Several months passed, but they failed to receive word from Lady Tango concerning their agreement. Slowly the truth dawned on them. Lady Tango, in collusion with Minamoto Michichika, Go-Toba's menoto, had proposed the match to prevent the regent Kanezane from assuming full power should his pregnant daughter bear Go-Toba a son. She had a daughter, and soon after another consort, Michichika's step-daughter, gave birth to a son, thereby assuring Michichika of the favored position he had sought. Yoritomo and Ōhime were no longer needed in his power game. Masako was upset at being exploited by the court, and the hapless Ōhime took ill again. Yoritomo still nursed his hopes of placing her alongside the emperor, but before these hopes could be realized, Ōhime died, at the age of nineteen, in the early summer of 1197.

Masako experienced intense grief at her daughter's death, a grief that must have been complicated by feelings of remorse for not being able to alleviate Ōhime's despondency after the loss of Yoshitaka.

With Ōhime gone, any hopes Yoritomo might have had of securing influence at court were dashed for the time being. Within a year, his closest remaining friend in Kyoto—his brother-in-law Ichijō Yoshiyasu—also died. Michichika's machinations in the capital, ousting Kanezane and engineering the enthronement of a new emperor, also worked against Yoritomo. By elevating Go-Toba to the position of ex-sovereign and setting his step-daughter's son in his place as Emperor Tsuchimikado, Michichika gained for himself the most influential position in Kyoto. All this was done without the consent of Kamakura.

Yoritomo had no choice but to plan a third trip to the capital, hoping that a show of force would help him regain some of the power he had lost. There is also evidence that Yoritomo had not entirely given up his plan of getting a daughter into the palace as imperial consort. His aims now centered upon the thirteen-year-old Sanman.

Dowager Nun

Before he had time to start preparations for his planned march on the capital, Yoritomo died. The manner of his demise was ironic for a man who was the leader of a military government and the head of the Minamoto clan long renowned as the horse-riding land force: he fell off his horse. When he could not be revived after the fall, he was immediately brought home to Kamakura. He never regained consciousness and breathed his last in early 1199.

The accident occurred after the opening ceremony for a bridge on the Sagami River commemorating a late sister of Masako's. The shogun's untimely death originating in such a public event gave rise to rumors that he had been assassinated. Legend has it that the spirits of Yoshitsune and the Heike noblemen he had destroyed in his rise to power appeared to him, including the ghost of the boy Emperor Antoku; Yoritomo then fell sick and died soon after, not of ordinary illness but by the curse of these spirits.[19]

Another legend popular in Tokugawa times, over five hundred years later, holds Masako responsible for her husband's death: She must have become so obsessed with jealousy at his philanderings that she lost control of herself. Or, as some versions tell it, her anger and jealousy grew so fierce that her spirit detached itself from her body and haunted Yoritomo to death. Since the Tokugawa shoguns claimed

Minamoto descent, popular storytellers, in their effort to vindicate Yoritomo's seemingly poor horsemanship, blamed someone or other for a variety of plots, from spooking his horse to poisoning Yoritomo. There seems to be little doubt, however, that he died of natural causes, a cerebral hemorrhage.

Barely recovered from Ōhime's death, Masako was so distressed, according to historical accounts, at the loss of her husband that she considered joining him in death and would have committed suicide had she not been held back by concern for her three remaining children: seventeen-year-old Yoriie, fourteen-year-old Sanman, and Sanetomo, who was just seven.[20] As the widow of a man of high status, she probably had little choice except to become a lay nun. She took that step right after her husband's death.

If Masako had hoped that by taking orders she would be relieved of worldly concerns to better mourn the deaths of her husband and daughter, she was mistaken. A more active role in shogunate politics would be forced upon her by her husband's death. As Yoritomo's widow and as mother of two successive shoguns, Masako would inherit the responsibility of making certain decisions that only she could enforce. Several years would pass, however, before she would be called upon to play this role.

A little more than a month after the funeral, Sanman took ill. The chances of getting her installed in the imperial palace as consort diminished with her father's death, but many retainers refused to give up hopes of improving Kamakura's relationship with the court through her. Go-Toba sent a prominent court physician to Kamakura with special instructions to care for Sanman. Her condition, which had remained serious for several months, was noticeably relieved by the medication he brought. Within a month, however, her illness took a turn for the worse. Several weeks after her doctor returned to Kyoto, Sanman died.[21] The scale of her funeral, which far exceeded Ōhime's, reflected the disappointment of Kamakura vassals.

Masako had lost two children and her husband in the short span of two years. Moreover, any hopes she might have had of finding consolation in her son Yoriie's responsible conduct of affairs as heir to his father in the position of shogun were dashed soon after he took the supreme office. Not two weeks passed after Sanman's death before an ugly incident began to unfold.

The new shogun summoned Adachi Kagemori, the son of Morinaga (one of his own menoto from the Nun Hiki's family), and ordered him to lead an army to Mikawa province, where Yoriie alleged that bands of outlaws were causing havoc. Kagemori was the *shugo* (provincial constable) for Mikawa, an office whose duties included routing bandits. During his one-month absence, Yoriie had one of his close retainers abduct Kagemori's concubine, a beautiful young woman from Kyoto, and bring her to his palace. Kagemori, who had found nothing amiss in Mikawa, returned to discover Yoriie's scandalous ruse.

Furious as he was at Yoriie's unjust conduct, Kagemori was prohibited from taking revenge. To explain why, we must examine changes that occurred in the shogunate directly after Yoritomo's death. Yoriie was not of the same mettle as his father. This quickly became clear to top members of the Kamakura government when he began to exercise his powers in judging suits. Without good cause, he would allot lands to sons and other relatives of his menoto Hiki Yoshikazu, whose daughter Lady Wakasa was his wife and the mother of one of his children. A regent council of thirteen members was immediately set up to take over the judicial functions.[22] Yoriie reacted to this reduction of his power by issuing an infamous pronouncement forbidding anyone from chastising his four companions, all sons or nephews of Hiki Yoshikazu. The retainer involved in the Adachi incident numbered among them.

Far from being as guilt-ridden as the Biblical King David was for coveting his vassal's wife Bathsheba, Yoriie and his four cohorts gathered forces to attack Kagemori in an attempt to forestall his possible revenge. But before Yoriie could put his plan into action, Masako made an unexpected move. Kagemori's father Morinaga had faithfully served Yoritomo since his days in Izu, and it was he who had carried clandestine letters between Masako and Yoritomo at the beginning of their courtship. Masako proceeded to Morinaga's house and from there dispatched a letter to Yoriie. The missive, which began with a reference to the recent deaths of Yoritomo and Sanman, reminded Yoriie how much his late father had valued Morinaga's services. "If you plan to kill Morinaga and his son, aim your first arrow at me," read the famous conclusion of her letter. Masako spent the night at the Adachi residence. Only when Yoriie's army had dispersed did she return home, carrying with her a written oath in which Adachi denied any intention of treasonous conspiracy. Unlike the fateful union of David and Bathsheba divinely vindicated by the birth of the great King Solomon, Yoriie's sorry affair ended quite anticlimactically a few days later, when he returned the abducted lady to Kagemori.

Masako's swift intervention had prevented a love triangle from mushrooming into full-fledged civil strife. Now known as *ama midai* (dowager nun), she was the only person who could control Yoriie. As shogun, he was immune to chastisement by his vassals, but not to that by Masako. Her authority derived not from any personal intimacy in the mother-son relationship, but rather from her position as widow of the founder of the Kamakura shogunate. Although Adachi Morinaga and Hiki Yoshikazu were related by marriage to the Nun Hiki's daughters, and both men were Yoriie's menoto, the two families were far from close. This incident shows how much animosity must have been growing against Yoshikazu, not only among Yoritomo's old retainers but within the Hiki clan itself. It is important to note that Masako sided with a retainer who had been loyal to Yoritomo rather than with her son. The Adachi incident helped make the rift in Masako's relationship with Yoriie more pronounced.

Yoriie, the Unfit Shogun

Masako's intervention had an untoward result. It pushed Yoriie away from his mother and the Hōjō and cemented his dependence upon Hiki Yoshikazu and his sons. He also began to show renewed interest in his neglected Hiki wife, Lady Wakasa. Dissatisfied with her son's conduct in public and private affairs, Masako blamed Hiki for insulating him from her edifying influence. Meanwhile, Hiki Yoshikazu kept on bolstering his power. In 1200 his powerful colleague Kajiyama Kagetoki dug his own grave by attempting to set up a rival shogunate with a candidate of his own choice. Kagetoki was another of Yoriie's menoto, but instead of supporting him the Hiki headed the forces sent out to kill Kagetoki and quell what amounted to a treasonous uprising.[23] It was around this time that Yoshikazu built a new dwelling on his own estate for Lady Wakasa and Ichiman, her son by Yoriie, no doubt certain that this grandson would succeed Yoriie as shogun.

Soon, Yoriie's overfondness for women was outmatched by a zeal for *kemari*, a sport popular among the aristocracy which was played by several players who took turns kicking a deerskin ball.[24] Critics, including the authors of *Azuma kagami*, frown on Yoriie's addiction to kemari, taking it as proof that he had little aptitude for the more serious shogunal responsibilities. This may have been true, but more important was the fact that Yoriie had all too quickly become a puppet of Yoshikazu, who encouraged his interest in kemari to keep him occupied with a harmless aristocratic pastime instead of interfering in political matters.

Masako once called a halt to a kemari game in early 1202, when she learned that Yoriie planned to play not ten days after the death of an old and distinguished vassal, Nitta Yoshishige. In another incident, Yoriie was called away from a kemari game to judge a land suit at the special request by a high-ranking vassal Hatakeyama Shigetada. Annoyed by the interruption, he showed no interest in listening to Hatakeyama's explanation of the situation and, to the chagrin of all concerned, settled the suit by arbitrarily drawing a line through the map to divide the land in dispute into two parts. Then he rushed back to his game. These two accounts, reported by *Azuma kagami*, portray Yoriie as unfit for the position of shogun. The Nitta and Hatakeyama families later supported the Hōjō in ousting Yoriie and the Hiki, so it is quite possible that *Azuma kagami* fabricated these incidents.

At least initially, Masako may not have been as hostile toward Yoriie as *Azuma kagami* would have us believe. Masako did spend one day watching kemari and attending a party held afterward. *Azuma kagami* authors, however, emphasize Masako's anger at the syncophant kemari expert from Kyoto who presumed to suggest that one of Masako's younger brothers change his name from the one given him by Yoritomo.

If we are to believe *Azuma kagami*, Yoriie was a capricious, tyrannical, short-tempered, unfeeling egotist who wasted his days away playing ball, enjoying the company of women, and drinking with his cohorts. Not one redeeming personality trait did he display. Throughout the ages, he has been consistently damned, dismissed as a despicable young man unfit for his exalted position. This interpretation is in turn reflected in works about Masako. Critics either strive to explain away her concern for him or see in her concern a testament to strong maternal affection: Why didn't she sever relations with Yoriie, why did she bother to attend his game, unless she loved him?

The description of Yoriie in *Azuma kagami* is reminiscent of the tendency in Chinese dynastic histories: rulers who lost their hold on power are usually condemned as having been morally corrupt. The Hōjō-based compilers may have borrowed this concept of "kingship by moral mandate'' to discredit Yoriie and his Hiki supporters in order to vindicate the Hōjō, who murdered them several years later. Like his Chinese counterparts who were deprived of power due to their own moral failings, Yoriie is presented as tyrannical and debauched, rather than merely unfortunate or weak. Nevertheless, his fondness of kemari, which at first glance would seem to prove that he was not the man his father was, may have served a crucial purpose.

Shogunate relations with the court had reached an all-time low by the time of Yoritomo's death. Kamakura, under Yoriie and now at a distinct disadvantage, had to look for new channels of communication with the court. Kemari probably served as an important means of mending fences. Of course it was not the only one, but the diplomatic value of the informal affiliations established through kemari cannot be overlooked. Yoriie, in fact, secured the services of a famous instructor of kemari at Go-Toba's recommendation. Many a political missive may have traveled between Kyoto and Kamakura as a postscript to an exchange of opinion about kemari. Masako's second son Sanetomo would use the genteel art of poetry for similar purposes in his term as the third shogun. Kemari helped considerably in smoothing relations between Kamakura and the powerful ex-emperor Go-Toba and his court. Masako may not have understood the fine points of a kemari game, but there is no evidence that she condemned Yoriie for playing.

No matter what Masako's true feelings toward her son may have been, the momentum was building to depose Yoriie and set up his younger brother Sanetomo as shogun. Retainers who had been loyal to Yoritomo but found their lands being confiscated for little or no reason took a dim view of Yoriie and the Hiki. Yet as long as Yoriie was alive, there was nothing that anyone could do short of an outright insurrection, or so it seemed to everyone but Hōjō Tokimasa and Ano Zenjō. If Tokimasa could dispose of Hiki Yoshikazu, actual political power would fall into his hands. Zenjō and his wife (Masako's sister Lady Awa) also knew that their charge Sanetomo could never inherit the shogunate with Hiki Yoshikazu alive.

Zenjō was the only one of Yoritomo's half-brothers to survive him. Having earned himself the nickname "Reverend Gritty of Daigo Temple,'' this stalwart warrior-monk nevertheless took no part in the war against the Taira. Instead, he chose to stay close to Yoritomo in Kamakura and became his trusted adviser. He is known as Ano Zenjō after the former Ano Manor where he resided. Nagai Michiko's interpretation is that Zenjō was cunning enough not to overstep his bounds. This was true at least while Yoritomo was alive; with him gone, Zenjō saw a chance to take power into his own hands through his nephew, and to that end he now began to encourage Hōjō Tokimasa to move against Hiki Yoshikazu.

The Hōjō Against the Hiki

Hiki Yoshikazu had his own plans centering on his five-year-old grandson Ichiman. Yoriie had been officially appointed shogun by the court in 1202, although he had been heading the shogunate in name since his father's death. His intention to bequeath his position to Ichiman became evident in the precedence accorded the young son over Sanetomo on the occasion of the new-year visits to Tsurugaoka Hachiman Shrine in 1203. Soon after, Yoriie fell seriously ill. Yoshikazu had Yoriie issue an order that Zenjō be brought to the palace by force and charged with treason. Later, armed men were sent to capture Lady Awa as well, but by then she had already fled for protection to Masako's residence together with her ward Sanetomo. If anyone could save Zenjō, his wife, and Sanetomo from their sudden predicament, it was Masako, for she alone stood outside of Yoriie's sphere of authority. Tokimasa trusted that his daughter would act in his favor when he rushed to her residence and urged her to protect Lady Awa and free Zenjō.

Hiki Yoshikazu's son, who headed the troops milling around outside her residence, presented Yoriie's order that she turn over Lady Awa, who was accused of treason. Masako refused to comply, but she took no action to save Zenjō. Sent into exile to Hitachi province, Zenjō and his son were executed one month later. The deaths of Yoritomo's half-brother and his heir left the Hōjō and the Hiki as the most powerful contenders for real power in Kamakura.

Thereafter, Yoriie's illness grew progressively worse, and it was obvious that his days were numbered. In the autumn of 1203, he fell into a coma. In the face of his imminent death, the rights to his shogunate manors were divided between Ichiman and Sanetomo. Furious that his grandson had not been accorded exclusive inheritance rights, Hiki Yoshikazu gathered his forces; Lady Wakasa reported the injustice to Yoriie when he regained consciousness, and he called Yoshikazu to his bedside to make concrete plans for destroying Hōjō Tokimasa and his family. According to *Azuma kagami*, Masako overheard the conversation through the paper doors. She immediately dispatched a letter alerting her father. He and several allies made counter plans. Yoshikazu was invited to participate in the religious services to aid Yoriie's recovery. He was ambushed and murdered on the way. Yoshikazu's sons made preparations to attack Masako's residence, but the Hōjō and their supporters assaulted the Hiki before they could carry out their plan. All the Hiki sons were killed, and their mansion burned. Lady Wakasa and Ichiman died in the flames. This incident has come to be labeled the Hiki Rebellion.

Nagai Michiko questions the credibility of the account as summarized above. She believes that *Azuma kagami* fabricated Hiki's inheritance complaint and attack plans to shift the blame for the bloodshed onto Yoshikazu away from the Hōjō. The scene in which Masako overhears through the paper doors Yoriie and Yoshikazu plotting to overthrow the Hōjō is too contrived to be credible. Nagai has found no other contemporary reference to corroborate the report in *Azuma kagami*, and she purposely omitted this particular scene from her novel.

The Hōjō coup d'état would not have been successful had Yoshikazu and Yoriie been in close communication. If Lady Wakasa and Ichiman had been at Yoriie's side at the time of the attack, the Hōjō would not have been able to kill them. *Azuma kagami* does not make clear where the attack occurred. Wakasa and Ichiman were residing at the *kogosho* (minor palace), which sounds at first as if it were part of Yoriie's residence, the *gosho* (palace). Nagai argues convincingly that the "minor palace" was actually part of the Hiki estate, and that it was so called because Ichiman, the shogun's son, lived there. Yoriie had two other children by two other women; none of his consorts, including Lady Wakasa, actually lived with him.

Where was Masako during the attack? What role did she play in it? Did she approve of the plan to kill Ichiman and Yoshikazu? *Azuma kagami* claims that it was she who ordered shogunate vassals to attack the Hiki and eventually convinced Yoriie to take the tonsure and pass the title to his brother Sanetomo. Nevertheless, I tend to agree with Nagai, who maintains that Masako probably had little to do with the Hōjō coup d'état. As soon as Yoriie fell into a coma, she took charge of nursing him and stayed by his side, anticipating his imminent death. Masako had already lost her husband and two daughters; precisely because she had not had access to Yoriie until what seemed to be his last moment, she now dedicated herself to caring for him. She presumably knew of her father's plans, but she was not directly involved in their formulation or execution.

Why would Masako agree to the coup d'état? The traditional view holds that when forced by circumstances to choose between her son Yoriie and her own natal family, she chose the latter. Nagai does not agree. She concludes that if Masako did make a choice, it was between the Hiki and the Hōjō.[25] Yoriie's death was believed imminent; therefore he was no longer in the picture. A new shogun had to be chosen between two contenders who were still children. Ichiman would become a Hiki puppet even more manipulable than Yoriie, whereas Masako felt true affection and intimacy with the youngest of her children, Sanetomo, who had been living with her since Zenjō's death. If Masako decided not to oppose the Hōjō plot, she may very well have done so for Sanetomo's sake, little aware of the tragic end to which her choice would lead.

Women in Power*

In the aftermath of the Hiki Rebellion, Yoriie was deposed and Sanetomo was appointed shogun by the imperial court in 1203. Within a year, Yoriie died in exile in Izu. In 1205, an attempt by Masako's father and his wife Lady Maki to depose or possibly kill Sanetomo and install their son-in-law in his place was thwarted by the coalition of Masako and her brother Hōjō Yoshitoki. After exiling their father to Izu, Yoshitoki became regent and ran the shogunate together with Masako for the next two decades. They consolidated the Hōjō regime, which would wield de facto power until the fall of the Kamakura Shogunate in 1333. All this would have been impossible without Masako's approval and help. Not only did she legitimize Yoshitoki, a non-Minamoto, in taking the helm of the shogunate as her deputy in form, but she also shared with him the power and the responsibilities in policy making and administration.

Masako's favorite younger son, the third shogun Sanetomo (1192–1219), proved to be no more amenable to her wishes or fit for the leadership of a warrior government than his elder brother. Attracted to

_____
*This section was written by Chieko Mulhern.

the sophisticated court culture, the twelve-year-old shogun rejected the arranged marriage to Masako's niece and married instead the daughter of a court noble from Kyoto in 1204. He showed more interest and talent in pursuing such aristocratic vocations as poetry, music, and kemari than in carrying out his shogunal duties. In the long run, however, the shogunate's loss turned out to be literature's gain. Sanetomo matured into a superior poet to win praises from the renowned poet-critic Fujiwara Teika (1162–1241). His extant poems number 753, including a collection entitled *Kinkaishū*. Elegant in style, lofty in vision, and masculine in tone, some of Sanetomo's *waka* are well known even today. Perhaps the most famous is the following in the *Shinchokusenshū* (New imperial anthology; 1232 or 1235, compiled by Teika):

> *Let the day come*
> *When the mountains fall asunder*
> *And the oceans run dry.*
> *Never will I waver*
> *In my devotion to the sovereign!*

The sovereign admired by the young shogun is no doubt the ex-emperor Go-Toba (1180–1239; r. 1183–98), who had ascended the throne at age three and had continued to reign even after abdication. Not only was Go-Toba related to Sanetomo through their consorts, but they were bound by a common passion. Go-Toba himself was a superb poet and respected critic who actively participated in the compilation of the great imperial anthology *Shinkokinshū* (1205) and was known for his powerful and majestic poetic style.[26] One of the most autocratic and daring of Japan's emperors, Go-Toba was nevertheless susceptible to the influences of an exceptional woman who plunged headlong into the thick of court politics, eventually finding herself pitted against Hōjō Masako. It was not one of Go-Toba's many consorts but his menoto, (Fujiwara) Takakura Kaneko (1155–1229).

Kaneko had an immediate predecessor and role model in Lady Tango (d. 1216; a favorite concubine of Go-Toba's grandfather Go-Shirakawa), who had once promoted and then prevented the match between Masako's daughter Ōhime and Go-Toba. Lady Tango's power base had been made secure through her unmarried royal daughter, who was endowed with a vast estate and honored with a highest rank for women, normally given out only to mothers of emperors. But Kaneko was not an imperial consort, nor had she any children of her own. Though traditionally a line of scholars in the middle-level aristocracy, Kaneko's family connection was impressive enough at the time. Her sister was another menoto to Go-Toba, and two of her nieces were Go-Toba's consorts and mothers of emperors Tsuchimikado and Juntoku. Kaneko derived her power, nevertheless, primarily from her uncanny ability to understand her charge Go-Toba's personality and anticipate his every wish. It seemed for some time that awards of positions and promotions at Court depended virtually on Kaneko's recommendation alone. In 1207, she received the Junior Second Rank, equivalent to the rank of the Three Ministers (the First Rank was only for the chancellor).

Kaneko's political career can be traced back to 1199, coinciding with Masako's new start as a dowager nun. The forty-four-year-old Kaneko surfaced in the court roster of that year as Naishinosuke (deputy director of the Handmaids' Office). Left a widow in 1203 by her first husband (head of Go-Toba's Imperial Household Office; Great Councillor), she married in 1205 a former chancellor who was serving as a mentor to Go-Toba's son Juntoku and as Lord Superintendent of the estates of Lady Tango's daughter by Go-Shirakawa, as well as those of Go-Toba's beloved mother, who was the sole owner of thirty-five manors and the famed Minase Palace. Soon Kaneko helped arrange for her step-daughter to become consort to Emperor Tsuchimikado. She also managed to marry her two foster daughters to the most exalted men of her time, Go-Toba and the shogun, Sanetomo. She came close to engineering dramatic changes in Japan's political structure twice in her old age, with Masako cast as her costar first and then as the ultimate victor over her.

The two elderly women met in 1218, when Masako journeyed to Kyoto and conferred with Kaneko on a major matter of state. Sanetomo, the shogun, was given to grand but distinctly eccentric schemes: a year earlier, for instance, an ocean-going vessel built by his order failed to float at its launch, scuttling his unrealistic plan to visit Song China. The handsome but frail and unpopular shogun was childless. Faced with the imminent extinction of the Minamoto main line, Masako and her brother at last agreed that one way to ensure the continued health of the Hōjō regime and maintain the dignity of the shogunate was to install an imperial prince as heir to its supreme position. Personally taking on this sensitive and critical mission, Masako made what would be her last trip to the capital to seek Kaneko's advice and assistance. Masako's request was not disadvantageous to the court, and Kaneko secured Go-Toba's promise to grant his son by Kaneko's foster daughter to Kamakura as heir to Sanetomo. The joint effort of these formidable women, both in their sixties by that time, would have added a new chapter to Japanese institutional history by establishing a blood bond between the imperial court and the warrior government

Their success, however, was destined to be nullified within a year by a bloody stroke of fate. In 1219, Sanetomo was assassinated by his nephew Kugyō, the second son of the second shogun Yoriie by the Hiki daughter. Probably in the hopes of weakening the shogunate through succession disputes, Go-Toba promptly rescinded his promise to send his son to Kamakura. The assassin and his two half-brothers perished subsequently by suicide and execution, and the male line of the main house of the Minamoto came to an end, no doubt much to the satisfaction of Hōjō Yoshitoki. For their next figurehead, he and Masako settled on a court noble's son whose grandfather had been a son-in-law of Yoritomo's sister. Since the fourth shogun-to-be, Kujō Yoritsune (1218–56; r. 1226–44), was barely one year old, Masako found herself a veritable dowager shogun, obliged to assume the shogunal duties herself on behalf of the infant heir.

Dowager or not, she fully lived up to the weighty position as de facto head of a warrior government. In 1221, Go-Toba issued a mandate proclaiming Hōjō Yoshitoki as an enemy to the throne. Leading the hawks at the ex-emperor's court, Kaneko urged Go-Toba to empower an army to chastise the shogunate and regain hegemony. At Kamakura, Masako took an equally aggressive stance: overruling her brother's cautious plan to wait in defensive readiness, she adopted the offensive strategy proposed by Yoritomo's old vassals. Her tactical decision was vindicated one month later by the total victory of the shogunate forces in skirmishes with the imperial insurgents. The conflict, called the Jōkyū Incident, resulted in the lifetime exile of Go-Toba and his ex-emperor sons Tsuchimikado and Juntoku to remote islands.

Historical records are uniformly critical of Kaneko for instigating a military action that proved to be foolhardy and futile. In contrast, Masako's reputation was greatly enhanced. Her famous address to the council of vassals exhorting them to rise to the occasion in the name of their fealty to her late husband is an impassioned speech of high literary quality, as recorded in *Azuma kagami* and other sources. A school of thought does exist that suspects the speech to be a composition by the editors of *Azuma kagami*. Nevertheless, the preconceived image of Masako, which stereotypes her as an unrefined, rustic Bandō woman, is obviously unfounded, judging from the poignant style and the strong yet elegant hand gracing her letter, which still exists in possession of Kongōsanmai Temple at Mt. Kōya.

Masako demonstrated her mettle and political acumen time and again in her own right. When her brother died in 1224, his second wife and her natal family moved to monopolize major posts in the shogunate. Masako's prompt countermeasures foiled their attempt and wiped out all forces that might threaten her nephew Hōjō Yasutoki's new regency. Masako's cause, the shogunate, thrived for more than one hundred years, until it was toppled by the onslaught of events triggered by unusual disasters—the Mongol invasions of 1274 and 1281, the only direct assault on Japan by foreign powers before World War II. The combined Mongol and Korean fleets were narrowly held back by the coastal defenses and virtually destroyed by the godsend typhoon (*kamikaze*) each time.

The enormous military expenditures depleted the shogunal treasury, however, and the lack of spoils gave rise to dissatisfaction and disputes among vassals over the customary reward for meritorious service, irrevocably weakening the administration. Thereupon, another enterprising and resolute emperor, Go-Daigo (1288–1339; r. 1318–39), made repeated tries over nine years and finally succeeded in reclaiming political power in 1333, causing the downfall of the shogunate. A Kamakura vassal of a Minamoto branch line, Ashikaga Takauji (1305–58), eventually annihilated the Hōjō and established a new shogunate at Muromachi in 1336 to continue warrior rule for another century and a half.

The Ashikaga, or Muromachi, Shogunate produced the only close counterpart to Masako, albeit a negative one. Two and a half centuries after Masako's death, the eminent court scholar Ichijō Kanera (1402–81; chancellor, 1446–50; regent, 1447–70) was tutoring the eighth shogun Ashikaga Yoshimasa (1430–90; r. 1449–73) and his wife Hino Tomiko (1440–96). In *Sayo no nezame* (Sleepless evenings; 1479), an intellectual tract expounding his views on literature, on women in general, and on women in politics, Kanera cites Hōjō Masako as an exemplar: "At the time of the Jōkyū Incident, it was at the command of Lady Second Rank [Masako] that Yoshitoki took the leadership of vassals. This goes to show you that woman is not to be taken lightly." Ironically, Hino Tomiko by then had already played out her own major role, which was to brand her one of the most notorious women in Japan's history.

Tomiko had removed the legitimate heir to secure the shogun's post for her own son, Yoshihisa, by setting powerful factions against one another in armed confrontations. Unlike Masako, who is credited with the tactical insight to put a swift end to the Jōkyū Incident, Tomiko is blamed for touching off the lengthy and widespread military strife known as Ōnin Wars (1467–77), which devastated Japan for ten years, escalating into clashes among major vassals over the succession disputes of their own houses as well as the shogunate's. The Ōnin Wars turned the capital and major cities into battlegrounds, reduced them to ruins, and spelled the effective end of the Ashikaga hegemony, though the shogunate continued in name for another hundred years. Hence, Hino Tomiko has been labeled *keikoku no bijo* (beauty who wrecks the country).

Masako's age abounded in romantic and heroic tales of beautiful women. Yoshitsune's tragic mistress Shizuka had commanded admiration and popularity as a dancer with her exquisite charm as well as her talent and cool dignity. The woman warrior Tomoe, who served Yoritomo's cousin-turned-enemy Kiso Yoshinaka, was famous as much for her feminine beauty as for her invincible skill in martial arts. Even more notable in some ways was Masako's nemesis and a leader of the antishogunate faction at court, Lady Tango. A breathtaking beauty even in her thirties when she captivated the ex-emperor Go-Shirakawa and bore him a princess, Lady Tango was often compared to Yang Guifei (719–56; known as Yōkihi in Japanese), one of the best-known *keikoku no bijo* in China. When it comes to Hōjō Masako's appearance, however, historical sources are suddenly and mysteriously silent. Even *Azuma kagami*, which is generous in describing other women's looks, offers no hint as to what Masako looked like. Yoritomo has been portrayed as a man of princely mien and neat features not lacking in masculine attractiveness. No reliable source, however, has even attempted a guess at Masako's looks. Few people would imagine her to be a raving beauty in any case, but none would doubt the sincerity of her passion for Yoritomo, her one and only love, which motivated her actions throughout her adult life.

As for her personality and character, her own behavior speaks louder than contemporary comments. While she was in Kyoto negotiating for a shogunal heir, Kaneko moved Go-Toba to grant Masako the Junior Third Rank and delivered the decree herself. Masako was already a lay nun, and the award of court rank to a person in tonsure had had only one precedent—the award to the priest Dōkyō by the controversial woman emperor Kōken-Shōtoku in the eighth century. Any other recipient would have been grateful, but when Kaneko made an additional effort to arrange an imperial audience, Masako declined to be received by Go-Toba, according to *Azuma kagami*, on the ground that "such an honor is of no use to an old country nun such as herself." She promptly returned to Kamakura. This incident is a veritable study in contrasts, the actions of the two women revealing what made each such a success in her own milieu. While Kaneko displayed the quick wit and mastery of social stratagem highly valued in court circles, Masako demonstrated the rugged pride of Bandō warriors unbeguiled by such empty honors as court ranks and imperial audience, as well as their pragmatic attitude that business was no more than business and personal gain or indebtedness should be avoided.

Masako died at the age of sixty-eight in 1225, leaving the shogunate founded by her husband on a steady course steered under the tutelage of her natal family. Nepotism or not, the succession of Hōjō regents vindicated her judgment by proving themselves to be far better administrators than the Minamoto scions. Under them, Japan stabilized and prospered. The manorial feudal system, with its codified laws to govern the warrior lords, stimulated developments in agriculture, commerce, and the arts. Masako's achievements were constructive and beneficial not only to her family but also to her country.

Notes

1. Watanebe Tamotsu, *Hōjō Masako, Jinbutsu Sōsho*, vol. 59 (Tokyo: Yoshikawa Kōbun-kan, 1961).

2. Nagai Michiko, *Tsuwamono no Fu* (Tokyo: Bungei Shunjū-sha, 1978), p. 25.

3. Minoru Shinoda, *The Founding of the Kamakura Shogunate: 1180–1185* (New York: Columbia University Press, 1960), p. 36. Such other important families of the region as the Hatakeyama, Kawagoe, Miura, Chiba, and Ōba were also of Taira descent.

4. Jeffrey P. Mass, *Warrior Government in Early Medieval Japan* (New Haven: Yale University Press, 1974), p. 39.

5. Nagai Michiko, *Hōjō Masako* (Tokyo: Kōdansha, 1969), p. 24.

6. My interviews with Nagai were done in Japanese; I have translated her remarks myself.

7. The nephew, Miyoshi Yasunobu, was at this time a low-ranking official in Kyoto. Later he would hold important positions in Yoritomo's government. His aunt was Yoritomo's *menoto* (wet nurse).

8. Despite its obvious bias in favor of the Hōjō, who later ordered its compilation, *Azuma kagami* is the most reliable source for the period and the one used most extensively by Nagai Michiko.

9. Shinoda, *Kamakura Shogunate*, p. 60.

10. *Azuma kagami*, a partial translation by Shinoda in *Kamakura Shogunate*, p. 199.

11. Shinoda, *Kamakura Shogunate*, p. 238.

12. There are several readings for the characters in Lady Kame's name. Kame no Mae is the most frequent. Shinoda, however, uses the reading Kizen in his translation of *Azuma kagami*.

13. Kaionji Chōgorō, ed., "Hōjō Masako," in *Nihonshi Tanbō* (Tokyo: Kadokawa Shoten, 1973), 2:118–19.

14. *Azuma kagami* does not contain any entries for the year 1183, but later sections refer to Yoshitaka and Ōhime as married. See Shinoda, *Kamakura Shogunate*, pp. 263–64. Nagai, in *Hōjō Masako*, pp. 107–16, describes the close relationship between the two children and relates rumors to the effect that they would be married at some future date. She does not believe that they were married. My description follows Nagai's.

15. Nagai expands on this incident in *Hōjō Masako*, pp. 151–57. In her story, Masako is furious because of Yoritomo's dalliance but hesitant at being responsible for any more deaths. She therefore gets word to Nohagi of the scheme through her brother, and Nohagi leaves Kamakura. This is certainly one interpretation, but there is no evidence that it is the only one.

16. Ivan Morris, *The Nobility of Failure* (New York: Holt, Rinehart and Winston, 1975), p. 78. A chapter on Yoshitsune gives a thorough account of the legend.

17. Quoted in Watanabe, *Hōjō Masako*, pp. 53–54. The poem contains several plays on words. In Japanese, it reads "Shizu ya shizu / Shizu no odamaki kurikaeshi / Mukashi o ima ni / Nasu yoshimo gana." The most obvious word play is the repetition of the phrase *shizu*, an alternative reading of Shizuka's name. The reference to the spool of thread is a set poetic phrase, used with the word *kurikaeshi* (repeat), and alludes to a poem in the *Ise monogatari*.

18. Nagai, *Hōjō Masako*, p. 179.

19. Nagai, *Hōjō Masako*, p. 84. The legend is found in the fourteenth-century book *Hōreki kanki*.

20. Ibid., p. 83, quotations from *Jōkyūki*.

21. Nagai, in *Hōjō Masako*, p. 216, reports the rumor that the doctor sent from Kyoto was instructed to poison Sanman. This is indeed a possibility, but there is no hard evidence to support this theory.

22. Nagai, in *Tsuwamono no Fu*, pp. 323–38, relates that the strongest family

in the council was the Hiki family and their relatives. Other menoto were also included, as were Hōjō Tokimasa and Yoshitoki. Jeffrey Mass, in the *Development of Kamakura Rule: 1180–1250* (Stanford: Stanford University Press, 1979), argues that from Yoritomo's death until 1205, Tokimasa was the chief power in Kamakura. After 1203 this is true, but before that date the Hiki family was supreme. The Hōjō risked losing all power to the Hiki until they eliminated Yoshikazu and his family in 1203.

23. Another interpretation, which does not negate Yoshikazu's role, is that Lady Awa instigated the events resulting in Kagetoki's death in the hope of seeing the shogunal position passed onto her charge, Sanetomo. Nagai, *Tsuwamono no Fu*, p. 244.

24. The objective of the *kemari* game was to keep the ball from touching the ground. A player's skill was determined by the number of times he succeeded in kicking the ball, by the course the ball took, and by his way of kicking it. The players wore special leather shoes and played on a square section of the garden, over two hundred square yards in area and marked on four corners by four different kinds of trees.

25. Nagai, *Tsuwamono no Fu*, pp. 259–60.

26. Go-Toba, "Emperor Gotoba's Secret Instruction on the Art of Poetry," trans. Chieko Mulhern, *The Denver Quarterly* (Summer 1977), pp. 107–19.

6

HANI MOTOKO
The Journalist-Educator

CHIEKO IRIE MULHERN

HANI MOTOKO (1873–1957; née Matsuoka) was born into a turbulent, transitional age. In the year of her birth, Japan officially switched from the lunar calendar to the Western calendar as part of national modernization policies following the Meiji Restoration barely five years earlier, but the samurai class did not give up their swords for another three years. The 1971 statute abolishing men's top-knots took an entire decade to enforce.

Growing up in this period of constant, often drastic changes, Motoko experienced both the excitement and the challenge of being the first or the only female in each sphere of her activities throughout her life. She was among the minority group of girls (comprising less than a quarter of the two million pupils as of 1873) in Japan's modern elementary school system established by the Education Act of 1872; and she finished the eight-year program as the only girl in her grade. She was also in the first graduating class of Tokyo First Higher Women's School, a pioneer public higher school for women in Japan. In her career, she became a trailblazer as Japan's first newspaperwoman. She published a number of magazines, including the prominent *Fujin no tomo* (Women's friend), the longest-surviving women's publication in Japan. She founded a unique school, Jiyū Gakuen, dedicated to a progressive goal: the cultivation of individuals endowed with self-awareness, a sense of mission, and a spirit of independence, all of which at the time were discouraged in women, if not positively denounced as character failings.

Pioneer Women in Early Meiji

Fortunately for her and for Japan, Hani Motoko was by no means the only woman to establish self-identity, independence, and individuality in modern Japan. November 1871, two years before Motoko's birth, marked a significant occasion in the history of Japanese women: five young girls crossed the Pacific with the Iwakura Mission to study in the United States. The youngest among them was seven-year-old Tsuda Umeko (1867–1929), who would eventually graduate from Bryn Mawr College, go on to teach at Women's Higher Normal School and Peers School for Women in Japan, and found the Women's English Institute (today's Tsudajuku Women's University) in 1900. The motto of that institution was "All-round Woman" [sic]. Nagai Shigeko, nine years old at the time of the trip, returned to Japan in 1881 and eventually married Admiral Uriu Sotokichi. Ueda Teiko and Yoshimasu Ryōko, both fifteen and unable to acclimatize themselves, soon returned to Japan due to ill health. Ryōko died before long, but Teiko married a scholar of Dutch studies, Katsuragawa. (Teiko's nephew is the eminent translator and poet Ueda Bin.) Yamakawa Sutematsu (then twelve) graduated from Vassar College in 1883. She became the wife of Field Marshal Ōyama Iwoa (1842–1916, army minister in six cabinets and supreme commander in the Russo-Japanese War of 1904–5). As widow and mother of their only son, Sutematsu had the misfortune of being cast in the role of the archetypal heartless, domineering mother-in-law in Tokutomi Roka's explosive bestselling novel *Hototogisu* (Never to return: 1898–99). It was in a sense an ironic by-product of her nurse's license earned in the United States, which compelled her to remove her tubercular daughter-in-law to detached quarters within their estate and shield her naval officer son against contagion.[1] Education was still a hazardous thing for women in Meiji Japan, but there is no denying that the surviving four of the five girls all played significant roles in modern Japan, either through their own work or as wives of prominent men.

In the political field, the brightest blossom was Nakajima Toshiko (1863–1901; née Kishida, pen name Shōen) from Kyoto. She was probably the first woman to deliver public speeches and command the admiration of audiences who were generally all males. The Public Assembly Act, issued in 1880 to suppress the people's rights movement, stipulated in particular that military personnel, policemen, teachers, students, and women were prohibited from joining political organizations or attending their meetings. (These restrictions were further tightened by the 1890 Public Assembly and Political Organizations Statute, which continued to deprive women of the right to political activities until 1926, when it was amended at the insistence of women's organizations.) In 1883, Toshiko was jailed briefly when she was invited as guest speaker at the Liberal Party meeting and her speech, "Overprotected Daughters,"[2] supposedly an "academic lecture" on the state of women, was declared by police observers to border on political discussion. Thereafter she turned her efforts to expounding on women's causes through fiction. In 1885 she married Nakajima Nobuyuki (1846–99; successively, deputy chairman of the Liberal Party, chairman of the Constitution Party, first president of the Lower House). Banished from Tokyo for three years in the 1887 expulsion of certain intellectuals, the couple moved to Yokohama and engaged in teaching and writing until Nakajima's election to the Lower House in 1890.

Among the women directly inspired by Toshiko was Fukuda Hideko (1867–1927; née Kageyama) from Okayama. She was imprisoned until 1889 along with 138 codefendants for her involvement in the Osaka Incident of 1885, a plot to stage a military coup for the purpose of establishing a constitutional state in Korea free from Chinese interference. After a brief common-law marriage to the key figure of the incident, Ōi Kentarō (1843–1922; champion of the Liberal Party's radical left), she married Fukuda Tomosaku, a University of Michigan graduate. She was widowed within eight years. In 1907, she inaugurated Japan's first socialist women's publication, *Sekai fujin* (Universal woman), advocating freedom for women in politics and love. Around 1911 she opened a handicraft school in the Shinjuku district of Tokyo to teach women means of self-support.

In the meantime, Japan's first full-fledged women's association, the Tokyo Women's Temperance Society, was formed at the direct urging of the World Women's Christian Temperance Union of the United States. In 1893, the Tokyo unit developed into the Japan Christian Women's Temperance Society (Nihon Kirisutokyō Fujin Kyōfū Kai) with a nationwide network. It advocated monogamy, abolition of prostitution (more to protect women against inhumane exploitation than to stigmatize prostitutes), women's equal rights, and temperance. This organization mounted successive campaigns for the peace movement during the Russo-Japanese War, for women's suffrage, and more recently against nuclear weapons. Their postwar victory was the passage of the antiprostitution bill in 1958. The founder and first president, Yajima Kajiko (1832–1925) from Kumamoto, had become a teacher and a Christian after her divorce from a violent alcoholic husband at the age of forty-one. She eventually headed a renowned Christian women's school, Joshi Gakuin, between 1889 and 1914. She represented Japan at temperance union conferences in Boston (1906) and in London (1920).

Even more dramatic was the impact of women's achievements in the literary field at the time, when teaching in a girls' school was almost the sole means of livelihood open to educated women. Hani Motoko's aspiration toward a writing career was widely shared among educated or awakened women after 1888, when Miyake Kaho (1868–1943; née Tanabe, alumnus of Meiji Women's School) electrified the imagination of aspiring women by earning the staggering sum of 33 yen and 20 sen for her work of fiction *Yabu no uguisu* (Nightingales in the grove) when Japan's per capita net annual income was 52 yen. Kaho's theme was the conflict between traditional values and the new aspirations of Meiji women, though she clearly favored the former. Scarcely half a year later, in January 1889, the *Yomiuri* newspaper began to carry a serial novel, *Fujo no kagami* (Paragon of female virtues), by seventeen-year-old Kimura Akebono (1872–90; graduate of Tokyo Women's School). Frustrated by restrictions imposed by her famous restauranteur father, Kimura took vicarious pleasure in letting the heroine accomplish her own dreams: to study at Cambridge University, to open a factory in Japan to employ the poor, and to run a nursery to help women. In the following months, the influential fiction magazine *Miyako no Hana* published *Sankan no meika* (Exquisite blossoms in the mountains), a fictional account of a young woman's effort to aid political activists and advance women's causes, written by Nakajima Shōen, a graduate of Ferris Women's School.

A pamphlet entitled ''Meiji Literary Women'' announced the results of an 1892 poll ranking notable women in literature. Leading the list in order of high score and identified typically by their relationship to eminent men were ''Tanabe Kaho, daughter of Tanabe Taichi the statesman; Nakajima Toshiko, wife of Nakajima Nobuyuki; and Koganei Kimiko, sister of Mori Ōgai the novelist-bureaucrat.''[3] A year or so before Motoko's employment with the *Hōchi* newspaper, the first-rate fiction magazine *Bungei kurabu* offered a special issue on women writers (December 1895), which proved such a success that the format was repeated again in January 1897.

Family Background

In many cases, a woman owed her success in any field to the under-standing, insight, and idealistic visions of enlightened men whose paths happened to cross hers at each critical juncture of her life. In the family structure of the Meiji period, the first and perhaps most crucial formative factor in a girl's life was the paternal figure. The five girls sent to the United States all had fathers progressive enough to be interested in Western studies in one way or another. Two of them had been abroad before the Restoration: Tsuda Sen to the United States in 1867, and Ueda to Europe in 1862. Fukuda Hideko's brilliant mother served as her mentor and model in place of her passive father. She ran a private school until she was appointed instructor of the first prefec-tural school for women in 1872. She helped her son and Hideko to establish a school in 1883. (This school was closed down by govern-ment orders within a year, in connection with Hideko's involvement in the Liberal Party's women's auxiliary activities.)

At the conservative end of the spectrum but no less active than Hideko, Yajima Kajiko was blessed with an impressive family back-ground. Her father was an innovative village leader and samurai mag-istrate in Kumamoto, and her brother was a top disciple of Yokoi Shōnan (1809–69).[4] One of Kajiko's elder sisters was Shōnan's wife; another, married to his disciple, founded Kumamoto Women's School; and yet another was the mother of the journalist-social critic Tokutomo Sohō and the novelist Roka. After her divorce from a Shōnan disciple, Kajiko was invited to Tokyo by her brother, who exposed her to the intellectual atmosphere enlivened by his young followers and encour-aged her to earn a certificate from the teacher training center.

The founder of Tokyo Women's Medical College, Dr. Yoshioka Yayoi (1871–1959; née Washiyama), also grew up with the support of a father who was moving ahead of the times. A physician, he was one of the three subscribers of Tokyo newspapers in town. He opened the first elementary school in his village in Shizuoka and sent his daughter Yayoi to the medical school in Tokyo along with two elder sons and a promising disciple.

In the literary field, the champion of the Romantic revolution in Japanese poetry, Yosano Akiko (1878–1942; née Ōtori or Hō, depend-ing on the reading of the one-character family name), owed her educa-tion to her father. He was a confectioner of scholarly bent who demonstrated a progressiveness exceptional among the merchant class. He not only sent his heir to Tokyo Imperial University to become an engineer instead of succeeding him in the distinguished family business, but also put his daughter Akiko through Sakai Women's School and another through Kyoto Higher Women's School.

Motoko was equally fortunate. The Matsuokas were a samurai family in the service of a sublord of Nanbu clan at Japan's northeastern tip, which was a true frontier—geographically, strategically, and culturally. The clan's distinction derived primarily from being the privileged purveyor of famed Nanbu horses to the Tokugawa shoguns. Thanks perhaps to their rural setting and modest rank, which had probably necessitated that they seek supplementary farm income before the Restoration, the Matsuokas seem to have survived the loss of their hereditary samurai employment better than most and emerged as relatively well-to-do landed gentry in the Meiji period.

Motoko's father was an adopted son-in-law (*yōshi*), but he was divorced and disinherited when Motoko was eleven. Thereafter, Motoko's grandfather looked after the family's welfare. This enlightened former samurai, sternly dignified but loving, saw to it that all of Motoko's siblings received education beyond the norm. Eventually all went on to distinguished careers. Motoko's sister married a doctor in her hometown and opened Chiba Gakuen, a sewing school for girls. One of their two brothers, Matsuoka Masao, was educated in Tokyo and America and served as vice president of the newspaper *Keijō Nippō*. He is perhaps better known as the father of Matsuoka Yōko (b. 1916), a Swarthmore College graduate who has served as founder of Fujin Minsei (Women's Public Welfare) Club, chief editor of their paper *Fujin minsei shinbun*, director of the Japan-China Friendship Association, and assistant to Edgar Snow.

Women's Education

Motoko was born in 1873, the same year in which Japan's modern school system was established. At that time, elementary school enrollments represented 46 percent of all school-age boys and a mere 16 percent of girls; four years later, the figures were still only 54 percent for boys and 33 percent for girls. The secondary level was separated into an all-male middle school (*chūgakkō*) and an all-female women's school (*jogakkō*) or "higher" women's school (*kōtōjogakkō*—usually on the same level as *jogakkō* but public and, therefore, more prestigious). Nationwide, there were nine women's schools at the secondary level with a total of 600 students in 1885, which increased to only 15 schools with 2,897 students in the next ten years. Motoko, who entered Tokyo First Higher Women's School in 1889, was one of the few highly educated young women of the day by any standard. It was not until 1932 that female secondary school enrollment reached 50 percent of that of males.[5] (The college-level ratio has made an even poorer showing: 0.2 percent in 1945 and 21.9 percent in 1977.)[6]

In early Meiji Japan, there were very few schools that took women students. Technically speaking, the first government-run secondary school for women was Tokyo Women's School (1872–77), but in reality, its students were limited to the upper class girls who could afford to pay the monthly tuition of two yen (when one yen bought 1.5 bushels of rice, enough to sustain an adult for four months). Moreover, its sole purpose was to teach refined manners and the social affairs of foreign countries. Eventually this school was incorporated into Gakushūin, the Peers School. The first truly public secondary school for women was Tokyo Women's Normal School, opened in Ochanomizu in 1874 (today's Ochanomizu Women's University). Publicly financed general education became available to female students in 1889 with the inauguration of the Tokyo First Higher Women's School, the first graduating class of which would include Motoko.

Women's education on an even higher level was formalized in 1901, when the Christian educator Naruse Jinzō founded Nihon Women's College. In 1911 Arai Tsuruko, a graduate of the college, became the first Japanese woman to earn a doctorate. She received her degree from Columbia University, with a dissertation on psychology entitled *Mental Fatigue*, which was published by Columbia University Press the following year and later translated into a number of European languages. Tsuruko did not have a long life, but she was successful in combining marriage and a career. Returning from the United States in 1911, she married Haraguchi Takejirō, a professor at Waseda University, and began teaching at her alma mater. After her death, Haraguchi wrote a brief biography of his wife.[7]

When Motoko completed her secondary education in 1891, no college in Japan admitted women as yet. Meiji Japan did have one alternative, however, which was available exclusively to women. The honor of pioneering Japanese women's education belongs indisputably to

British and American Christian missionaries and their schools, and Motoko was to benefit from a Christian education. The first Christian school for women was Ferris Women's School, which opened in 1870 as the girls' division of the James Hepburn Medical Clinic and Language School. Its moving force was Mary Kidder (1834–1910). Nakajima Shōen was a graduate of and professor at Ferris. Within the same year, Ferris was followed by Tsukiji A No. 6 Women's School, which absorbed a few other schools to become Joshi Gakuin in 1889. Yajima Kajiko once served as its president. Kyōritsu Women's School (1871) evolved from the American Mission Center under Mary Bryant. (All three have college divisions today.) Between 1877 (when Tokyo Women's School was incorporated into the new Peers School, Gakushūin) and 1889 (when Tokyo First Higher Women's School opened), women's secondary education in Japan was carried on all but exclusively by eleven Christian schools funded by foreigners. There were also three non-Christian schools for women in existence: one was a sewing school; Atomi Women's School was an expansion of Miss Atomi's father's former *terakoya* (premodern neighborhood school); and nothing is known about the third, the Ueda Women's School.

The Christian schools had no restrictions as to the students' age (anywhere from nine to twenty) and the period of study (some are known to have stayed as long as nine years). They were dormitory schools, unprecedented in that they trained students in the discipline of daily living as well as in academic subjects. Unlike the public women's schools that proliferated quickly and still espoused the Confucian and feudal female virtues, Christian schools aspired to mold "modern" individuals and advance women's social status by encouraging their ability to play a full role in society. Thus, these schools contributed immeasurably to women's causes by producing dedicated leaders of women's movements and education. They propagated the idea of monogamy (against the socially sanctioned custom of keeping concubines) and cultivated women's self-identity as individuals. The Meiji Women's School, which Motoko chose for herself, was also one of the few that had been founded by foreign-educated Japanese Christian missionaries. Such Protestant values and ideals as espoused by Christian schools—dedication to labor, self-reliance, responsible work ethic, and a sense of mission—were readily accepted by the students, who found them not much different from samurai ethics.[8]

Meiji Women's School and *Jogaku Zasshi*

The second man to play a crucial role in Motoko's career was Iwamoto Yoshiharu (1863–1943). He was principal of the Meiji Women's School and chief editor of *Jogaku zasshi* (Women's learning) both six years old in 1891, when Motoko managed to get herself admitted to the school and employed by the journal simultaneously by virtue of her pertinacious appeal to Iwamoto. Iwamoto envisioned "women's learning" as encompassing knowledge in all fields that would contribute to the liberation and welfare of women, and he believed in expansion of women's rights. His image of the ideal woman can be termed the "good wife and wise mother," a combination of the Christian concept of familial roles and Confucian moralism, as expressed in his inaugural declaration: "The purpose of *Jogaku zasshi* is to educate women by providing them with a model of ideal womanhood in which both the Western concept of women's rights and Japan's own traditional female virtues are embodied." More concretely, he played important roles in the lives of four literary women: he found a teaching position for Nakajima Shōen, married the translator Wakamatsu Shizuko, arranged the marriage between Tanabe Kaho and the nationalist Miyake Setsurei, and indirectly helped Higuchi Ichiyō by starting the Romanticist literary journal *Bungakkai*, which not only published her best work but also introduced to Japan the Christian Romantic worship of women. The first, most prominent Meiji journal dedicated to the enlightenment, liberation, and happiness of women, *Jogaku zasshi* was supported by two types of readers. The majority were women who sought enlightenment and aspired toward better social status. The more significant were small yet articulate groups—progressive men with understanding and sincere sympathy for women's causes, and a number of women whose education and self-awareness matched that of educated men.

Granted, no Meiji man was more dedicated to women's education than Iwamoto, and Motoko was certainly a most resolute pursuer of goals throughout her life. But the direct and determined appeal to an influential person was one drastic measure resorted to by other ambitious Meiji women as well, often with great success. Fukuda Hideko obtained an introduction to Itagaki Taisuke (1837–1919, head of the Liberal Party) in 1884 and through his help found a philanthropist to finance her education at Shinsakae Women's School (later Joshi

Gakuin). The first Japanese woman to proclaim herself an anarchist in court, and the only woman in Japan's history to be convicted and executed for treason, Kanno Suga (1881–1911, later Kōtoku Shūsui's wife) also secured the position of *Osaka chōhō* reporter by approaching the novelist Udagawa Bunsui (reigning over the Osaka literary circle at the time) for help in 1902. Ten years later, another anarchist-feminist, Itō Noe (1895–1923), obtained an education at Ueno Women's School financed by the popular novelist Murakami Namiroku, who was moved by her letter to her uncle pleading for help. Later she was hired as assistant editor of the ill-fated feminist journal *Seitō* (Blue stockings) by its founder, Hiratsuka Raichō (1886–1971), who had been deeply impressed by Noe's fervent letter and ensuing interview. Within three years Noe, at age twenty-one, took over the helm as managing editor. A sensational scandal involving her and anarchist Ōsugi Sakae spelled the end of the journal in 1916.

Motoko's plea to Iwamoto, however, could not have come at a more opportune time. There was an ongoing controversy over the feasibility of women's higher education, which came to a head at a meeting of the Japan Women's Education Association when Katō Hiroyuki (then president of Imperial University) made a speech denouncing as optimistic and impracticable any attempts to apply men's higher education to women.[9] An advocate of Darwinian social evolutionism, Katō was speaking for the majority opinion in Meiji society. One of his most vocal and impassioned antagonists was none other than Iwamoto Yoshiharu, the champion of women's education. Iwamoto promptly counterattacked by declaring that the early Imperial University freshmen would have been easily matched in intellectual achievement by the present sophomores in Meiji Women's School. It was a confidence of no small measure, but he was deadly serious.

Motoko was admitted to the school and given a part-time editing job on the journal to pay for her room, board, and tuition. For reasons that are not clear, she withdrew before the end of the two-year advanced program, but her brief period there provided valuable experience that ultimately shaped her career. Her life in the Christian residential school taught her that a set of ideals and values could serve as working principles in the operation of the small-scale yet organic social unit that was a school. The training and ideals absorbed at Meiji Women's School eventually bore fruit in Jiyū Gakuen, which she founded with her husband. But Motoko's initiation into the world of publishing was to have an even more immediate impact on her life's course.

The Job Market for Meiji Women

Thanks largely to Christian missionaries and a handful of dedicated Japanese educators, advanced education was available to most women who wanted it badly enough. But the job market was entirely another matter. Aside from such marginal professions as teaching music, hairdressing, and midwifery, there were few decent careers for respectable women. Perhaps the most prestigious was schoolteaching, which became available to women after the passage of the 1872 Education Act. Also possible was a position as printing machine operator at the national mint, which the government opened to women in 1874. The traditional post of lady-in-waiting in the Ministry of the Imperial Household was still available, as it had been since the beginning of Japan's history, but the small number of posts and strict qualifications down to impeccable family background made it an unlikely career for most women. A nurse's training center established in 1882 opened the field of health care to women, but nursing was not for everyone.

It is no coincidence, then, that nearly all the women mentioned in this chapter were teachers, at least during part of their careers. Fukuda Hideko, for example, was appointed associate teacher upon finishing elementary school at the top of her class around 1880 with an astonishingly high starting salary of three yen a month. This high income is cited as one of the factors that enabled her to reject proposals of marriage tendered in 1881 by two men from her hometown—Inukai Tsuyoshi and Fujii Kōichi, future prime minister and admiral, respectively.[10]

In 1891, teaching was still a privileged profession for women, who comprised 5.9 percent of all teachers. (The figure would reach 48.2 percent in 1951, and 55 percent in 1977.)[11] After withdrawing from Meiji Women's School in 1892, Motoko became a teacher at an elementary school in her hometown of Hachinohe, Aomori prefecture. But she found no intellectual satisfaction or challenge in teaching at the public school or at a Catholic girls' school in Morioka, where she subsequently taught and lived among nuns from abroad. Sometime around 1895, she left her position to marry a Kyoto man, but the marriage proved a disastrous mismatch, and Motoko dissolved it within half a year and left for Tokyo.

Determined to support herself, Motoko first took a menial job as a live-in maid, by happy coincidence in the household of Dr. Yoshioka Yayoi. During her brief term as servant and then as a ''live-in student,'' Motoko had the opportunity to observe an ideal marriage between two individuals who believed in equality of the sexes. She also came in contact, if circuitously, with a number of career women, probably including Yoshioka's friend, Dr. Okami Kyōko, a graduate of Pennsylvania Women's Medical School.

Medicine was one male domain that had opened its reluctant door to women quite early in response to the dogged efforts of a single determined female, Ogino Gin (1851–1913). Having been infected with a venereal disease by her husband and then divorced, Gin resolved to become a physician to spare other women from the humiliation of being treated by male doctors. She hammered away at the Ministry of Home Affairs until eventually they gave in and conceded the eligibility of women to take the medical practice qualifying examination in 1884. The following year, at the age of thirty-four, Gin emerged as Japan's first woman doctor. Others followed. The national medical school, Tōkō (today's Tokyo University Medical College), remained exclusively male, but the only private medical school, Saisei Gakusha, began to admit women after a direct appeal was made to its founder-president Hasegawa Tai by Takahashi Mizuko, a thirty-six year old midwife. Virtually forcing her way in, Takahashi graduated in 1887 to become the third woman doctor in Japan. She later studied in Germany.[12]

Washiyama Yayoi, who later graduated from Saisei Gakusha along with fifteen other women, passed the two-stage examination in 1893. She was the 6,898th physician and the 27th woman to join Japan's medical profession. Intending to follow Dr. Takahashi to Europe, she attended Shisei School, a German language academy run by Yoshioka Arata (1868–1920). Before long she married Yoshioka and opened the Shisei Clinic across the street. Thus she was able to integrate her career with her husband's, for German was the required language in Japanese medicine. Yoshioka's language academy assumed an especially important role after 1900, when Saisei Gakusha reverted to an all-male admissions policy, and Yoshioka Yayoi turned her clinic (then with four students) into Tokyo Women's Medical Institute (today, Tokyo Women's Medical University).

In many ways, Yayoi is a close parallel to Motoko, who was two years her junior. Yayoi succeeded in making marriage and career compatible and mutually enriching without overshadowing her husband. There was much indignant criticism leveled against women engaging in such "grossly unladylike" practices as dissection of cadavers. She countered such arguments through her school's paper, *Joikai* (Women doctors' world). Both her medical school and her newspaper are alive and thriving today, headed by her physician son, although her alma mater Saisei Gakusha lasted for only twenty-seven years and closed in 1903. During Yayoi's fifty-year tenure as president, her school produced over seven thousand women doctors. She believed firmly in the "do and learn" principle, and her students were even present to benefit from the experience of her own childbirth and her miscarriage. Motoko's own *Fujin no Tomo* and her school Jiyū Gakuen betray a strong affinity for the practical approach and character of Yayoi.

Career in Journalism

Motoko had been favored with a head start in editing experience on Iwamoto's journal, and the stimulating atmosphere of Yoshioka's intellectual salon inspired her to seek a rewarding career of her own. But above all, her search for a challenging job was facilitated immensely by favorable social trends and, more specifically, by the caliber of men who happened to be in the position to decide her fate at the outset of her writing career. The man who interviewed her at the *Hōchi* newspaper was Tanomogi Keikichi, who would serve as minister of communications in 1936 in the Hirota Kōki cabinet. The chief editor who agreed to hire her was Tagawa Daikichirō, who later became mayor of Tokyo.[13] Their decision to hire a woman as copy editor and then to promote her to reporter is remarkable in view of the history of Japanese journalism.

In becoming Japan's first newspaperwoman, Motoko was only thirty years behind her male counterpart, Ōtsuki Fumihiko (1847–1928). A samurai from Sendai, he had the distinction of being the first native reporter to be hired by the first Japanese-language newspaper to carry domestic news, *Bankoku shinbun*, founded in 1867 by British missionary Buckworth M. Bailey. This paper did not survive into the modern era, ceasing publication in 1868, the year of the Meiji Restoration and the beginning of Japan's modernization. Nevertheless, its coverage of domestic affairs established an example of journalistic reportage to be followed by full-fledged modern Japanese newspapers, clearly distinguishable from the newsletter type of pre-Meiji papers that primarily transcribed foreign news items. The "new" newspapers attracted talented men, many of whom went on to prominence in other fields, such as politics, literature, and education. Japan's first news-paperman, Ōtsuki, whose most memorable report was on the capture of Abraham Lincoln's assassin, is better known as a scholar and compiler of the monumental *Genkai* (Ocean of words, 1891), the first modern dictionary of Japanese language, which is still in use today. The *Hōchi*, which took the unprecedented step of hiring a woman for a prestigious position in a relatively young profession, could boast a particularly notable roster of reporters whose subsequent career accomplishments became history. Motoko was by no means an exception in blazing a trail of her own.

Around 1897, when Motoko eased the first female foot into the editing room of the *Hōchi*, this newspaper happened to be in the pro-cess of rapid expansion. Its circulation was rising from a low of 22,000 in 1894 to what would be its high of 50,000 in 1900.[14] Inaugurated in 1872 as *Yūbin hōchi shinbun*, it had gradually taken on the character of a people's rights proponent as the staff swelled with young reporters who aspired to political careers. Among them were Ozaki Yukio (1859–1954), who later served as ministers of education and justice and became mayor of Tokyo, and Inukai Tsuyoshi (1855–1932), who was destined to become prime minister, only to be assassinated in the May 15 naval officers' coup. (His granddaughter Inukai Michiko is a prominent and prolific social critic and a highly respected interpreter of Western thoughts and social trends.) In 1881, the *Yūbin hōchi* was purchased by Yano Ryūkei (1850–1931: statesman, journalist, novel-ist), who turned the paper into the unofficial organ of the Constitu-tional Progressive party, formed the following year by Yano, Ozaki, and Inukai, among many other prominent activists.

During the 1880s, the literacy rate was still low—only about half of the adult population could read even the plebeian "small" papers (*shōshinbun*) aimed at the least sophisticated readers. A monthly sub-scription, furthermore, was expensive, at twenty to seventy sen (a half bushel of rice sold for sixty sen). (The literacy rate for draft-age males is recorded at 45 percent in 1900; it rose to 75 percent in 1912.) But in the 1890s, proliferating public newspaper reading rooms and "milk halls" (coffee shops) provided easy and free access to papers. Soon they found their way into barber shops and various waiting rooms.[15] As readership expanded and grew more diverse, inevitable changes had to be made in editorial policies.

In 1886 Miki Zenpachi had been entrusted with the marketing and management of *Yūbin hōchi* to boost its sagging circulation. When he became president eight years later, he took "Yūbin" out of the name in a symbolic change of image. On November 26, 1894, the new *Hōchi shinbun* embarked on what was to be a forty-eight year course. (It was absorbed by the *Yomiuri shinbun* in 1942 and survives today as the popular sports paper *Hōchi*.) A grand editorial manifesto in 1894 promised that it would be transformed from an intellectual ideological "large" paper (*daishinbun*) into the "most unpretentious, sophisticated, highly principled, and universal" paper possible: in short, it would become a *chūshinbun*, a popular but not banal "medium" paper.[16] The *Hōchi* readership thereafter consisted predominantly of teachers, students, government employees, soldiers, landed genry, farmers, factory workers, and merchants—segments of the population that preferred entertainment and information, such as fiction and domestic news, to political proselytizing.[17] (The first four categories of readers were prohibited by law from participation in political activities.) Miki had the marketing expertise and journalistic insight to build up the *Hōchi*'s annual distribution total from 1,715,000 in 1885, ranking eighth of all Tokyo papers, to the lead position with 6,640,000 in 1888.[18] Miki had enough practical incentive, if not purely idealistic vision, to present female viewpoints, a fresh perspective that would appeal to the new and expanding readership. An observant employer, he bestowed personal commendations on Motoko when her article raised much reader response. Motoko, on her part, squarely met both his expectations and the new reader demands.

In the early 1900s, an increasing number of women reporters were hired, spurred on by the sudden boom in newspaper journalism following the Russo-Japanese War. As a rule, however, their assignments were little more than inconsequential society tidbits and fill-in spot articles meant for female and juvenile readers. These women themselves seem to have had little to offer in the way of experience, qualification, or motivation to engage in full-fledged reporting. From time to time, male reporters poked fun at their female colleagues by slipping tongue-in-cheek personal gossip about them into the papers. The realities of the profession and the general state of women were such that even Motoko was less than optimistic about the chances for a woman in journalism. In an article entitled "New Professions for Women" in *Jogaku sekai* (January 1905), she listed some reasons why women's careers often failed to materialize. She cited the small demand for women reporters and pointed out that even if there were more demand, the majority of contemporary Japanese women were woefully lacking in common sense, life experience, and even basic knowledge, not to mention reporting skills. She lamented that the social status and the state of education at women's schools promised no immediate way out of the deplorable situation.[19]

Even in July 1913, an article on "Women Reporters in Tokyo" in *Chūō kōron*'s special issue on women (no. 294) was still saying that women reporters generally have no opinions or convictions of their own to express. Hence, it added, a woman needed no particular talent or skill to become a reporter, because all she would end up doing would be running errands for the paper or fetching a finished manuscript from a guest contributor. But the author of this article did cite a few prominent exceptions: Hani Motoko of *Fujin no tomo*, Nishikawa Mitsuko of *Shin shinfujin* (New true woman), and Shimoyama Kyōko of *Jiji shinpō* (News of the times).[20]

As a woman journalist, Motoko more than deserved the notice. She had brought competence, experience, and ambition to her post. Besides being among the small cadre of highly educated women, she was already independent and mature far beyond her twenty-four years. Her perspective had been tempered by such personal traumas as her father's marital complications, his brushes with criminal indictment and litigation in connection with business dealings, as well as by her own unfortunate marriage. She also had the instinct of a thoroughly innovative professional.

At a time when the newspaper reporter was facetiously defined as someone who described anything *as if* he were an eyewitness, Motoko's pragmatic "see and tell" approach and conscientious leg work were refreshingly original. Instead of such universal staples as tear-jerker "true stories" or popular society news, which amounted to little more than gossip about upper class ladies or glorification of their supposed virtues, Motoko endeavored to find wisdom in mundane settings. After thorough research, she wrote in a straightforward, succinct style that contrasted sharply with the pedantic bombast then prevailing in newspapers.[21] As she describes in her autobiography, which follows, she pursued social problems rather than personal anecdotes or gossip, and investigated each subject personally. She appealed to the intellectual curiosity of literate but average men and women, dealing with issues close to their daily life such as family relationships, child care, and religion in the life of laymen.

Hōchi executives and readers were not alone in their recognition, admiration, and appreciation of Motoko's talent. The president of the House of Peers, Prince Konoe Fumimaro (1891–1945) commended her for an article on the Okayama Orphanage, the largest of its kind in Meiji Japan. This orphanage, with a capacity of 1,200, was founded by Christian physician Ishii Jūji and financed by the president of Kurashiki Spinning Company, Ōhara Magosaburō (1880–1943). In view of the deep-seated Japanese aversion to caring for or adopting the children of strangers, Motoko's coverage of the institution in a national paper proved a valuable social service. Its benefactor (and the founder of the famous Ōhara museum in Kurashiki City), the philanthropist Ōhara, was delighted by her accurate and thorough representation of his cause. Some years later he voluntarily provided the necessary capital when Motoko and her husband were about to launch their first independent publishing venture, *Fujin no tomo*.[22]

Love and Marriage

Under the Meiji family code, a woman was considered virtually the property of the head of the household, and ironically, divorce often had the positive effect of freeing a woman from family control, if she were capable and aggressive enough to make her own way. For some, like Ogino Gin, Yajima Kajiko, and Hani Motoko, divorce was the event that enabled them to seek careers of their own. Not even the radicals Kanno Suga and Itō Noe were free from family pressures until they took the initiative to dissolve marriages forced upon them in their late teens.

Successful marriage played an even more significant and constructive role in the lives of many prominent women. In an age of arranged marriages, these women usually had the courage to marry for love, and they sought partners with whom they shared mutually supporting convictions and goals. Belying the persistent belief to the contrary, love matches did prove secure and fruitful in the cases of Yoshioka Yayoi, Wakamatsu Shizuko, and Hani Motoko. Perhaps the most celebrated was the union of poets Yosano Tekkan (1873–1935) and Ōtori Akiko. Akiko defied convention by falling in love with Tekkan, a married man, and shocked even the permissive literary world with her passionate love poems. Akiko eventually married Tekkan and went on to become the star of her husband's poetry journal *Myōjō* (1900–1908). Even after *Myōjō* closed, she continued to write prolifically, turning out poetry, essays in support of the women's movement, and even a translation of the voluminous *Tale of Genji* into modern Japanese. She also raised eleven children. Her accomplishments closely paralleled Motoko's. She was a cofounder and faculty member of Bunka Gakuin, which opened its doors in 1921 and eventually expanded to include today's college division.

At their most unfortunate, love matches often led to tragic endings, as in the case of Kanno Suga. In 1906 she married Arahata Kanson (1889–1981), a Christian-turned-Bolshevik and a colleague on the radical socialist paper *Muro shinpō*. A few years later Kanson was imprisoned, and during his incarceration, Suga became romantically involved with anarchist Kōtoku Shūsui. Ultimately she implicated him in an aborted plot to assassinate the emperor, which ended in death sentences for both of them. Similarly, in 1916, Itō Noe abandoned her husband, Dadaist writer Tsuji Jun (1884–1944) and one child, to live with anarchist Ōsugi Sakae. This notorious union, which resulted in the cessation of the feminist journal *Seitō*, was cut short seven years later when both were murdered by the dreaded *kenpeitai* (thought-control police) in the aftermath of the Great Kantō Earthquake.

Motoko's marriage was by no means sensational or adventuresome, but it was no less fateful. Hani Yoshikazu (1880–1955) came into her life sometime during her four years at the *Hōchi*. Their courtship was far from smooth for various reasons. Motoko was divorced and older than Yoshikazu by seven years. She was also from the northeast, a region considered culturally disadvantaged, and she was not a raving beauty by any standard. Yoshikazu was the tall and handsome son of a samurai family of the former Chōshū domain, which had considerable prestige then, thanks to the powerful Chōshū clique in the Meiji government. Even before he joined the *Hōchi*, Yoshikazu won an essay contest in Tokyo, but the panel of judges included socialist Sakai Toshihiko (1870–1933, later a member of the Japan Communist party and antiwar leader of the Labor and Farmers party). Even this indirect contact with a known socialist was enough for the public middle school to force Yoshikazu to leave. He went to Tokyo, lived for a time at Yano Ryūkei's house as a live-in student, and began working as a reporter on his paper.

Both equally talented, ambitious, and independent, Yoshikazu and Motoko were able to marry without family interference from either side, but the newspaper was not yet ready to condone a love match within its offices.[23] Soon after marrying Yoshikazu in 1901, Motoko resigned under unspoken social pressure, and Yoshikazu was transferred to head the Niigata bureau of the *Mainichi shinbun*, then under *Hōchi* management. In 1903, however, he was invited back to Tokyo as editor-in-chief of the new *Denpō shinbun* (1903–6).[24] Short as they were, Yoshikazu's *Denpō* days had a significant bearing, if obliquely, on Motoko's life. Among Yoshikazu's subordinates were the poets Kubota Utsubo and Kawai Suimei, both older than he. Their continuing friendship eventually yielded the most comprehensive biography of Motoko to date. It was written by Suimei's novelist wife, Shimamoto Hisae (b. 1893), and is available in her book, *Meiji no joseitachi* (Meiji women, 1966).

Meanwhile, Motoko worked for the journal published by the Women's Education Association, and in 1903 she inaugurated *Katei no tomo* (Friend of the home, 1903–8) and became its sole editor and writer. When the *Denpō* was sold in 1906, ultimately to merge with the powerful *Tokyo nichinichi shinbun* (today's *Mainichi*), Yoshikazu joined Motoko at *Katei no tomo*. In 1908 they parted with their publisher and set out to launch the *Fujin no tomo*, which is today the longest surviving periodical for women in Japan.

Women's Publications

After Iwamoto Yoshiharu pioneered in the field with *Jogaku zasshi*, a host of monthlies rode the wave of the women's movement as it gained momentum in the 1880s. Women's publications around the turn of the century fell roughly into two types. The majority consisted of commercial magazines put out by large publishing houses that supported nationalist sentiments by reaffirming the traditional family, the established social structure, and customary female roles. Their readership was predominantly upper middle-class women.[25] More significant, however, was a small but diverse group of privately financed publications that appeared early in the century: *Katei zasshi* (Home magazine, 1903) was edited by radicals including Sakai Toshihiko, Osugi Sakae, and his wife Hori Yasuko; close behind followed Fukuda Hideko's socialist monthly *Sekai fujin* (1907), the Hanis' *Fujin no tomo* (1908), and the feminist journal *Seitō* (1911). Different as their causes were, these publications each urged women to establish self-identity, while denouncing the traditional "way of women."

Sekai fujin continued for thirty-seven issues, its pages providing a platform for political activists Kōtoku Shūsui, Sakai Toshihiko, and Katayama Sen. In the struggle for revolutionary social reform, they blazoned the banner of radical freedom, advocating the liberation of women from all traditional laws, customs, and moral codes that would "enslave" and destroy their potential. *Sekai fujin* was shut down by a government injunction within two and a half years because of its socially constructive campaigns, such as fund raising for pollution victims in the Ashio Copper Mine incident, and a petition to amend the repressive Public Peace Preservation Statute. This spelled an effective end to the political career of the paper's publisher-editor, Fukuda Hideko.

Seitō, the first women's journal published solely by women, announced the birth of the "new woman" in Japan. Its first editor, Hiratsuka Raichō (1886–1971, real name, Okumura Akiko), shocked the intellectual world with her celebrated inaugural declaration (September 1911): "In the beginning, woman was the sun, the genuine human being. Now she is but a moon—dependent on others for existence and unable to do anything more than reflect the glory of others—an infirm pallid moon. . . . She must return to her original state of glory." Inevitably, Raichō's call for women to regain the equal, if not superior, status enjoyed by Japan's mythical Sun Goddess Amaterasu was answered by her comrades most conspicuously in the form of explicit pursuit of sexual freedom. Raichō herself made public her own cohabitation with a younger painter in 1914.[26] The image of the "new woman" was irreparably tarnished when a tour of the red-light district and public drinking by the *Seitō* members provided a sensational cause célèbre for the hostile press's moral crusade, inflaming public outrage and suspicion against radical feminist movements. In the end, however, what undid *Seitō* was its own slogan of free love. Raichō's protégée and successor Itō Noe abandoned her editing duties in 1916 when she moved in with anarchist Ōsugi Sakae. Ōsugi insisted on maintaining his relationship with another *Seitō* member, Kamichika

Ichiko (1889–1981), as well as with his legal wife and comrade, Hori Yasuko. The complex four-way affair led to the arrest of Kamichika, who knifed Ōsugi. In the aftermath of the scandal, *Seitō* failed to resume its publication for lack of a managing editor.

The radical leaders of the feminist movement and their publications succeeded in their initial purpose of awakening Japanese society and raising women's consciousness, if by sheer force of shock alone. The careers of many women were launched through these publications, and some went on to make lasting marks as politicians, journalists, educators, and novelists. Yet there is no denying that their creeds, actions, and methods were often counterproductive, actually retarding the attainment of their goals, as well as impeding later women's movements. Their objectives were carried out to real and permanent success by less flamboyant organizations such as the Japan Christian Women's Temperance Society and the Shinfujin Kyōkai (New Women's Association). The latter in particular produced prominent political figures who championed women's causes in society's main arena: Ichikawa Fusae (1893–1981), who in 1953 began her long and distinguished career as a Diet member; and Oku Mumeo (b. 1895), the highly visible and effective leader of the powerful Housewives League, which she helped organize in 1948 and built into the respected consumer lobby it is today. On another front, emotional, if not sexual, freedom was not only propagated more effectively but even crystallized into a passionate apotheosis of life and humanism in the sensuous splendor of Romantic poetry by Yasano Akiko. While giving expression to long-repressed female sensuality, she had the courage to sing against the ideology of fanatic patriotism and its glorification of death during the Russo-Japanese War, as in her daring poem, "Die Not, My Brother."

Although far less spectacular by comparison, the contributions to women's welfare made by politically neutral magazines such as *Fujin no tomo*, *Fujin kōron* (Women's forum, 1916), and *Shufu no tomo* (Housewives' friend, 1917) have been significant and continuous, as attested to by their very survival today, over seventy years hence. *Fujin kōron* originally catered to a readership of well-educated, often single, career-oriented younger women, while *Shufu no tomo* attracted less ambitious home-bound wives and future brides. Both journals, however, have adjusted their editorial policies and format to respond to the changing times. Today, neither is above resorting to such circulation-boosters as contests for the best account of "my first sexual experience" or pseudo-medical sex counseling. Nevertheless, they successfully disseminate knowledge of all kinds and encourage new research into issues neglected by scholars and journalists. These publications provide nationally prominent and prestigious platforms for free-lance women reporters, and they have launched the careers of many nonfiction writers. As more women armed with bilingual competence (considered in Japan to be an aptitude predominant in females) join the ranks, these journals carry an increasing amount of foreign news. *Shufu no tomo*, for example, sent a noted "single career girl turned nonfiction writer," Kamisaka Fuyuko, to interview Nancy Reagan soon after she became First Lady. (The customary "introduction" fee paid by this magazine later played an unwitting role in the resignation of presidential adviser Richard Allen.)

Most Japanese women's magazines are far more substantial in volume and content than American ones. *Fujin kōron*'s monthly issue is soft cover but about the size of an average hardcover book, with four to five hundred pages. They boast diverse authorship, including scholars, politicians, physicians, and social and household critics, in addition to well-known writers. They cover subjects ranging from nuclear disarmament to the discussion of whether or not tea serving in the office should continue to be considered part of every girl's job. *Shufu no tomo* is larger, with the same sheet dimensions as *Time* magazine, but nearly three hundred pages long every month. It offers an even wider range of content, including travel abroad, flower arrangement, monthly poetry and essay contests, and investigative reports. All the magazines carry at least two serial novels by famous authors.

Of the countless magazines for women thriving in Japan's literary market today, *Fujin no tomo* is unique: it has preserved its journalistic dignity into the 1980s and remains a refreshing and reassuring, if somewhat didactic, source of practical wisdom in daily life. The readership is still the same—women of all ages, well-educated, with upper middle class family status and financial standing. In short, *Fujin no tomo* has been carrying on the visions of its founders. Under Motoko and Yoshikazu, this magazine took up issues such as the liberation, employment, and emotional life of women; it discussed consumer unions and women's suffrage and dealt with problems of agriculture, household budgets, health control, and family maintenance, in addition to marriage and education of children.[27] Ultimately, the motto of *Fujin no tomo*, "daily life in itself is education," led to the creation of a school meant to be a viable organic milieu in which pupils learn through the experience of running their own lives.

Gestalt Education

Jiyū Gakuen, founded by Motoko and her husband in 1921, was not the first school to espouse so-called free education (free in the sense of independence from Ministry of Education directives). Four years earlier, Seijō Gakuen had been opened on the principles of respect for individuality, self-study, and self-control. But Jiyū Gakuen was managed and taught by the Hani family themselves, who were not professional educators. Their success, nevertheless, was acknowledged by their peers in 1932, when Motoko was chosen to represent Japan at the World New Education Conference in Nice. Motoko is sometimes called the mother of free education. One of the wonders in Jiyū Gakuen's history is how it managed to retain the nearly taboo word *jiyū* (literally, freedom or liberty) in its name throughout the repressive wartime period. The answer may lie in the nature of its "free education" and the meaning of the word jiyū.

At the outset, in the heyday of Taishō (1912–26) democracy, Jiyū Gakuen's name was often misconstrued to mean a school where students were free to study completely without guidance or restraint. Motoko was frequently obliged to explain that jiyū at her school was diametrically opposed to the liberalism based on individualism or the willfulness of libertinism, and that the school's name was derived from a passage in the New Testament (John 9:31–32): "If ye continue in my word, then are ye my disciples indeed; and ye shall know the truth, and the truth shall make you free."[28] In an article entitled "Goals and Methods of Education" (1947), Motoko states that the ultimate goal of education is to create a truly free individual (*shin no jiyūjin*).[29] She elaborates on her statement with biblical quotations from Matthew (6:26, 28, 34): "Behold the fowls of the air. . . . Consider the lilies of the field, how they grow . . . for the morrow shall take thought for the things of itself. Sufficient onto the day is the evil thereof."

Motoko's concept of jiyū, however, was not exclusively Christian or Western-oriented. Her husband Yoshikazu in particular had had a solid knowledge of Chinese classics instilled at an academy of Chinese learning before he became a newspaper reporter at the age of seventeen. After prayer services at Jiyū Gakuen, he often discussed quotations from the Analects of Confucius that corresponded to the passages in the Bible and told the students to memorize them in pairs.[30] When invited to speak at the commencement of the boys' division in 1943, social critic Miyake Setsurei made a speech on the concept of freedom, stressing that the word jiyū was not a translation of an idea imported from abroad after the Meiji Restoration. As an example of the pre-Meiji use of the term jiyū, Miyake quoted a poem by Hashimoto Sanai (1834–59), a samurai scientist executed for political activism: "Is a lord with fine fur coats and stout horses to be revered? Nay! For I am freer."[31]

In their character, their conviction, and their lives, Motoko and Yoshikazu synthesized the Protestant and Confucian ideals of self-sufficiency, hard work, and proud independence. The first campus building at Jiyū Gakuen, designed by Frank Lloyd Wright in 1922 and still standing in Mejiro (today housing the alumni craft shop), symbolizes the tranquil yet powerful interplay of Western and Oriental cultures which the Hanis sought to encourage. A photograph of Motoko in volume 14 of *Hani Motoko chosakushū* (Complete works of Hani Motoko) bears the Jiyū Gakuen motto in her own handwriting: "Thinking, Living, Praying." The Hanis' concept of jiyū might be summed up as "freedom to believe in Christ, freedom to think for oneself, and freedom to shoulder life's responsibilities." The social climate of the day, however, defined female virtue as silent, unquestioning obedience, which suggests the enormity of their task in educating young girls in particular. They created a school that would serve as a gestalt of actual living where students not only study and pray but function as social beings. At the time it was almost revolutionary to suggest that sheltered children of privileged families carry out all menial tasks such as cleaning and cooking at school, but at Jiyū Gakuen such work was part of the curriculum.

For the first fourteen years, the Jiyū Gakuen in effect strove to cultivate the "good wife and wise mother" who could function without depending on servants, that is, a typical middle-class housewife by today's standards. At the time, however, it was decidedly too progressive an idea to be accepted by society at large. It was only through the material privation and hardship brought on by World War II and continuing in the postwar period that Jiyū Gakuen's philosophy was vindicated. After the boys' division was added in 1935, the students built Japan's smallest hydroelectric plant on the campus, established and staffed childcare centers in six prefectures, bred hogs and trout, and developed a farm at Nasu that supplied food for their dormitory. As the war progressed, older students were assigned to work in arms factories, but the remaining students earned a six-year grant from the Gakushi-in imperial academy for their research project on frost (which may have been considered beneficial to military efforts in controlling frostbite).[32]

In view of such worthy activities, even the militarist authorities probably failed to find any reason to insist that the word jiyū be dropped from the school name. True, students' parents included bureaucrats, intellectuals, and well-to-do people with influence, but a primary factor affecting official consideration may well have been their branch school in China, Jiyū Gakuen Peking Seikatsu Gakkō (Living School), opened in 1938. Until the end of the war, Jiyū Gakuen teachers and students provided postelementary school instruction in craft and housekeeping to Chinese girls from underprivileged families in Peking. Of the first twenty who finished the program, seven were chosen to go to Japan for further study. Three other groups were sent to Japan in the seven years of its operation. Official recognition of their private philanthropic project came as early as 1939 when Prince Takamatsu, on a tour of Peking, presented a monetary award from the Imperial Privy Purse.[33]

Conclusion

In many ways, Hani Motoko was a unique figure in the history of Japanese women. Along with other successful women of her period, she shared the influence of Christian education, a driving sense of mission, and the belief that women could earn a meaningful place in modern society by making individual contributions. Nevertheless, unlike the five girls who went to the United States, and unlike Tanabe Kaho, Kimura Akebono, and Nakajima Shōen, who were born in wealthy or influential families, Motoko was totally without social advantages. She faced a competitive metropolitan society and established a place for herself through individual effort and intelligence alone. Unlike women who benefited directly or indirectly from their husbands' fame and guidance, Motoko built her reputation as publisher and educator in a joint effort with her husband throughout the course of their marriage. Unlike Tsuda Umeko, Higuchi Ichiyō, and many other women who forfeited marriage by choice or circumstance,

Motoko chose her own mate. Not only did she make her marriage compatible with her career, but she even succeeded in making marriage and career mutually enriching. She wrote in her autobiography, "Our home has been the center of our work, and our work has been an extension of our home life: the two are completely merged without demarcations of any kind. I am truly grateful for this ideal union that is the very essence of both our work and marriage. Together, we have found our place in life."

Unlike Shōen, Shizuko, and Akebono, who all fell victim to tuberculosis at regrettably young ages, Motoko was fortunate enough to retain her vitality till the end of her eighty-four years. Still more fulfilling, her ideal marriage was blessed with outstanding offspring. Her eldest daughter, Setsuko (1903–87), became a social critic, wife of the leftist scholar Hani Gorō (1901–83), and mother of film director Hani Susumu (b. 1928). Motoko's youngest daughter, Keiko (b. 1908), headed Jiyū Gakuen and supervised publication of *Fujin no tomo*. Most important of all, Motoko's accomplishments are very much alive and thriving today. Eight decades after its inception, *Fujin no tomo* still enjoys a wide circulation and is staunchly supported by a nationwide group of loyal readers, the half-century-old Tomo no Kai (Friends' Association) of some thirty thousand members. When this association held conferences on home economics at 331 locations in 1971, the meetings were attended by more than fifty thousand participants.[34] Jiyū Gakuen, which began with twenty-six girls in 1921, is now a highly respected institution offering continuous coeducation from kindergarten through college.

Motoko on Motoko

The following translation of Hani Motoko's autobiography, *Hansei o kataru* (Speaking of my past; August 1928), is abridged so as to chronicle the life of an enlightened Japanese woman. It primarily covers her childhood, education, family life, career experience, and ambitions, up to her marriage. The second short piece, *Kaiko to tenbō* (Reflections and perspectives; March 1928), sums up her next quarter century, in which her goals were attained and her causes were shared and carried on by her readers and students. Since both pieces are addressed to the readers of *Fujin no tomo* and parents of Jiyū Gakuen students, her style is often didactic, personal, and informal. Toward the end in particular, her tone takes on the fervor of a rousing speech, but it reflects the urgency and sincere concern felt by the Japanese under the mounting tension and ominous shadows of impending crisis, as Japan and all of East Asia were plunging into chaos.

A half century later, Hani Motoko and her husband are far from forgotten or relegated to the past. In recent years, Yoshikazu's life and contributions have caught the attention of women's studies specialists in their search for more cooperative and constructive male-female relationships as workable alternatives to the antagonistic ones advocated by the feminists of the 1960s or the doomed efforts of Meiji and Taisho radicals. Exceptional as her life may be, Hani Motoko's narrative vividly illuminates the state of women in modern Japan and provides some answers to universal issues concerning the integration of personal life and career, and the reconciliation of female self-awareness and traditional roles.

Notes

1. Kimura Ki, *Kaigai ni katsuyakushita Meiji no josei* (Meiji women abroad) (Shibundō, 1963), pp. 58–59.

2. Reproduced in Itoya Toshio, *Josei kaihō no senkushatachi* (Pioneers in women's liberation) (Shimizu Shoin, 1975), pp. 37–45.

3. Quoted in Shioda Ryōhei, *Meiji joryūsakkaron* (A study of Meiji women writers) (Nara Shobō, 1965), p. 65.

4. Yokoi Shōnan was the leader of Jitsugakutō, a late-Edo progressive reform faction advocating pragmatic learning, an end to the isolation policy, and alliance of the imperial loyalist with the shogunate supporters. He was assassinated in 1869.

5. Ōi Minobu et al., *Nihon joseishi* (A history of Japanese women) (Yoshikawa Kōbunkan, 1962), p. 245.

6. Yamashita Katsutoshi et al., "Kinryoku sengoshi" (A history of postwar monied power), *Shūkan Asahi*, August 25, 1978, p. 154.

7. Kimura, *Kaigai ni katsuyakushita Meiji no josei*, pp. 188–98.

8. Murakami Nobuhiko, *Meiji joseishi* (History of Meiji women) (Rironsha, 1973), 1:374.

9. History repeated itself in the 1960s, if with more journalistic fanfare and a chorus of agreement from many quarters, when a professor published an article warning that women students would cause the downfall of the nation. His worry: females, with their generally higher examination scores, seemed to be crowding late-blooming males out of the extremely limited space in Japan's colleges.

10. Koyama Itoko, "Fukuda Hideko," *Jinbutsu Nihon no joseishi*, (Famous women in Japanese history) (Shūeisha, 1978), 11:128.

11. Murakami, *Meiji joseishi*, 3:353–54.

12. Nishikawa Yūko, "Yoshioka Yayoi," *Jinbutsu Nihon no joseishi*, 12:288–30.

13. Yoshimi Kaneko, "Hani Motoko," *Jinbutsu Nihon no joseishi*, 12:205.

14. Yamamoto Taketoshi, *Shinbun to minshū* (Press and the people) (Kinokuniya, 1973), pp. 132–33.

15. Ibid., p. 50.

16. Ibid., p. 74.

17. Ibid., p. 138.

18. Nishida Taketoshi, *Meiji-jidai no shinbun to zasshi* (Shibunsha, 1963), p. 13.

19. Quoted in Murakami, *Meiji joseishi*, 3:316.

20. Ibid., pp. 318–21. *Jiji shinpō* was founded by Fukuzawa Yukichi, the progressive intellectual leader, in 1822 and was published until 1936.

21. Ibid., 2:315.

22. Shimamoto Hisae, *Meiji no joseitachi* (Meiji women) (Misuzu Shobō, 1967) p. 414.

23. It was not until the 1970s that a woman won a suit against a firm that had fired her but not her husband on account of their office marriage; she was not reinstated, but the court's monetary award to her was considered a major victory by feminists and her supporters.

24. Shimamoto, *Meiji no joseitachi*, pp. 416–19.

25. Nishida, *Meiji-jidai no shinbun*, p. 221.

26. Takenishi Hiroko, "Hiratsuka Raichō," *Jinbutsu Nihon no joseishi*, 11:63–64.

27. Takana Natsumi, *Fujin no tomo* in *Nihon kindai bungaku daijiten* (Encyclopedia of modern Japanese literature) (Kōdansha, 1977), 5:351–52.

28. Hani Keiko, *Jiyū Gakuen no kyōiku* (Education at Jiyū Gakuen) (n.p., n.d.), p. 90.

29. Ibid., p. 91.

30. Ibid., p. 99.

31. Ibid., p. 100.

32. Ibid., "Chronology: 1921–1975."

33. Ibid., p. 114.

34. "Tomo no Kai News," *Fujin no tomo* (January 1972), pp. 266–69.

STORIES OF MY LIFE

HANI MOTOKO

AUGUST 31, 1923: It is an uncommonly clear day on the Karuizawa plateau as I sit tranquilly at my desk, here to unroll the scroll of my life, a scroll dear to my heart, but far from neatly delineated.

Childhood

I was born on September 8, 1873, in the former Nanbu clan castle town of Hachinohe. The local climate was by no means ideal, inflicting such stubborn and common native ailments as frostbite and ague. Luckily, none of the children in our family suffered from any of these indispositions. I was considered a particularly hardy child, but in my early teens I developed a drawn-out case of scrofula that necessitated regular visits to the local outpatient clinic. Environmental hygiene and personal cleanliness in those days left much to be desired. Today ague is rare even in my home town, and children enjoy better health thanks to improved sanitary conditions. My mother had pockmarks on her face, a reminder of childhood smallpox, but I remember being vaccinated at a local clinic along with other small children, most of whom were crying. I seem to have been an observant child; the doctor reported later that I had called him *ojii* [grandpa] because he was about the same age as my grandfather, my mother having presented her father with a grandchild before he was forty years old.

In elementary school, each pupil carried a wooden identification tag hanging from his or her *obi*. Every so often I would gleefully read out the notation on my tag: "No. 6, Nagayoko-cho, Hachinohe, Aomori prefecture; Granddaughter of Tadataka, former samurai: Matsuoka Moto, 5 years, 9 months old." The new school year must have started in May those days (rather than in April as today), for the record of my age on the tag indicates that I entered elementary school in May 1879. It is winter in our region for almost half a year. Toward the end of April and the beginning of May, plum, cherry, peach, and pear trees

---

"Hansei o kataru," in *Hani Motoko chosakushu*, vol. 14, pp. 1–93 (Fujin no Tomosha, 1974); abridged and translated by Chieko Irie Mulhern.

begin to bloom, and adults and children also come to life, once again enjoying the warmth of the sun and the firmness of snowless earth under their feet. As a new first grader, I, too, must have been exhilarated.

On my way home from school one day, I left my umbrella leaning against a fence near the school and wandered away in search of pebbles to play with. By the time I returned, my umbrella was gone. I began to look for it, and then two older girls told me that a man had taken it to the police box nearby. I was surprised, but more chagrined. I had left the umbrella there only for a moment. Why did anyone have to turn it in, as if it were an item for the lost and found? I hesitated, and then marched indignantly into the police box and demanded my umbrella back. After a few questions, a smiling policeman behind the front desk gave it to me. Even now I remember the frustration of being unable to convince him that I had not lost it but simply left it there until I retrieved it later. It seems that I was not a sweet or endearing child, and I never even told my family about the incident. It eventually came out when a rice dealer dropped by our house and mentioned in passing that the policemen were still talking about the brave little girl who had come alone to claim her umbrella.

In school, upperclass girls ruled the younger pupils with an authority second only to the teacher's. While most of my friends ingratiated themselves with the older ones and enjoyed the benefits of their patronage, I failed to gain favor and was constantly tormented by their spiteful bating. "Whenever you-know-who shows up, I get a nosebleed," a ringleader once announced to her group, flaunting a piece of paper stained with red ink in my face. An older cousin of mine frequently needled me to the point of tears, and then she would try to humor me by making a big joke of it all. Rather than go crying to my family, at such times I mused about why people disliked me; but childish and naive, I never did find out. I suppose older people found my subjective nature irksome, for I clung tenaciously to my own ideas and beliefs. Had I been open enough to confide the umbrella incident to my mother, for instance, she might have explained to me that the roadside is no place to leave one's possessions, even for a while. Already at that age, I was fully capable of rational and logical thinking; with proper guidance I might have learned to be grateful to the person who picked up my umbrella and to the busy policeman, as well as suitably remorseful for having caused them needless trouble. Unfortunately no such moral guidance was forthcoming to correct my willful self-centered tendencies. My family was not uncaring nor negligent, but in those days no one, even in the more educated families, knew better. Not until many years later did I realize that my mother was particularly naive and untutored.

Another handicap I bore throughout my life was an incredible lack of manual dexterity. I was good at bouncing a ball, but juggling bean bags, shooting marbles, or skating defied all my efforts. Drawing class, in particular, was exquisite torture, for while my hands were slow and clumsy, my brain was meticulous. In drawing, I could not tolerate the slightest deviation from the model, but it was a painful as well as hopeless task trying to satisfy such fastidious standards with my awkward hands. I would accept nothing less than perfection in anything. I must admit that the best of my natural attributes were nurtured by this peculiar idiosyncrasy, but at the same time, it stifled lesser talents, depressed me, and inconvenienced people around me. How I wish my parents and grandparents had been alert enough to do something about the stubborn and self-defeating proclivities of their little girl! I do not mean to sound resentful, but childrearing should begin with careful attention to such needs and idiosyncrasies.

I had enormous difficulty reciting the simplified forms of the addition tables. Instead of chanting "one and one is two" by memory I must have been laboriously computing them in my head, "one plus one equals two." For days I agonized over addition, until one evening I finally confided in my grandmother. Crying with rage, "Why can't I do it?" I roved from room to room pulling her by the hand. My grandfather tried to pacify me by going over the addition tables, but I was too distraught and obstinate to listen or understand. Finally, in the middle of the night, he lit a paper lantern and went to call on the school principal for advice.

For most school subjects such as history, geography, science, Japanese literature, *kanbun* (Chinese writing), and arithmetic, there were readers, and I poured studiously over them, applying myself as best I could. All through my school years, I received perfect grades on examinations and quizzes and double and triple circles of excellence in composition. I do not recall ever consciously competing with other pupils. In retrospect, I think this lack of competitiveness came from my impulse to pursue knowledge for its own sake in all fields and from my need for self-satisfaction—it was steadfast perfectionism on the one hand but a troublesome quirk on the other. I was inspired with growing intellectual curiosity that was quite unrelated to class standing or grades, and I even developed a taste for Chinese classics after avid reading on my own, though my teachers provided no historical perspective.

In my day, elementary school was divided into four lower grades, two middle and two upper grades. Boys' and girls' schools were separate, but in our area the number of girls dwindled to five or six by the time we reached the fifth grade, and so we were absorbed by the boys' school. In the eighth (and last) grade, I was the only girl in my class, although there had been at least three girls in previous senior classes. My thirst for knowledge intensified as I grew older. The experience of coeducation helped expand my horizons beyond a small subjective cosmos, enabling me to assess people and the world around me objectively. Every morning as girls entered the school gate, the boys would harass us from the upstairs windows, shouting nicknames they had assigned to each of us—I was known as "sweet roll." At first it was distressing. The teachers were either unable to control the boys or did not consider the situation serious enough to intervene, and the pestering continued. Before long, however, we became aware of a curious phenomenon: whenever we passed any of the boys alone on the street, he would usually look away or blush, except for a few brave ones who scoffed roguishly. Thus we discovered male vulnerability. It was enlightening to discover that the boys who were most abusive and loud in a group tended to be the most helpless when alone. Once several girls from different classes joined forces to waylay one particular boy on his way home and teased him with silly comments. "Look, what a big mouth he has," we derided him.

One incident in sixth grade left an indelible mark on me. The class was composed of two dozen boys and a handful of girls. We were reading aloud from a geography textbook filled with exotic names such as Hottentots and Bichambumbs, when someone near the teacher's dais broke wind audibly. The pupils roared with laughter and the teacher hurried out of the room clutching his book, probably to avoid laughing in front of the class. The boys pointed at a girl named S, seated behind me. I alone called out the name of the boy sitting next to S, whose guilty expression gave him away. But S, too, was blushing profusely—a reaction quite understandable under the circumstances. In the end, I somehow lost confidence and let myself be overridden by the boys. Stuck with an embarrassing nickname, S grew pale and with-drawn, dropping further and further behind in her grades.

I now regret that I failed to assert my almost certain knowledge of the culprit. On the one hand, I learned never to let an opportunity to slip away, but to grasp it firmly and quickly. On the other hand, I was sorry that if S was indeed innocent, she lacked the courage and confidence to defend herself against unjust accusation. I remember watching afterward to see if the boy B would use S's newly acquired nickname. And he used it as loudly and brazenly as the other boys. If, as I believed, he had been the guilty one, perhaps he secretly suffered as he witnessed the fate of S who carried the burden of his "crime." How horrible if he was shameless enough to feel no pangs of conscience!

It was nothing more than a trifling incident in a classroom. Today [1928] youngsters with a sense of compassion and more cultured manners would be considerate enough not to make an issue of such an indelicate occurrence—or so I would like to believe. Our class magnified the trivial incident all out of proportion, to the point where a decent young girl was condemned to despondency and anguish—though we cannot be directly blamed for her death. Why did I not make the effort to find out the truth from S? If she was being tormented in B's place, I should have comforted her, or I should have enlisted the help of the other girls in confronting B until he publicly vindicated S. Despite my conviction that it was B, I lacked the integrity and judiciousness to do anything on S's behalf, while she was in no position to speak up for herself. She moved up to the seventh grade with me, but died before the end of the school year after prolonged illness, leaving me the only girl in my grade.

The boys' attitude toward me gradually changed until I was no longer harassed. Perhaps the S incident had affected them too. Fortified by two years of experience in coeducation rather rare in those days, I was not afraid to be alone among them. By no means gregarious by nature, I developed no close association with any of them. I sat a little apart from the rest of the class, observing the boys quietly. Some were ingenuous and open, others remarkably intelligent, some were good-natured but not bright, others boisterously cheerful or somewhat sly. In the course of such attentive observation, an unobtrusive and unconscious affection seems to have developed between us. I dimly remember one occasion when we were taking turns giving short speeches in front of the class. After two or three boys had delivered theirs, one suggested politely, "Why don't you go next?" A bit surprised, I promptly rose and spoke my few formal words. I am convinced that even on elementary and middle school levels, coeducation can work to the advantage and benefit of both sexes as long as proper guidance is given.

In 1881, Emperor Meiji visited the northeastern region. On that very hot day, school children lined the main road leading into the town to welcome His Majesty. I have no recollection of the occasion except that our elementary school served as the imperial rest stop. It was probably then that we were taught to sing to a Western melody for the first time, by a teacher who was also a Shinto priest. The lyric was a thirty-one-syllable Japanese poem written in incomprehensible classical language:

Aogi kite	*Even foreigners*
Totsukunibito mo	*Seek to come*
Sumitsuku ya	*And settle in our country.*
Waga hi no moto no	*It must be the radiance*
Hikari naruramu	*of our sun.*

The teacher kept time by striking two small blocks of wood together. Every time we sang this song, I longed to know the meaning of the words, but for some reason could not bring myself to ask the teacher to explain them.

It took me years to learn that the first five syllables meant "seek to come." The next seven, "even foreigners," remained a puzzle for a long time. The most mystifying was the verb, *sumitsuku*. Our *Tohoku* (northeastern) dialect, which makes no phonetic distinction between *su* and *shi* sounds, happens to lack the word *sumu* (dwell) in its daily vocabulary. Hence, *sumitsuku* ("take up residence" in standard Japanese) could only be *shimitsuku* in our dialect, "freeze hard"! The imagery of the "radiant sun" at the end of the poem, therefore, made no sense to me.

In most families nowadays, everyone gathers together at the same table at mealtimes. If it had been so then, I might have had a chance to ask my grandfather or father about the poem. But the idea of women and children sitting at the same table with men was inconceivable in those days.[1] My grandmother and mother were totally illiterate, as were most women of the samurai and commoner classes in general, excepting perhaps those from top-ranking samurai or extremely wealthy merchant families. In fact, it was commonly believed that a woman who learned to read would come to a bad end. Unfortunately I had no elder siblings who might have shared similar questions or encouraged me to speak to my teachers. Today, so many years later, I have a better perspective. Preoccupied by the meaning of the words at the time, I failed to appreciate the spirit of people singing as a group. Willing participation in activities is a prerequisite to making one's own individual contribution to the group.

From time to time, officials from the district government bureau would visit our school and select a few top pupils from each grade to take "incentive examinations." Sometime around 1884, the Ministry of Education presented awards to pupils who excelled in academic performance or moral conduct. I was fortunate enough to be among the three who were nominated by our school, and was surprised to realize that despite my peculiarities, my teachers recognized my good qualities. The ceremony was grand. One boy and I each received a copy of the Chinese classic, *Xiao jing* (Book of filial piety). Another girl, cited as a model of filial piety, was presented an even better prize. After the ceremony, a huge crowd gathered in the school yard to watch a magic show.

Family Life

Memories of family life are clearer than those of my school days. Much of my character seems to have been cast in the mold of my maternal grandfather. The genealogy of my family goes back only to my great-grandfather, whose samurai rank was not high enough to compel us to live in a formal, ceremonious fashion. That left us relatively free of the strict observance of conventions, and grandfather ruled the family in a straightforward, rational and pragmatic manner. My grandmother was an affable and competent household manager, but absolutely lacking in intellectual or mathematical inclination. She served her husband faithfully and obediently, and their marriage was harmonious, his awesome dignity and inaccessibility were complemented by her warmth and openness. She was my mother's stepmother and had no children of her own, but was a truly good person.

When I was eleven, tragedy struck. In a desperate effort to stem the tide, I did everything within my limited power, but the situation proved to be beyond repair. My father had been adopted into my mother's family and made the legal heir (*muko yōshi*). Complications in connection with an extramarital affair[2] developed, and he was divorced and disowned. A few months before, I had overheard my mother and one of her friends discussing my father's affair. The woman in question was one of three Tokyo geisha who had come to work at a local restaurant. The management of that particular restaurant came into question and, in the course of police investigations, my father was, or was about to be, subpoenaed. I heard only a part of the story and by chance, but it was enough to make me feel ashamed and wretched.

One evening a few days after overhearing that conversation, I found my father stretched out on the tatami floor reading a newspaper in a room near the street side of the house. Anxious to talk with him, I hovered about. Suddenly someone with an unfamiliar accent called out: "Hidé, you shouldn't!" Rushing outside, I saw a woman peering over the latticed top section of the fence into our house. It was not difficult to guess who it was. The startled woman bowed and quickly went off to join another woman waiting some distance away. I immediately reported the little incident to my father, adding that I could not bear the thought of him being involved with a woman like that. When I insisted on having a serious discussion, he must have become angry at my impertinence, for I fainted and later found myself in bed in another room.

Several days later, while hunting fireflies with some friends near my grandmother's brother's house, I ran into my great uncle and learned that my father was not at his law office that day. I pleaded with my great uncle to take me to the restaurant, and he acceded, saying "Well, I have some urgent business with him; might as well take you along. Would you like to go home and change first?" "No, I will go as I am," I said, somehow wishing to preserve the spontaneity of my action. At the restaurant, my great uncle and I stated that my father was needed at home. He came down from upstairs followed by a number of women and went into what appeared to be their living quarters. The eldest of the women offered me a pretty box, saying, "Poor little dear, you need not worry about your father. We are taking good care of him." I refused stiffly. "Thank you, but I don't want your gift." Shortly after I returned home, father came back as promised.

Father's brother was manager of the largest bank in town. From a poor family, he had risen to an impressive position and had acquired a great deal of wealth. At the time of these events, he had just built a large house right behind ours, the first three-story house in the town of Hachinohe. A short plump man with pockmarks, my uncle was sociable even toward women and children, but greed and overconfidence were the unfortunate by-products of his ambitious nature. As a respected lawyer with a law office of his own, my father was often called upon to become involved in his brother's self-seeking and questionable ventures, and my family constantly worried that someday he would get himself into trouble.

My grandmother's brother-in-law, named Minamoto,[3] was an influential man later elected to the newly established Diet. He was given the task of persuading Father to straighten out his personal as well as business affairs. Even he was unsuccessful, however, and after Minamoto's second visit, grandfather sent for grandmother, mother, and myself. "I regret having to say this, but I have decided that I must disinherit Tōtaro in order to protect our family name," he announced. My mother submitted, saying, "Forgive me for all this trouble. I have been ready for your decision." I was grief-stricken; I felt as if my father had been deprived of his place in life.

Later, in connection with some bank business, charges were brought against a number of men, including my father and his brothers, and they were placed under arrest. When my father alone was dismissed of charges at the preliminary hearing, my grandfather rejoiced, saying "I knew he was incapable of committing a crime." It is not enough merely to be incapable of misconduct. If one is not capable of taking positive action, misfortune is sure to follow.

My father remarried after the divorce, but he was never able to live in a house as large as ours or employ as many servants. Because of ill health during his incarceration and trial, he progressively lost weight so that every time I saw him he looked like a different person. Whenever I was in his neighborhood or passed by his home, I was torn by conflicting emotions—the desire to see him and the restraint of the circumstances of our separation. I met his second wife on the street on several occasions and she always kindly invited me to drop in. While I was burning with love and longing for my father, he rarely showed affection or pleasure at seeing me. Perhaps he was uncomfortable at the abruptness of such encounters.

After finishing elementary school, I stayed home for a year devoting myself to the serious study of English and to the task of convincing my grandfather to send me to school in Tokyo. Studying English was very popular at the time, and a number of teachers taught reading and translation classes usually consisting of a handful of girls and a score of boys, among whom I was one of the youngest. When our class was translating [Peter] Parley [Samuel Goodrich, 1793–1860] I memorized the meaning of every word. [Probably excerpts which were published later in 1912 as *Readings from Peter Parley's Universal History*, Kōbunsha, 163 pages; the original book is 718 pages.] My teachers emphasized the verbatim translation method rather than a broader comprehension approach, so this study did not prove as useful as it might have. This period was the height of my enthusiasm for academic pursuits, which ended with the termination of my English studies.

In early February 1889, I went to Tokyo by sleigh, "Santa Claus" style, so to speak. An avid reader of the *Choya shinbun*, my grandfather had found an announcement of the opening of the First Women's Higher School and decided to enroll me there. We set out early so that I would have enough time to adjust to life in the metropolis before the academic year began in April. But my grandfather was as anxious to witness the promulgation ceremony of the Constitution, scheduled for February 11 [a national holiday commemorating the enthronement of the legendary first emperor Jinmu] as to see me settled in Tokyo.

Railroad lines did not yet reach Hachinohe, and the sea route was the shortest way to Tokyo in those days. For some reason, however, my grandfather chose the land route. Accompanied by a Pure Land monk, we rode in a horse-drawn carriage for five days to Sendai. From there, Tokyo was only one day away by train. But on the second day of our journey, it snowed heavily and we had to cross the Nakayama Pass [in Iwate prefecture] by sleigh. February is the coldest month in northern Japan and the snow was already deep enough to conceal low growing trees and bushes. We called to each other to keep in touch and our two sleighs proceeded through falling snow, arriving safely at an inn after dark. The lamplight of the inn was bright and the burning fire warm and inviting. From Ishinomaki to Shiogama, we took a small steamship. My aesthetic sensitivity had not yet matured then, and in the rain and snow I failed to appreciate the natural beauties of the famous scenic islands of Matsushima.

At Sendai Station early the next morning, how exciting it was to see a train for the first time in my life! Newly arrived into this bright land out of the gloomy northeast, I gazed at everything with a sense of wonder and joy. It was a clear day with a brilliant sun. Outside the train window, tree leaves gleamed. The people in the crowded car were all strangers, all so very different and so fascinating to a girl from a town where everyone knows everyone else. Curiously enough, when I travel to and from my hometown today, I notice only uniform local characteristics in people's attitudes, appearance, manners, and accent. On that first occasion, however, each passenger seemed refreshingly unique. When I stepped out onto Ueno's amazingly wide Hirokoji avenue, I knew I had finally arrived in Tokyo. Our lodging was a pleasant inn overlooking the Sumida River. Until school opened, my grandfather took me out every day sightseeing and kept up a running account of the changes that had taken place since the days when he served as a samurai in his lord's Edo residence.

I was eventually placed in a boarding house near the Eitai Bridge with other girl students from the northeast. The house was run by unpretentious, quick-witted Tokyo townsmen; this gave me an excellent opportunity to observe their vernacular, manners, and daily routine, and to acquire a whole new variety of practical wisdom.

Higher School in Tokyo

At school too, new experiences rushed at me. The First Women's Higher School was a new school offering a three-year program for graduates of eight-year elementary schools. Each grade was subdivided into upper and lower sections so that there would be a graduating class every half year. Based on entrance examination scores, twenty-four of us were placed in the lower section of the second grade, the highest class in this new school, and we were to become the first graduates two years later.

I was still a good student, but my earlier enthusiasm for study had waned, while my interest and curiosity were captured by the metropolis around me. The first Imperial Diet session imminent, frequent political meetings were held in Welfare Hall and there were several women among the speakers. I went to listen to the speeches, but less often after the school advised us not to attend political gatherings. Once, at the home of the friend who had first taken me to Welfare Hall, I was introduced to some of those women speakers, but the encounter left no particular impression.

From time to time, street circulars appeared announcing lecture meetings held at Christian churches in the vicinity of the school. The lecturers included some persons whose names often appeared in the famous journal, *Jogaku zasshi*, of which I was a regular reader. I vaguely entertained the thought of attending those lectures, but somehow failed to make the effort. Around that time, a new student joined our class who would fold her hands and say grace before lunch, undaunted by the obvious disapproval and sneers of her classmates. I was impressed by her courage, and talking with her one day, I learned that she had been attending a church at nearby Akashi-chō. At her suggestion, I accompanied her the next Sunday and discovered yet another new world.

A number of Western men and women delivered sermons in cultured Japanese and extended me a warm welcome. Many Japanese there seemed to understand English, and two of the women were even dressed in Western clothes. After the service, several men and women rose to make various announcements. The teacher of the Sunday school class to which I was assigned was, to my surprise, a well-known woman named Ushioda Chiseko.[4] The minister's lectures on Christianity were enlightening and easy to understand. Before long, I was baptized.

My ambition at the time was to go on to higher normal school and eventually become a teacher—the only meaningful way of life that I knew. Tokyo Women's Higher Normal School was then about to graduate its first class and their senior class came one day to observe our school. To us, they were magnificent, heavenly beings, dressed in Western-style uniforms, with dignity and refinement that left us speechless. In 1890 two classmates and I took the entrance examination for this school; I alone failed. I had begun attending church before that and was baptized sometime afterward.

Among the members of our church were students from a Christian women's school located in the foreign residential district, a school whose atmosphere seemed quite different from our public higher school. As an admirer of the periodical *Jogaku zasshi*, it was natural that I aspired next to enter Meiji Jogakkō (Meiji Women's School), said to embody the ideals of the magazine. I wanted to enroll in their three-year higher division upon graduating from the First Women's Higher School. Unlike my first choice, the government-supported

Women's Higher Normal School, the private Christian Meiji Women's School charged tuition. The main reason for my grandfather's initial hesitation in sending me to Tokyo had been simply arithmetic—my younger sisters and brothers were waiting their turns. I could not expect him to spend any more money on the education of his eldest granddaughter.

Having set my mind on Meiji Women's School, therefore, I searched for a financial solution of my own. Finally, I wrote a letter to Iwamoto Yoshiharu, chief editor of *Jogaku zasshi* and president of the school. Impatient, I wrote a second letter and, without waiting for a reply, paid a visit to the editor's office located next to the school campus. I had no appointment and could not see Mr. Iwamoto that day, but he later specified a date by letter. The outcome of my interview with him was that I was admitted to Meiji Women's School with a tuition waiver and a job that would finance my dormitory room and board.

My work assignment was to supply *furigana* (phonetic syllabary to indicate pronunciation) for *kanji* (Chinese characters) in the manuscripts appearing in *Jogaku zasshi*. Among the contributors to the journal, the novelist Shimazaki Tōson[5] always provided his own beautiful *kana* in red ink alongside neat, legible characters. Mrs. Iwamoto [Kashiko], better known by her pen name, Wakamatsu Shizuko,[6] wrote her manuscripts in an accomplished hand that was more difficult to decipher. When her most celebrated translation [1891] of *Little Lord Fauntleroy* [1886, by Frances Hodgson Burnett] was published by Jogaku Zasshisha, I had the honor of copyediting the manuscript.

About one hundred students lived in the dormitory of Meiji Women's School. At seven in the evening, we would gather in the auditorium for a prayer service and stay on to study until nine o'clock. I worked on manuscripts during this period. Fairly well-read for my age, I could handle my job, but it was only through the sheer kindness of Mr. Iwamoto that I was given a job which could have been done easily by a regular employee. Now I find myself in a position similar to Mr. Iwamoto's, managing a school and a journal simultaneously, and appreciate more than ever the extra consideration extended to me when I needed it most.

At the school I learned of the benefits for mind and body of a regimented daily routine. For a country girl like myself, it was not easy at first to get up early in the morning, to wash in a crowded washroom, and to eat and bathe expeditiously. I took up the challenge and reaped an unexpected dividend: stubborn headaches I had suffered throughout my First Women's Higher School days from constant, indiscriminate reading late into the night stopped. I was cured, moreover, of the bad habit of snacking ingrained as a child growing up in the countryside, where constant nibbling was a way of life. Instead, I found new pleasure in filing a request for sweet potato soup with our delegate to the weekly menu committee, or in her information that rice cakes would be served the next week.

One of the dormitory supervisors, a Mrs. Kuroyanagi, was a widow who combined the graciousness of her native Kyoto with the high spirit worthy of a Tokyoite. Her competent management and creative imagination contributed immensely to our health and enjoyment. The chief maid was a stocky authoritative woman; under her direction, rice for one hundred boarders was cooked to perfection three times daily. The term "maid" has since been replaced by a more respectable word "helper." In our day, though, it did not occur to anyone to attach the honorific "san" to our maid's names; yet we enjoyed a good rapport with them. they were kind and attentive, remembering which girls liked the crispy browned rice from the bottom of the pot or which disliked raw fish. (I was among the latter and they would give me fish cakes instead.) The most popular dishes included beef vegetable stew and dumpling soup.

How clearly I recall the old handyman carrying a large cloth bundle on his back. Every Saturday, he would come hurrying down the dormitory hallway delivering the sweets we had ordered. We were allowed to buy three sen worth of snacks per week. On Saturday mornings, we could each make out a list including such favorites as roasted sweet potatoes, rice cakes, sweet rolls, and salted beans. The room leader would collect and submit our orders to the supervisor, who would send the old man off to fill them. Wednesdays and Saturdays were our bath days, and it was one of our greatest pleasures to gather in our rooms after bathing, to nibble at our sweets and let forth volleys of girlish chatter. One sen bought six roasted potatoes or two rice cakes, so three sen worth was enough to last the weekend. Fruit is my present favorite, but I do not recall ever ordering fruit—perhaps fruit was not as plentiful then as today.

During my years at Meiji Women's School, I met many prominent people in literature, religion, education, and other fields. Once I was sent on an errand to the house of Professor Kato Hiroyuki[7] with a message concerning the date of a meeting. It was an extremely hot summer day, but the elderly scholar greeted me in a formal black *haori*, worn over his cool white summer kimono. I was deeply impressed by the good manners and courtesy he extended to me, although I was only a young girl. I had met Professor Kato once before when he came to the First Women's Higher School. The visit of this illustrious university president caused much excitement then. After a short speech, our principal had called upon a few students to speak on behalf of the student body, but no one responded. So he called on me. Feeling very awkward with my northeastern accent, I was startled, but mounted the rostrum with hesitation. I have no idea what I said. More than ten years later I consulted Professor Kato's son, who was an imperial physician, about something to do with childcare information in our magazine. From time to time, Mrs. Kato also provided advice on household management, and we have maintained a close association ever since. Our two families are of quite different persuasions—one bound by religious faith, the other by a philosophy of atheistic materialism—yet I know now that mutual respect and friendship can grow as long as each is secure and confident in their own values.

The students of Meiji Women's School attended Sunday services at a church established by Uemura Masahisa [1857–1925, perhaps the single most influential Protestant minister-theologian in late Meiji Japan]. Just as much as the other students, I was spellbound by the Rev. Uemura's impassioned sermons, although in retrospect I seem to have understood very little. As usual, I was obsessed with such ordinary questions as how the Devil could exist in God's realm. I asked many questions during Sunday school classes and eventually fell into a state of "ungratefulness" which grew out of my own peculiar logic: I had been brought into this world and forced to live, but I could have been spared all this trouble had I not been born in the first place. Some Sunday afternoons, as a gesture of defiance, I even went to hear sermons at a nearby Buddhist organization called Byakurensha [White Louts Society, perhaps a group studying the Lotus Sutra].

A belief prevailed among the students that Dr. Uemura would discourage girls who expressed the desire to receive baptism on the grounds that women would probably forget the faith after marriage and could not be true believers. Despite numerous questions and the impulse to turn to him for help, I was never able to muster the courage to talk to him for fear that he might ask me why I had been baptized while still unable to understand the fundamental questions.

In our school we were fortunate to have among our instructors Hoshino Amachi [writer and editor of *Bungakkai* magazine], who lectured on the *Book of Poetry* and *Anthology of Tang Poems*; the poet Ōwada Tateki; and the scholar Suzuki Kōgyō, who taught Japanese poetry and the *Pillow Book*. Every day after lunch we assembled in the auditorium to hear Mr. Iwamoto, the principal, discourse on current events or literature, religion, and a variety of other topics. These talks were extremely informative and inspiring, and were enlivened by his eloquence, insight, dignity, sincerity, vision, and enthusiasm for learning.

In the summer of 1892 I returned to my hometown (the railroad had extended past it by then). For some reason I no longer remember, I stayed on to become a teacher at Hachinohe Elementary School. My mind had been wholly occupied with intellectual pursuits before I moved to Tokyo, and I had been captivated by the city. In other words, despite the unique experience of coeducation in elementary school and the relative freedom accorded us in the boarding house environment during my higher school days, there had been no room in my life for emotional involvement with the opposite sex. By contrast, my seven months as a teacher offered little intellectual challenge or all-involving activity, but at that point, I fell in love.

One evening, a former First Women's Higher School classmate came to visit and asked me to take over her teaching position in a girls' school in Morioka, which she was leaving to get married. Love beginning to bloom within me, I moved into the dormitory of the Catholic school. The nuns were most kind and gentle; even the slightest cold was tended by a physician nun. They pitied me, the nuns said, because as a Protestant I was denied Paradise, and they often took me to mass at a church near the school. The midnight High Mass at Christmas was especially memorable. At Meiji Women's School we had been taught Christian thought but not faith. The religion of the nuns was inspired by a mystic longing, but it was not a faith meant for beings of flesh and blood. Although drawn to religion even before my baptism, I had never embraced a true and vital faith. I considered myself a Christian then, but in retrospect, it merely meant that I had made the choice to live by the Christian moral code.

At any rate, the most powerful emotion I felt during this period was my love for a man. Despite the separation of distance, our attachment grew stronger, and finally he made a formal proposal of marriage to my family through a properly qualified intermediary. My grandfather, who knew nothing of his character or our feelings for each other, replied that he intended me to be his heir and as such, he explained, I was expected eventually to marry a man who would take our family name. It was as simple as that. My grandfather lacked the wisdom and foresight to ask how and why a man from a distant city had appeared so suddenly with a marriage proposal. I did not have the courage or sense then to plead our case, and we had no choice but to wait.

In contrast to Meiji Women's School, which had had an open and socially active atmosphere, the Catholic school was isolated, an unworldly realm after school hours. I lived in a narrow, high-ceilinged, second-floor room with a tatami floor; there was a bed by the wall and a large desk by the north window. A similar room across the hallway facing south belonged to an Italian nun. In this sentimental, introverted atmosphere, so detached from the outside world, my sole pleasure consisted of reading a collection of Japanese literature. Not even the study of French suggested by the nuns interested me. It was the most passive, unproductive period of my entire life. Around this time, my estranged father died, ending his unfortunate life at the young age of forty-two. He had great resourcefulness and personal warmth; it seemed terribly sad that his later years were darkened by adverse circumstances.

Career in Journalism

While teaching at the Catholic school, I faced yet another source of anxiety. The man I loved took a new job in town near Kyoto, and I began to detect a gradual but radical shift in his thinking and tastes. Belying his former puritanical simplicity, he grew extremely vulgar. I felt compelled to leave my teaching position and marry him in order to save our relationship before it was too late. This time, when I pressed my case with my grandfather, he gave me his blessing. My grandmother told me later that even before that, he was already aware of the circumstances and had become sympathetically disposed. The man I wanted to marry, on the other hand, rapidly lost his earlier zeal; his reluctance and coolness grew more and more pronounced despite his efforts to conceal his true feelings.

Years later, a newspaper account of my life ventured to speculate that the reason for our divorce within half a year was incompatibility between my mother-in-law and myself. It concluded confidently that the clash between new and old, which destroyed our love, actually helped make me into a strong and resolute woman. My ex-husband's poor mother, however, is the victim of false accusations, for she never even lived with us, much less caused any conflict. The truth was that as an educated woman from the northeast, I found Kansai taste intolerably vulgar, while my husband eagerly assimilated it. Not fortified with sufficient determination and unprepared to manage in a society so diametrically opposed to all that was familiar, there was little I could do to save our marriage. The half year was painful; full of unpleasant experiences and an anguished sense of helplessness.

Being, by nature, a small fish wishing only to live in pure water, I could not even contemplate trying to thrive in mud. My husband was basically a good man, but he turned out to be all too susceptible to outside influence and temptation, a quality which surfaced only after he took to drinking. Eventually I made the drastic decision, "as if giving up my own life," to relinquish my love. No one who has not experienced the depth of desolation beyond hope can ever fully appreciate the profound implications of that cliché. It was difficult, but bidding farewell to the dear but cold corpse that was my love, I set forth to find a more meaningful way of life.

Boarding the Tokyo-bound train at Kyoto Station, I tingled with anticipation at the unknown battles to come. The man who had been my husband stood by the window, saying over and over again, "I know you will make something of yourself." I could not help but respect his humble repentance. I have always feared that this painful episode of my life, of which I am ashamed even today, might jeopardize the effectiveness of my public service. Not for a moment, however, do I regret my decision to liberate myself from the enslaving hold of emotion, for my life had been rendered meaningless by the selfishness and profane love of another. I am grateful for the power that granted me fortitude when I most needed it.

The following few years were as challenging and fascinating as scaling a mountain. We made an agreement to keep our divorce and my move to Tokyo secret from both our families and friends for a time. Although our silence might have seemed arrogant and reckless, it was motivated by the wish to spare our families unnecessary concern, at least until I settled myself in a proper situation. I also refrained from seeing any of my former classmates or friends in Tokyo. Out of genuine kindness and a lingering sense of responsibility, my ex-husband arranged with a friend to provide me temporary lodging. His consideration was touching, but under the circumstances, accepting his help would have been awkward as well as against my principles.

I decided to seek a position as a live-in maid, with the ulterior motive that such an experience might be valuable in realizing my long cherished ambition of writing fiction. An agency happened to find employment for me with the prominent family of Yoshioka Yayoi [1871–1959], one of the first women doctors in Japan and the founder of Tokyo Women's Medical School. Across the street from her clinic was a private German language academy run by her husband, Dr. Yoshioka Arata. Among my co-workers were a reticent but efficient head kitchen maid and a rickshaw man always attired in a formal black *haori* with the Yoshioka family crest. Above me in rank were a young woman druggist with dark, alert eyes and a woman doctor who also handled the accounts.

I performed my duties as best I could, and soon the Yoshiokas took notice of me. I couldn't bring myself to confide all the facts of my still fresh and painful past, but they were sympathetic enough to guess from what little I revealed. They encouraged me to pursue my ambition and changed my status to the equivalent of live-in student. Despite my initial ambitious and heroic resolution, the life of a maid had proved to be humbling. Thanks to the generosity of the Yoshiokas, I was released from this menial existence after only one month and allowed to join the family gatherings around the brazier in the largest room in the house. Listening to them talking about everything from medicine and men's schools to the ambitions and dreams of the Yoshiokas, I was struck with the contrast between that cheerful, optimistic world and the depressing Kansai environment I had just left behind. Even the quiet north country of my birth was very different. My elation was accompanied by a sense of awe; I drank in the stimulating atmosphere and found it soothing to my invisible wounds.

The Yoshiokas permitted me to seek outside employment. My search through newspaper ads yielded only one unsuccessful interview for a clerk's position. Then, to our mutual surprise and joy, I happened to meet the daughter of Mrs. Kuroyanagi, the Meiji Women's School dorm supervisor. As a result of an introduction from her mother, I obtained a teaching position at an elementary school in the Tsukiji area, and soon moved into Mrs. Kuroyanagi's house.

My real ambition, however, remained a writing career. On my way to school each morning, I stopped at the main office of the *Hōchi shinbun* to look through their employment guide. Then, passing the *Yamato shinbun* office one day, I found a notice that a copy editor was wanted. I rushed home to prepare a letter and a résumé and ran back to the *Yamato* office. The sleepy-eyed receptionist informed me that the position had just been filled. My enthusiasm instantly deflated, I nevertheless learned a valuable lesson from the receptionist—his attitude clearly announced that no woman would ever be considered for the employment. Thereafter I carried a statement among my application papers explaining why, as a woman, I wished to be a copy editor. Within a week, the *Hōchi* want-ads announced an opening for a copy editor at their office. I arrived at the reception desk too early in the morning and was met not by a receptionist but by the head janitor, who said, "Are you applying for the opening yourself? A copy editor is a man's position, you know." "No, I was asked to deliver this to the person in charge," I replied in desperation and handed my papers to him. Since then, I have often tried to convince myself that the lie was forgivable because I had no bad intentions, only a desperate wish. Nonetheless, I was ashamed of having lied to the honest old man.

The following day, I received a postcard from the *Hōchi* summoning me to an interview. My elation was quickly quelled when I entered the shabby, small waiting room to find several men, obviously other applicants for the same position. I was the last to be interviewed. I no longer remember the details of the meeting, except for the impression that the interviewer had apparently read my papers with care and was giving me fair consideration. He proposed a one-day trial. Then and there, I was taken to the copy desk in a corner of the editing room and introduced to the unsmiling middle-aged man who was the chief copy editor. Without a word, he pushed toward me some copies of an advertisement which he had been busily correcting. I did the best I could on them, discovering the excitement of reading sections of a newspaper before they were printed. Toward evening, the chief dismissed me with a trace of a smile and said, "That's it for today. Come back around ten o'clock in the morning. You'll probably do."

I began work the next morning. Later in the day, I was called to the conference room to meet Mr. Miki Zenpachi, long-time president of the *Hōchi* and a leading journalist. At the time, I was totally unaware of the tremendous social standing of the man sitting before me; but his face and words are still etched in my memory. He said, "We are very impressed with you. The chief copy editor claims that few men could do the job with your accuracy. You are hired as of today, but as the first woman to work in our editing room, you will have to prove yourself." I received his permission to work afternoons only until a replacement was found to fill my teaching position. Luckily, our private school was more flexible and liberal than public schools, so I was free from my duties after morning classes.

At the beginning I heard comments coming from the printers, who worked in a room separated from the editing room by a screened window. "Hey, there's a woman in the zoo now," they quipped, using the editing area's nickname. But I was too happy in my new job to mind their teasing and it soon stopped, thanks, no doubt, to the editing room staff who spoke to the printers in my defense.

The *Hōchi* was then carrying a very popular column entitled *Fujin no sugao* (Portraits of leading women), featuring sketches of the lives of married women of high society. Reporters were already assigned to this column, but, even though I was only a copy editor, I developed a desire to write a similar article myself. I recalled that one of my former teachers at the First Women's Higher School, a beautiful young lady with crisp speech and a positive outlook, had been concurrently living in the home of Viscount Tani Kanjō as a tutor to his children. She had often related to our class stories she had been told of Lady Tani's experiences in the besieged castle during the Satsuma Rebellion of 1877 (when her heroic husband successfully defended Kumamoto Castle against a formidable rebel army) and how hard she worked at home, even weaving her own kimono material.

My teacher was married by then, but with her help, I was able to interview Lady Tani, who chatted quite freely with me and even showed me around her house. I arranged the collected material into an article of four or five installments, and submitted it to the editor in charge of the "Portraits of Leading Women" column. Not only was it accepted immediately, but it brought me praise of Mr. Miki. (To be sure, he was more than generous with praise where genuine talent was concerned. Every time he was pleased with an outstanding article, he would drop into the editing room and shower its author with superlatives, his usually fearsome face melting into a smile.)

This article was directly responsible for my dream coming true sooner than I had expected. Only half a year after returning to Tokyo following my drastic decision to leave my husband in 1897, I had resigned from the teaching position and found myself a full-fledged reporter. Most people seem to be under the impression that I endured severe hardships, but the truth is that opportunity always reached out before suffering could claim me.

Next I wanted to write about a prominent Zen priest named Nishiari who was the son of a poor bean-curd vendor in my hometown. He was well known for his eccentric ways as well as his saintly virtue. I made the rounds of large temples in Tokyo until I learned that he was at a quiet temple in Shizuoka recuperating from an illness. Mr. Miki granted me one week's leave to visit the priest in his temporary retirement. In addition to the usual press pass, I was given a special credential certifying me to be a *Hōchi* reporter, since a woman was likely to encounter skepticism regarding the legitimacy of her press pass.

I had heard much about the priest Nishiari since my childhood, and once in my hometown I had caught a glimpse of him from the back of a crowd. When I finally met him in person, not only did he fulfill my expectations, but my respect for the old man deepened. Talking with an appealing openness and grandfatherly kindness, he confessed that he had welcomed my letter and was looking forward to my visit. He gave me a great deal of thoughtful and personal attention, which touched me deeply. For all my valiant determination to achieve my ambitions on my own, I was still helplessly vulnerable and the scars of my recent divorce were still fresh. The days with Nishiari are among the most precious experiences of my life, and they proved to me again that as long as a person does not lose courage and faith in himself, he will find the soothing balm of sympathy and understanding to heal his wounds. For three days I listened to the aged master by his bedside. At night a monk would escort me by the light of his lantern back to a parishioner's house where Nishiari had arranged my accommodations. His reminiscences of childhood were suffused with love and sympathy for his strong-minded mother, who had raised a large family and quite loyally assisted her good-natured husband. Again and again he stressed how valuable women were.

Despite my still immature, untrained writing style, my report on the priest Nishiari was serialized over a month in the top column of the prestigious city news page. The Yoshiokas and Mrs. Kuroyanagi were delighted at my new start in life, and at last I could now break the news of my divorce to my family and report on my recent activities. I moved into quiet, sunny rooms in a boarding house with my brother, who had come to Tokyo to enroll at Keio Gijuku. The feeling of inadequacy and shame which had kept me away from my former teachers and friends fell away; I was happy and at peace, though my daily schedule made it impossible to renew friendships immediately.

I searched for worthy projects for the paper on my own, eager to contribute creative ideas, and I found more than enough. Not only everyday social notes, but even information brought back by police reporters often yielded items that begged for the woman's touch, the woman's point of view, and the woman's pen. Reader responses proved me right, and I was rewarded with the satisfaction of knowing that I filled a vital role in society.

Ambitions Realized

In the thirty-odd years since my career began, I have lived very much in the public eye. Naturally, Japanese society did not exactly welcome its first newspaperwoman with open arms. In retrospect, however, I realize that any hostility toward me or harassment was essentially the expression of undefined fear, jealousy, dissatisfaction in life, or lack of ideas. But I also received much encouragement, empathy, and help from persons of integrity, sincerity and insight. The occasions when I encountered great kindness and total support far outnumbered instances of open malice or lack of understanding. It was always gratifying when my articles elicited response from readers. Even the editors were pleased when my coverage of a childcare association inspired some women to join that worthy organization. While another article on the Okayama Orphanage was being serialized, I had an opportunity to interview Prince Konoe Fumimaro, then president of the House of Peers. "You are the author of the orphanage report, aren't you?" he commented. "It is good to see an article written by a woman, so rare in newspapers. You should be proud. Continue the good work," the prince said with sincerity.

By that time, Nishiari was installed in a new temple bearing his name in Yokohama. One summer he taught at a Sōtō Zen academy in Azabu, Tokyo, and I attended his morning lectures every day, the only woman among a host of monks. At the time, I toyed with the idea of becoming a nun. In the excitement of my job, I was perhaps unaware of a deep-seated loneliness. This and my thirst for social recognition were part of my motivation in aspiring to be a nun, for Nishiari had told me that there were nuns long ago who were so highly respected that they were allowed audiences at court and exerted far-reaching spiritual influence on society. I even investigated a little and found out something about convents from a certain monk of Nishiari's acquaintance. During a visit home after a long absence, Nishiari made time in his tight schedule to call on my grandfather and inform him of my latest desire [to become a nun]. (I only learned of their meeting later.) "I have tried not to interfere with her wishes in the past," my grandfather said to him, "But I wish she would reconsider this time." The priest commiserated. I benefited much from his guidance; despite his advanced age—he was past eighty then—and his exalted position as the head of a Buddhist order, he gave me much compassion and help.

Hani Yoshikazu [1880–1955], who was to become my life's companion, joined the *Hōchi* some time after me. He also enjoyed praise and commendation from Mr. Miki. We were married in 1901 and my love and ambition found a single, perfect means of fulfillment. Ever since, our home has been the center of our work, and our work has been an extension of our home life, the two merging completely. This unity bespeaks the essence of our work and our marriage; together we found our place in life.

Reflections and Perspectives[8]

This April it is already twenty-five years since we began to speak to our friends the world over through the pages of our magazines, which I edit and my husband manages. In 1903, I was editor-clerk-manager of the journal of the Fujin Kyōikukai (Women's Education Association), which was the most influential women's organization at the time. I was pregnant and I had heavy responsibilities for the journal, but I was so healthy and enthusiastic that I continued working until two days before the birth of our first daughter on the second of April. How symbolic that the inaugural issue of our first magazine *Katei no tomo* (Friend of the home, 1903–8) came out the very next day! It contained only thirty-two pages and was written entirely by one person—myself. It must have been difficult to launch a new magazine almost simultaneously with giving birth to my first child, and I must have been concerned about the next issue. But all I remember now is the excitement, not the difficulty.

While trying to manage as an unsophisticated housewife and brand-new mother, I enlisted the help of prominent people with some kind of special experience or vocation to get material for the journal. After questioning them as thoroughly as I could and learning about their viewpoints and knowledge, I then tried to convey the essential facts on a subject or the underlying principles of a problem in the way most comprehensible and useful to housewives. Such an approach had never been attempted before by any magazine, and the style as well as material we printed was completely new to readers. I would like to believe our work was as welcome to society as it was satisfying to us.

Stimulated by first-hand observation during years of newspaper reporting, our concern extended beyond the limited scope of household advice, and we began to include discussion of social mores and the psychological aspects of family life. Our fourth issue carried the story of how a loyal and loving wife of a gifted man helped her husband break his drinking habit and restored him to professional productivity. This issue was extremely popular and went into a third and even a fourth printing. The story brought us numerous new readers who wanted to have back issues as well. Eventually then, we established a bond with our readers, and our contribution to society grew more and more meaningful.

One day on the street in the foreigners' residential section in Tsukiji, a group of foreign children playing, dressed comfortably in Western clothes, caught my attention. They made me think how unfortunate our own youngsters were, encumbered by restricting kimono. Immediately I went to a nearby kindergarten and learned all I could about Western clothes from its superintendent, Mrs. Tapping. Our magazine introduced the idea of dressing children in Western clothes and encouraged readers to try them. We instructed them in how to cut material and sew Western clothes, how to wear them, and how to launder them. Over the years we included follow-up reports on the experiences of those who actually used Western clothes, including information on the costs involved. We even held study classes on this and many other subjects, all as part of our editorial policy.

Being parents, we were deeply concerned with the education of children. When our elder daughter Setsuko entered elementary school, we began to entertain visions of setting up the "ideal" school. But it was almost ten years later, when our younger daughter Keiko finished elementary school, that we were finally able to realize that dream. In 1921 we founded our own school, Jiyū Gakuen [literally, Garden of Free Learning], for graduates of elementary school. The world needs social critics and commentators, but the mission of our own magazine, *Fujin no tomo* [1908–present], lies somewhere beyond mere theorizing. It is our ultimate goal to give concrete form to our visions and to substantiate our theories in practice. Sometimes this takes a long time, because our standards are high and progress on our projects is often slow.

Jiyū Gakuen is our life now. Today the world seem withered, and threatened by the shadow of self-extinction,[9] but signs of hope are appearing in all fields—politics, finance, education, religion. Individuals, too, are awakening to new visions. We do not believe that it is necessary to destroy the dominant image of traditional man in order to create a new man, nor that the existing system must be totally discredited before a fresh one can emerge. If we aspire to create a viable new order and pull out of the stagnation of our contemporary world, we must join the forces of our hopes and prayers in a continuous and united battle against our own attachment to outmoded values. Let us search and test more educational methods which will be conducive to genuinely free development of the individual and replace time-worn, rigid educational methods.

Within Jiyū Gakuen, which is a small society in itself, everything—administration, human interaction, consumption, production—is intended to move forward toward the ideals of the new world we envision. The transition from one period of time to another should be like the regeneration of a lawn in the spring. Fresh green leaves shoot forth not from withered, dead grass, but from roots awakened from winter slumber. Recognizing that social transformation is imminent, we must rejuvenate the fundamental life force within each of us that lies dormant under the suffocating weight of the old system. Social enterprises, families, and individuals will serve as the vanguard of the new age—in Japan and abroad, among rich and poor, and, of course, among men and women. We are proud that Jiyū Gakuen will be one of these brave pioneers of a new age.

In essence Jiyū Gakuen and *Fujin no tomo* are one and the same. That is to say, *Fujin no tomo* is you and I; and Jiyū Gakuen is the ground where the seedlings planted by *Fujin no tomo* germinate. The initial purpose of the publication was simple: to transmit practical knowledge indispensable for the improvement of our daily lives, basic information useful to everyone. Eventually we began to feel the need to practice what we preached. The convictions we asserted in our magazine concerning education led, after ten years of planning, to the founding of a school. In the seven years since its establishment, Jiyū Gakuen has become a small beacon of truly free education in a darkening age. It has grown into a vital nucleus of a working model with which we can try out our theories for a new society. Jiyū Gakuen enables *Fujin no tomo* to propagate, now with reinforced confidence, a dynamic way of life which can adjust to changing times.

Social transition is inevitably accompanied by problems in education, livelihood, and distribution of wealth. These are at once problems of society and of the individual. Both rich and poor must be humble in the concerted search for workable solutions. The anxiety of parents is particularly acute today, and it is a challenge to *Fujin no tomo* to try to answer their need for information and moral support. Recently the quality of many women's magazines has seriously declined and I sense that we face a grave battle to preserve the ideals we stand for and to act on the message we impart.

As we celebrate the twenty-fifth anniversary of our journalistic association, let us renew our faith and determination to pursue this mission. Bless the borderless kingdom of *Fujin no tomo*, for it is founded upon the combined aspirations, faith, and prayers of publisher and readers.

March 1928

Notes

1. For a portrayal of mealtime in a Tōhoku samurai household, see Dazai Osamu's autobiographical novella, *No Longer Human* (1948). He describes the painful memory of a mealtime scene in the hero's childhood where a family sits at individual trays lined up in two rows facing each other in order of age. They eat in oppressive silence as if undergoing punishment or penance.

2. The Edo period family codes for the samurai class recognized no female heir, though commoners were allowed to have female heads of household with male guardians. In 1873, the Meiji government recognized the legality of a female head of household, but upon marriage, all her rights and property automatically

passed to her husband. Similarly, the wife's right to sue for divorce in a contested case was qualified by the consent of her parents and/or grandfather (also needed for marriage) and by their physical presence when she appeared in court. Four legitimate grounds for a wife's request for divorce were: (1) desertion for a period of over two years; (2) criminal conviction of her husband involving imprisonment of more than one year; (3) profligacy by her husband; and (4) malignant disease or advanced psychosis.

In the case of Motoko's father, as the head of the household the grandfather had the right to disinherit and divorce him. It would have been extremely difficult to remove the father after he himself became household head and acquired the almost immutable rights under Meiji civil law. Having concubines was not in itself a cause for divorce. The Japanese word for "profligacy" in legal terms is *hōtō*, which means dissipation, dissolute living, and debauchery, among other things—conduct much more promiscuous and prodigal than merely keeping concubines.

Divorce was surprisingly common in the late nineteenth-century Japan. *Kokumin no tomo*, no. 6 (July 1892) lists the ratio of divorce to the number of marriages as follows: 1885, 41 percent; 1886, 45 percent; 1887, 38 percent; 1888, 36 percent; 1889, 32 percent; 1890, 39 percent, all for Tokyo only. The local figures are presumead to be lower by about 7 percent.

3. It is safe to assume that Motoko's relative, Mr. Minamoto, was one of the extremely wealthy landholders who dominated membership to the Lower House.

4. Ushioda Chiseko (1844–1903) entered a Christian school in 1883 after she was widowed and eventually became president of the Tokyo Women's Temperance Society and the founder of the Tokyo Women's Charity Association engaged in child education and Christian missionary work. She later opened a rescue mission for prostitutes.

5. Shimazaki Tōson (1872–1943), poet and novelist, was a teacher at Meiji Women's School in 1892.

6. Wakamatsu Shizuko (1864–96) was the only student in the first (1882) graduating class of the higher division of Mary Kidder's Ferris English-Japanese Women's School at the James Hepburn Medial Clinic in Yokohama. Kidder, 1834–1910, was the Dutch Reformed Church missionary who taught the women students of Hepburn's language school. Shizuko remained at the school as a teacher, published English poems (of her own composition as well as translations) in *Jogaku zasshi*, and married Iwamoto Yoshiharu in 1889. She died prematurely of tuberculosis. Her translation of *Little Lord Fauntleroy* enjoyed the acclaim of critics and immense popularity. It was reprinted over 100 times by 1910.

7. Baron Katō Hiroyuki (1836–1916) was a jurist who exercised great influence on the formative political structure of Japan. A student of Sakuma Shōzan, Katō served in the Tokugawa shogunate's western books investigation center and after 1861 he began writing a series of works introducing and advocating constitutional government which were to spearhead the early people's rights movement. In 1874, however, he reversed his position and opposed the proposal for the establishment of a legislative assembly, saying that it was premature. He occupied positions of power such as first president of Tokyo Imperial University, member of the House of Peers, and president of the Imperial Academy (Gakushiin), and

became a central figure representing the Tokyo University faction and the government's official stand. Greatly influenced by Western philosophy, he championed an anti–people's rights stand. He published *Jinken shinsetsu* (A new theory on human rights) in 1882 based on Darwinian social evolutionism.

8. "Kaiko to tenbō," *Hani Motoko chosakushū*, vol. 14, pp. 82–93.

9. Hani was writing at a time when Japan and all of East Asia were in turmoil. In the wake of the financial panic of 1927, the economy was unstable and government suppression of opposition elements was growing more forceful, as illustrated by the mass arrest of Japan Communist Party members in March 1928 and the placement of special political police in the prefectures in July.

7

TAKAMINE HIDEKO
The Actress

JAMES O'BRIEN

TAKAMINE HIDEKO, who was born in 1924, made her movie debut at the age of five. A winsome girl, she quickly became a popular child actress, affectionately known in her own country as "the Japanese Shirley Temple." In retrospect she might be compared to Deanna Durbin or, better yet, Judy Garland. Unlike Shirley Temple and most other child stars, Takamine Hideko managed to avoid the pitfalls that always seem to await the popular child performer trying to sustain a career beyond the period of natural charm and into adolescence. Takamine sustained her career right through adolescence and into adulthood, a feat she attributes—with unwarranted modesty, it must be said—to the fact that she appeared infrequently in featured roles during her adolescence. While remaining somewhat in the public eye during this period, she wisely capitalized on her partial respite from the lime-light to master specific skills that would make her a considerable per-former as an adult. When she was in her mid-twenties, the Japanese cinema entered one of its greatest periods. It was the 1950s, and the country was beginning to recover from the ravages of the Second World War. Takamine emerged as a mature actress, often working with directors highly skilled at depicting femininity—Ozu Yasujirō (1903–63) and Naruse Mikio (1905–69), to cite the two most conspic-uous examples. She has played, under these and other directors, an astonishing variety of roles: the cheerful and sympathetic elementary

The author is grateful to Professor David Bordwell of the University of Wis-consin and Professor David Desser of the University of Illinois for their advice on the preparation of this chapter. He also wishes to thank Chieko Mulhern for her help in gathering information and answering questions.

school teacher in *Twenty-four Eyes* (1960), the ill-fated mistress of *Drifting Clouds* (1955), the stern mother-in-law of *The Doctor's Wife* (1967). Takamine Hideko's performances have won her a considerable number of awards. Now in her sixties, she lives in semi-retirement with her husband, the well-known movie director, Matsuyama Zenzō (b. 1925).

Ms. Takamine is more than a talented and successful actress, however. She is also an accomplished author, her most notable work being an extended series of autobiographical articles written for a Japanese weekly magazine during the mid-1970s. These installments were eventually collected and published as a two-volume book entitled *Watashi no tosei nikki* (A journal of my life).[1] The recipient of a prestigious award for nonfiction writing, the book describes the interplay of chance and personal drive that enabled a girl of low birth and provincial background to become a child star almost overnight and to sustain a movie career for as long as she wished it to continue. That such a career could be fashioned in a country still very much dominated by men and in an industry where careers are fragile is remarkable. In *A Journal of My Life*, Ms. Takamine tells her story in a straightforward fashion. Her narrative sheds light on how she was able to succeed in Japanese society. More important, it demonstrates that, in the midst of her success, she was able to have a personal life enriched by numerous and varied friendships.

Ms. Takamine's journal is not one of those ghost-written products so standard with Hollywood figures and former politicians in this country—the autobiography of Shirley Temple, by coincidence, being one of the latest entries in this mostly dreary procession. Although dealing with the recent past and the present, Takamine's book harks back to a long tradition of personal writing in Japan. Her very title, *Watashi no tosei nikki* (literally, "A diary on making my way in the world") echoes one of the earliest personalist writings in Japanese letters, the *Tosa nikki* or *Tosa Diary* of the early tenth century. The *nikki*—literally, "daily record"—is a somewhat poetic and, in spite of its label, semifictional species of writing prominent during the Heian period from the ninth through the twelfth centuries. Written almost exclusively by women, especially ladies of the imperial court, the nikki as a specific genre came to an end shortly after the Heian period. Personalist writing of various kinds survived, however, and the travel journals of the haiku master Matsuo Bashō (1644–94) are one example well known even to Western readers. In the present century the personalist tradition is seen both in the preponderance of journal and diary writing and in the *watakushi-shōsetsu* (the "I"-novel), a loose form of narrative generally based on the author's own experience, but admitting a degree of fiction. In fact, Western scholars of Japanese literature have recently replaced the literal translation of *watakushi-shōsetsu* with the more pertinent designation, "personal fiction."

Takamine Hideko's autobiography provides much factual background on the life of the actress. Inasmuch as she wrote it entirely on her own, the very style of the autobiography conveys much of her personality. Like most other instances of the genre, Takamine's autobiography follows a chronological pattern. She gives her attention almost exclusively to the years of childhood, adolescence, and early adulthood. Though written when the author was about fifty, *A Journal of My Life* essentially ends with her marriage to Matsuyama Zenzō at the age of thirty. There are occasional reflections on her life with Matsuyama and a few anecdotes from the period, but this material is inserted by and large into the narrative of the author's earlier life. In short, the autobiography follows the pattern of a Bildungsroman, being primarily a record of Hideko's coming-of-age.

The word anecdotal, mentioned above, might be taken as characterizing Takamine's style of autobiographical writing. This statement should not be construed as negative in the least, either. Anecdotal writing might not, as a rule, organize experience into what Westerners are overly fond of calling "art." Nonetheless, there are various kinds of anecdotal writing—from the flat, meandering kind seen in *Something of an Autobiography*,[2] a chronicle by the famous Japanese director Kurosawa Akira (b. 1910)—to the scintillating and pointed kind well exemplified in Takamine's work. Hideko's generally anecdotal method does not amount to an interpretation of her life, nor does it give a perspective for viewing it. Nevertheless, the narrative is an instructive and varied one that holds the reader's interest. Put in the simplest terms, Takamine Hideko evokes what happened. She thus leaves her experience open-ended in a way that invites musing in the reader, musing rooted in the standard or typical matrix of the history and forms of life in twentieth-century Japan. Educated, thoughtful Japanese share a deep interest in this cultural material, and Hideko's writing provides the opportunity for a replay, with variations appropriate to her individual case, on a story the general outlines of which are already well known.

Idiosyncrasies of Japanese Autobiography

Autobiographical writing in modern Japan can give an impression of being overly factual or, especially in the case of late nineteenth-century work, of adhering to a fairly rigid set of conventional attitudes and responses. In his *As We Saw Them: The First Japanese Mission to the U.S.*,[3] Masao Miyoshi slights the Japanese bureaucratic functionaries he writes of for their inability to record in their journals the totally different realities they were encountering in America. Other autobiographical writings from early modern Japan transcend the conventional perspective of the emissaries' works. Nagai Kafū (1879–1959), a fine writer of faintly decadent tales, has left an exact and amusing account of his dallyings in a personal diary;[4] and the great Meiji educator Fukuzawa Yukichi (1835–1901), in perhaps the most celebrated autobiography in modern Japan (*The Autobiography of Fukuzawa Yukichi*),[5] has vividly portrayed the struggles and mishaps of a life devoted to popularizing Western ways and knowledge. In neither Kafū nor Fukuzawa, however, does one find a sustained attempt to convey a particular and striking image of the self. The highly focused and closely defined portraits of the self, familiar to the Western reader from such classic autobiographies as those of Cellini and Rousseau, are worlds apart from the indirection and modesty of the typical Japanese self-portrait. If these Western examples seem too different from the Japanese works just mentioned and from Takamine's book as well, one could cite instead, especially with the actress in mind, the two-volume autobiography of someone like Artur Rubinstein.[6] In some respects Rubinstein portrays himself as a picturesque hero, free to move from one adventure to another on his own initiative. Like most of her fellow autobiographers in Japan, Takamine portrays herself as constrained by both public and private circumstances. Kafū and Fukuzawa are doubtless greater literary talents than Takamine; and, as men in Japan, they could exercise more control over their lives. As surely as in her case, however, the agenda of their lives, even as portrayed by themselves, seems given by historical circumstances rather than determined by the impulse to achieve a self-realization of sorts.

Along with this focus on circumstances as opposed to individuality, the modern Japanese autobiographer or diarist seems somewhat reluctant to express personal feelings and judgments, even on his or her own experience. But, precisely because this is so, a deviation, when it does occur, can be all the more effective. What reader can forget the scene in which the young Fukuzawa takes his first step on the road to a rationalist outlook on life by trampling on an amulet with the name of a god and throwing the object into the toilet? Takamine, not to be outdone, indites certain passages with surprising self-assertion. In fact, part of the appeal of her writing comes from the alternation between her characteristic attitude of self-effacement and periodic manifestations of confidence and pride. Among many examples of this alternation, one could mention her confessions of ignorance about many subjects as an example of modesty; and, as an instance of pride, her rather offhanded mention of a childhood ability to memorize easily an entire script so that even the adult performers came to rely on her for stage prompting.

Family Background

Early in her life story, Takamine Hideko gives a brief survey of the recent history of her family. Her paternal grandfather, a jovial, carefree man named Hirayama Rikimatsu, was the owner of a small-town restaurant in Fukui Prefecture. By the time he went off to fight in the Russo-Japanese War of 1904–5, Rikimatsu was the father of three children, the youngest of them a girl named Shige who would play a crucial role in Takamine Hideko's life. After Rikimatsu returned from the war, he left his wife for a nineteen-year-old girl. This move meant the downfall of his business, for small-town residents in those days would censure a man who abandoned his wife. In 1907 Rikimatsu sold the restaurant and moved to Hakodate, a port town at the southern tip of Hokkaido. A great fire had recently leveled an extensive area of Hakodate, a tragedy that afforded new opportunities to any enterprising person. Unfortunately, while his new restaurant was being built, the purse containing the entire proceeds from the sale of the earlier business was pilfered, leaving the unlucky man virtually destitute.

Thereupon Rikimatsu dismissed the two maids he had brought to Hakodate and became a day laborer while living in a hut by the sea. His youngest daughter Shige was sent to live with a family of strangers, but she wept so incessantly that the family returned her to Rikimatsu. Rikimatsu's new wife bore her husband a total of thirteen children. Only five of them survived their childhood, however. Nonetheless, both the short-lived and the surviving children constituted a considerable burden for the family, much of which fell on the young shoulders of Hirayama Shige. In fact, as Shige was the only child from Rikimatsu's earlier marriage to remain with her father, she felt quite isolated while carrying out her nursing and cleaning tasks. Despite the problems, she managed to live with her father and stepmother until the age of seventeen. Rikimatsu tried to help matters by occasionally slipping the girl a few coins for spending money. But he saved most of his earnings—enough to eventually purchase a café and restaurant. By the time he opened a small theater as well, he was too busy to bother about Shige. Thus the girl was left to fend for herself in the hostile environment of her stepmother's home.

In 1918 Shige eloped to Niigata Prefecture with a ne'er-do-well named Ogino Ichiji. Ogino worked as a *benshi*, a professional reciter in the movie theaters in Japan during the era of the silent film. (The benshi would narrate the story and deliver the lines of the characters while the story unfolded on the screen.) Shige herself became a female benshi, assuming the professional name, significantly, of Takamine Hideko. Shige had not run away for love, but merely to escape Hakodate. When the couple eventually moved to Tokyo, she found herself neglected while Ogino traveled about in his new occupation of artist's agent.

In the meantime events were transpiring back in Hakodate that would eventually give a new direction to the life of Hirayama Shige. Rikimatsu's oldest son Kinji had married and become the father of three boys. On March 27, 1924, he again became a father, but this time the child turned out to be a girl. During this latest pregnancy of her sister-in-law, Shige had asked that she be allowed to adopt the expected child, a request that could be made quite readily in Japan in view of the widespread use of adoption for various social purposes. Kinji, believing that his wife was destined to bear only boys, promised that Shige could adopt the child. When a girl was born instead, Shige immediately called her Hideko after the professional name she herself had taken. Despite the promise made to her, Shige was not allowed to adopt Hideko right away. The couple in Hakodate did pledge to give her up in two years, leaving Shige no choice but to return to her lonely life in Tokyo.

Four years went by before this pledge was carried out. During this time Hideko apparently led a mostly uneventful life. Like her grandfather Rikimatsu, Hideko's father Kinji also ran a restaurant. Geisha would arrive there in the evening and befriend little Hideko during a lull in their duties of entertaining customers. Hideko remembers one dramatic event from those days—setting fire to her hair while playing with matches. Fortunately she was only singed and no permanent scars were sustained.

Hideko's first few years hardly suggest a potential for anything out of the ordinary. Hokkaido, the northernmost of the four main islands, was cut off from Japan's cultural and political life more drastically than the southernmost island of Kyushu. To the Japanese themselves, Hokkaido had been frontier country until the present century, a land identified with the alien culture of the Ainu and mostly valued as a barrier against Russian expansionism. Hideko, a child of the lower classes, might well have ended up as a waitress or a maid, had her life followed a typical pattern of a girl in her station.

In *A Journal of My Life* she portrays her family as caught up in circumstances largely beyond its control. The main activities would seem to be bearing children and making ends meet. If one allows the imagination free reign, one can even picture the adolescent Hideko being sold to a procurer of prostitutes, a common enough means by which families—especially those in the northern stretches of the country—tried to alleviate their poverty.

Hideko was plucked out of her early surroundings by pure chance. In 1928, intent on putting an end to Shige's insistent requests, Hideko's mother journeyed to Tokyo to tell her sister-in-law that the girl would remain at home. Shortly after her return to Hakodate, however, Hideko's mother became seriously ill with pulmonary tuberculosis. Within a short time Shige was summoned to Hakodate, this time to attend the funeral of the woman who had refused to fulfill the adoption pledge. Takamine describes the funeral in her book:

> A frightening spectacle leaped into view when I entered the inner parlor to take leave of my mother. A large coffin had been placed in the center of the room, and Mother's face loomed above it. (I must mention that, in Hakodate, the coffin stood on end, and the dead person appeared to be seated in a chair.) A white cloth was arranged about the body of the deceased, and this made the head appear to hover of its own accord. I let out a fearful scream and clung to Aunt Shige as she approached the dead woman. Afterward I clung to my aunt's sleeve even in the washroom and slept through the night in her arms.

Hideko's father willingly gave up the child for adoption. A younger son, too, was adopted by the dead woman's sister. Three other sons remained with the father, the oldest of whom would eventually play a brief role in the life of Takamine Hideko.

At Rikimatsu's insistence Hideko's father Kinji married again. This marriage failed, but not before three children had been born. Leaving two of his children with Rikimatsu, Hideko's father chose another wife who eventually bore him an additional three children. He also started a tea shop in Hakodate, but another great fire destroyed the business in 1939. Though she left Hokkaido at the age of four, Hideko had not seen the last of her father. He remained poor until his death in the 1950s, and there were times when Hideko seems to have been the main, if not the sole, means of support for the entire family.

With travel between southern Hokkaido and Tokyo difficult, Hideko was cut off from the various branches of her family and—if one chooses to read between the lines of the autobiography—not overly inclined to keep in touch with them. Nonetheless, after she got established in film, Hideko often enough found herself with unwelcome family guests in the house. Shige was willing to support these guests, and Hideko herself, as she grew up, undoubtedly felt an obligation to assist the bumbling and helpless members of her own family.

With Shige filling the void created by the death of her mother, Hideko could look back on these early days of their life together as fairly benign ones. By featuring the part Shige played in the history of her recent ancestry, Hideko suggests a degree of sympathy that some-times gets obscured in the account of their final years together. The author is acutely aware of the difficult time Shige had after being deprived of her own mother. Hideko too might well have been victim-ized by a stepmother, had she remained as Shige did with her father. Although she does not say so directly in her autobiography, Takamine does imply by the ordering of her narrative that Shige rescued her as a child from the hazards of living in a house that might not have pro-vided real parental love. Shige may have wanted a child of her own, and Hideko became available just in time to play this role. Regardless of how possessive Shige would prove to be later on, or how jealous of Hideko's youth and success, she did provide protection for the girl during the most vulnerable years of her childhood and early adoles-cence.

Indeed, the most striking example of Shige playing the role of mother occurs at the moment of the girl's very initiation into adolescence. Hideko relates the episode in brief but telling detail.

> That morning I was unable to get off the toilet, for a red thread kept streaming out from underneath. It was blood, and it came out exactly like red thread being unwound from a skein. Was the blood going to flow out of my body entirely? I turned pale at the very thought and fled from the bathroom.
>
> "Mother, something's broke down there."
>
> "Huh? Down there?" She stood up, staring at me. Slowly her wide open eyes narrowed, and she began to snicker. "Oh, that's nothing," she said. "You just became a woman."
>
> "A woman?"
>
> "That's right. You're not a child any more, you're a woman. From now on the blood will come out every month, maybe for as long as a week. This is a happy occasion, and we'll celebrate this evening with red beans and rice."
>
> She went to the closet and got out a clean towel. Tearing this in half, she made a kind of diaper. She placed thick cotton on the diaper and put it between my legs.

Although Hideko at first resisted becoming a woman, Shige was always at her side to help her negotiate the inevitable shoals of growing up.

Almost one year after her arrival in Tokyo, an event occurred that would alter the course of Hideko's life more drastically than the move from Hokkaido had done. Her Aunt Shige was still married to Ogino, the benshi with whom she had eloped years before. One day Ogino took Hideko along when he paid a visit to the studio of the Shōchiku Film Company, located in the Kamata district of Tokyo. At that very moment the director Nomura Hōtei happened to be auditioning a large number of children for a role in an upcoming film. Apparently on impulse, Ogino placed little Hideko in the line of children waiting to be auditioned. Nomura quickly recognized the girl's appeal and selected her for the role.

The film, entitled *Mother*, was the first of many in which Hideko would appear as the little daughter. For a child who had just lost her own mother and been taken from her surroundings by a relatively unknown aunt, this type of role was far from ideal. The Shōchiku Studio operated from early morning until well into the night, shooting a number of films at the same time. Hideko found herself playing daughter to several different actresses from one hour to the next. Before she was barely comfortable with her Aunt Shige, she had to regard—at least during those long hours of work—Kirishima Sumiko on one film set and Kawata Yoshiko on another as her "mother." In her account of those early days, Ms. Takamine tells how she tried to suckle at the breast of one of her "mothers." This scene, however, was being played onstage in the Kabuki manner, with the role of her mother being taken by a male actor.

Her Aunt Shige seems to have accompanied Hideko to the studio on a daily basis. One can readily imagine her feelings at this turn of events—happy for Hideko, perhaps, and not averse to the additional income, but presumably bereft too at a kind of defection on the part of her adopted daughter. Hideko says very little about Shige's role at the studio. This in itself suggests how monopolized Hideko's own time was—mostly in the filming process itself, but also in getting taken about to restaurants and other places of entertainment by studio people in the brief time left over for leisure.

Takamine's overall view of those early years in the movies is ambivalent. Certainly there were many problems aside from the confusion over her mother. In the absence of child labor laws, the long hours proved trying for the girl. She had to follow a special diet to maintain her stamina, a diet that ran to such unappealing fare as fried garlic and herbs of all kinds. For her own protection, Hideko learned that she must pretend to fall asleep when midnight rolled around or else the director would keep the camera turning. Since her home was some distance from the film studio, Hideko had to leave early in the morning so the make-up personnel had time to ready her for the day's filming. Needless to say, she was kept out of school, and she seldom had any companions her own age to play with on the studio lot. In looking back on those days, Ms. Takamine remarks that the child she saw most often was an albino girl who regularly ventured out on the neighborhood street as she herself left for work. Hideko felt a certain bond with this girl; after all, neither one had any playmates, and now that she was appearing in films, Hideko too was stared at. Though drawn to the unfortunate girl, Hideko did not even have the time to greet her.

Unlike the albino girl, however, Hideko enjoyed a number of benefits in return for the hardships she had to endure. *A Journal of My Life* does not skip over these benefits, either. As a child star in a nation that adores children, she was petted and entertained by a host of interesting people in the movies. Besides Nomura, the Shōchiku Studio employed such famous directors as Gosho Heinosuke and Ozu Yasujirō. These men were very generous to those who worked under them and would occasionally give lavish parties for their staffs. Hideko was a great favorite, and, when time permitted, she would be taken around to cafés on the Ginza and even to the geisha houses in the Yoshiwara district. Even though she was not in the occupation by deliberate choice, Hideko evidently found acting an enjoyable activity in spite of the grueling work schedule. She vividly recalls certain plays in which she appeared—*Manchuria*, for example, a drama based on the Shanghai Incident of 1932 in which the young actress sat on an emperor's throne while mysterious talk about military matters went on around her.

Hideko was also paid well, at least by the rather low standards of the acting profession in prewar Japan. At the same time the studio scheduled work as tightly as possible in order to utilize its personnel for maximum effect. In retrospect the author of *A Journal of My Life* seems acutely aware of how she was used by various adults. The studio overworked her in order to profit from her popularity with Japanese audiences. While her salary matched what a graduate of a prestigious university could command, the entire sum was under the control of her aunt and adoptive mother, Hirayama Shige.

Takamine Hideko's sense of how adults could use and even defraud a child was sharpened by a strange affair that extended over nearly two years of her childhood. One of the many entertainers who came into contact with Hideko was a popular singer of the day named Shōji Tarō. After performing in a skit with the girl, Shōji asked her Aunt Shige whether he and his wife could adopt Hideko. In his mid-thirties at the time, Shōji had two boys from an earlier marriage. He wanted a daughter too, but his present wife had not borne him any children. Shige, wary of being deprived of Hideko's company even more, turned down the request. Shōji Tarō was persistent and clever, however, and eventually he agreed to having Shige herself live in his house as Hideko's guardian. Shige saw an opportunity to rid herself of the unwanted Ogino, and she therefore acceded to the plan.

The move occurred in 1934, when Hideko was ten years old. During the almost two years that Hideko and her Aunt Shige stayed in Shōji's house, the girl's film career was virtually suspended. Instead of acting, she accompanied her new foster father on his tours throughout Japan. In retrospect, Hideko claims that Shōji's wish to adopt her might have been more to further his career than to fill a void in his life. This idea might seem somewhat far-fetched to the reader of A *Journal of My Life*, given the author's own description of how Shōji and his wife virtually competed with one another in showering the girl with affection.

Though Hideko was kindly treated, Shige herself was not shown even elementary courtesy. From the very beginning she was kept in a different part of the house from Hideko; eventually she was more or less turned into the household maid.

The departure of Hideko and Shige took place under strange circumstances. One New Year's Day Mrs. Shōji gave Shige some kimono fabric as a gift. She evidently did this with the best of intentions, but the gesture suggested a traditional ritual carried out between master and servant. Hideko claimed aversion to the look of the particular fabric and insisted that she and Shige leave the Shōji house immediately. This decision exemplifies a fairly common motif in Takamine's life—the sudden change, resulting either from a deliberate decision or from an accident, which orients the life in a new direction. In this instance, the immediate reason for the departure seems rather trivial; but the stated reason could possibly be the straw that broke the camel's back. Shōji had pledged to send Hideko to school and to give her piano lessons. He did neither; and, when pressured to provide some kind of assistance for Hideko's schooling and household expenses after the breakup, he temporized and ended up doing nothing.

In her autobiography, Takamine Hideko adds a postscript to the account of her sojourn at the Shōji house. Shōji died in 1972 at the age of seventy-four, a few years before Takamine began to write. To balance her ultimately negative treatment of his personal qualities, the author has recourse to his professional gifts. On the above-mentioned tours, Hideko would wait in the wings while Shōji went through his routine on stage. She expresses immense admiration for his stage presence and for his disciplined approach to rehearsing.

Adolescence

In the mid-1930s Japanese cinema made the transition from the silent film to the talkie. At about the same time, certain studios consolidated their operations and began working on a larger scale. Several independent companies merged under the name Tōhō and built a huge, Hollywood-style studio in the Seijō area of Setagaya Ward in Tokyo. Hideko's company, Shōchiku, moved its quarters out of Tokyo to the town of Ōfuna in Kanagawa, a prefecture to the south of the capital city. Several of Japan's most talented directors, Mizoguchi Kenji for one, began their careers at this time as well. A "star" system came into being, and the reputation of actors and actresses as "riverbed beggars," inspired by the unsavory origins of the Kabuki theater in the seventeenth century, began to fade.

Hideko worked just a few years at the Ōfuna studio before she and Shōchiku parted company. Actually the break was the work of Aunt Shige, rather than a move taken by either Hideko or the studio. (As will become clear, Shige was to prove quite ready to interfere in the life and career of her adopted daughter from this time on.) Shige was in need of money, partly because her brother Rikimatsu, following another disastrous fire in Hakodate, had arrived penniless in Tokyo with his household of nine people. Part of Hideko's salary supported this group, and Shige hoped to invest additional funds in a boarding house to augment the girl's income. An impetuous woman, she went directly to an official at the studio and demanded an advance on Hideko's salary. Outraged when the official refused, Shige looked for ways to strike back. When the Tōhō people happened to send a representative to sound out the possibility of luring the girl away from Shōchiku, Shige leaped at the chance for vengeance. Tōhō's offer seemed generous, for Hideko's salary would be doubled, and she would be allowed time off to attend school. Without this latter provision, the girl would not have assented to the move.

Takamine Hideko writes of her early days at Tōhō in positive terms. She and Shige were given a new house in Seijō, the pleasant Tokyo suburb where the studio was located. Hideko could walk to work, enjoying the trees and shrubs along the way and listening to a piano playing classical music somewhere nearby. She finally realized her long-time dream of attending school, commuting in the beginning with some regularity to the Bunka Gakuin campus in northern Tokyo.

In retrospect, the school and the studio each proved to have a highly egalitarian spirit. Although Americans today regard Japanese schools as strict and academically oriented—in comparison to their own, at least—there was far more regimentation in them before World War II than at present. Indeed, discipline was the order of the day, in behavior as well as in school work. The Bunka Gakuin, a progressive school, was the exception to this rule. Students were encouraged to call their teachers, and the principal too, by their first names. Social dancing was part of the daily routine, and academic instruction was quite lax. Famous since her days as a child star, Hideko was constantly being asked to pose for the drawing class. She had come to the Bunka Gakuin to learn, but she found it impossible to turn down her teacher's invitation to leave class and pose for the budding artists. About the only thing the school apparently would not tolerate was truancy. Eventually Tōhō proved no more willing than Shōchiku had been to allow such a valuable property as Takamine Hideko time off during the day to attend school. After a time the girl was absent so often that the school gave her a choice: either attend regularly or withdraw. Perhaps Hideko was disillusioned with the school for its laxity; or maybe she was already reconciled to the necessity of, as she puts it several times in her autobiography, "learning by ear," that is, learning from the diverse and talented group of people who surrounded her every day. By this time Hideko felt financially responsible for Shige and for her father's family. She opted for her career and dropped out of school.

The studio did not allow its employees the same degree of freedom as the Bunka Gakuin granted to its students. In other ways, however, Tōhō represented a distinct improvement over the Shōchiku system of that time. According to Takamine, Shōchiku had an autocratic system that segregated the stars from the other actors and from the production staff as well. Tōhō, on the other hand, rejected the traditional Kabuki-inspired notion of a hierarchy of acting professionals. Instead, the acting staff at Tōhō was divided into equal groups, each assigned one large dressing room with one of their number designated a kind of overseer for three months at a time. Hideko was too young to assume such duties, but she found herself in a group guided by such famous actresses as Hanabusa Yuriko, Hara Setsuko, and Chiba Sachiko.

Like Shōchiku, Tōhō saw to it that Takamine Hideko earned every yen of her larger paycheck. During her first two years at the new studio, she appeared in twelve movies. Often Hideko had to memorize two or three scripts at one time; and, when one film was completed, she would be whisked off to another set where the next film was already being made. Normally thirty to forty days of intense work went into each movie, although longer and more complex films might be a year or more in the making. Takamine mentions that her favorite film during these early years at Tōhō was *Tsuzurikata Kyōshitsu* (The Writing Class), a piece directed by Yamamoto Kajirō and based on an autobiographical story by Toyota Masako, a girl almost the same age as Hideko herself. She also mentions that, during these years of middle adolescence, she realized that a film represented the collaboration of many people, from the producer and director down to the most menial laborers on the crew. Each employee of the Tōhō Studio felt a personal responsibility to produce the best possible work. Without such an esprit de corps, no worthwhile film could really be achieved.

The Beginnings of Maturity

During the 1930s the Japanese Army became more and more involved on the Asian mainland, and life in Japan grew increasingly difficult. Material goods were scarce, and the government started to crack down on behavior that deviated from a strict nationalism. Hideko was too young to understand political issues, but she was affected in special ways because of her status as a child star. Japanese women during these years would send soldiers various gifts—vests with one thousand stitches, each stitch the work of a different woman, or comfort bags containing trinkets of various kinds. A photo of Takamine Hideko might be included among these effects, and she often received letters from the soldiers who kept her photo. These letters, many addressed merely to "Takamine Hideko of Japan," wring the heart with their simplicity. One soldier wrote that he had discovered a portrait of Hideko pasted to the ceiling of a house in which he had sought refuge. About to take the photo with him, he decided in the end to leave it for the benefit of whichever soldier wandered in next. On another occasion Hideko's photo was returned inside an envelope, with an apology from the soldier for its soiled condition. He went on to explain how loathe he was to have her likeness strewn on the battlefield with his own corpse. Once a letter arrived from Osaka with a wrinkled photo and a brief note of explanation: the family's son, killed in action, had left the photo among his effects. In describing these experiences from the years of her adolescence, Takamine Hideko also recalled a visit she made to Peking well after the war had ended. Even while showing her a display of miscellaneous effects from Japanese soldiers killed in action, the Chinese guide advised her to forget about the war. For the

Chinese themselves, the guide went on, the war was merely a small episode in their immensely long history.

Other experiences remain deeply etched in Takamine's memory from those trying years of mobilization and war. Especially after Japan joined with Germany and Italy in the Triple Alliance in 1940, such frivolous pleasures as dancing and curled hair were forbidden to the populace. When the use of English words was also banned, Hideko realized that her collection of classical and pop records was doomed. Rather than allow her records to be carted off and destroyed, Hideko decided to do the job herself. She threw them one by one into the garden and then ground the whole lot to bits, crunching each disk beneath her wooden clogs.

With the advent of the General Tōjō's cabinet in 1941, jingoism set in and further rigid measures were undertaken by the government. The Hawaiian steel guitar was proscribed as effeminate and sentimental. American and British films were banned at this time as well, and the chorus-line singer-dancers performed on the Takarazuka all-female revue stage were forbidden to dress in men's clothes. Two meatless days per month were decreed, and tobacco and salt were rationed. Despite her status as a celebrity, even Hideko was compelled to gather branches and twigs in the woods to heat her bath water.

Even during these difficult times, however, there were many lighter moments. Takamine points out that, by a not uncommon irony, the general somberness of the era gave rise to renewed interest in various kinds of comedy. All sorts of entertainers, especially professional comedians, were given ample opportunity to demonstrate their talents. Hideko came to know two comedians particularly well, Enomoto Kenichi and Furukawa Roppa. Enoken, a familiar designation linking the personal name and the surname, was a friendly man who would invite the entire filming crew to his dressing room for drinks after a hard day's work. Sometimes his own drinking got the better of him, and then he would frighten everyone off by brandishing a prop sword about. The next morning he would set things right, bowing apologetically to each member of the staff who came to the studio. Roppa had a more aristocratic makeup. He once declared that he preferred to eat alone in order to savor his food properly. After the war, when the American forces occupied the country, Roppa switched to a different diet—working his way from beginning to end of an English dictionary and swallowing each page after he had memorized it. As one might expect, Roppa was utterly chagrined to discover that the English he had learned in this unique fashion was useless.

Another good friend and talented actor from Hideko's late adolescence was Ōkōchi Denjirō. In spite of his fame, Ōkōchi lived a reclusive life at his home in the Arashiyama Hills west of Kyoto. In between films he spent his days performing Zen meditation and decreeing that journalists and women must keep their distance. Since Hideko was still young, she was not included in this interdiction. As an actor, Ōkōchi seemed to Hideko to capitalize upon his limitations. He was nearsighted and uncoordinated; furthermore, he did not remember his lines easily. Still, his eyes had a thoughtful look, and his performance seemed all the more powerful for the regular pauses he employed in order to recall his lines. In the final scene of a film about the hero Tange Sazen, a lengthy shot shows Tange fleeing along a river bank, one arm cut off as a consequence of his duel with the famed swordsman Chiba Shōsaku. His balance adversely affected by the loss of his arm, Tange leans forward, so far that he seems to be scurrying ahead on his knees.

Impressed by the ability of Ōkōchi and many other actors and actresses whose work she encountered every day, Hideko began to think about her own training. Recognizing the advantages of a set of skills, she began in late adolescence to develop techniques that would help make her an adult professional in the cinema. She took lessons in voice and elocution, studying under two teachers whose own abilities virtually overwhelmed her. One voice teacher could drown out the sound of nearby commuter trains, and the vocal power of the second teacher made Hideko compare her own voice to the cry of a mosquito. She learned a number of useful techniques from these mentors—for example, to incorporate all her breath into vocal expression in such a way that a candle flame placed right in front of the mouth would not even waver. She also learned other skills, some of them quite mundane, for particular films. For her eight films in 1939, for example, she had to learn, among other things, to ride a bicycle, to ice skate, and to speak Kyoto dialect. In one of the films she had to play the thirteen-stringed *koto* by herself. To help her with this task, she received a lesson in the instrument from the leading performer of the day, the blind master Miyagi Michio.

One must keep in mind, too, that the general condition under which movies were made in prewar Japan were primitive in comparison to

the present. The studios had neither central heating nor air condition-
ing; the performers simply endured the cold and heat. Furthermore,
films for the summer were often shot in winter, while those for winter
were shot in summer. Often the dress required for a given scene was
totally inappropriate for the season when the filming was being done.
During the winter Hideko and her colleagues would suck on ice to
prevent their breath from appearing white on the film. In the summer
they could do nothing about the perspiration that the hot kleig lights
brought on.

One of the strongest motivations behind the writing of A *Journal of
My Life* bears on the ordeal of acting. Although a versatile and subtle
actress, Hideko by and large eschews comment on such matters as the
psychology of acting and the inner rewards associated with the activity. In a number of passages she contrasts the physical hardship of the
profession as she has known it with the relative comfort in which
contemporary performers carry out their tasks. Part of this difference is
no doubt traceable to the overall rise in the standard of living in Japan
during the past several decades. Actors and actresses are no longer
considered "river beggars"; on the contrary, they enjoy some of the
same privileges as their Hollywood counterparts. Against the popular
notion of the glamour and luxury of the profession, Takamine insists
on the struggle and hardship as the general lot of performers at the time
she achieved fame in the movies.

The Kurosawa Incident and the End of the War

By this point in her adolescence Takamine Hideko was appearing in
more grown-up roles. One of her films was entitled *Horse* and was set
in northern Japan, which compelled her to master the unfamiliar dialect
of the region in order to play her role. The film was of epic length and
took three years to make. Hideko would be rushed up north on overnight trains from Tokyo when the weather for shooting certain scenes
turned favorable. While shooting one scene that required her to plow a
field, she fainted and had to be taken to the hospital. She was obviously suffering from exhaustion—and, as it turned out upon examination, from dry pleurisy and appendicitis as well. She returned to Tokyo
and took a long rest in a hospital.

While working on *Horse*, Hideko came to know well a man who
was to play an important role in her life in both personal and profes-

sional terms. At the time Kurosawa Akira (b. 1910) was an assistant director, a sort of apprentice who does miscellaneous tasks for the film director while learning the techniques of the trade. Already Kurosawa displayed the discipline that would help him become one of the world's greatest film directors. According to Takamine, Kurosawa would go to extreme lengths to study in the evening. When on location, he would seclude himself with a book or scenario in a closet at the inn where the film crew would be lodging.

During her adolescence Hideko had enjoyed Kurosawa's company on a number of occasions. They wrote rather casual letters to one another, and Kurosawa turned out to be the first face she recognized when coming out of her fainting spell during the filming of *Horse*. The relationship, however, suddenly took on a different cast one evening during Hideko's late adolescence. As her Aunt Shige played mahjongg with several male friends downstairs (a practice she followed assiduously after the move to Seijō), Hideko came to the conclusion that she could no longer live with her aunt. Kurosawa's apartment was nearby, and that is where Hideko fled, apparently on impulse. When she reached the apartment, she was welcomed inside. However, Kurosawa and Hideko had hardly sat down opposite one another before the door opened and Shige walked in. She glared at Hideko, evidently in a fit of jealousy; then she let out a scream and fainted.

Hideko was taken home and confined to her room an entire week. When she finally got back to work, Kurosawa snubbed her. Rather than find out what the problem was, Hideko decided to ignore him. Presently she learned that the newspapers had announced an engagement between them; rather than thrash out the problem with the haughty Kurosawa, the girl decided to concentrate on her career—to become an actress worthy of the professional standards of this prodigy of a director.

One other encounter with a man warrants mention at this point. An older brother named Minoru had gone to Manchuria during the 1930s to work for a drilling firm. One day, shortly before war broke out between Japan and the United States, Minoru strolled into Hideko's residence completely unannounced. After washing up, he told his sister to purchase five hundred miniature "skull rosaries," the kind sold at the bazaars in Tokyo. He also bought some of the tiny skulls himself, intending to return to the continent and sell them at a considerable profit.

One night, while Shige was away at the public bath, Minoru be-
haved far more outrageously. Alone with his sister, he suddenly threw
himself on the girl as she lay in bed reading. He declared his love for
Hideko and said that the two of them would marry in their next life
cycle. Minoru departed shortly thereafter, leaving Hideko with several
gem-like stones and a Mongolian knife. After the war he returned to
Japan, but he was by then an utter derelict.

These two episodes represent the closest thing to a physical encounter with a man described by the author of *A Journal of My Life*. In the
last two decades Japanese writing has explored the sexual—indeed, the
perversely erotic—with little heed for the reticence of an earlier age.
(In fact, certain foreign observers would appear to believe that the
mass media in Japan, especially television, have made the erotic more
accessible there than anywhere else.) Takamine, however, was raised
at a time when reticence still regulated the relation between the sexes,
especially during adolescence and early adulthood. Even when she
describes the courtship between Matsuyama Zenzō and herself, little if
anything emerges as to how the couple felt about one another, let alone
how intimate they ever became with each other.

In this context the two encounters described above, the one with
Kurosawa and the one with Minoru, take on added meaning. Both
were brief and unusual. Neither seems to have affected Hideko except
in a momentary way. (To repeat an earlier point, however, it should be
remembered that the failure of the Kurosawa affair did play a role in
Takamine's commitment to acting.) It should also be stressed here that,
in general, Hideko writes quite casually about the men she has known
socially and professionally. Those who appear in her autobiography,
even in the chapters dealing with her adulthood, are old enough to be
her father. They offer her friendship and guidance rather than excitement and romance. Even when Hideko emerges as a mature actress,
playing the role of a virtual femme fatale (the bar madam in *When a
Woman Climbs the Stairs*, for example), in her personal life she seems
to maintain a highly deliberate and realistic outlook on the opposite
sex.

By Hideko's late adolescence, Japan's war with the United States
had reached a climax. The Japanese film industry continued to operate,
but much of its production was along patriotic lines. Although there
was little opportunity for Takamine to star in the nationalistic films
that featured highly masculine actors, she did appear in certain roles. In

one film, for example, she played the girlfriend of an airforce pilot—actually a member of the elite kamikaze corps who must keep his identity a secret even on the night before his scheduled suicide mission.

Although Takamine appears apolitical in *A Journal of My Life*, she does seem to have been skeptical about certain claims the military authorities made about the progress of the war. Late in the war years she was engaged in the filming of a production entitled *Full Tilt Toward America*. Even as the film was being shot at a provincial location east of Tokyo, however, American planes were carrying out regular and devastating bombing raids against a nearby air base. The actress had other experiences during the war that sowed doubts about the validity of the militaristic propaganda. In one instance, captured American films were shown to a select audience of government officials and studio personnel, including Takamine. After viewing *Gone With the Wind* and Walt Disney's *Fantasia*, Hideko wondered—probably with the other Japanese who had access to them—how Japan could be at war with a country capable of producing these splendid films.

By the time *Full Tilt Toward America* was being filmed, Japanese cities had already been devastated by B-29 bombing raids, and the government had issued its directive that the populace should fashion bamboo spears to defend itself against an expected invasion of Allied forces. Shortly after the Tōhō crew arrived on location, the Americans began bombing the area daily, evidently aiming at the nearby airfield. During one of the raids Hideko decided to stay in her room at the inn rather than take shelter in one of the ineffectual foxholes scratched out on the beach. Here is her description of a raid:

> The heavy thud of a bomb echoed in the distance; then a carrier-based fighter skimmed over the rooftop with a screeching sound. The plane repeatedly dove, its machine guns blasting away until the whole area was enveloped in acrid smoke, and the smell of gunpowder invaded my nostrils. Glass shattered in the distance and, somewhat closer, roof tiles crumbled and fell. Before my very eyes planes engaged in a dog fight. Was that fighter plunging and bursting into flame an American one? Or one of our Zeroes? My mind was quite composed, as though I were watching a film, but I nonetheless crouched down as if bound hand and foot. Outside, it was truly a battleground.

Finally, with the famous broadcast by the emperor in August 1945, the war came to an end. Takamine was still at work on *Full Tilt*

Toward America when the populace heard an imperial voice for the first time in history. The night after the surrender was announced, she saw and heard something of the despair of the Japanese soldier, suddenly deprived of the very center of his existence.

That evening the streets were in an uproar. There were explosions of ear-splitting magnitude, and planes flew in low over the rooftops dropping leaflets like snowflakes. The ink of the printing press was still fresh, and the message clear. *Resistance to the Utmost! We Shall Fight Till Death.* Also, several officers I knew by sight and who only that morning had vigorously saluted me now rushed into the garden brandishing their swords. Their eyes were bloodshot and they smelled of liquor. With piercing shouts they slashed wildly at the trees that had been placed in an aesthetic arrangement about the pond. Some trees crashed to the ground while others fell into the water. To me this spectacle was more frightening than the air raids and dog fights I had recently witnessed. When the noise finally subsided, I put on my pajamas and got under the mosquito net. Until the previous night, the shutters had to be kept shut in spite of the heat, and a black cloth draped over every lamp. Tonight, however, the lamps shone so brightly that one could hardly recognize the place.

I wondered how things would go from tomorrow. But thinking about it wouldn't change anything, and eventually I fell asleep. Suddenly the roar of a plane filled the air. It was already past midnight, and I leaped from bed. One after another the planes roared by overhead. Finally the sounds died out over the ocean, and the inn fell quiet once again.

Brought up only to fight, indoctrinated to wage war and die, these young men had suddenly been deprived of a foe. There was nothing for them to do anymore, but was suicide the only way out of despair? I did not know how many bombs these planes held in their bellies, but the fuel of a Zero fighter was quite limited. The dark, endless ocean toward which the planes had flown would become the graveyard for each pilot when the final drop of gasoline ran out. Why . . . when the war had ended . . . ? The thought was unbearable. I merely crouched beneath the mosquito net, hugging my knees as I listened to those roaring planes pass over the roof.

The American Occupation

With the unconditional surrender of Japan, the dreaded invasion by a vengeful American military force never materialized. Rather than a bloody series of pitched battles, the Japanese experienced a remarkably peaceful occupation by American forces under the direction of General Douglas MacArthur. As a public figure, Takamine Hideko came more directly into contact with the occupation than the average Japanese citizen. In general, the encounters with American officers and troops that she recounts seem pleasant enough, even frivolous at times. For example, she sang for the soldiers at a theater in Tokyo named after the noted war journalist, Ernie Pyle. The applause and whistling that greeted the end of her performance seems amusing, though hardly overwhelming, to Takamine the author. When some nisei Japanese-American GI's showed up in her dressing room, she invited them to come to her home someday to have riceballs. Much to her surprise, an entire bus load of troops pulled up to the house shortly thereafter. Even though they came tramping in with their boots on, a conspicuous violation of Japanese custom, Hideko seems to have found the nisei enjoyable company.

As a celebrity she was called upon to perform a variety of services during the years of the occupation—from throwing out the first ball to open the professional baseball season in Tokyo to helping the emperor plant a few trees in the Hakone mountains. This last experience is described in amusing terms in the autobiography. Hideko was driven by jeep up the Hakone Pass without being told what was in store. The jeep came to a halt where a sizable crowd had gathered. A number of saplings were lying about, along with a few shovels. Eventually a procession of black limousines pulled up, and the emperor himself alighted from one. According to Hideko, the emperor seemed quite bewildered as the ritual planting began. He held a shovel, and the actress took hold of one of the saplings. The emperor then looked at her as if asking to be told where the hole should be dug.

There were difficulties as well as pleasures during these years. Unlike countless Japanese citizens, Hideko did not have to worry about either her next meal or a place to spend the night. The problems she did encounter were trying ones, but they did not bear on her survival. A major psychological problem—one which appears to have resolved itself by chance—concerns labor troubles at the film studio. To nullify the authoritarianism that seemed behind Japan's ill-advised war effort, the officials of the American occupation established conditions favorable to the growth of democracy among the people, one of these being the freedom for workers to organize as labor unions. Takamine

Hideko, who seems generally apolitical, does not deal with the politics of the situation. She did participate in a strike against the Tōhō Studio and was part of a group of actors and actresses who set up a rival studio called Shin Tōhō, or New Tōhō.

The Great Artists

If her autobiography is any indication, Takamine Hideko does not define her life with reference to social ideas and movement, on the one hand, or to such varied and discrete experiences as sharing a meal with *nisei* soldiers or planting a tree with the emperor, on the other. Like a significantly large number of Japanese, she views herself in the context of her personal ties, especially with those she admires and cherishes. Certain ties from her childhood and adolescence have already been mentioned. As an adult she continues to cultivate friendships among movie people, but her circle of acquaintances broadens to include artistic people from beyond the world of the cinema.

A Journal of My Life has a cover portrait of the actress by Umehara Ryūsaburō, a celebrated Japanese painter who died in 1987, just one year shy of his hundredth birthday, and whose Western-style works were well represented in the recent exhibition, "Paris in Japan." Takamine knew Umehara before sitting for the portrait, but her most pointed remarks on the painter revolve around the making of this work. A public figure from childhood, Hideko believed she must maintain a cheerful exterior in public, even when this meant hiding her deeper feelings. Posing for Umehara in early adulthood, Takamine instinctively assumed her usual public personality. But when she looked at her image as drawn by the painter, she realized that he had seen right into her. Thereafter the two became totally open and frank with one another. Takamine tells of eating and talking with Umehara, and she even quotes a number of brief letters she received from him. (Umehara had been to France as a young, aspiring painter, where he studied with Renoir; he had also traveled extensively in other European countries and lived for a time both in Taiwan and in mainland China.) Umehara had a truly gargantuan appetite. When the mood struck, he was entirely capable of picking up an entire dish and devouring the food directly off the plate.

Another famous artist with a huge appetite also became a close friend of Takamine Hideko. Tanizaki Junichirō (1886–1965) is best known in the West for his massive social novel *The Makioka Sisters* (1948), and for a number of sardonic shorter works, among them *The*

Diary of a Mad Old Man (1962) and *The Key* (1956). Hideko made Tanizaki's acquaintance when offered a role in the film version of *The Makioka Sisters*. Hideko suspects that Tanizaki treated her with paternal solicitude because she played the youngest of the four Makioka sisters. In any event, Tanizaki often invited her to his house. She would bring a package of rice crackers, knowing that Tanizaki would expect such a gift when he met her at the door. Without even thanking her, he would open the package and begin stuffing the crackers into his mouth. When he had eaten his fill, he would carefully wrap up the remaining crackers and store them in the cupboard. Only then was Hideko allowed to greet the author's wife and daughter, both of whom embodied the gentle ways and precise manners often associated with traditional Japanese women.

According to Hideko, not many people were aware of the author's infirmities. In addition to a heart problem, Tanizaki had trouble with one of his hands. By his late seventies he had lost much of his vigor. Then he underwent an operation and suddenly was his old self—eating, drinking, and going off to see the sights. To the great surprise of his friends, however, he died several months later, at age seventy-nine. Hideko was saddened by his death. It was hard to realize that such an energetic man could really be dead. Hideko also confesses to feeling indignant toward him for abandoning his beloved wife Matsuko, on whom Tanizaki had based many of his unforgettable heroines.

Both Umehara and Tanizaki stand larger than life in Takamine's evocation of them. Their abundant energy and contempt for conventional form and decorum come through in the author's description of their gustatory habits. In Umehara's case, Takamine also experienced the utter concentration with which the painter worked. His eyes would take on a sharp, focused expression, and his cigarette would invariably burn his lip before he realized he was even smoking. Takamine did not have a like opportunity to observe Tanizaki in the throes of composition. Nonetheless, Tanizaki does emerge in her pages as a heroic figure, his stature enhanced by the void that his death leaves in his family. Umehara was almost ninety when Takamine wrote *A Journal of My Life*, and he was still going strong. He seems yet more heroic than Tanizaki by virtue of his amazing longevity as an artist and bon vivant.

Two other older men who also impressed Takamine Hideko were the directors Ozu Yasujirō and Naruse Mikio. Ozu directed certain of Hideko's early films, and during the late 1940s and 1950s director and actress collaborated on such works as *The Munakata Sisters* (1950) and *Early Summer* (1951). Ozu died of cancer in 1962, and Hideko evokes his memory in the autobiography she wrote more than ten years later. Ozu had a quiet dignity about him, and the film crew, normally jovial and boisterous, would inevitably fall silent when he was present. During the filming of a movie, even veteran performers were cowed by Ozu's presence. While playing a certain scene with the veteran actor Ryū Chishū, Hideko noticed that the teacup in her companion's hand was quivering. Though Ryū had often worked under Ozu's direction, so awed was he by the director that his hand shook. This, at least, was the conclusion that Takamine Hideko reached. Perhaps she was especially sensitive to the effect Ozu had on her older colleagues because of his indulgent manner toward her. Playing the role of a child or even of an adolescent, Hideko should appear to act naturally. The grownups, however, should exemplify the reserve and discipline common to Japanese at that stage of life—or at least, to those Japanese who appear in Ozu films.

Naruse Mikio, who died just seven years after Ozu, also directed in an understated manner. Indeed, despite her immense admiration for his talent and respect for his memory, Hideko does not hesitate to complain of Naruse's taciturnity. Unlike other directors, Naruse never told or showed anyone how to play a scene; all he did was indicate when he was satisfied. Although much of what she has to say about Naruse seems negative—on longer trips to location, he might sit in morose silence for hours on end—Hideko evokes his presence in virtually religious terms. As with Ozu, she talks freely about his death, particularly her last visit to see him during his final illness. As she was leaving his house, he made a cryptic remark about a film—a purely black-and-white film played against a blank background—that he had earlier hinted he would like to make with the actress. Takamine left not knowing whether Naruse meant they must still make the film, or whether, because of his illness, he had lost his chance to do that. The actress adds that she has never visited Naruse's grave because of her feeling that he still lives within her. In spite of her comments about the director's lack of method, it is clear that Takamine believes that her magnificent performances in such films as *Floating Clouds* (1955), *Her Lonely Lane* (1962), and *When a Woman Ascends the Stairs* (1960) were inspired by this great director.

Takamine Hideko depicts her women friends in *A Journal of My*

Life in quite different terms. Unlike Umehara and Tanizaki, the women in the book are vulnerable rather than heroic; unlike Ozu and Naruse, they are also very intimate with Takamine. These features are especially evident in Takamine's treatment of the two most significant women in the second volume, the novelist and social critic Ariyoshi Sawako (see chapter 8 of this book), and the actress Tanaka Kinuyo (1910–77).

In her treatment of the former, Takamine expresses great admiration for the writer's abundant energy and realistic concern for the kinds of social problems most people would rather forget. The only extended episode involving Ariyoshi, however, concerns a trip to Mexico that she took along with Takamine and a group of other well-known personalities. Ariyoshi, having just finished her justly acclaimed novel on the problem of aging in Japan, was utterly worn out. During several days in Mexico City, she was afflicted with a raging fever. Mostly she remained in bed, perspiring profusely and barely able to crawl to the door whenever the worried Takamine came to look in on her.

The woman most fully evoked in positive terms by Takamine Hideko is the actress Tanaka Kinuyo. The two became close friends when the adolescent Hideko was invited to live at Tanaka's house in Kamakura shortly after Shōchiku moved its studio to Ōfuna. Though Kinuyo was twenty-seven and Hideko just twelve, they were both the same height. Kinuyo let Hideko wear her clothes and treated her like a younger sister. Indeed, this relationship was duplicated in one of the films the two actresses appeared in together—*The New Road*, by the famous director from the days of the silent film, Gosho Heinosuke.

Hideko's most poignant pages on Tanaka Kinuyo concern an ill-advised journey that the older actress made to Hollywood. With the American occupation in force in Japan following World War II, an opportunity arose for Tanaka to spend some time in Hollywood. Thought by many Japanese to be a symbol of traditional feminine modesty and reserve when she departed, Tanaka returned to Japan in January 1950, her personality seemingly transformed by her sojourn in a radically different culture. Sporting a Hawaiian lei and sunglasses, throwing kisses to the crowd of well-wishers gathered to welcome her back at Haneda Airport, she seemed a Hollywood actress of the most vulgar kind. The press reacted violently to what it saw as a betrayal of native values. Tanaka was scathingly criticized for several years thereafter for almost every role she played. One day, while the two women were working together on Ozu's *The Munakata Sisters*, Tanaka confided to her younger friend that she had seriously thought of committing suicide. Eventually she overcame her depression and went on to try her hand at being a movie director as well. Her acting was finally recognized for its true worth and brought her a number of prizes.

Awakening in Paris

Although Takamine Hideko does not make the connection explicitly, the thought of what happened to Tanaka Kinuyo in a foreign culture could well have been on her mind about a year and a half after her friend's return to Japan. By this stage in her career, Takamine had established her own credentials as a mature actress. Acting, however, was the only life she had ever known. It was not a life she had chosen, either, and the best way to get beyond it was to leave the country where she was so familiar to everyone. With this in mind, Takamine sold most of her possessions and left for Paris in the summer of 1951.

This step was not as easy as it might seem today. The American occupation was just coming to an end, and foreign travel for Japanese citizens was severely restricted. With the help of the French journalist Robert Guillain, Takamine received permission to go to France on the pretext of attending the Cannes Film Festival. There were financial problems, too, beyond the restrictions on the amount of currency that one could take out of the country at the time. Takamine remarks that she had little money or property, her financial affairs having been controlled since the beginning by the irresponsible Aunt Shige. (Some embezzling, too, had been perpetrated by an official at her studio.) To finance her trip, she had to sell one of the two houses she owned at the time. Besides the possible fear aroused by the fate of Tanaka Kinuyo in going abroad, there was always the potential loss of her popularity that might come about through her absence. Stardom in Japan, as in other countries, can be very short-lived.

Hideko went to Paris to be alone, to see what life would be like without her friends and the constant pressure of work. Her very arrival in Paris taught her how dependent human beings could be on one another. The landlady who was supposed to meet her at the Invalides Terminal was late in arriving. With virtually no ability in French, Hideko began to panic. When the landlady finally came rushing up and gave her a hug, Hideko felt a surge of gratitude.

For the next six months the celebrated Japanese actress Takamine

Hideko lived anonymously in her own room in a fifth-floor Parisian apartment. The landlady and her mother were extremely kind, introducing Hideko to various wines and showering her with kisses. One of the few dissatisfactions was the limit of one bath per week—with lukewarm water to boot. Like most Japanese, Takamine preferred to bathe daily, and in water that might scald the average Westerner. The landlady showed such solicitude in testing the water she drew for Hideko's weekly bath that her tenant didn't have the heart to complain.

Late in the summer the two ladies left for their annual holiday, and Hideko was left to fend for herself. The other residents had left too, and so had the concierge. The elevator had been shut down, and the actress had to climb up five flights of steps, groping for the switch at each landing that would light the way up the next flight. Hideko's only company during this period were some Japanese university students who happened to be living in cheap hotels in the neighborhood.

One day, as Hideko rested in bed, she let out a yawn—virtually, it might seem, the first time she had ever felt bored in her entire life. She had to do something, and so she seized her purse and rushed out of the apartment. She took a bus to a department store near the Opera. Entering the store, she went to the toy department and picked out a male doll for herself. This being a Western country, the doll was almost bound to have blue eyes. This particular doll also sported a handsome blue cap with silver embroidery. Hideko could not resist his charm. She had never owned a doll before and, even though the price was equivalent to a month's rent, she impulsively handed over the money. Then, as she herself says,

> I took the doll back to the apartment in a large cardboard box. I placed him on the mantle, with his suit nicely arranged. His cheeks were dimpled, and two small teeth were visible between his slightly parted lips. Since the doll couldn't speak, I spoke to him in my heart. Just having him around gave me a feeling of comfort.

Hideko even took the doll to bed with her that night. When she awoke the following morning, the sun was shining through the window, and the doll was lying by her side. She was startled by the closed eyelids, for she hadn't realized that the doll could appear to sleep also.

The above passage, evoking an emotional void in the author's life, is unique in the autobiography of Takamine Hideko. Leaving much unsaid, Takamine does not explain what prompted her return to Japan at the end of 1951. Possibly another experience, this one very different from the experience with the doll, taught her something about the type of life suited to her. During a Sunday outing with the landlady and her mother, Hideko was taken to the zoo. Her companions taught her the French words for the various animals, and even treated her to an ice cream cone. As the sun warmed her back, Hideko looked at the crowds strolling about the park as if they hadn't a care in the world. Hideko suddenly realized that most people pass their lives in this desultory way. To her such a life seemed trivial. Better by far to be so immersed in work that you didn't have time to catch your breath. Her own career as an actress now seemed to be surpassingly worthwhile.

Hideko was met at the airport in Tokyo by a number of well-wishers and reporters. Aunt Shige was also there, and she remarked rather cryptically to Hideko, ''I hope you've learned to appreciate your mother now.'' Shige had habitually acted as if she owned whatever had been bought on Hideko's income. This attitude had grown quite pronounced well before Hideko went to Paris. Once Hideko was back, Shige began to act as a landlady might. One evening, after the dinner tray had been taken from the table, the maid brought Hideko an itemized bill. ''This covers your first week . . . ,'' she began. Hideko does not indicate whether or not she paid this bill. However, she doubtlessly had had enough of Shige's high-handedness. She left the house soon and, after spending several weeks in hotels, settled into her own residence.

The Marriage

For some years Takamine Hideko had toyed with the notion of marrying at the age of thirty, years past the most eligible time for the normal Japanese woman of the period. (A thirty-year-old bride, as Takamine puts it, is hardly an exciting prospect for a man.) This independence of mind is also evident in the way she went about the business of choosing a husband for herself. Naturally, the men she knew best worked in some capacity for the film companies. Two assistant directors in the Tōhō Studio especially engaged her attention.

After sending her maid around to ferret out the gossip about the two eligibles, Takamine thought over her options with a characteristic sober-mindedness and realism. Yes, she mused after hearing out the maid, assistant director Kawagashira Yoshirō had good color and a well-fed look. And there was something generous and optimistic about the way he worked. He was the sort of person who had always been well off. Matsuyama Zenzō, the other assistant director, bustled nervously about the studio lot, and his cheeks had a sunken look.

Perhaps Hideko was allergic to wealth. She figured that one could always work hard and earn money. The wealthy might have money, but they worried about losing it, too. Shouldn't one be free of such worries? Finally, Hideko concluded that Matsuyama was the better prospect.

After the wedding in March 1955, Takamine Hideko greatly reduced her acting commitments. Now she must divide her time between her profession, on the one hand, and her private life as a Japanese wife, on the other. She writes of the bantering that takes place between husband and wife, depicting Zenzō as an intimate friend—in Hideko's terms, a Tanaka Kinuyo rather than a Tanizaki or Umehara. Hideko herself would be a cheerful companion and try to grow old gracefully along with her husband. In her autobiography, the years of the marriage are glossed over. It is the prospect of aging and death that engages her interest.

Both husband and wife were over fifty when the autobiography was written; at present, some ten years later, they are both still in good health. One assumes that the following conversation, related by Takamine, might be taking place now, but with the added gravity that a decade or more of life can add to one's reflections on mortality.

> We began to talk about our own deaths after I played the role of Teruko in a film based on *The Twilight Years*, a novel by Ariyoshi Sawako. At first we would joke about the subject, as something in the distant future. Lately, however, the thought of death has become more real to us. If I go first, I'm not sure how my husband will dispose of my cremated bones. But, if he goes first, I have no intention of burying his remains beneath a cold, square gravestone. It would be better that he rest beneath the large magnolia in our garden. He loves this tree which blooms so beautifully each spring. My husband likes cosmos flowers, and these I could place in his coffin. If he dies outside of summer, I'll be in trouble. And, if I don't bury him, what would I do instead? I'd place his bones in his favorite Korean vase and keep him always by my side. I've even thought of placing in a handy drawer the bones that are too big for the jar. With his low blood pressure, my husband will probably be cold in the jar, so I'll order a special one. I will fail as a woman if I do not persevere in my project of protecting the bones of this man who, in sunshine and shadow, has for decades cared for his simpleton of a wife.

Notes

1. (Tokyo: Asahi Shinbunsha, 1980).

2. Trans. Audie Bock (New York: Knopf, 1982).

3. (Berkeley: University of California Press, 1979).

4. Edward Seidensticker, *Kafu the Scribbler* (Stanford: Stanford University Press, 1965).

5. Trans. Eiichi Kiyooka (Tokyo: Hokuseido Press, 1960).

6. Rubinstein, *My Young Years* (New York: Knopf, 1973); *My Many Years* (New York: Knopf, 1980).

8

ARIYOSHI SAWAKO
The Novelist

MILDRED TAHARA

DURING the past twenty-five years, a number of women writers have risen to prominence on the Japanese literary scene, among them Ariyoshi Sawako (1931–84), Sono Ayako (b. 1931), Kurahashi Yumiko (b. 1935), Ōba Minako (b. 1930), and Kōno Taeko (b. 1926). These women, many of them prolific writers, have been fully recognized for their high intellect and outstanding literary talent.

Of the above-mentioned writers, Ariyoshi Sawako was perhaps the most versatile and representative of contemporary Japan, and her works appeal to men and women of all ages. Although Ariyoshi could boast an output that is incredible in terms of both quality and quantity, it was not unusual for her to spend years planning and doing research for a particular work, be it a historical novel or a work treating a modern social problem. The first full-length Ariyoshi novel to be translated into English was *The Doctor's Wife* (Kodansha International, 1978). Another was *The River Ki*, published by Kodansha International in 1980. In the spring of 1985, *The Twilight Years*, which treats the universal problem of caring for the elderly, was published by Peter Owen. *Kae*, the French translation of *The Doctor's Wife*, was published by Stock in 1981; it became a bestseller in France. As of this writing, Ariyoshi's works are available in twelve countries. Slowly but steadily she is becoming a world-famous literary figure. Certainly she is one of Japan's most talented and respected writers.

Life

Ariyoshi Sawako was born on January 20, 1931, in Wakayama City. Her father, Shinji, was employed by the Yokohama Specie Bank and

297

stationed at the bank's New York branch. Her mother, Akitsu, came from a family in Wakayama; she remained behind in Wakayama for the birth of her daughter. Besides Sawako, the couple had two sons.

Ariyoshi's father returned to Japan in April 1935 when Ariyoshi was four, and the family subsequently moved to Tokyo. In 1937, he was sent to Batavia in Java (Jakarta, Indonesia). The family soon joined him there and enjoyed a privileged life for the next few years. While in Java, Sawako enrolled in the Japanese Elementary School. Being a precocious child, she read such intellectual fiction as *The Collected Works of Natsume Sōseki* and *The Selected Works of Arishima Takeo* when she was in the second and third grades.

In March 1940, the family returned to Wakayama City, where Ariyoshi transferred to the third grade in Kinomoto Elementary School. Less than a year later, the family moved back to Batavia; in May 1941, however, with the war clouds gathering ominously, the family returned to Tokyo. Ariyoshi, who was a sickly child, was often absent from the five different elementary schools she attended. It was rare for girls her age to have moved so many times and to have lived abroad. Her unique childhood experience no doubt helped expand her perspective and the horizons of her imagination. As a writer, she was to become known for exploring social problems and issues before they caught popular attention, and for experimenting with new literary forms and techniques that would often challenge the accepted definitions in a particular genre.

In April 1943, Ariyoshi entered Takenodai Women's School. During the bleak postwar years, her father, sensing her loss of faith in her own country, introduced her to the Kabuki theater. This was the beginning of Ariyoshi's lifelong interest in the traditional Japanese theater. She graduated from Tokyo Municipal Higher Women's School in March 1949 and entered Tokyo Women's Junior College in April of that year, majoring in English literature. When she was nineteen, she had to interrupt her formal education for reasons of health. Her father, who was fond of the theater and an avid reader, died in July 1950.

Ariyoshi resumed her studies in April 1951 and developed a deeper interest in the modern theater and the traditional performing arts; at about this time, she became a member of the Kabuki Studies Group. In May, she entered an essay contest sponsored by a magazine and was recognized for her outstanding essays on actors. She also joined student groups that studied such proletarian writers as

Kobayashi Takiji (1903–33) and Miyamoto Yuriko (1899–1951). In February 1952, shortly after celebrating her twenty-first birthday, Ariyoshi was employed on a part-time basis by a drama journal, *Engekikai* (Theater world) and edited a special issue on Kawatake Mokuami, a traditional Kabuki playwright of the late Tokugawa and early Meiji eras. Many years later, she was to write plays and adaptations of her own novels for stage performance. After graduating from Tokyo Women's Junior College in March, she joined the editorial staff of Ōkura Publishing Company in August. It was during this phase of her career that she contributed to a literary coterie magazine, *Hakuchigun* (Idiot horde); she also became a member of the fifteenth *Shinshichō* (New thoughts) group, where she made the acquaintance of Miura Shumon and his wife Sono Ayako, who would later become novelists as popular and successful as Ariyoshi herself.

In July 1954, she was hired as a correspondent of the Azuma Kabuki Association, headed by a unique female Kabuki performer, Azuma Tokuho. She worked for this group, performing secretarial duties and assisting in stage production, until May 1956.

Debut and *The River Ki*

Her first story, "The Blindman" (*Mōmoku*), was published in *Shinshichō* in August 1955. Before long, Ariyoshi's short stories began to be published regularly in such leading monthly journals as *Bungakukai, Mita bungaku, Shinshichō*, and *Bungei shunjū*. In September 1956, a short story "Jiuta" (*Ballad*) won the *Bungakukai* New Writer Award and was nominated for the thirty-fifth Akutagawa Prize. "Ballad" is the story of the daughter of a blind ballad master who is a professional dancer in her own right. She marries a Japanese-American against her father's wishes and is disowned. The setting is postwar Japan, and the work ends with the father going to see his daughter off at Haneda Airport as she leaves for the United States with her husband. Vividly depicted in this skillfully told story is the world of the traditional arts of ballad chanting and dance; at the same time it is a moving story of a father and daughter who go through emotional upheavals of love, imagined betrayal, estrangement, and uneasy reconciliation.

In 1956 Ariyoshi's dance drama based on the Noh play "Aya no tsuzumi" (The damask drum) was performed at the prestigious Shimbashi Embujō Theater. In Ariyoshi's version, the hero driven mad by an unrequited love is a handsome youth, instead of an old man as in the fourteenth-century Noh play. Her original puppet drama was also performed at the Osaka Bunraku Theatre. At this early stage in her career, Ariyoshi's two loves were already literature and theater. In the ensuing years, besides writing original plays or adaptations of other authors' works, Ariyoshi saw her novels adapted for the stage, the cinema, and television.

Throughout 1957 Ariyoshi continued to write works of fiction for numerous journals. *Masshirokenoke* (White all over), a collection of short stories, was published by Bungei shunjū. In the same year she wrote "Ishi no niwa" (The rock garden), a television script for NHK, Japan's national broadcasting company. For this script she was awarded the Minister of Education's Fine Arts Festival Award, the first of many awards she was to receive.

In April 1957, "Akaiko monogatari" (The tale of Akaiko) was published in *Shinnyoen*, a women's magazine. The story is set in ancient times. One day Akaiko, a young maiden of sixteen, meets a handsome prince. The prince, who subsequently ascends the throne as Emperor Yūryaku (r. 456–79), requests that she not marry anyone, for he will one day summon her to his palace. In the ensuing years, Akaiko rejects all the young men who come to woo her. The emperor's promise to her is transmuted into an ideal that sustains the heroine for eighty long years. Never marrying, she quietly weaves white cloth as a means of livelihood. As an old woman in her nineties, Akaiko finally requests an audience with the emperor to present him with the cloth she had woven. He, now 113 years old, has absolutely no recollection of her. Akaiko recounts her story and he is moved by the withered old woman standing before him. In his arrogance, he is completely blind to his own ugliness in his dotage, and he sincerely believes that Akaiko still cherishes a deep love for him.

The touch of ironic humor at the end of the story is characteristic of Ariyoshi. Akaiko cannot help but be amused by the emperor's conceitedness. No, she did not love him. She is eternally grateful to him, however, for the promise he had made, for it had become an ideal that had given her strength to reject all her suitors. It had also enabled her to see through each and every suitor; she had seen with utmost clarity that each one, deep in his heart, had looked down upon women. The emperor was no exception. Even when he was too old to sleep with a woman, his heart was full of pity for Akaiko. It was beyond his imagination that a woman was capable of living for an ideal. In the closing lines of the story, Akaiko can hardly suppress her laughter as she regards the foolish old emperor, arrogant to the end and utterly blind to the reality of the situation.

In 1958 Ariyoshi was nominated for the thirty-sixth Naoki Prize for her short story "Shiroi ōgi" (White fan), later retitled "Hakusenshō." Though she continued to publish short stories, she also had a novel *Geisha warutsu Italiano* (The Geisha Italian waltz), serialized from May to December 1958 in *Shūkan Tokyo*, a weekly magazine. One memorable short story, "Eguchi no sato" (The village of Eguchi), was published in *Bungei shunjū* in October 1958.

The main character in "The Village of Eguchi" is a Catholic priest called Gounod. After spending years in Japan mastering the difficult language, he is quite disenchanted with his parishioners, whose unbending puritanism is intolerable to him. A beautiful woman, Sakai Satoko, begins to attend mass regularly, seeking spiritual guidance from Father Gounod. She brings a touch of beauty into the priest's colorless daily routine of interminable meetings and sermon writing. The woman, moreover, contributes generously to the church. Half a year after her first appearance, a self-righteous church member storms up to Father Gounod, demanding to know why he wishes to baptize a geisha of Yanagibashi. He learns that Satoko had been born to a poor family in the neighborhood and that she had been sold as a child to a geisha house, where she received training in various performing arts. Known as Kofumi, she was a courtesan of the highest class.

Father Gounod is not at all disenchanted upon learning of the beauty's profession. When he asks her why she wishes to be baptized, Satoko replies that she has been inexplicably drawn to the church, which she entered for the first time thirty-five days after the death of her mother. She further explains that in her heart she feels that her mother is calling her. Though she is not ashamed of her profession, Satoko sincerely believes Father Gounod's words and in the teachings of the scriptures. Near the end of the story, Satoko invites Father Gounod to a dance performance. She performs with two other women in "Saigyō in the Rain," and her role is that of a prostitute in the village of Eguchi who offers the priest Saigyō, a famous twelfth-century poet, lodging for the night. Completely captivated by the beauty of the dancer, Father Gounod is overcome by the feeling that in the remote past he had actually seen Satoko in the village of Eguchi.

Against the backdrop of classical dance and the overlapping atmosphere evoked by a poetic legend, Ariyoshi unfolds the encounter between a celibate Western male symbolizing spirituality and a geisha who is the quintessential female. Neither melodramatic nor didactic, Ariyoshi delineates the contradictions and hypocrisy inherent in contemporary society and human values. At the same time, she affirms the empathy between soul and flesh in an unassuming quiet way.

Another fine longer story, "Ningyō jōruri" (Puppet drama), appeared in *Chūō kōron* in December 1958. This work is based on an actual event that took place in the modern history of the puppet theater when two master puppeteers, Yoshida Bungorō and Kiritake Monjūrō, temporarily established rival troupes because they disagreed on how the puppet theater should be run. The protagonist, Tamajirō, is modeled after the real Monjūrō, and it is with great regret that he breaks with his master to form the Tripod Troupe (Kanae Kai), so named because its policy was to treat equally the three principal performers in each puppet play: the shamisen player, the chanter, and the puppeteer. The members of the Tripod Troupe undergo great hardship just to survive before finally receiving recognition. Especially well depicted is Tamajirō's anguish as he struggles to be independent of his master, Usaburō, whom he continues to hold in awe. At the climax of the story, the master and his disciple are reconciled, and the two groups decide to merge. It is interesting to note that Ariyoshi wrote this story before meeting Bungorō and Monjūrō. Much to her surprise, 820,000 copies of the Chinese translation of this work sold in mainland China.

In February 1959, "Kitō" (Prayer) was published in *Bungakukai*. In this work, Ariyoshi quietly attacked discrimination against and social exclusion of victims of radiation disease. Michiko, an attractive woman, marries the older son of an impoverished Tokyo widow. Michiko had been in Nagasaki when the atomic bomb was dropped there in August 1945, and she occasionally experiences fainting spells. She requires constant blood transfusions, but she gives birth to a son who becomes the joy of the entire family. When the boy is taken ill with a mysterious fever, however, tensions mount. Everyone expects the baby to die, but they fervently pray for his recovery, and by some miracle their prayers are answered. Ariyoshi skillfully describes Michiko's silent anguish and the silent tears she sheds when the crisis is over. "Prayer," together with "Namayoi" (Half drunk), well represent the works on social problems for which Ariyoshi is remembered.

"Half Drunk" was published in *Shōsetsu shinchō*, a journal of "new" or "middle" fiction aiming at the level in-between serious and popular fiction, in November 1959. The story treats the long-lasting and deadly effects of the atomic bombing of Hiroshima on August 6, 1945, from a man's point of view. As she does in "Prayer," Ariyoshi describes the physical and emotional suffering of the survivors. Though other writers have movingly described the immediate aftermath of the holocaust, Ariyoshi focuses on the less dramatic but long-term aftereffects on ordinary people years later.

In "Half Drunk," a young man from Tokyo visits Hiroshima on August 6, 1959, the fourteenth anniversary of the bombing. While drinking at a bar, he learns of the sufferings of victims of the bomb from an older man, who is unable to get drunk, no matter how much he imbibes. The older man rambles on and on about how he met his wife. Both the man and his wife Yoshiko had been exposed to radiation when the bomb exploded over Hiroshima. They are innocent victims who have to live with their own worries about their health as well as the social stigma and discrimination against them regarding marriage. The couple keep the radiation exposure a secret from each other, and tensions intensify between them to the extent that the man begins to suspect that his wife had been involved with another man in the past. A crisis occurs when Yoshiko becomes pregnant, and the couple finally confess to each other the truth about their past. A second problem the couple have to cope with is their concern over the health of their daughter. The child carries the inherent risk of radiation disease, which might destroy the happiness of the family. The man continues to drink in a futile attempt to drown his sorrows. Toward the end of the story, he announces that his wife is pregnant again, thus suggesting that he will have his second child's welfare to fret over as well in the years to come.

Ariyoshi continued to be active in the theater. Her own adaptation of her original television script "The Rock Garden" was performed at the Kabukiza Theatre in June 1959. At about the same time, what would become the first of Ariyoshi's best-known early novels, *Kinokawa* (The River Ki) was serialized in a leading women's journal, *Fujin gahō*, from January to May 1959; it was made into a film by Shōchiku in 1966.

The River Ki involves a family history of three generations that sweeps through Japan's entire modern period from the Meiji and

Taishō to Shōwa eras. The theme of conflict between two generations of women in a family is one of the author's ongoing themes, and it appears again in *Incense and Flowers* (1962) and *The Doctor's Wife* (1967). *The River Ki*, like the river of that name that flows through Wakayama Prefecture (where Ariyoshi was born), moves along at a leisurely pace. For centuries Japanese women had been confined to the home, kept virtually in bondage by feudal conventions and female roles. In this work, we see how the past continues to have a strong hold on the lives of women in modern Japan.

This novel consists of three long sections. Hana, who represents the Meiji woman, is the main character, and it is her life story that is told in the pages of this book. Hana had been brought up by her grandmother, Toyono, who was born in 1854, still in the feudal age. Like Toyono, who had read translations of Dostoevsky, for example, Hana read intellectual books and journals and was considered up-to-date and highly educated for her time. Hana eventually marries into the Matani family. The description of her grand wedding procession—part of the way in boats down the River Ki—as she makes her way to her new home is colorful and vivid as well as being distinctly symbolic. We then follow Hana through her child-bearing years as a gracious and devoted wife to Matani Keisaku, the capable eldest son of a respected local leader and powerful landed gentry. When, in time, Keisaku becomes a member of the prefectural House of Representatives, Hana conducts herself with proper decorum in public while efficiently running her household. She also sees that her children receive a good education. Though Hana is constantly beset by one worry or another, she seems to grow in stature after weathering each crisis, and through the years she slowly becomes an integral part of the Matani family. Hana's strength and fortitude are such that she is not overwhelmed by her onerous burdens and responsibilities. In fact, she resembles the River Ki, which on the surface appears calm and gentle but tends to draw everything into its waters.

Part 2 concentrates on Fumio, Hana's willful daughter. Fumio goes away to Tokyo to study at a women's college when Taishō democracy is in full flower. Having become a progressive young woman, she rebels against her mother. It is in the conflict between Hana and Fumio that we see two generations of women, both considered modern in their respective day, clashing because of the changes brought about by time. Fumio eventually falls in love with and marries an elite employee of a bank and goes abroad with him. Even after becoming a mother, Fumio shocks Hana with her modern ways. However, the grief and guilt over the death of a son causes Fumio to be increasingly attracted to old beliefs and customs.

In part 3 we see Hanako, Fumio's daughter, growing up. Hana's husband Keisaku eventually becomes a member of the national parliament and leads an active political life; however, he dies suddenly on the eve of the Pacific War. Sweeping changes take place following Japan's surrender. The family property is confiscated during the American occupation. Despite the slow but steady decline of the Matani family, as seen in the dilettante Kōsaku (Keisaku's iconoclastic younger brother) and the apathetic Seiichirō (Hana's eldest son), we see Hana's courageous spirit being transmitted to her daughter and granddaughter. Soon after the war, Fumio's husband dies, and Fumio is sustained through this critical period by her children and grandchildren. All too soon, Hanako leaves childhood behind and goes to work as an editor for a magazine. Hana, by now an old woman, falls gravely ill and awaits death. She is the last of the Matanis, and with her death approaching, the very soul of the family is in danger of being extinguished. Hanako takes a leave of absence from her editorial duties to visit her bedridden grandmother. While reading to her from the ancient history book *Masukagami*, young Hanako realizes that the same family blood of generations past runs also in her veins.

The novel is rich in local color, like others of Ariyoshi's works set in Wakayama Prefecture, an area noted for steadfast yet feminine women. Moreover, the dialect is authentic and the historical details accurate, so that the matrilineal heritage is distinctly etched against the flow of time, changing social milieu, and the status of women in general. It is interesting to note that the model for Hana was the author's own grandmother; that for Fumio, her mother; and that for Hanako, the author herself. *The River Ki* is the closest Ariyoshi has come to writing an I-novel, but the author's artistic detachment and the descriptive passages in a beautiful literary style attain universality and make this a tribute to all Japanese women who have lived through the same period of time as mothers and daughters.

In November 1959, Ariyoshi was invited to the United States under a Rockefeller Grant to study at Sarah Lawrence College in New York during the winter and spring terms. During her stay there, she studied the playwright Christopher Fry, whom she eventually interviewed in

London a few months later. In August 1960, she made her way to Europe and returned to Japan via the Middle East after spending nearly a year abroad. Two novels, *Not Because of Color* (Hishoku) and *Puerto Rico Diary*, were written as a result of her residence on the East Coast for nearly a year; both probe into the problem of racial discrimination in the United States.

Racial Prejudice and a Social Issue Novel

In June 1961, Ariyoshi was invited to mainland China with a group of writers headed by the literary critic Kamei Katsuichirō. The group included the prominent novelist Inoue Yasushi and the critic Hirano Ken, among others. This trip yielded "Sumi" (The ink stick), a short story. It concerns a classical dancer by the name of Kajikawa Haruko, who is known by her stage name Harutoyo. She is an exquisite beauty but painfully aware that she is no longer young; she therefore takes great pains in selecting her cosmetics and costume. Maeda Kōkichi, an old artisan who paints gorgeous kimono designs for Haruko, uses his treasured Chinese ink stick, which he had purchased for a vast sum of money when he was young. He tells her, only half in jest, that his life will expire when the ink stick is used up. Not too long afterward, Haruko visits mainland China as a member of a dance troupe. Her kimonos, especially the one by Kōkichi with a magnificent peony design (China's national flower), are a great success and the focus of attention at each gathering. During her stay in Peking, Haruko succeeds in getting the perfect gift for Kōkichi: an ancient ink stick. Kōkichi is so inspired by Haruko's thoughtfulness and kindness that he begins immediately to paint elaborate kimono designs for the beautiful dancer, whose life he feels is coursing through his veins, giving him a new lease on life. The man dies of sheer exhaustion before the last of four magnificent kimono designs is completed; Haruko does not learn of Kōkichi's death until after his funeral, but the Chinese ink stick that she had given him is bequeathed to her as a keepsake.

In this work the author juxtaposes the youthful and beautiful dancer against the dedicated old artisan; for a while the paths of these two people cross, bringing to each a touch of beauty. Lovingly described are the splendid dance costumes with extravagant designs of a multitude of cherry blossoms with gold centers, gigantic irises in full bloom, and a flower cart laden with a variety of flowers. Dancing and acting are new careers that opened for women in modern Japan, for the traditional Noh and Kabuki theatres in the medieval and feudal periods were forbidden to employ women as performers. Also, professional secrets of artisans were handed down to male heirs only. The glorification of the dancer in "The Ink Stick" is magnified by the triumph of the artisan, whose work would be of little value without the female beauty that gives life to it.

The short story "Sambaba" (Three old women) was written in 1961. The major theme of this unusual work is women as survivors, and the man in the lives of these three old ladies is already dead at the beginning of the story, which is set in the bleak postwar years. The situation is unique: to make ends meet, the man's widow, his younger sister, and his geisha mistress come to settle each in a separate tea ceremony cottage within the sprawling estate left by the deceased merchant. These women continue to live on and on, bickering among themselves, growing old together, and observing drastic changes occurring as Japan recovers from the devastation of the war and begins to prosper.

Also published in 1961 was the fascinating short story "Kiyū no shi" (The death of Kiyū), in which Ariyoshi describes the pathetic fate of a woman who dies in the 1860s and is turned into a symbol of patriotism by the loyalist samurai faction desperately striving to expel the foreigners from Japan's shores. Women throughout Japanese history had been used by men for public causes as well as for personal expediency. Ariyoshi was later to write a novel about an imperial princess who was also used by men who wielded power and influence, but in this story she tells of a gentle and melancholy prostitute who is so terrified of foreigners that she commits suicide to avoid becoming the mistress of an American. After her death, she is glorified as "the maiden flower of Yamato [Japan]," thus becoming a legend and a subject of wood-block prints.

The story also delineates a vivid picture of life in the pleasure quarters and of the women who sold their favors to both Japanese and Western patrons. Kiyū's story is told by Sono, her confidante and colleague in a house of assignation in Yokohama. A survivor in a man's world, Sono eventually marries an honest man and lives through the Age of Enlightenment following the Meiji Restoration of 1868. During her lifetime, the shogunate falls and the antiforeign samurai, who had once threatened her life, become powerless, but the late

Kiyū becomes so famous she is mentioned in school textbooks.

The plight of a prostitute in any country and in any period is a wretched one. At a time in Japan when foreigners were not considered to be human beings, some prostitutes sold their favors to vulgar seamen and merchants from abroad, and some became the mistresses of foreign residents in Japan. They were treated like pariahs in Japanese society for the rest of their lives. In describing how even prostitutes were segregated into two groups—those for Japanese customers and those for Westerners, Ariyoshi began to explore racial prejudice, a serious social issue that she would take up at greater length in *Not Because of Color*.

From January 1962, she began serializing *Sukezaemon yondaiki* (The four Sukezaemons) in *Bungakukai*, completing this ambitious work in June 1963. It is a dynastic saga concerning a 250-year feud between two great families affected by a fearsome curse. She remained active in the world of theater, too, and in that year, the Bungakuza Troupe performed her historical play *Kōmyō kogō* (Empress Kōmyō), about the famous eighth-century empress and mother of the female emperor Kōken-Shōtoku (see chapter 2). "Puppet Drama" and "Kuroko," her first works to be translated into a foreign language, came out in Chinese that same year.

The novel *Kōge* (Incense and flowers) was published in December. It belongs to the category of family saga and to that of the life story of professional entertainers. This lengthy novel describes three generations of women. The central figure is Tomoko, and it is through her eyes that we see her grandmother Tsuna and her mother Ikuyo. Tsuna, widowed in her early forties, adopts Tomoko in order to carry on the family name. Ikuyo remarries, against her mother's wishes, and sees very little of Tomoko thereafter, except for a period when Tomoko is forced to live for a time with her mother and stepfather following her grandmother's death. Throughout her life, Tomoko is haunted by the memory of her grandmother, who died a wretched death, cursing Ikuyo for being unfilial. Ikuyo's second marriage turns out badly, and she becomes a prostitute in Shizuoka, where Tomoko had earlier been sent to be an apprentice geisha. The world of the geisha and the prostitute is depicted in great detail as we watch Tomoko grow up. Perhaps because her relationship with her own mother had been cold, Ikuyo has no motherly warmth and shows no affection for her children. In her youth, Tomoko falls deeply in love with a promising student in a military academy, but when it is discovered that her mother had once been a prostitute, their marriage becomes impossible. When Tomoko becomes a successful geisha and restaurant owners, Ikuyo clings tenaciously to her for support. It is Tomoko's unhappy fate that, though she has two elderly patrons who dote on her and help her become established in the profession, she is prevented from leading a normal married life and having a child of her own. Nonetheless, Tomoko is undaunted by any misfortune that comes her way. Her patrons die in the years that follow, and as she grows old, she is forced to struggle on alone, especially after her establishment is totally destroyed by the Tokyo air raids.

The novel begins in Wakayama and moves on to the vicinity of the Yoshiwara red-light district in Tokyo, where Ikuyo and her second husband make their home. The setting then shifts to Shizuoka, back to Akasaka, and to Tsukiji in Tokyo. There are superb descriptions of each locale, and the dialogues are in the dialect of each area. The work covers the half-century between 1900 and 1950. Figuring prominently in the novel are events such as the Tokyo Earthquake of 1923, the China incidents of the 1930s, and the bombing of Tokyo during the Pacific War. Also described vividly are the bleak postwar years. It is during the Allied occupation that Tomoko manages to see her former sweetheart, the only man she had ever loved, before he is executed as a war criminal. Still later, she receives the ashes of the executed war criminals whose corpses were cremated en masse, and she places his memorial tablet on her family altar next to an urn containing her mother's ashes and the tablets of her devoted patrons. At the end of the novel, Tomoko, who has a nephew to look after, prays for the repose of the souls of the war criminals. The title of the work refers to the incense and flowers she offers to those who have preceded her in death. A stage adaptation of *Incense and Flowers* was performed at the Tōhō Geijutsuza in September 1963.

In November 1963, a daughter, Tamao, was born to Ariyoshi and her husband Jin Akira, director of the Art Friend Association, whom she had married in March. While Ariyoshi was pregnant, she was busily serializing her novel *Aridagawa* (The River Arida) in a monthly journal, *Nihon*, from January to December, and another novel, *Hishoku* (Not because of color), in *Chūō kōron* from April 1963 to June 1964.

The heroine of *The River Arida* is a strong-willed woman, and the novel traces her life from childhood to old age. The only child of the Tsukuno family, Chiyo believes she is their real daughter. When a little sister is born, however, Chiyo overhears a conversation and discovers that she had actually been adopted, that as a baby she had been carried by the flood waters of 1889 to the childless couple. Though she adores her baby sister, Chiyo runs away in the confusion accompanying another flood, and she becomes a servant in the household of tangerine growers. In the years that follow, Chiyo learns all that she can about the care of tangerine trees, earning the respect of everyone in the area. Even after having lived a sheltered life as a pampered only child, she gradually adjusts to a life of hard work and strict discipline.

In time Chiyo meets a young man, Kawamori Kanta. Just before their marriage, her adopted mother comes to her and once again Chiyo is reunited with her sister, who by then had grown into a lovely young girl of fourteen. Chiyo is married to Kanta in due time, and together they raise a family. A few years later, following a magnificent wedding ceremony, her sister leaves with her husband for Tokyo. Left behind in Arida, Chiyo becomes the pillar of her family and manages at the same time to keep up with the latest knowledge regarding the growing of tangerine trees. Her sister is widowed early and returns to Arida in the 1930s; during World War II, Chiyo loses her second son. At the end of the novel, Chiyo, now seventy-five years old, and her husband look back upon their life, which had been rich and rewarding.

Not Because of Color is a novel that tackles the problem of racial minorities in the United States. The heroine, Emiko Jackson, is a young Japanese woman who married a black soldier during the Allied occupation. Emiko and her husband, Tom, enjoy a few years of marital bliss in Japan, blessed with the birth of a little daughter Mary. The family does not remain together long, for presently Tom is shipped back to the States. For a few years Emiko is resigned to the fact that she had been abandoned by her husband like so many other Japanese wives of American servicemen. She somehow manages to eke out a living for herself and her daughter by working as a housemaid in a military housing area and by dealing in black-market goods. Distressed to see the misery and loneliness of Mary, who has no playmate and is mercilessly teased by the Japanese children in the neighborhood, Emiko decides to join her husband when he finally arranges to bring his family to the United States. Despite the coldness of her own mother and sister toward her, Emiko would probably not have left Japan had she not realized that there was no future for her dark-skinned daughter there.

On board a military transport Emiko meets three other Japanese war brides, who, along with their children, share the same cabin: Takeko, a friendly, down-to-earth woman with a black son; Shimako, a cold, haughty woman with a fair-skinned son; and Reiko, a fragile, doll-like beauty with a photo of her handsome young husband, whom all imagine to be a rich man's son. None of the four has any idea of the minority problem they are about to be confronted with in New York City, where they plan to make their homes. Upon arriving in the city, the four women and their families go separate ways, and for a time we follow Emiko through the difficult period of adjusting to life in a black ghetto. Emiko is forced to work as a waitress in a small Japanese restaurant in downtown Manhattan to supplement the meager salary her husband brings home as a male nurse working on the night shift. She commutes to work from their single-room apartment in Harlem. The years slip by quickly, during which her family grows in size. She is so busy working and having children that she sees very little of the rest of New York City, let alone the United States.

An elegant Japanese restaurant opens near the one she is employed at. When Emiko goes to work there, she finds her former cabin mates among the other newly hired waitresses. Takeko lives in Brooklyn, practically supporting singlehandedly her lazy husband and her brood of children; Shimako's husband is a poor Italian-American, so she finds it necessary to work; Reiko, a pale ghost of her former self, is also there, to the surprise of the other women. They soon discover that Reiko's husband is Puerto Rican, and that she is living under the most wretched conditions imaginable in the Spanish Harlem section of the city. Reiko, unlike the others, fails to face the reality of her situation and is driven to commit suicide when she becomes pregnant and learns that she cannot have an abortion in the United States.

Toward the end of the novel, Emiko goes to work as a live-in nursemaid in the home of an educated, stunningly attractive Japanese woman who is married to a Jewish college professor. She is then given an opportunity to observe closely the lifestyle of a privileged class and compare her charge with her own children. At one of the parties given by the professor and his wife, Emiko meets two educated Africans who consider themselves far superior to American blacks. It is at this point that Emiko decides to give up working altogether and to be with her family as much as she can. Through the eyes of a Japanese war bride living in New York City in the 1950s, Ariyoshi attempts to analyze the problem of race and social class in the United States and boldly asserts that discrimination is inflicted not because of the color of a person's skin but based on an individual's family and educational background. With *Not Because of Color* and *Puerto Rico Diary* (serialized in *Bungei shunjū* from July to December 1964), Ariyoshi takes a step forward into the contemporary scene to broaden her scope. She went on to produce a number of social-issue novels.

Ariyoshi and Jin Akira were divorced in 1964. In the following year, *Hidakagawa* (The River Hidaka) was carried in *Shūkan bunshun*, a weekly magazine, from January to October, and a stage adaptation of *The River Arida* was performed at the Tōhō Geijutsuza in March. In May, Ariyoshi left for mainland China to study the role of the Roman Catholic Church in China, returning in November. Between December 1965 and January 1966 she visited Hawaii and the U.S. mainland.

Hanaoka Seishū no tsuma (The doctor's wife) appeared in November 1966 in *Shinchō*. It was made into a movie by Daiei Studios in 1967. Ariyoshi also adapted this novel for the stage to be performed at the Tōhō Geijutsuza in 1967. This novel vividly describes the intense rivalry between a mother-in-law and daughter-in-law for the affection of a physician, Hanaoka Seishū (1760–1835), who was the first surgeon in the world to successfully perform a breast cancer operation under general anesthetic. The women vie with each other to serve as guinea pigs for the doctor's experiments, and the wife, Kae, eventually loses her sight as a result of taking large doses of his experimental anesthetic. Kae endures with fortitude her mother-in-law's machinations and does her utmost to be a devoted wife of the famous doctor. As the ultimate survivor, she emerges triumphant, basking in the love and respect not only of her husband but also of the people of the rural district. She dies in 1829 at the age of sixty-eight. As in her other historical novels, Ariyoshi read widely on Hanaoka Seishū, including his diaries and other writings to endow this work with great impact.

Between January 1967 and December 1969, *Izumo no Okuni* (Okuni of Izumo) was serialized in *Fujin kōron*, a leading women's magazine. This fictionalized biography of a seventeenth-century woman dancer encompasses three volumes. The changes occurring in Japan during the late sixteenth and early seventeenth centuries are dramatically described in this award-winning novel, which is being translated by James Brandon.

Umikura (Darkness of the sea) was serialized in *Bungei shunjū* from

April 1967 to April 1968. The setting of the novel is Mikurajima, an island off the coast of the Izu peninsula, which the author describes as being totally cut off from the main islands of Japan. Ooyon, the stubborn heroine, is an old woman of eighty with ten great-grandchildren. She is at once the matriarch of the island and the symbol of its traditions. Having acquired great wisdom through experience, Ooyon is not one to listen to what she considers nonsense. The old woman, who has never been away from the island, is bewildered by the changes brought about by the passage of time and distressed that the young find it necessary to leave the island upon graduating from intermediate school. It appears likely that eventually only the elderly will be left on the island. Ooyon, who is the very heart and soul of Mikurajima, gets deeply involved in any event of significance concerning the island and fearlessly voices her views.

The author describes in great detail the heroine's reaction to the news that the Japanese government is considering giving the United States permission to use the island, which has a population of two hundred, for bombing practice. Newspaper reporters fly out to the island by helicopter to interview the natives, whereupon Ooyon adamantly declares that she will never move away, even though bombs begin raining upon her. She refuses to leave because she cannot imagine life away from her beloved island. Blindly attached to the land, Ooyon is disgusted with the husband of one of her granddaughters, who is interested in the money the government is offering each citizen who is willing to leave the island. The author skillfully juxtaposes Ooyon, who values above all else the land and its traditions, with the younger islanders who are willing to sell it for a large sum of money. At the end of the novel, however, the reader is left uncertain as to which side Ariyoshi supports. The annual income of each islander is less than 10,000 yen, and the young dream of leaving for Tokyo, where they can enjoy a higher standard of living. They are happy to leave behind the boxwood trees and everything else that symbolizes Mikurajima's heritage. Although the two factions clash with one another, in the end the Japanese government decides against using the island for bombing practice. Members of both factions are disappointed by this decision; it means that the island is so utterly worthless it cannot even be used for bombing practice.

Despite the uncertain note on which the work ends, the author succeeds in creating a memorable character in Ooyon, a staunch pacifist who is vehemently opposed to the Japan-U.S. Mutual Defense Treaty. Ooyon vividly remembers being told shortly after Japan's surrender that under the new constitution the Japanese will never have to send their sons off to war again. Toward the end of the novel, Ooyon's son, who originally had no intentions of leaving the island, moves away. What seems to be suggested here is that although Mikurajima will remain unchanged topographically, it will gradually become modernized along with the rest of Japan, despite the old matriarch's protest and prayers.

In mid-January 1968, Ariyoshi traveled to Cambodia and Indonesia. She then decided to visit New Guinea since, according to the map she had checked, it was two inches away. She stayed for about a month in the jungles of New Guinea with a Japanese woman anthropologist. During her stay, Ariyoshi lost her toenails and had to be carried out of the jungle in a hammock by tribesmen. Not at all comforting was the thought that cannibalism was still practiced by some tribes. Ariyoshi returned to Japan in April. Having contracted malaria in New Guinea, she fell gravely ill during the months of May and June and was hospitalized for a time. Her adventures in New Guinea are described in *Onna futari no Nyuu Ginia* (Two women in New Guinea), serialized from May to November in the weekly magazine *Shūkan Asahi.*

The Twilight Years and Princess Kazu

From April to December 1970, *Yūhigaoka sangōkan* (Number 3 Yūhigaoka), which focuses on the lives of wives of white collar workers, was serialized in the daily newspaper *Mainichi shimbun,* which enjoys wide circulation. In November 1970, Ariyoshi accepted an invitation to join the faculty of the University of Hawaii at Manoa as a scholar-in-residence. There she presented a graduate seminar on the Japanese theater of the late Tokugawa period, for which she had her students read the plays of Tsuruya Namboku IV. Several years earlier, she had begun to study gerontology when she realized that she, too, was growing old. During her stay in Hawaii, she visited numerous homes for the elderly and observed the aged firsthand. She extended her visits to nursing homes in other cities in the United States and Europe. In March, Ariyoshi left Hawaii for the U.S. mainland and Europe, spending time in London and Paris. She returned to Japan in August 1971. During her absence, Shinchōsha published the first set of her selected works, *Ariyoshi Sawako senshū*, consisting of thirteen volumes. In September, "Narayama bushikō" (1953; The song of oak mountain), a story about the ancient custom of abandoning old women to die, written by Fukasawa Shichirō (1914–87) which Ariyoshi adapted for the stage, was performed at the Kabukiza.

In June 1972, *Kōkotsu no hito* (The twilight years) was published by Shinchōsha. The focal character is Shigezō, an eighty-four-year-old man in his dotage. In this poignant work, which takes up the serious problem of caring for the elderly in Japan, the author traces Shigezō's mental deterioration during the last eighteen months of his life, and the hardship that the other members of the family—particularly his daughter-in-law—undergo as they do their utmost to see that Shigezō is cared for at home until his last moments. As in her earlier novels, Ariyoshi finds tragic beauty in old age, and Shigezō, as he becomes as helpless as a toddler, is described as being god-like.

Throughout the novel, Shigezō's son watches helplessly from the sidelines as his wife Akiko stoically, although grudgingly at first, takes care of his father. His sister is coldly unsympathetic. It is Akiko who matures. While holding a full-time job as a typist in a law firm, she becomes a deeply compassionate caretaker, despite her memory of harsh treatment at the hand of Shigezō in the past. Akiko's affection for her father-in-law grows daily as she watches him grow weaker. Although she knows full well that he will never recover, she does all she can to keep him happy and comfortable. After all, when a Japanese dies, it is still generally believed that he joins other family members who have preceded him in death. When at last Shigezō dies, his son and grandson are of no practical assistance, but Akiko remains cool and collected, surprising even herself. She prepares Shigezō's body for the funeral and makes arrangements for the service. In fact, she conducts herself with such dignity and composure that the heroine in chapter 1 and the heroine in the last chapter are indeed a study in contrast. *The Twilight Years* is available in translation by Mildred Tahara.

The original title of this novel means "Man in Ecstasy." For a cogent term to describe Shigezō's condition, Ariyoshi searched widely in Western and Japanese sources. In *Nihon gaishi*, a historical work by Neo-Confucian scholar-poet Rai San'yō (1780–1832), she found the work *kōkotsu* (ecstasy), referring to the state of an old man. *The Twilight Years* created quite a sensation. Ariyoshi touched a responsive chord in the reading public, for Akiko's experience is by no means unique in today's Japan, where countless families are faced with the same task and anguish, currently or in the future. *The Twilight Years* was a huge commercial success, selling over a million copies before the end of 1972. Because of its tremendous sales, the novel earned royalties of more than 100 million yen (at the time approximately $300,000) within six months of its publication. Ariyoshi sought to give the entire sum to nursing homes to benefit the aged, but she was prevented from doing so by tax agents, who wanted the money for the government's coffers. After a series of protesting articles appeared in the Japanese press, the tax bureau allowed her to give 22 million yen to the elderly. Because of the furor over the case, the government began to liberalize its restrictions on charitable donations.

Because the novel turned out to be a bestseller, many of the established literary critics belittle the work as a potboiler. Nonetheless, it is a thought-provoking novel that prompted the Japanese to become keenly aware of the plight of the elderly and their caretakers. It is predicted that by the beginning of the twenty-first century, the population of those over sixty-five in Japan will reach thirty million. In effect, this means that each working member of society will be supporting four elderly.

A historical novel, *Managoya Omine* (Omine of the Managoya), was serialized in *Chūō kōron* from January 1973 to August 1974. From October 1974 to June 1975, *Fukugō osen* (Compound pollution) was serialized in *Asahi shimbun*. *Compound Pollution* is a semidocumentary that focuses on the dangers of the cumulative effects of agricultural chemicals and food additives. In the United States and other advanced nations, special studies have been conducted on the harmful effects of mercury poisoning, dioxin, heptachlor, DDT, and so forth. Ariyoshi suggests in her work, however, that we cannot begin to measure the total harm of all these dangerous chemicals and toxic wastes interacting in the human body. This work has generated great interest among environmentalists. Readers of this lengthy study—many of them housewives—voiced their apprehensions and besieged government ministries with queries as to what the Japanese government intended to do if chemicals and additives currently used showed harmful effects in the future. To write this work, Ariyoshi read widely and conducted numerous interviews with experts on the subject. In the summer of 1978, Ariyoshi, now widely regarded as an expert on environmental pollution in her own right, spent several months traveling extensively through rural China. She lectured the Chinese on the dangers of agricultural chemicals such as DDT, still being used in China.

Kazunomiyasama otome (Her Highness Princess Kazu), written in 1978, illustrates well the pains Ariyoshi took to research the history and language of the late Tokugawa period; it also demonstrates that she was one of the most talented storytellers in Japan. On January 20, 1979, her forty-eighth birthday, Ariyoshi received the prestigious Mainichi Cultural Prize for this work. The novel was adapted for television and telecast nationwide in January 1980. Different stage adaptations of the work have been performed, and the novel has been translated into English by Mildred Tahara.

It is set in the period just before the Meiji Restoration of 1868. The main action of the story takes place in 1860–61 when the shogunate sought to restore its prestige by uniting the court and the shogun. To bring this about, Kazunomiya (1846–77), an imperial princess, is forced to break her engagement to Prince Arisugawa (1835–95; later statesman and army general), to whom she had been engaged since the age of six. Plans are made for her marriage to Tokugawa Iemochi (1846–66), the fourteenth shogun, including arrangements for a large party to accompany the princess to Edo.

According to Ariyoshi's novel, the real Princess Kazu (the daughter of Emperor Ninmyō, half-sister of Emperor Kōmei, and aunt of Emperor Meiji) was replaced by a lowborn maidservant before her retinue left Kyoto. The maidservant was later replaced by another, and it was this second substitute who died in 1877 as the widow of Iemochi and whose remains were found in the Tokugawa mausoleum in recent years. Whether or not a substitute was involved, many women were uprooted from the palaces of the nobility in Kyoto and made to face an uncertain future in the shogun's castle in Edo.

Tragically, these women suffered all in vain, for the Tokugawa shogunate was doomed. Historically, Princess Kazu survived her husband by eleven years. As a young widow, she witnessed from within the shogun's palace the fall of the shogunate and pleaded for clemency on behalf of the Tokugawa family, who soon abandoned her. At one point she traveled back to Kyoto with a small entourage, only to return to Tokyo to live out the rest of her life in a palace in the Azabu district of the city, which by then had become the new capital of Japan. Princess Kazu is one of Japan's highest-ranking tragic heroines.

In May 1977, Ariyoshi suffered from overwork and was hospitalized for a time. Between August 1977 and August 1978, the second thirteen-volume series of the *Selected Works of Ariyoshi Sawako* was published. *Akujo ni tsuite* (All about an evil woman) was serialized in the weekly magazine *Shūkan Asahi* between March 1978 and September 1978; at the same time, it was serialized on television. In April 1978, Ariyoshi left for France to work on a translation of a French work by Benoite Groult; the translation was subsequently published as *Saigo no shokuminchi* (The last colony). Shortly after her return to Japan, Ariyoshi visited China, where she toured seven communes and actually lived and took her meals with the Chinese. She returned to Japan in July. A book about her impressions of and experiences in China, *Chūgoku repooto* (China Report), was published by Shinchōsha in March 1979.

From April to August 1979, *Aburaya Okon* (Okon of the Aburaya) was serialized in the *Mainichi* newspaper. In this work, which is set in the late 1700s, the author took up the problem of prostitution. The serialization was left incomplete, however, in part because of public protest that the work bordered on pornography.

A Personal Glimpse

In February 1981, Ariyoshi traveled to Europe and spent some time in Paris. In April 1981, *The Doctor's Wife* was performed on stage in Beijing and other cities in China and was well received. In 1982, Ariyoshi's first mystery, *Kaimaku beru wa hanayaka ni* (The bell at curtaintime rings merrily), was published by Shinchōsha; an adaptation of this novel about a prominent and long active actress was telecast in January 1983. Years earlier, the author had read all of Agatha Christie's mysteries, and she was familiar with works by Rex Stout. Those in the United States who have discovered the riveting mystery fiction of Amanda Cross know that this literary genre had earned a respectable place in the world of fiction. Ariyoshi certainly had the potential to develop into Japan's counterpart to any of the leading writers of mystery and suspense fiction in the West.

Ariyoshi was also a playwright, and a number of her novels have been adapted for stage, television, and the cinema. A woman of great wit and intelligence, she entertained millions with her spell-binding stories. Furthermore, as a social critic, she has made her readers think seriously about the many ills with which society is beset. Needless to say, the works that tackle contemporary social problems are of great interest, but students of Japanese literature will be drawn to Ariyoshi because of her deep affection for Japan's rich cultural heritage. Her profound knowledge of the classical theater—the Noh, Bunraku, and Kabuki—is astounding. Moreover, she was knowledgeable on the subject of the tea ceremony and had a fine personal collection of tea utensils. That she was extremely well-read in the cultural history and the arts of the Azuchi-Momoyama and Tokugawa periods (late 1500s to 1868) is obvious to anyone who has read her historical novels.

For the Japan P.E.N. Conference held in Tokyo and Kyoto in November 1972, Ariyoshi played an instrumental role in arranging to have the Noh actor Teshima Yazaemon perform "Shōjō." In a magnificent kimono, she also performed the tea ceremony at a tea cottage on the grounds of the Hekiunsō, featuring priceless tea treasures owned by the Yabunouchi school. The main theme of the gathering was "Three Literary Women": Murasaki Shikibu represented the name of the flower in the alcove; the nun Abutsu (thirteenth-century poet and diarist) was pictured in a scroll with a sutra fragment in her hand; and Ariyoshi herself was the hostess who prepared "thin" tea for her guests.

In the summer of 1973, Ariyoshi hosted a formal *chaji* on the theme of boat and stars, since it was held at the time of the Tanabata Star Festival. One of the scrolls on view was by novelist Natsume Sōseki (1867–1916), on which was written the haiku *Natsugusa ya / shita ni nagaruru / shimizu kana* (Summer grasses—flowing below, a clear stream). Ariyoshi personally owned a set of scrolls known as the *Bakumatsu sanshū* (Three shū or boats of the late Tokugawa period), referring to three great samurai thinkers—Katsu Kaishū, Takahashi Daishū, and Yamaoka Tesshū. For the occasion, she had her guests view a Chinese poem by Katsu Kaishū. Still another scroll in the *machiai* was one by Shiba Kōkan, a Western-influenced painter and scholar of Dutch Learning of the late Tokugawa period. Among the guests were several foreigners, an editor, a businessman, and a movie actor (to represent a star).

One of the flowers on display was "cat's whiskers," to suggest Sōseki's novel *Wagahai wa neko de aru* (I am a cat). One course of the elegantly prepared meal featured a boat made of bamboo leaves that contained about ten "fish stars" (*uo no hoshi*) mixed with grated radish. Dressed beautifully in a kimono, Ariyoshi prepared for her guests both thin tea and thick tea and later actively participated in the haiku composition session.

It was sometimes extremely exhausting to chat with Ariyoshi, for she would be talking about golf and baseball (she played a good game of golf and was an avid baseball fan) one minute, then would plunge without warning into a discussion of Princess Shikishi and Fujiwara Teika, *waka* poets of the *Shinkokinshū*, a poetry anthology compiled in the early thirteenth century. A woman with a deep love for Japan's rich cultural past, she would take the time out to visit places of interest in western Japan: the Tatsuta River, a place famous in *waka* poetry; the Myōkian Taian, a tea room in Yamazaki associated with the tea master Sen no Rikyū (1522–91); Meiji village near Nagoya; and the Nagara River to view cormorant fishing. Also knowledgeable in Japanese art history, she visited countless museums; she commented at length on artists, living and dead, and their works. Her deep interest in the theater led her to explore the Western opera, and she spoke glowingly of the tenor Jose Carreras and the highlights of Cilea's *Adriana Lecouvreur*. On the other hand, she complained of Debussy's *Pelléas et Melisande* for its lack of memorable scenes or arias. As further proof of her versatility, she adapted Father Daniel Berrigan's antiwar play, "Catonsville Nine," and put it on stage in Tokyo in 1972. She also wrote a musical based on Japanese folklore. In fifty-three years, Ariyoshi accomplished a great deal.

Ariyoshi Sawako died in her sleep in 1984, a most eventful year for her. Plays based on her novels were being performed throughout Japan, and she had traveled to London in April when *The Twilight Years* was published by Peter Owen. Unlike other Japanese women writers, Ariyoshi did not write love stories, for she believed that there were other more important issues for a professional writer to take up. She had often mentioned to friends that she had poured all her creative and literary talents into writing *Her Highness Princess Kazu*. She may have experienced despair, feeling that she was losing her creativity during the last few years of her life, and privately she described herself as being a manic-depressive. In the highly competitive literary arena where new young writers were being acclaimed and the reading audience was dramatically shrinking in number, it would certainly have been difficult to remain a literary luminary indefinitely.

Ariyoshi lived through a remarkable half century of modern Japanese history. As a child, she observed Japan at war on the Asian continent; in her teens, she saw the war end in total defeat and all that had been drummed into her at school denounced or negated. No person of sensitivity could have emerged unaffected by these traumatic events, and Ariyoshi maintained a strong antiwar stance for the rest of her life. Having lived for years in a Japanese colony, she was exposed firsthand to the prejudice with which the Japanese regarded other non-Japanese. Though proud of all that the Japanese had achieved since the end of World War II, she was conscious of the country's many social problems and sympathized with the innocent victims suffering in silence, whether she was writing about racial prejudice or radiation disease.

As a divorced woman bringing up a daughter, Ariyoshi thought deeply about the position of women in Japanese society throughout the centuries. Feudal institutions die hard, and Ariyoshi wrote about women ranging from an imperial princess used as a political pawn to an illiterate prostitute who, through no fault of her own, was forced to lead a miserable life. It is because women have to struggle harder than men that they emerge as final victors in many of her works. Perhaps the adversity that women have to face in their childhood and adulthood enables them to cope with the problems that develop as they grow older. Women in the next generation will doubtless benefit from the struggles of the generations of women who preceded them, bearing in their breasts the hope that those who follow will find the struggles of life a little easier to bear.

In January 1986, the media announced that an Ariyoshi Sawako Memorial Museum was to be established in Wakayama City. The plans for the museum and adjacent branch of the Wakayama Municipal Library were made by the Wakayama Municipal Government and the author's devoted fans. Ariyoshi's mother consented to turn over her daughter's personal possessions and original manuscripts. These efforts are being made by the residents of Wakayama in gratitude to the author for her many outstanding literary works, a number of which were set in Wakayama. The museum will play an important role in helping students of Japanese literature appreciate and understand Ariyoshi's works more fully. That this talented writer, known for her high intellect, is being honored in this special way in the home of her maternal grandmother, the setting of *The River Ki*, is most fitting. Ariyoshi will certainly be remembered as a unique writer who admirably carried on the great tradition of outstanding Japanese women writers into our time.

English Translations of Works by Ariyoshi Sawako

"Ballad" (*Jiuta*, 1956), trans. Yukio Suwa and Herbert Glazer, *Japan Quarterly* 22, 1 (1975):40–58.

The Doctor's Wife (*Hanaoka Seishū no tsuma*, 1961), trans. Wakako Hironaka and Ann Siller Kostant. Kodansha International, 1978.

"Her Highness Princess Kazu" (*Kazunomiyasama otome*, 1978), trans. Mildred Tahara, in *Translation—The Journal of Literary Translation*, 17 (Fall 1986):164–83.

"The Ink Stick" (*Sumi*, 1961), trans. Mildred Tahara, *Japan Quarterly* 22, 4 (1975):348–69.

"Prayer" (*Kitō*, 1959), trans. John Bester, *Japan Quarterly* 7, 4 (1960):448–81.

The River Ki (*Kinokawa*, 1959), trans. Mildred Tahara. Kodansha International, 1980.

Selected Works by Ariyoshi Sawako, comp. and ed. Mildred Tahara, forthcoming. This anthology will include English translations of *Kurogo*, *Sambaba*, *Sumi*, *Namayoi*, *Kiyū no shi*, *Akaiko monogatari*, among other stories and chapters from longer works. "The Tomoshibi" (*Tomoshibi*, 1961), trans. Keiko Nakamura, in *The Mother of Dreams*, ed. Ueda Makoto. Kodansha International, 1986, pp. 240–57.

The Twilight Years (*Kōkotsu no hito*, 1971). Translated by Mildred Tahara. Kodansha International, 1984.

"The Village of Eguchi" (*Eguchi no sata*, 1958), trans. Yukio Suwa and Herbert Glazer, *Japan Quarterly*, 18, 4 (1971): 427–41.

References on Japanese Women Writers

Encyclopedia of Japan. Tokyo and New York: Kodansha International, 1985.

Hisamatsu Sen'ichi, ed. *Biographical Dictionary of Japanese Literature*. Tokyo and New York: Kodansha International, 1976.

Mulhern, Chieko. "Japan: A Survey of Women Writers Past and Present," in *Longman Anthology of World Literature by Women*, ed. M. Arkin and B. Shollar. New York and London: Longman, 1988.

———, ed. *Japanese Women Writers: A Bio-critical Source Book*. Westport, CT: Greenwood Press, forthcoming.

INDEX